PORTRAITS OF AMERICAN WOMEN

Volume II
From the Civil War to the Present

G. J. Barker-Benfield
State University of New York at Albany

Catherine Clinton
W. E. B. Du Bois Institute at Harvard University

St. Martin's Press
New York

To all students in women's history, past, present, and future.

Senior editor: Don Reisman
Production supervisor: Katherine Battiste
Text design: Nancy Sugihara
Cover design: Darby Downey

For information, write:
St. Martin's Press, Inc.
175 Fifth Avenue
New York, NY 10010

ISBN: 0-312-02431-2

Acknowledgments

"Charlotte Perkins Gilman" by Carol Berkin. Berkin, Carol Ruth, Mary
    Beth Norton. *Women of America: A History.* Copyright © 1979 by
    Houghton Mifflin Company. Used with permission.
"Crystal Eastman" by Blanche Wiesen Cook. Courtesy of Blanche Wiesen
    Cook.
"Eleanor Roosevelt" by William Chafe. Courtesy of William Chafe.
"Georgia O'Keeffe" by Sarah Whitaker Peters. Sarah Whitaker Peters ©
    1989.
"Helen Gahagan Douglas" by Ingrid Winther Scobie. Parts of this essay were
    previously published as "Helen Gahagan Douglas: Broadway Star as
    California Politician" *California History,* Vol. LXVI, No. 4 December
    1987.

Photo Credits

Cover and page 310, "Charlotte Perkins Gilman." Courtesy of Bryn Mawr
    College Archives.

Photo credits and copyrights are continued at the back of the book on
page 617, which constitutes an extension of the copyright page.

Preface

The title of our book reveals much about our goals. The word *portrait* emphasizes the individuality of a particular woman and the historian's representation of her. By combining *American* and *women*, we include the general features of the cultural life that individuals shared with others who were American and who were women. Scholars always have to balance two dimensions of their subject: the distinctive and the common, the exceptional and the representative. So in each "portrait" the reader will find references to many other women as well as generalizations about the period in which they lived. Our text attempts to paint a picture of not only women's history in general, but the history of gender roles and relations in the United States, in the context of the broad scope of social history. Clearly, women's lives provide a vital perspective through which the great panorama of social change in the American past can be understood.

We have placed introductory essays before each grouping of portraits to provide connections between our subjects and their times. Insofar as it is possible to do so in so brief a space, these essays aim to locate the histories of women and men together by period and to provide a sense of their continuities through the whole gallery of the American past. We hope these introductory passages will make the major themes of American history and women's role in these significant transformations accessible to general readers. Until recently, the "womanless" American history was the norm. But in fact, without a history of women we neglect consideration of gender dynamics, sex roles, and family and sexual relations—the very fundamentals of human interaction.

We want to emphasize that the individuality of each portrait is a distinguishing feature of the book. We decided on this for two reasons. First, the portraits demonstrate the sheer quality and variety of women's experiences and contributions throughout American history. The way in which individual women have been able to push beyond the ideological myths attempting to define them as the "second sex" provides absorbing material. Perhaps one of the most notable developments in the history of the American nation, one which can be detected in the following pages, has been the mass "awakening" of women.

Second, it could be said that our portraits are representative in that they represent for many women the possibilities of their historical circumstances. At the same time, we do not mean that these women "typify" female experience in the American past. A typical woman was more subordinated to productive and reproductive labors and was denied the possibilities of finding her own voice and of leaving us a record of it. It was only recently that, inspired by the changes of the 1960s, social historians developed ingenious ways of recovering the pasts of the uneducated, the poor, and the oppressed; we applaud these efforts, which enrich our historical horizons through their studies of women of color and others who left behind only the faintest traces of their lives.

There are many paths to the past, and we wish to provide you with some of the principles that shaped the composition of our gallery of portraits. First and foremost, we decided to include in our collection women who made significant contributions in the public realm. The second was the availability of accessible source material to allow us a viable portrait of our subject. In a few cases we could find neither suitable primary papers nor scholars involved in biographical research to undertake such a project. In some instances, we found a few previously published essays that suited our needs, and we adapted these to our text. But the majority of our portraits are commissioned pieces written by scholars engaged in ongoing research on their subject. Our selection process was also guided by our desire to maintain as diverse and balanced a group as possible to represent coverage within each chronological era. The portraits are fashioned to appeal to a wide range of readers, but all include sound scholarship and accessible prose and raise provocative issues to illuminate women's lives within a broad range of historical transformations.

Our second goal in thus presenting a series of individual histories is derived from our experience as scholars and teachers. Students of American history seem to find biographical approaches very appealing, and we obviously share that view. As exciting and revealing as other approaches to women's history have been over the last quarter century—and we have incorporated these findings where relevant—the lives of individuals continue to defy generalizations and to create compelling reading.

Our portraits are of women who realized their potential more than did the majority of their sisters, for a whole range of reasons, which we challenge you to consider. Between the introductory essays and the portraits, we would like our readers to ponder the question, What distinguished each individual woman portrayed from other women of her time and place? By making our intentions and assumptions about the book explicit, we encourage you to question our choices and think of alternatives. Most of all, we want *Portraits of American Women* to stimulate you to fresh ways of thinking about the history of women, of America, and of yourselves.

We would like to thank the following scholars for their anonymous but very welcome reviews of an early draft of our manuscript: Jo Ann Argersinger, University of Maryland, Baltimore County; Kathleen Berkeley, University of North Carolina, Wilmington; Victoria Brown, San Diego State University; Miriam Cohen, Vassar College; Janet L. Coryell, University of Dayton; Barbara Epstein, University of California, Santa Cruz; Barbara L. Green, Wright State University; Jaclyn Greenberg, University of California, Los Angeles; Susan M. Hartmann, Ohio State University; Ann J. Lane, Colgate University; Carol Lasser, Oberlin College; Joanne Meyerowitz, University of Cincinnati; Fred M. Rivers, Towson State University; Jean R. Soderlund, University of Maryland, Baltimore County; and Margaret B. Wilkerson, University of California, Berkeley. We would also like to thank all those at St. Martin's Press who helped to produce this book: Elise Bauman, Don Reisman, Abigail Scherer, Heidi Schmidt, Bob Sherman, Jean Smith, and Richard Steins.

All of our friends and colleagues give us indispensable support, but several gave generously of their time and skills in specific ways: Anne Braden, Ellen Fitzpatrick, Jacqueline Jones, Debbie Neuls, Tammy Rich, Angie Simeone, and Bennett Singer. We received invaluable institutional support from the Department of American Studies at Brandeis University, the W. E. B. Du Bois Institute at Harvard University, and the Department of History at the State University of New York at Albany.

We thank our families, Patricia West, Daniel Colbert, and Drew and Ned Colbert for their sacrifices and support.

Our part introductions are the distillation of courses we have taught for years, and the best aspects of them represent the fine work of historians whose gratifyingly large number make them impossible to specify here. But we can single out the fellow scholars whose work makes up this volume. They have given us much more than their chapters. Along with the inevitable challenges of the process which they helped us meet, they strengthened old friendships, established new ones, and reaffirmed our faith in the great enterprise of writing women's history.

G. J. Barker-Benfield
Catherine Clinton

Contents

Preface v

PART V

The Reform Era *299*

Charlotte Perkins Gilman (1860–1935)   Carol Ruth Berkin   311

Jane Addams (1860–1935)   G. J. Barker-Benfield   339

Ida Wells-Barnett (1862–1931)   Paula Giddings   367

PART VI

The Transition to Modernity *387*

Rose Schneiderman (1882–1972)   Annelise Orleck   399

Crystal Eastman (1881–1928)   Blanche Wiesen Cook   423

Alice Paul (1885–1977)   Christine A. Lunardini   449

PART VII

New Horizons *471*

Eleanor Roosevelt (1884–1962)   William H. Chafe   483

Georgia O'Keeffe (1887–1986)   Sarah Whitaker
                                        Peters 509

Margaret Mead (1901–1978)   Rosalind Rosenberg 527

PART VIII
Contemporary Lives *547*

Helen Gahagan Douglas   Ingrid Winther
  (1900–1980)   Scobie 561

Ella Baker (1903–1986)   Catherine Clinton 581

Betty Friedan (b. 1921)   Donald Meyer 599

About the Authors 618

PART V

The Reform Era

The range, variety, and success of women's efforts in caring for the sick and wounded of America's explodingly expansive cities and industries allow us to describe the period from 1877 to 1914 as "the reform era." These efforts remained consistent with the nineteenth-century social idea of "separate spheres"—the private sphere of home and motherhood for women and the larger public sphere of everything else, with which men identified themselves. Because women had specialized in morality in the family and housekeeping, most claimed to enter the public sphere in order to clean up its "sins." Before the Civil War, they had started with prostitution, drunkenness, and slavery.

After the Civil War, the public world to which women brought such traditional values changed with dramatic intensity. Changes included the growth of mechanized farming, the massive expansion of industry and the growth of cities, and of the immigration that industry stimulated. By 1900, the oil, iron, steel, railroad, milling, mining, manufacturing, and merchandizing industries had been transformed into interlocking monopolies, creating a single, standardized national economy. The direction taken by women reformers cannot be understood without taking note of these major changes in American society.

The mechanization of farming allowed farmers to produce vast quantities of cotton and cereals for a world market, as well as for the burgeoning American cities. The transportation, marketing, and financing of these crops were in the hands of corporate businessmen. When supplies of farm products outstripped demand, there was a steady and disastrous fall in prices that resulted in foreclosures, indebtedness, and an increase in the number of landless tenant farmers. Starting in the 1860s, farmers banded together as the "Grange," an economic self-help organization, in which farm women played a significant role. Managing separate "female" concerns, women also had full voting rights in the organization. Not so in the Grange's successor organizations, the Farmers' Alliances, which created the populist movement, one of the largest democratic mass movements in American history. While populist women lectured, organized locally, and helped educate masses of rural people in the innovative, cooperative economics proposed by the alliances, they were denied organizational voting rights and any voice at the national level. In response, in 1891 Fannie Mc-

Cormick and Emma Pack started the National Women's Alliance. Supporting the economic reforms demanded by their male counterparts, they also endorsed women's suffrage and temperance, as had Grange women before them. Both issues were refused support by male Populists.

White Farmers' Alliances did cooperate with the Colored Farmers' Alliances, which counted a million members in the South, but the relationship was a vulnerable one, succumbing to the racist attacks launched by the enemies of Populism. And the farmers' groups never managed to form the largest alliance at which they had aimed: one with urban workers.

Between the Civil War and 1900 there was a huge increase in the number of wage-earners employed in heavy industry and transportation. The number of female wage-earners went from 2.5 million in 1880 to 8.5 million in 1900. Moreover, the proportion of women employed as domestic servants, laundresses, and cooks dropped as their employment in the public service sector of the economy increased, for example, as clerical and retail workers. Women comprised 4 percent of the clerical work force in 1880; by 1920 they comprised nearly 50 percent. While women earned far less than their male contemporaries, their income was essential to the family income because living costs kept ahead of wages, even though wages increased over this entire period. A large number of children were drawn into paid labor for the same reason. Much wage-earning was seasonal, and all of it subject to the tidal waves of economic depression, notably in 1873–78, 1884–85, and 1893–97.

The rich got richer and America produced more and more millionaires. Employers kept wages as low and hours as long as they could. They had a free hand to dictate working conditions because the prevailing economic ethos among society's leaders was laissez-faire. While this policy claimed to be minimum action by government in the marketplace, in fact the U.S. government has always given lavish assistance and protection to business. In accordance with the same ideology of laissez-faire, "individualism" was preached from the top to the bottom of society. The "self-made" man was exemplified by the male heroes of Horatio Alger's novels. Such a male ideal existed in sharp contrast to the domestic ideology of harmonious and moral relations with which women were supposed to identify themselves, and which were preached in such novels as *Little Women*. One result of laissez-faire capitalism was the failure to consider even the most basic safety of workers; industrial accidents killed and maimed hundreds of thousands of workers each year. In 1913, 1 million workers were injured and 25,000 were killed, even after employees began to respond to the reform campaigns which women led and joined. Protective legislation was one result of their efforts.

In facing terrible living as well as working conditions, female and male industrial workers, the majority of whom were immigrants, were sustained by the traditions of their various ethnic heritages, ranging from age-old religious beliefs to equally strong secular political beliefs. People banded together in churches and clubs, keeping their old ways alive in their marriage patterns, religious festivals, and ethnic newspapers. These traditions were diversified even more with the changing proportions of immigrants—less arrived from the northern and western countries of Europe, while huge numbers poured in from the eastern and southern countries (the shift from the so-called Old Immigrants to the New Immigrants). It would take several generations before immigrant groups achieved social mobility by way of property ownership, education, or both.

The flood of European immigrants had been drawn to America by industrialization's demand for labor. For years, workers, union organizers, and other reformers decried the living and working conditions of industry's employees, which were appalling by any standard. At the same time, urban political machines played an important role in fostering city services, brokering different interests, and disbursing a wide range of charity where no one else would. These political machines were rooted in ethnic constituencies and were self-interested in the good as well as the bad they did. Such self-interest laid the machines open to middle-class reformers' charges that the machines were corrupt. In attacking political machines, reformers claimed that they were applying neutral, social-scientific standards to bring about progress. There was another dimension to the reformers' attack, one that linked it to the campaign for female suffrage. Political machines and clubhouse politics were imbued with traditional masculine values. Symbolically, voting took place in bars and taverns. What room was there in such machine politics for women? Jane Addams's early conflicts with Chicago's bosses were symbolic of the conflict.

In opening her campaign in the city, Jane Addams undertook a formidable task. Chicago, like many American cities, was growing rapidly. The nationwide urban population increased five-and-a-half times between 1870 and 1920, by which time 54 million Americans (a clear majority of the total population) lived in cities. The living conditions of the urban working class were, as Addams observed, "horrid." The influx of people exceeded housing supplies; people were crammed into filthy tenements. In many cases tenements were workplaces, too, especially for women in the needles trades, desperately combining family care with work, trying to scrape together some income. Reformers like Jacob Riis publicized the terrible overcrowding and unsanitary living conditions experienced by the working class.

Cities were transformed in shape as well as size because mass transit systems facilitated the sprawling of cities into suburbs. There the single-family, suburban home would be made into the all-American ideal. Among their other achievements, reformers Addams and Charlotte Perkins Gilman were pioneers of alternative living arrangements. Addams's settlement house—a community of reformers established in working-class neighborhoods—and Gilman's kitchenless apartment house symbolize the alternative ways of organizing which were being explored within the larger and traumatically transformed urban spaces of late nineteenth- and early twentieth-century America.

Women rose to the challenge posed by the careless individualism of self-made men with an outpouring of "expanded domestic housekeeping" and "social mothering." They qualified themselves for such a challenge by their successful inroads on the male bastions of higher learning. The Morrill Act of 1862 had sponsored the founding of coeducational state universities. Although many of these universities maintained a gender differentiated curriculum, by 1879, nearly half of all American colleges were coeducational. Stanford and the University of Chicago, both founded in 1890, were open to women. Women went on to demand entry into the professions for which their education now qualified them; they became natural scientists, social scientists, academics, and lawyers, despite meeting obstacles at every turn. Female doctors were the most successful of professional women before 1900, but this was because they concentrated their careers in obstetrics and gynecology and many based their claim on women's "natural" proclivity for nurturance. They were trained largely in separate colleges and hospitals. Many women patients preferred women doctors. In short, women's modest success in entering the medical profession must be explained by its congruence with Victorian, separate-sex culture.

Some men supported women's educational advance, but many found it deeply threatening. One form of resistance to equal education for women was an updating of the traditional argument that women were physically incapable of being educated. This was the context within which one must place Addams's struggle to go to medical school. The attitude that she and women with ambition like hers challenged was represented by Dr. Edward Clarke, a trustee of Harvard's medical school (which at the time faced women's insistence on being admitted). In 1873 Clarke published *Sex in Education*, an attack on women's having any college or high-school education. Clarke said that young women could not compete intellectually with men and develop their ovaries at the same time. Clarke's additional suggestion that female factory workers' reproductive capacity was damaged by similar "unnatural" demands on their system was developed by Dr. Azel Ames in *Sex in Industry* (1875). Ames had been instrumental in making these views the rationale for a 1874 Massachusetts law attempting to limit women's factory-work hours to ten a day. While exceptional and unenforced, this law was an early effort at "protective legislation," aimed at "protecting" women in the paid workplace. In addition to shorter hours (to protect women's reproductive and mothering capacities), later "protective" laws aimed to establish minimum-wage requirements (better wages meant shorter hours and therefore more time for mothering); restrictions on nightwork (again, to leave more time for mothering); the provision of places and seats to rest (to protect women's health); and separate toilets. In short, while it was based on apparently medical and therefore "scientific" evidence, "protective legislation" in fact expressed middle-class Victorian gender values.

Throughout the century, courts and legislatures continued to upold the sanctity of laissez-faire capitalism against the effort of reformers. Lawyers and labor organizations tried and failed to limit the hours of industrial workers but were defeated by the courts. Government, said the courts, could not intervene in the freely entered contract between employer and employee. Finally, the reformers decided to use the tactic of appealing to the gender ideal embodied in protective legislation. In their successful 1908 brief, *Muller* vs. *Oregon,* lawyer Louis Brandeis and his sister-in-law Jacqueline Goldmark cited that 1874 law rationalized by the Clarke-Ames argument. (Oregon had passed a law limiting a woman's daily work hours to ten, which a commercial laundry operator named Muller,[12] had ignored.) Brandeis and Goldmark amassed apparent proof that extended hours of work damaged menarche and healthy menstruation. Those processes represented *potential* motherhood—menstruation was common to all women—therefore, the argument was a way of classifying women by way of reproduction, whether they became mothers or not. By upholding the Oregon law, the Supreme Court placed motherhood above laissez-faire.

The case also symbolized the acceptance of medical and social-scientific authority as the arbiter of social policy. After the Civil War, the study of society, claiming to have the authority and prestige of hard science, began to flourish in the new and growing research universities. Social science provided careers and a rationale for reformers. Eventually entering higher education in significant numbers, women had come to combine their moral claim to reform, which was based on a highly idealized motherhood, with the language, authority, and institutions of social science. This fusion made late nineteenth-century reform significantly different from women's reform activities earlier in the century. Women shed their more genteel outlook in order to increase their influence on public affairs. They began forming female clubs and associations. In 1890, they organized themselves into the General Federation of Women's Clubs; by 1910, 800,000 women had joined this national network. Members collected data for the solution and protection of large-scale social problems. Their efforts and those of many others, including settlement-house workers, helped to desentimentalize motherhood and to make it more "scientific." One illustration was the supposedly biological rationale for protective legislation.

While concerned with the circumstances faced by workers of both sexes, women reformers were particularly focused on the plight of women. For example, the Woman's Christian Temperance Union (WCTU), founded in 1874, addressed the terrible damage that men's alcoholism did to their families, that is, to most

women's primary concern at the time. The WCTU was the largest women's organization of the nineteenth century. It had roots
among women in country and city. Its combination of middle-
class, "female," Protestant, and social science values was typical
of its era. Its greatest leader, Frances Willard, recognized the only
effective way to bring power to bear on national social problems
was politics. Temperance reformers, like settlement-house workers, embraced suffragism.

Fostering education, establishing settlement houses, and forming pressure groups, educated women became central to Progressivism, the loosely defined movement that culminated in the "reform" presidencies of Theodore Roosevelt (1901–1909), William
Howard Taft (1909–1913), and Woodrow Wilson (1913–1921). Following in the wake of populist reformers, Progressives aimed to
check the excesses of corporate power, from the abusive railroad
rates charged farmers to the monopoly of city power companies.
Feminist Progressives exposed the terrible conditions of women
factory workers and attempted to reform them through labor legislation. These efforts were consistent with Progressive journalism's "muckraking" of the meat-packing and oil industries and
the passage of laws to check those abuses, and its cleansing and
opening of politics by way of the secret ballot, the initiative, referendum, and recall. Women's demand for suffrage can be seen as
part of this whole progressive thrust.

Female reformers' identification with motherhood was sometimes at odds with other impulses in reformers themselves and
in popular culture at large. Americanization and greater material
prosperity can be correlated with declining family size, an increasing number of women choosing not to marry, and an increasing rate of divorce. While celebrating marriage and motherhood
for women generally, Jane Addams never married; Charlotte Perkins Gilman eventually sent her child to her husband to raise;
and late in life, the great suffragist Elizabeth Cady Stanton was to
identify herself with "The Solitude of the Self" even in the experience of motherhood. "Alone" she wrote, woman "goes to the
gates of death to give her life to every man that is born into the
world; no one can share her fears, no one can mitigate her pangs."
Perhaps the most dramatic expression of this appetite for individual identity is Kate Chopin's 1899 novel, *The Awakening*. Its
heroine "awakens" to sensuality and individual consciousness—

in short, to freedom—which she chooses over conventional marriage and motherhood. But such clarity was rare; far more characteristic of women's intellectual lives was the conflict between, on the one hand, subordination of self to larger entities (family, society, or "womanhood") and, on the other, the assertion of individual freedom.

African-American female reformers shared certain characteristics of late nineteenth-century white female reformers. Educated, middle-class in comparison to most African-Americans, and struggling with some success to enter the professions, black reformers also established settlement houses and a national network of women's clubs. Ida Wells-Barnett's extraordinary work against lynching may be seen as both muckraking and as the social-scientific gathering of data. But as her targeting of lynching illustrates, black women's intellectual orientation was fundamentally different from white women's. Pervasive and continuous racism affected African-American women and men in every dimension of their lives, whatever the success of their attempts to resist it and maintain their cultural identity.

As white, urban-dwelling women left paid domestic service for the tertiary sector, African-American women took their places because they were excluded from other kinds of work. In the southern states, they were allowed into the booming tobacco industry only in the hardest, dirtiest, and worst-paid jobs. The vast majority of African-American women worked as sharecroppers and farmers. In many places they were visible as convict labor on the roads as well as in the fields. Nonetheless, a few African-American women fought their way into middle-class jobs, most notably into teaching. Lucy Craft Chaney established the Haines Institute in Augusta, Georgia, in 1886, which trained African-American women for teaching and nursing. Middle-class black women formed clubs to foster the same goals (child care, health care, relief for the impoverished, moral and educational reform) that were fostered by white women's clubs. When the white General Federation of Women's Clubs rejected black women's clubs, black women formed their own national organizations. They also founded suffrage associations, which similarly faced rejection by white suffrage associations, most notably in 1919 at the hands of Carrie Chapman Catt, the head of the National American Woman Suffrage Association. While some African-American women then rejected the suffrage movement altogether because of this racism, others continued to fight for the vote in local, regional, and national associations.

This era was in large part one of reform because of the large-scale emergence of educated women into public life. Overcoming resistance to their desire for higher education, arming themselves with social expertise, and banding together in overlapping networks of associations, middle-class women took on a daunting array of social problems that were largely the effects of unchecked capitalism. Ironically, perhaps, America's economic success provided its female reformers with the resources, of time and education, on which they depended. Jane Addams's inheritance from her "capitalist" father paid her way for the rest of her life. On the other hand, capitalism itself benefitted inestimably from the cheap labor of women, who provided at least one-fifth of the factory labor force throughout this period. It also encouraged and relied upon all classes of women to purchase consumer goods and services.

Charlotte Perkins Gilman
(1860–1935)

Carol Ruth Berkin

Charlotte Perkins Gilman was born July 3, 1860, in Hartford, Connecticut, to parents who separated soon after she was born. Following her own divorce from her first husband in 1894, Gilman moved to California where she began to establish her career of social reform by publishing in several literary forms and by lecturing to women's clubs and to socialist and working men's associations. In 1898 Gilman published Women and Economics: The Economic Factor between Men and Women as a Factor in Social Evolution, *a work that made her internationally famous and has remained the best known of her many writings. Gilman's goal was to end women's subjection to degrading and unpaid housework; child care, cooking, and cleaning, she argued, should be separated from other aspects of women's lives and assigned to paid professional specialists. Gilman's architectural plans for kitchenless living quarters were designed to facilitate this purpose. They stemmed from a long-standing tradition of socialist and feminist thought. With Jane Addams and other women, Gilman was a founder of the Women's Peace Party during World War I.*

Charlotte Perkins Gilman married her cousin, Houghton Gilman, in 1900. The couple lived together in New York and in Connecticut. Diagnosed as having terminal cancer, she committed suicide in 1935 in California, where she had moved to be with her daughter soon after Houghton Gilman's death in 1934.

Once upon a time, 10-year-old Charlotte Perkins wrote in 1870, the good King Ezephon and his besieged kingdom were saved by the heroic battlefield performance of Princess Araphenia, only daughter of the king. Araphenia had not vanquished the wicked enemy alone, however; she had magical help from the fabulous Elmondine, a beautiful visitor from a distant planet. Bejeweled and bewitching, Elmondine had come to a lonely Araphenia in the palace garden and had offered advice and assistance. To save the king and his kingdom, Elmondine created, out of thin air, an army of a thousand men. And to the young earthly princess, this fairy princess gave a magic sword with which to fight and an invincible horse on which to ride while disguised as a warrior-prince. When victory came, the brave girl threw off her disguise, and her astonished father embraced her.

Tales like this one appear in different versions throughout Charlotte Perkins's diaries.[1] The central characters remain the same in each story: a young woman who can, through some magic, overstep the prescribed boundaries of her life and enter into active participation in the great struggles between good and evil in her society; an older woman, resplendently female yet wise and independent and powerful, who guides the novice's path; and always a grateful father whose respect had been won.

Charlotte Perkins was a young girl with an active fantasy life and a lonely reality when she spun these tales. But as a mature woman of 50, she continued to write stories of wise, older women, strong and independent doctors or philanthropists, who appeared out of nowhere to guide some struggling girl to maturity. The setting was no longer fabulous, but the characters were unchanged.[2]

No Elmondine ever appeared in the life of Charlotte Perkins Stetson Gilman. But for many younger women—in her lifetime and today—she has seemed to play that fabled role herself. Writer, philosopher, socialist, and feminist, Gilman has come to stand for the potentialities of American womanhood. She appears very much the self-made woman, overcoming sexual stereotype and social pressures to emerge as a woman of depth and dimension.

Valuable as this Elmondine may seem to those searching for a model, Gilman did not come from a distant planet, free of the conflicts that a woman might have faced at the turn of the century or faces today. Nor was she magically transformed by any fabulous figure into a secure, stable, integrated personality without the marks of a difficult childhood. Her life bears witness to the difficulties of feminism, not as an ideology or a political commitment, but as a personal experience. Charlotte Perkins Gilman struggled for intellectual and emotional liberation, hampered through much of her life by an internalization of the very split vision of masculine and feminine

313

spheres and destinies that, in her work, she would expose as artificial. She struggled later in her life to achieve a balance between independence and an interdependence with others. This essay seeks to chart her personal confrontation with feminism, because it is in that experience that she may serve as a model for American women.

Charlotte Perkins was born on July 3, 1860.[3] Her parents' family trees, rooted in New England soil, were already intertwined, with cousins marrying cousins in discreet confirmation of their pride in association. Her father was a Beecher, grandson of Lyman Beecher, and nephew, as Charlotte put it, of twelve "world servers," a young man nearly smothered in the mantle of reform. Frederick Beecher Perkins's mother had been a rebel of sorts, the odd sister who had never taken any interest in public affairs.

Frederick Beecher Perkins struck a compromise between family tradition and maternal heresy; He dedicated himself to the pursuit of knowledge, thus satisfying his own personal desires in the interest of society. It was his world service to know everything, in case anyone might ask. He was quick-tempered, sensitive, with a well-mannered hostility to authority. He was never much of a financial success and never seemed to care. In 1858 Perkins married his 31-year-old cousin, Mary Fitch Wescott of Providence, Rhode Island. As a girl, Wescott had been "the darling of an elderly father and a juvenile mother," a naive, lovely, flirtatious girl who broke hearts and prompted numerous proposals at first sight. Her own branch of the family was known for its strong attachment to one another and its indifference to the outside world.

If Mary Fitch Wescott had been naive and frivolous as a maiden, her marriage cured her of both failings with cruel abruptness. Within less than three years she bore three children. The eldest died. Thomas Perkins and his younger sister, Charlotte Perkins, survived. When the exhausted mother was told that another pregnancy would kill her, her husband abandoned her.

The dissolution of the Perkins family worked upon the consciousness and character of each member differently. Despite the poverty, the humiliating dependence on family charity that kept her moving from home to home and city to city, Mary Perkins never voiced a word of criticism at her abandonment. Thus, her children were left to struggle with its mystery. Their father's motives could only be imagined and their mother's continuing attachment to him only accepted as a reality.

Mary Wescott Perkins kept her silence, but she drew from this marital experience a lesson that surely helped shape her daughter's life. She learned, she said, that affection was a fatal vulnerability.

What was true physiologically became for her psychologically true as well: Love could kill. She strove, therefore, with devotion and steely determination, to arm her own children against emotional disappointment. She resolved to nurture stoics, immune to rejection because no appetite for love had been developed. This denial of affection to her children was, of necessity, also self-denial; out of love for her children she kept her distance from them. "I used to put away your little hand from my cheek when you were a nursing baby," she once remarked with pride and regret to her adult daughter. But her stoicism was acquired rather than natural, and there were lapses; in secret moments, when she thought her daughter Charlotte safely asleep, she held and caressed and kissed her.

It was Charlotte Perkins—precocious, intensely lonely, isolated from other children by her family's nomadic life, and alienated from her brother by his teasing style and his "bad" behavior—who bore most heavily the burden of her mother's contradictions. From Mary Wescott Perkins she learned the unintended but crucial lesson that there was a public, rational, independent self and a secret, emotional, vulnerable self. The young girl took the public self to be estimable and held the private self suspect. By the age of 10 she had constructed this dichotomy.

Her childhood diaries reveal a self-consciously stoical Charlotte, a character ruthlessly creating itself, always disciplining and reprimanding, always self-critical, trusting in rigorous programs for self-improvement to overcome unacceptable character traits. This was, for her, the real Charlotte Perkins. Yet she indulged a secret self. At night she immersed herself in a rich fantasy life, allowing her imagination to transport her to beautiful and exotic paradises where (as she later remembered) "the stern restrictions, drab routines, unbending discipline that hemmed me in became of no consequence." But allowing free rein to her imagination provided more than an escape from drab situational realities. Her fantasy worlds were never so randomly constructed as she might have believed. Repeatedly she peopled them with open and affectionate maternal figures who provided her with the secrets to winning a father's affection and esteem.

As sustaining as she knew her fantasy worlds to be, Charlotte Perkins felt the need to prove that she kept her imagination under control. Unwilling to relinquish it, she struck a bargain with herself that would preserve it: "Every night," she wrote, she would think of pleasant things that could really occur; once a week, of "lovelier, stranger things"; once a month, "of wonders"; and once a year, of "anything."

This bargain held until her adolescence. When she was 13, as Gilman recalled in her autobiography, her mother discovered the evening fantasies and ordered her daughter to end them. To this, Gilman wrote, an obedient child instantly acceded. Perhaps, however, Charlotte Perkins demanded of herself that the fantasies be abandoned, or transformed into something less disturbing to her conscious self. Such a transformation did occur, for even as she dissolved the kingdom of Ezephon she began to nurture an absorbing enthusiasm for the "things that could really occur" in the world of science and sociology. Social "wonders," existing and potential, began to preoccupy her; physics, with the power of its absolute laws, made magic pale; and the plausible utopias the social reformer could design were "lovelier stranger things," than the fairy kingdoms had ever been.

The bridge between the old fantasy world and the new scientific one was her own role in them. In either setting, Charlotte Perkins's part was heroic. In the new and less-disturbing secret life that took shape, she dreamed of becoming a renowned world server, a major figure in the reorganization of her society. The shift in focus to the real world offered her a better chance to release her productive and constructive energies. But lost in this transformation was the expression of a desire for intimacy and the frank recognition that loneliness was a negative condition.

Her imaginary worlds had helped her confront her feelings. They were populated by individuals who came to cherish her and to love her and, thus, to end her emotional isolation. But in the new world of social realities, Charlotte Perkins saw herself befriended by no one in particular and a friend to no one but impersonal humanity. In such a self-image, loneliness was elevated to a necessity; it was transformed into the price one paid for the heroic self. Through the prism of her new ambitions, the years of stoical training at last revealed their clear purpose. Her mother had intended to prepare her for survival only; now Charlotte Perkins saw that self-denial and discipline prepared one not simply to endure life, but to perform great deeds in it.

As this perception of her life hardened into an ideology, Charlotte Perkins lost the power to discern genuine interests from defensive commitments. The attraction of social reform became a shield against the appeals and the dangers of personal intimacy. The two modes of living were forced into contradiction. Armed with a rationale for dismissing her feelings, she often refused to probe their meaning. Some emotions she could incorporate into or redefine within her heroic image. Responses and impulses she could not thus account for, she simply denied. Her conscious certainty masked her deep ambivalence.

Her new self-image and its ambitions drew Charlotte Perkins to a closer identification with her father. He loomed in her mind—as figures often do who are not familiar realities—as the embodiment of his ideals rather than his performance. His reputation as a humanitarian was as well known to her as he was unknown. His apparent dedication to public service contrasted, in her mind, with her mother's slavish commitment to her children and the narrow circle of domestic life. Certain that her mother led a "thwarted life," she became equally certain that her father did not.

Thus, attraction to Frederick Perkins increased, even as the key to gaining his attention seemed to be found. Charlotte Perkins had sought that attention before, appealing to him to write to her because she was lonely. Appeals for support and approval now gave way to requests for reading lists in history, anthropology, and science. To these came speedy and lengthy replies. In this manner she reached out to him, speaking of her intellectual isolation, not a personal loneliness but an absence of tutelage and collegiality. No one at home, she wrote, could understand as he could her ambitions to relate to social issues. It was in this shared breadth of vision that she pressed their kinship. But for all her efforts to rise above "personal pain or pleasure," her disappointment at his frequent coolness and distance slipped into the letters. "Should I continue to write," she asked after a long period without response from Frederick Perkins, "for I am anything but desirous to intrude."

Her mother conveyed a sense of danger in the admission of personal needs, and her father seemed simply to dismiss them as trivial. Thus, both parents denied the validity of feelings to their daughter. But without knowing it, mother and father conspired in a second way. The young Charlotte Perkins came to believe that the compensations for self-control and self-negation were real in the public sphere and were only a mean mockery in the circle of the home; that the avenue to satisfaction and the path to despair were as inevitably separated as this man and woman. She must choose between them. And she must be allowed to choose between them. The choice was a demand upon her own resources; the possibility of choice was a demand upon the society in which she lived. The Victorian society she encountered seemed more hostile than receptive to her pursuit of a public life, and this would direct her reformist energies to the place of women in American society.

The new self-image that took shape in the early 1870s may have cushioned Charlotte Perkins while family relationships and economic circumstances disintegrated further. In 1871, after a decade of separation, Mary Wescott Perkins began a suit for divorce. Her motives are unknown, but the decision brought a dramatic alteration in her public image. When the divorce came in 1873, Mary Perkins was no longer a loyal and suffering wife; she had become a scandalous divorcée. Once-sympathetic Beechers and Perkinses closed their doors to her, and she and her children were left entirely on their own.

In 1873 the three moved to Providence, Rhode Island. They spent a brief time experimenting in cooperative living. When this failed, the Perkinses settled into independent poverty. While her mother struggled to support the family, Charlotte struggled for autonomy. At 15 she openly challenged her mother's rule of complete obedience, with ironic success. Free of parental control at last, she promptly disciplined herself: She swore to give total obedience to her mother until she reached age 21.

Superficially the results of rebellion and of defeat were one and the same; in more ways than she yet understood, Charlotte Perkins remained a dutiful daughter. Her real rebellion was not in character but in the uses to which she intended to put the stern self-discipline and the dire vision of a woman's lot in the world that were her inheritance. Mary Wescott Perkins intended to protect her daughter from disappointment, and to prepare her for life. But that protection was situational: It was in marriage, as wife and mother, that Charlotte Perkins was expected to face her tests. Charlotte Perkins intended, however, to escape marriage, to avoid the despair and defeat it guaranteed, and to meet her test in a world her mother could not know or imagine.

The reality of her adolescent years offered few opportunities to test the meaning of her commitment to spinsterhood. Her mother's excessive restrictions on Charlotte Perkins's social life limited her access to men and even to women. Without any real attachments and always desperately lonely, she fell back upon her imagination for relief. She formed a wild and absorbing crush on an actor she had seen perform but had never met. She nursed an adoration of an older woman who had been only casually kind. In her diaries she regularly denounced love and marriage, yet she filled its pages with speculation: "Who will you marry?" "What will be his age?" "What will you wear on your wedding day?"

At the age of 18 Charlotte Perkins described herself in her diary: "18 years old. 5'6½" high. Weigh some 120 lbs or thereabout. Looks, not bad. At times handsome. At others, decidedly homely. Health, perfect. Strength—amazing. Character—ah! . . . I am not in love with anybody; I don't think I ever shall be." This was written in January 1879. In February a short diary entry reasserted her lack of attachments. "No Valentines! No Regrets!" Perhaps there were no regrets. But in March of that year, her mother allowed Charlotte to accompany her on a visit to relatives in Cambridge and Boston. Here, suddenly, the 18-year-old found herself the belle her mother had so often been in her own youth. She was surrounded by young college men, courted by Arthurs, Edwards, and Charles Walter Stetson, a "Nice boy . . . but young." She frankly enjoyed the flirtation, and when she returned home in July, her mood grew gloomy.

That fall she returned to Cambridge and then went to Connecticut, and again was faced with a happy embarrassment of beaux. Back home in November, she kept herself busy writing letters to her new male friends, among them a younger cousin from Connecticut, George Houghton Gilman. For several months letters passed between "Dear Ho!" and "Dear Chopkins," and it was to Houghton Gilman that she most openly wrote of the boredom and the tension of living under the heavy hand of her mother. On March 6, 1878, she had chastised herself in her diary: "I must really abolish all desire for comfort or any sort of happiness if I expect to have any peace." But back in Cambridge for New Year's Day 1880, she recorded with pleasure a day of excitement and expectation, the "best day of my life."

Charlotte Perkins was nearly 20 when this brief flurry of social life broke the monotony of her Providence existence. When the excitement ended, she settled once more into biding her time until, at 21, she could embark upon her own life. Even in her impatience, however, she knew that things at home had greatly improved. She had studied art, and recently had enjoyed some independent income through the sale of miniatures and other decorative pieces. She found release for her physical energies—and an opportunity for sorority—at a local woman's gymnasium.

And despite her mother's continuing interference with her life—reading her mail, intercepting and rejecting social invitations—Charlotte Perkins had established her first genuine friendships with other women. One of these women was Grace Channing, daughter of a noted New England clerical family, a girl with a background similar to Charlotte's. Together, Grace Channing and Charlotte Perkins wrote plays and poems to entertain themselves and their families. But most intimate and most important was the friendship formed with Martha Luther, a young girl who for almost four years held Charlotte Perkins's unguarded confidence.

These friendships were hard-earned. Charlotte Perkins was as deeply wary of them as she was eager for them, thinking affection to be a trap and a drain on one's energies, but feeling it as a voluntary vulnerability. To protect herself, she compelled Martha Luther to make a pact, pledging that their affection would be "permanent and safe." Even with such a guarantee, Charlotte worried that she would jeopardize the relationship either by excessive demands for affection or, conversely, by sudden withdrawals of affection. "I was always in a fervor," she later recalled, "that for a time I should want to see her continually, and that there would be spaces when affection seemed to wane."

Sometime before the end of 1881 Martha Luther married and moved from Providence. Perkins felt the separation keenly, experiencing the old isolation and loneliness more intensely after the years of sharing with Luther. She was, by her own account, in a vulnerable state when, in January 1882, Charles Walter Stetson re-entered her life. Like Perkins, Stetson had trained as an artist. Art was an immediate bond between them, though perhaps it involved more competitive tension than either thought to admit. Even deeper was the bond of circumstance. "He was," Gilman later recalled, "a great man—but lonely, isolated, poor, misunderstood." Stetson's state of mind and worldly condition seemed to mirror her own perfectly. The two quickly fell in love and, within a short time, Walter Stetson proposed.

The effect of Stetson's proposal upon Charlotte Perkins was deep and disturbing. It came in her twenty-first year, and thus it set her cruelly at odds with herself. She was, by the terms of her bargain with herself, free at last of parental control. She felt an urgency to give her past meaning by pursuing its heroic dreams. Her self-esteem depended upon an energetic dedication to her social goals. To abandon the pursuit of a life of world service before it had begun, and to embrace instead love and marriage, would be to shatter a self-image that had, despite its problems, been sustaining.

Just when she needed most to understand what she truly desired and what she might realistically work to have, Charlotte Perkins was most completely at a loss. She could not separate her genuine commitment to social reform from the power she had invested in it to justify her emotional isolation; and because she had invested her commitment with that power in order to defend against emotional rejection and disappointment, she could not risk disarming it in the face of a proposal of marriage, with its confusing threats and promises of intimacy. She loved Walter Stetson and wanted to be with him. But she could neither overcome the powerful image of her mother's thwarted life nor separate that image from the institution of marriage itself; the two concepts were merged.

In order to avoid confronting her confusion, Charlotte recast her dilemma. She posed the choice as one between two mutually exclusive duties rather than two strongly felt desires. She faced, she told herself and Charles Walter Stetson, a decision to be made between a duty to life and a duty to love. Thus she distorted her feelings and the issues entirely; she sacrificed any awareness of her positive yearnings for both choices in order to avoid the reasons for rejecting either. In her diaries and her letters to Stetson, she hid behind a rhetoric of obligation and self-sacrifice that not even she could resist in the end. She made no effort to accommodate both duties. She was protected from this approach not simply by her psychic patterns, but also by her sociological perceptions. For women, life and love were not overlapping spheres. Men could have marriage and careers; women, responsible for home and children, could not. A sense of injustice that she could not entirely hide sprang from the fact that it was exactly this social division of labor and duties that she intended to reform.

For months, Charlotte Perkins pleaded with Walter Stetson for delay. This she won in large part simply by her indecision. Although he suffered, she felt she suffered more, because she was torn this way and that, and had, she told him, no peace. "How often one duty contradicts another," she exclaimed when, in the midst of reading in order to acquire a "general notion of how the world worked," she stopped to write him a letter. "And what a world of careful practice it needs to distinguish the highest!" It was the skill required to distinguish the highest duty that she felt sorely lacking. And this, she argued, accounted for her delay.

"I am not a tenderhearted child," she assured him, and herself, "neither am I an impulsive girl: But a clearheaded woman who is weighing a life time in her hands." How could she know what she would lose or gain if she had no experience of either life? On marriage and motherhood there were, she knew, all-too-many voices of authority to guide her. "This is noble, natural and right," said "all the ages." Her own body, she admitted, urged her to yield. Against her independence ran "all the ages" as well, for "no woman yet has ever attempted to stand alone as I intended." The grandiosity of this statement was entirely innocent, although it did not reflect social reality.

In the 1880s American women of her race and region were experimenting with independence. The existing social currents for change had, in fact, suggested to her the role of public woman and reformer; her ambitions confirmed that the struggle had already begun. Of course, the general contours of her society reinforced both her notion of women's segregated sphere and the heretical quality of her career aspirations. But when Charlotte Perkins spoke of standing alone, it was the expectation of emotional isolation rather than the concrete problems of economic support or practical opportunities that gave force to her personal drama.

What did she want to do? She had taken care to bury the answers and could not now plumb her own depths. She tried to clarify her thoughts in letters to Walter Stetson, in soliloquy rather than conversation. But she could not explain—or understand—herself. Why, she wrote, do I hesitate? Life with him promised paradise, she said, but love seemed to ask "more than I can give." Repeatedly, and with an unwitting callousness for his feelings, she pressed for a relationship that was limited, a friendship, like the one agreed upon with Martha Luther, that would free her from the necessity of choice. Companionship and friendship would satisfy her; why must there be love and marriage? "I ought not to complain of being offered the crown of womanhood," she confessed, voicing her own and her mother's tenacious romanticism about all that they feared; but she did not fully wish to accept it.

Slowly the choice crystallized into one of duty to submit and endure, or duty to rebel. Posed in these terms, love lost all its positive potential, and independence had its romance restored. But at the last moment, with frustrating perversity, she denied even her own freedom and responsibility to choose. Instead she bowed to the moral imperative of finding one's "right duty." The "right duty" was surely the more difficult one. As she weighed each choice, her pride—and the hint of pleasure—in her insistence "that my life is mine in spite of a myriad lost sisters before me" made her crucially uneasy with the choice of independence: thus, she chose marriage. On December 31, 1882, she wrote in her diary: "With no pride, with little hope, with uncertain occasional happiness, with no glad energy and living power; with no faith or nearly none, but still, thank God! with firm belief in what is right and wrong; I begin the new year."

A deep nostalgia and a sense of loss showed in her diary for 1883 as she made plans for marriage. Self-pity, wholly shrouded from her own consciousness, marked every page. Dread—equally of unhappiness and of happiness—pervaded this secret record of events.

On May 2, 1884, Charlotte Perkins and Walter Stetson were married. Despite all her mother's care and preparation, despite her own, Charlotte Stetson entered marriage as an innocent and a romantic: "My Wedding Day . . . HOME. . . ."

> I install Walter in the parlor and dining room while I retire to the bed chamber and finish its decoration. The bed looks like a fairy bower with lace, white silk, and flowers. Make my self a crown of white roses. Wash again, and put on a thin shift of white mull fastened with a rose bud and velvet and pearl civeture. My little white velvet slippers and a white snood. Go in to my husband. He meets me

joyfully; we promise to be true to each other; and he puts on the ring and the crown. Then he lifts the crown, loosens the snood, unfastens the girdle, and then— and then. O my God! I thank thee for this heavenly happiness! O make me one with thy great life that I may best fulfill my duties to my love! to my Husband!

May was filled with diary reports of great personal happiness and a total commitment of energy and ego to cooking, baking breads, visiting, and house care. She aimed for perfection and was furious at any domestic failures. Culinary errors made her "disgusted with myself." By mid-June efforts to prove herself a perfect wife were interrupted by an illness that left her weak and bedridden. By June 25 she was miserable, not because of domestic failures, but now because her "old woe"—"conviction of being too outwardly expressive of affection"—had begun to fill her with fears of driving Walter Stetson away. Assurances by her husband could only temporarily ease her mind. In early August she learned she was pregnant.

Through most of her pregnancy, Charlotte Stetson was both sick and depressed. The physical incapacity and loss of the body tone she had acquired through hours in the woman's gymnasium disturbed her, and they no doubt contributed to her sense of unnatural lethargy and of a passivity she held in contempt. Holding herself in ever lower esteem as the months went by, she feared Walter Stetson must share her disgust with herself. But her husband—almost stubbornly— proved sympathetic and supportive. "He has worked for me and for us both, waited on me in every tenderest way. . . . God be thanked for my husband!"

The pregnancy brought her little pleasure. Still, as the months passed, Charlotte Stetson began to adjust to her child-to-be in the terms she best understood: in the language of duty. Her hopes, she wrote, were that the child she carried would be a "world helper" and that she herself could serve the world by a devotion to the child. "Brief ecstasy, long pain. Then years of joy again," she wrote on the morning of March 23, 1885, when Katherine (Kate) Beecher Stetson was born.

But pain and joy seemed to wage a confusing struggle that left her helpless. Despite desperate efforts to be a perfect mother, Charlotte Stetson had given over the care of her daughter to her own mother by August 1885. Depressed, ill, bedridden, she had few days without "every morning the same hopeless waking." She could not explain her deepening depression. Her child was lovely, her husband was loving; she berated herself for not regaining control over her emotions and carefully shied away from locating in her illness any hostility or anger. She was suffering, she was certain, from a new disease called "nervous prostration," and she came to fear that she had contracted an infection of the brain.

Walter Stetson, however, surmised that marriage and motherhood were his wife's problems. Although he did not understand why this was the case, he accepted it. That fall he offered her a separation. But with desperate insistence Charlotte Stetson refused this relief. "He cannot see how irrevocably bound I am, for life, for life. No, unless he dies and the baby die, or he change or I change there is no way out." The dilemma was once again, if not of her own making, at least one she would not allow to be too easily resolved. She could not permit herself to be relieved or consoled; she was invested in this painful punishment. And, with the unintentional blindness of the determined sufferer, she forced husband, daughter, and mother to participate in her nightmare.

Then, in the summer of 1886, Charlotte Stetson bowed to family urgings and left, alone, for California. She looked forward to a host of reunions, visiting her brother Thomas in Utah, her father in San Francisco, and her good friend Grace Channing in Pasadena. The trip restored her health and spirits almost magically. The lush, rich floral splendor of Pasadena satisfied her childhood dreams of beauty; to her, the city was Edenic.

But her return home brought immediate relapse into illness and despair. That winter her husband took her to the famous woman's doctor, S. Weir Mitchell, for treatment at his clinic. Here, her worst fears that either love or "her driving force" must be relinquished were given confirmation by a representative of that impartial science she had always trusted. Mitchell, famous for his belief that anatomy was a woman's destiny, argued that the passivity of the womb must be echoed in the woman's daily life in order for true health to be hers. He prescribed for Charlotte Stetson a totally domestic life, the constant companionship of her child, and an absolute end to any writing or serious reading. Determined to obey this dictum of absolute domesticity, Charlotte Stetson reached the dangerous edge of insanity.

This total collapse, with its admission of failure and its punishment, seemed to release Charlotte Stetson from her commitment to her marriage. Every effort had been made. Thus, in early 1887 she agreed to a separation from her husband. She had, in significant if shrouded ways, recapitulated her parents' marital history. Her mother's physical danger from childbearing found its counterpart in her own near-insanity. But the Stetsons' separation, unlike that of Frederick and Mary Wescott Perkins, had no taint of a husband's abandonment.

Walter Stetson remained nearby, visiting whenever his wife allowed, some weeks coming to see her every day. He brought her gifts, cared for Kate when his wife or child was sick, and, as Charlotte Stetson frequently recorded in her diary with gratitude, did not press any demands upon her. Yet when she looked at the examples of marriage and motherhood around her, she identified with the despair of vulnerable and abused women. "Talked with Mrs. Smythe," she wrote on February 20, 1887. "She is another victim! Young, girlish, unexperienced, sickly, with a sickly child, and no servant . . . ignorant both, and he using his 'marital rights' at her vital expense."

By the end of the year, Charlotte Stetson had begun to think again of California and its healing effect on both body and mind. In 1888, with her daughter and her mother, she set out once again for Pasadena. She had done her duty to love; now she meant to fulfill her desire "to have my utmost capabilities called out in some necessary work."

In this manner, the Charlotte Perkins Gilman known to us through her books, lectures, novels, magazine articles, and poetry began her career. If this were a fairy tale, the woman who left New England "ashamed, degraded and despairing" to become an independent woman and a leading intellectual and social critic of her day would have soon experienced the personal satisfaction and self-esteem her achievements should have brought her. But this woman was who and what she was, and like us all she carried her past into her present.

With her mother (soon to develop cancer) and Kate, Charlotte Perkins Stetson lived a precarious existence, economically and emotionally, in California. She was formally uneducated, and unskilled except in commercial art. This occupation she did not pursue. Her goal was a public life and her career the preaching of a gospel of reform. She tried to support her family by giving public lectures on reform topics, but the proceeds from a passed hat were small. Extra income came from taking in boarders. Debts piled up; soon the triad was moving from house to house in a nomadic pattern reminiscent of her own childhood. If her experience as the head of a husbandless household echoed her mother's years of struggle, Stetson's love life became an odd parody of her marriage.

In 1890 she formed a relationship with another woman writer. The affair was not necessarily sexual; the intensity of emotion did not demand, though it may have included, physical expression. Perhaps Stetson was only seeking a friendship similar to the sustaining one with Martha Luther, but with "Dora" she accepted the subservient and self-negating role she had always associated with "wife." The aspects that had driven her from marriage she now experienced with, even seemed to invite from, Dora. Dora was generous with money, and Charlotte, who would take no financial aid from her estranged husband, accepted assistance from Dora—with every string attached. In return for the money and the companionship, Charlotte provided Dora with her domestic services, "making a home for her," and with intellectual support, cheating her own career by "furnishing material for [Dora's] work."

But the companionship was not so gentle and constant as that she had received from "her dear boy," Walter. Dora was an openly abusive partner. She was "malevolent. She lied . . . she drank . . . she swore freely, at me as well as others. She lifted her hand to strike me in one of her tempers." This affair, begun with the decade, ended when Dora left Charlotte in 1893. From this demeaning experience, Charlotte Stetson refused to learn anything except disappointment. She did not examine her choice of loves or raise any questions about what the affair reflected of her needs and her insecurities. She would only chastise herself in her diary: "Out of it all I ought surely to learn final detachment from all personal concerns."

These private turmoils did not prevent, but coincided with, Charlotte Stetson's growing recognition as a public figure. Her skills at extemporaneous speaking had earned her little money in her early years in California, but they had brought her a reputation, just as her first essays and published articles had brought national notice. Her radical views on the rights of labor and of women, on child care, and other social reforms earned her influential friends in California, as well as the expected enemies. In an essentially conservative state, there were nevertheless several active women's organizations and a few lively communities of intellectuals and writers. These groups welcomed Charlotte Stetson without hesitation, helped her find speaking engagements, and encouraged her to develop and expand her ideas.

Through her work with women's organizations like the Pacific Coast Women's Press Association, she made contact with the national leaders of the women's rights movement—Stanton, Stone, and the settlement house organizer, Jane Addams. To these friends and associates Charlotte Stetson appeared as an energetic, creative, remarkably productive, and admirable woman. But this image contrasted sharply with her own critical sense of herself. In her public life, as in her private life, she seemed determined to demean herself. She was not to be applauded for her raw energy or its constructive channeling, she felt. In reality, she was no better than a cripple; illness, fatigue, and the accompanying mental lethargy that she insisted were the legacy of her married life had permanently damaged her intellectual abilities. She was certain never to realize her potential, and thus she was a disappointment to herself, as she should be to others.

In her first year in California, amid the confusion of establishing a new life, with financial worries and a young child to care for, she had written 33 articles and 23 poems. But this was not enough to bring a sense of satisfaction. In every possible way she seemed to flee the self-esteem her work could and, by her own declared philosophy, should provide. She was hampered by an inability to take her work (rather than herself) seriously. Her speaking and her writing she dismissed as "natural" for her and therefore not to be confused with true work. Work she defined as everything she could not do easily, well, or at all, and she could not hope to do such work because her nervous condition prevented it. Thus, she felt her marriage remained with her; she had not escaped.

It was not the marriage itself that Charlotte Stetson remained wedded to, but rather her concept of her feminine identity. This identity was rooted in disappointment and the thwarted life. As she moved into what she viewed as a masculine sphere, the world of the mind and of action, she would not abandon its opposite. Ironically, though perhaps not surprisingly, the very things she defined as legitimate, enviable intellectual work—"reading, going into a library, learning languages"—were her father's skills, joys, and professional duties as a librarian. And these were, she insisted (and thus it was so), the achievements her past made impossible.

But Gilman's abilities were extraordinary. Quick, creative, able to grasp immediately the essentials of an argument and to generalize from seemingly disparate particulars, she had trained and tutored herself well during her lonely youth. Her true genius lay in her ability to transform her personal contradictions into valuable and legitimate insights on social problems and on the institutions and ideologies that created and sustained the problems.

In her ability to bridge the gap from personal experience to social understanding, she liberated her intellect from the immobility she protested she suffered. What fueled the process was her conviction that social solutions could be found that would some day obviate psychological dilemmas like her own. In this there was potential irony, for she had committed her energies to the elimination of a source of her creativity.

The intellectual framework of her insight was that of the evolutionary and progressive social analysts of her era. Like Lester Ward, Edward Bellamy, and other social critics of the late nineteenth century, she believed that the always shifting patterns of social organization could be understood, predicted, and to some extent manipulated if the evolutionary laws Charles Darwin had discovered were properly applied to human society. By understanding the laws of sociology, human participation in the shaping of human destiny was possible—and, for the concerned citizen, imperative.

Charlotte Perkins Stetson Gilman, like her peers, wrote and lectured to suggest the appropriate actions. For committed evolutionist reformers like herself, change was synonymous with progress. No matter how dark or regressive they might seem, the past and the present always served as a useful and ultimately justifiable base for a better future. Thus, there was equanimity in her perspective, despite the tone of urgency or impatience in pressing reform or the polemical style of her argument. She was dedicated to prodding for changes she was convinced would eventually come. It was only a matter of when and how smoothly the changes would arrive.

Gilman's own work was devoted to the analysis of the relationship of women to their society.[4] Her ideas were not formally or systematically presented until *Women and Economics* was published in 1898, but they had been formulated many years before and were already introduced in the work of her California days. As a historical social anthropologist, she traced the rise and institutionalization of patriarchy as a necessary step in human growth and progress. Until the development of modern industrial society, this patriarchal structure with its rigid segregation of women into sex-related functions had been essential for race preservation. But modern society no longer required such a segregation, nor its aggrandizement to the male of privilege and power through the monopoly of the social sphere. The laws and customs sustaining male monopoly on socially productive activity were now clearly without legitimacy. This kind of social division of labor was neither permanent nor fixed by nature; permanent sexual differences did not, as social conservatives argued, mean permanent differences in capacity for social productivity.

Women's potential for contribution in the social—or, as Gilman called it, the human—sphere must now be released and realized. This would mean a radical restructuring of the society, which would be resisted by men jealous of their privileges and by women ignorant of their deprivation. But, she wrote in 1912: "Social evolution has never waited for the complete enlightenment of mankind."

Gilman's vision of the future did not eliminate the genuine sex-related functions. Reproduction remained woman's specific natural specialization, essential to the preservation of the race. But she wholly renounced the traditional social institutions and duties that surrounded this sexual function. In books like *The Home* or in her *Forerunner* essays, she entirely dismantled the imprisoning female sphere of home-making and child care.

Astute and direct, Gilman located the institutionalization of women's oppression in the home and the family, and in the conditioned mentality that channeled all love and all sense of responsibility and potential for self-esteem into limited personal relationships rather than social activities and humanitarianism. Women were not merely trapped in the home, but also psychologically crippled so that they must only hope to remain there. Not only was their world too narrow, but they could not hope to master it. The sphere itself, with its multiple and dissimilar duties, its undifferentiated requirements, its mystique that forbade systematic training for what was "natural"—this chaotic agglomeration called home and child care could not be successfully managed by the average woman.

The fault lay with the role, not with the woman, Gilman insisted. Only a total disassembling and rationalization of "women's sphere" would be acceptable, with each component of women's traditional roles transformed into a modern, scientific, and professional activity. Once this process had begun, women could abandon their old tasks with confidence that none suffered as a result. They could release their energies in the larger world. Professional "baby gardens" or nurseries, professional food services, and house-cleaning services—on these Gilman's hopes rested. Woman's role would thus disappear, and she would not be accused of deserting it.

Femininity itself would be redefined and attainable: "As women grow, losing nothing that is essential to womanhood, but adding steadily the later qualities of humanness, they will win and hold a far larger, deeper reverence than that hitherto vouchsafed them. As they so rise and broaden, filling their full place in the world as members of society, as well as their partial places as mothers of it, they will gradually rear a new race of men, men with minds large enough to see in human beings something besides males and females."[5] Gilman's woman of the evolutionary future would be Elmondine, female and independent, at ease with her sex and her work.

Yet, ironically, Gilman's new woman carried with her the crucial social and psychic trappings of the old. Gilman, like many of her contemporary feminists, could not ultimately envision woman liberated from the task of nurturance itself, could not imagine woman pursuing work for her own personal satisfaction or solely for its challenge to her mind and ambitions. Although she was genuinely radical in the surgery she wanted to see performed on society and all its sacred institutions in order to free women from a sex-defined sphere of domesticity, her goal was to expand the area in which women might serve, not be served. Admittedly she placed the same standard of morality upon men; a desire to cooperate with and to contribute to the welfare of the greater society was, if anything could be said to be, the defining impulse of true humanity.

Here was the reform vision of her century, perhaps, but those who struggled to meet its demands with an obliteration of self were too often women like Charlotte Perkins Gilman. Too many of her own psychic struggles were over defining *self*, its boundaries never stable, the distinction between self-fulfillment and selfishness never clear. She had married, driven to a great extent by a repulsion at her *pride* in defining herself as a woman different from others and independent. Her self-esteem was stifled once she achieved that independence because, to take pride in her own creativity and talents, to cherish them for their own sake, could only be understood as selfish. Surprisingly, she would have more success in her private life resolving this dilemma of self and selfishness than her intellectual work incorporated or revealed.

Gilman's feminist ideas were shared by other women of her generation. Although her radical programs, such as dismantling the home, were resisted by feminists and nonfeminists, her central analysis of women and society was embraced. In her thinking and writing, in the realm of ideas, she was not isolated from others, but had found companionship.

In 1895 Charlotte Stetson left California. Within those eight years she had established herself as a writer, admired in literary as well as intellectual circles and praised by social reformers across the country. She had lectured for socialist and women's organizations. She had edited a financially unsuccessful but intellectually exciting radical newspaper. She had helped organize and had participated in women's conferences that earned her a place among the leading ranks of international feminists. She had organized a unique employment office, through which "day work" domestics could find temporary jobs. She had written about evolutionary socialism, anthropology, history, and feminism. But at the age of 35, when she left for the East, she judged herself a failure.

Charlotte Stetson returned East alone. Her mother had died in 1894. That same year Walter Stetson had remarried, choosing his ex-wife's friend Grace Channing as his bride. To many people's surprise—and disgust—Charlotte Stetson appeared delighted with this match. Soon after their marriage, she sent Katherine to live with them.

The decision to relinquish Katherine had been characteristically a blend of rational considerations and deep emotional ambivalence. Her relationship with Katherine was so complicated by fears of failing to be a good mother, by self-conscious and rigid pursuit of a program of "good mothering," and by doubts about its success, that her daughter made her both anxious and guilty. Like her own mother before her, she found it difficult to express directly the love and sympathy she felt for Katherine, often because she feared it would burden the child in some way.

She chose, again as her own mother had, to be useful to her daughter, to protect her by building in her a "right character." She substituted the doctrines of "understanding and self-control" for Mary Wescott Perkin's "obedience and discipline," and she produced a perfectly behaved, sober, responsible, emotionally distant young girl. When in 1894 Charlotte Stetson decided to send her daughter to the more stable home of the Stetsons and thus to the care of Grace Channing, she refused to let Katherine see that the separation would hurt her. In this way, she said, she protected Katherine from any uneasiness at deserting her mother. The cost of this denial Charlotte Stetson thought only she had to absorb.

Nothing she ever did raised such hostility or brought her such notoriety as this act of voluntary separation from her child. She was labeled an unnatural mother, accused not of failing as a mother but of renouncing her duty to be one. Duty and self-indulgence seemed to reverse themselves in the public eye, like a reflection in the mirror: She thought she was helping Katherine by giving her up; the newspapers said she was freeing herself. Her critics' insight was only semantic: The freedom they spoke of, a self-conscious self-interest, was not yet within her reach.

The year 1895 was spent in Chicago, with Stetson working for Jane Addams in the Chicago settlement-house projects. In January 1896 she attended a suffrage convention in Washington, D.C., where she met and befriended the famous pioneer in American sociology, Lester Ward. Between January and July of that year she took to the road, lecturing and giving guest sermons at 57 different churches or meeting halls in the Corn Belt.

In the midst of a hectic schedule she found time in April to visit New York City where her father, now remarried, had settled. Stetson liked her new stepmother and her grown daughters. Her father seemed content, their meeting was warm, and she allowed herself the sweet contemplation of a home at last—with her father. But by November 1896, when she returned to New York, Frederick Perkins had been moved to a sanatorium. He was helpless, growing rapidly senile as the arteries in his brain hardened. Her own intellectual powers were on the rise; his had ebbed. He would not be there to welcome or commend her to the larger world he had so long symbolized.

The next two years were important ones in Stetson's life. Free entirely of personal ties, she devoted herself to her work. She kept up an extraordinary pace, traveling for months at a time, lecturing, attending feminist meetings and conventions, and in her uncommitted hours, reading and writing. Everywhere she went she was confronted by the tangible evidence of her success. Men and women greeted her in each town, receptive to her ideas and eager to be near the energy she radiated. Younger women confessed that she was their model of independent womanhood. Her litany of self-doubt and self-criticism was weakened by this daily routine confirmation that she was indeed what she had wished and worked to be.

Reality thus seemed to catch up with Stetson during these years, and the passage of time seemed to make her more comfortable in her chosen role as spokeswoman for reform. Yet surely this maturation process pointed to a new receptivity to self-esteem. Perhaps the loss of both her parents freed her from the need to view her life in the old pattern of dichotomous loyalties and aversions, a duality that allowed her no victory without its companion, defeat.

One thing is clear: The acceptance of her success changed her understanding of her personal loneliness. Loneliness lost its heroic quality and she came to feel it not as a necessity or a punishment or the price of success, but simply as an emptiness. This changed perception influenced the course of her renewed friendship with Houghton Gilman.

On March 8, 1897, Charlotte Perkins Stetson visited Houghton Gilman's New York office for advice on a legal matter. It had been almost 20 years since "Ho" and "Chopkins" had exchanged letters, yet Houghton recognized her at once. "This," she later wrote, "was the beginning of a delightful renewal of an earlier friendship."

George Houghton Gilman was seven years his cousin's junior, a handsome, courtly, intelligent man. He was gentle, steady, generally likable. He had for most of his life been burdened with responsibility that had tied him down, emotionally and financially, for his mother was an invalid, his brother Francis a dwarf. These family obligations, heavy enough to oppress others, seemed not to embitter Houghton Gilman or to produce in him any debilitating sense of lost opportunities. He may have lived a circumscribed life, but he nevertheless found enjoyable moments and interesting pastimes. He was modestly ambitious and honorable; he liked his work as an attorney. He was not politically active or much attuned to the issues that so engrossed Charlotte Stetson. But he very much enjoyed her company.

Charlotte Stetson was obviously pleased with the new friendship and could not stay off the subject of Houghton Gilman, even in a letter to her daughter. "Last week I made a delightful discovery!

Found a cousin! . . . This cousin is Houghton Gilman . . . he is now a grown man nearly thirty, but when I remember him he was just your age." Then, only a few sentences later, she found herself writing: "To return to my newly discovered cousin; he is in the 7th regiment, and is going to take me to see them perform next Tuesday."

By March 18 the cousins were corresponding again, as they had decades ago. Charlotte, full of things to say and feelings to show, chose to write them to "Ho" even though they were both in New York City. "In some ways," she explained, "paper is freer than speech." The paper served her well, for the letters are frank and intense. "What a good time I did have the other night!" she wrote on March 18. "You now float and hover in my brain in a changing cloud of delectable surroundings."

Enjoying Houghton Gilman's company and his confidence seemed to reinforce Charlotte Stetson's awareness of how carefully she had repressed her feelings over the last several years and had escaped dealing with them by a frenzy of activity. "These years, when I stop doing things and my mind settles and things come up into view, most of these are of so painful a nature that I have to rush around and cram them back into their various (right here I have to stop and write a poem on 'Closet Doors' . . .)." But Gilman had created a mental space for her. "Now when I am quiet," she wrote, "there's a pleasantest sort of feeling—warm and cosy and safe."

Although her friendship with Gilman had allowed her room to test her capacity for affection once more, and helped her come to terms with its long absence, she was still wary and insecure. She often insisted that the relationship was platonic, familial, with herself the idiosyncratic but interesting older cousin and him the elegant and courtly young boy who found her educational and amusing in a maiden-aunt fashion. "I am looking ahead and wishing most earnestly and tenderly that you may have such a house as you deserve and one of the very charmingest of wives," Charlotte Stetson typically included in a long and effusive letter, using her pose as "Aunt Charlotte" like a talisman against disappointment.

As the odd courtship continued, these letters became—as those to Walter Stetson had once appeared to be—an open battleground for her conflicting emotions. But Charlotte Perkins Stetson had grown. There may have been defensive cul-de-sacs and charades, but there was nevertheless a true effort to discover her feelings, to know her desires, and to act as she wanted to act rather than as she ought. She knew that Houghton Gilman made her feel good about herself, good enough for her to admit how very low her self-esteem had always been. "Truly Houghton, for all the invulnerable self-belief and self-reliance which I have to have to live at all, you have no idea how small potatoes I think of myself at heart, how slow I am to believe that anyone's kindness to me is other than benevolence."

Houghton Gilman could not help but know. She had revealed her insecurity in every letter, in a transparent flippancy that was too earnest to be coy. "It won't surprise me in the least when you get over liking me as they all do," she had written, and in a hundred different forms she repeated the same fears over the next years. It was an appeal for reassurance woven into the letters with others. "Do [my letters] annoy you? I couldn't write for a week 'cause this fear depressed me," she wrote while in Kansas; "*Say* you like me if you do—often!" she added to a letter that summer.

For four years Charlotte Stetson confided her present and her past to Houghton Gilman, in a dialogue largely with herself. And, although much of the content was self-denigrating and self-pitying, there were moments of a new comfortable feeling about herself. She began to treat herself well, to buy clothing, and to indulge in gratuitous touches of luxury. She had begun to celebrate herself. Although this delight in self would previously have repelled her, now she began to accept personal pleasures that harmed no one by their fulfillment. Most important, she re-examined the very basis of affection.

Duty, she discovered, could not always promote or sustain love. "I have loved many people, in various ways, mostly because they needed it," she wrote Houghton, "but . . . the way you make me feel is different. It is not merely in the nature of wanting you—in the sense of a demanding personal affection, or even of—well, any kind of hungriness. And it is not at all in the sense of wishing to serve . . . the uppermost feeling is of pure personal gratification because you are so!"

What surprised Charlotte Stetson most was that the frank commitment to love did not destroy the sense of commitment to her life's work. Self-denial and self-satisfaction were not after all mutually exclusive rulers of character and destiny; there was room in her to accommodate both states. Her work improved, she told Houghton, her energies increased, her desire to write was not diminished but intensified. She had moments of genuine optimism. "The new charmed being now accepted by Madam Conscience, who has been struggling violently to choke it up for some time past, works admirably and I begin to see my way to let out more love towards Kate, too."

In truth, Charlotte Stetson was at the peak of her career when she wrote these letters to Houghton Gilman. *Women and Economics* was published in 1898 and won instant international acclaim. Even before it was published she was at work on a second book. In the summer of 1899 she returned to England, a star among equals at the international women's conference. Her lecture tours at last showed a profit, with Houghton Gilman acting as her agent and adviser. Her personal philosophy, equating living with growing, had once located growth in the soil of pain, denial, and disappointment. Now she conceded a growing that was expansive and inclusive. What could be a clearer sign of the changes in Charlotte Perkins Stetson than that she had at least developed a sense of humor. The heroic figure could now laugh a little at herself.

In June 1900 Houghton Gilman traveled to the Midwest to meet Charlotte Stetson. She was in the midst of a speaking tour; he had taken the summer away from his law practice. They had not seen each other for almost a year. On June 11 they were married. Of this wedding day, Charlotte Perkins Gilman, now 40, wrote:

> Monday . . . Our Day . . . the end of waiting, not to let the happiness blind and mislead me—dull my sensitiveness, check my sympathy, stop my work. It will not, I know; it has not so far and it will not. On the contrary I shall do more work and better. . . . I suppose I shall get used to love and peace and comfort and forget to be grateful everyday! But I doubt it. The other life has been too long. . . . I have liked as well as loved you from the first. . . . So strong and quiet and kind . . . to your pure and noble Manhood I come humbly, gladly full, bringing all that I have and am—willing to be taken as I am. . . . I am coming to be your happy Wife.

Gilman's new confidence in the harmony possible between her public and private lives proved well founded. For 34 years her personal happiness neither hampered her work nor eroded her feminist perspective. When, on August 17, 1935, she ended her own life to avoid debilitation by cancer, she was no longer an influential figure in the world of ideas or politics. The war and the decade that followed had destroyed the world she knew. The era of optimistic reform had passed; and the search in the 1920s by young women for self-gratification and satisfaction without any commitment to public service had made her militant but nurturant feminism obsolete. Despite her eclipse, Charlotte Perkins Gilman continued to write and to advocate the restructuring of society. Her last book, however, was not social anthropology but autobiography, charting an inner odyssey to both independence and interdependence. It was a conscious effort to mark the path for other, younger women.

In the end, Charlotte Gilman's philosophy and her psychic needs seemed, after all, to be one. She sought a social and psychological androgyny: a full humanity, to be experienced by each individual, that would create harmony among them through shared experience rather than the isolation and dualism of the sexually segregated world into which she had been born. She sought the pride in contribution and participation that ensured self-esteem, and the condition of independence that ensured equality. She sought the integrated self, and even at those moments when she felt it impossible for herself in her own lifetime, she was determined to secure it for future generations of women and men.

Notes

[1] In this essay, all materials from Gilman's diaries and personal correspondence with family and friends are drawn from the Charlotte Perkins Gilman Papers, Schlesinger Library, Radcliffe College, Cambridge, Massachusetts.

[2] See, for example, the novelettes serialized in *The Forerunner* (1911–1916), reprinted by Greenwood Press, New York, 1968.

[3] Gilman's own account of her family history and her life, from which much of the information in this essay is drawn, can be found in her autobiography, *The Living of Charlotte Perkins Gilman*, D. Appleton-Century, New York and London, 1935.

[4] Gilman's books, published between 1898 and 1935, are: *Women and Economics*, Small, Maynard, Boston, 1898; *In This Our World*, Small, Maynard, Boston, 1898; *Concerning Children*, Small, Maynard, Boston, 1900; *The Home: Its Work and Influence*, McClure, Phillips, New York, 1903; *Human Work*, McClure, Phillips, New York, 1904; *What Diantha Did*, Charlton, New York, 1910; *The Man-Made World*, Charlton, New York, 1911; *His Religion and Hers: The Faith of Our Fathers and the Work of Our Mothers*, D. Appleton-Century, New York, 1923; *The Living of Charlotte Perkins Gilman*.

[5] Charlotte Perkins Gilman, "Are Women Human Beings? A Consideration of the Major Error in the Discussion of Woman Suffrage," *Harper's Weekly* (May 25, 1912).

Jane Addams

(1860–1935)

G. J. Barker-Benfield

Jane Addams, born in 1860, was the founder of Hull House in 1889. This was one of the earliest of American "settlements," community houses established in poor urban neighborhoods to stimulate social reform. Addams publicized the goals and achievements of settlements in hundreds of lectures around the country, which she used as the basis of a dozen books published between 1902 and 1930. In 1895 she collaborated with her fellow workers on Hull House Maps and Papers, *one of the first sociological studies of tenements and sweatshops. She published* Twenty Years at Hull House *in 1910. Addams's reform impulses led her to suffrage, to political progressivism, and to help establish an international peace movement during World War I (1914–1918). The latter activity subjected Addams to jingoistic vilification. She was expelled from the Daughters of the American Revolution, but elected the first president of the International League of Peace and Freedom in 1919. Further resisting conformist pressures, Addams was a founder of the American Civil Liberties Union in 1920 and worked for it for most of the rest of her life. She also continued to work for peace and remained a controversial figure throughout the 1920s. Addams maintained her relationship with Hull House and in 1930, she published* The Second Twenty Years at Hull House. *In 1931, Addams shared the Nobel Peace Prize with Nicholas Murray Butler, the noted educator, and was frequently named the "Greatest American Woman" by public opinion polls. Her political heritage and her work with Herbert Hoover's relief agency in Europe during and after World War I led Addams to support Hoover for presidency in 1928 and 1932. Addams died of cancer in 1935.*

The following essay examines the decisive phases of Ad-

dams's life in order to cast light on how middle-class women overcome opposition to their entering public life. The essay challenges the reader to do two things: to follow Addams's own detective work in diagnosing her illness; and to watch carefully for the connections between this intimate story and the larger social changes of which it was part.

Jane Addams came from a family with deep roots in Pennsylvania and Quaker history. She was born in 1860, in Cedarville, Stephenson County, northern Illinois, to John and Sarah Addams, who had moved there from Pennsylvania right after their marriage in 1844, nine years after the first white settlers had arrived. Staked by his own father, John Huy Addams (1822–1881) had bought a saw and grist mill which, in the primarily lumbering and agricultural region that he helped link to Chicago by rail, provided the basis for his economic success. He moved into banking, investment, and politics, where he was an associate of Abraham Lincoln.

Jane was the youngest of the five children who survived infancy: Mary, born in 1846; Martha, 1850 (she would die at 16); James Weber, 1853; and Alice, in 1854. Their mother, Sarah Weber Addams (1817–1863), who had attended "boarding school" in Philadelphia, was "accomplished in music and drawing," and was pregnant nine times, her last pregnancy terminating with her death.[1] The bereaved family was augmented in 1868 by John Addams's marriage to the widowed Anna Haldeman; she brought two sons into the household from her former marriage. Harry,* then aged 18, and George, at 7, close to Jane Addams's age. From 1868 until they went to college in 1877, Jane and George were "inseparable companions."[2] Like her siblings, Addams had attended the one-room school house in Cedarville, her education there supplemented by private lessons in music and drawing. While George went to Beloit College, Jane followed her female siblings to Rockford Female Seminary (1877–1881). She then successfully completed the first year of medical studies at the Pennsylvania Woman's Medical College in Philadelphia (1881–1882). But in her autobiography she would include that year in the period of sickness and uncertainty that lasted, she wrote, "from the time I left Rockford in the summer of 1881 until Hull House was opened in the autumn of 1889."[3]

While traveling in Europe in 1888, Addams visited Toynbee Hall

---

*Harry Haldeman married Alice Addams in 1876 and therefore bore the double relation of stepbrother and brother-in-law to Jane Addams.

in London, an all-male "community of University men who live there, have their recreation and clubs and society all among the poor people, yet live in the same style they would live in their own circle." This visit seems to have crystallized Addams's purpose, which she would share with many others: the establishment of reform centers, or "settlements," to bridge the social gulf that had opened up in American cities as the result of the expansion of industrialism and the immigration which it sucked in. Addams's achievement was to do for women what she often said Lincoln had done for men: open up a "channel through which the moral life of his countrymen might flow," a channel that is, into public life.[4]

By 1900 there were over a hundred settlements in American cities.[5] Addams became the leader of this national movement, and in 1911 was elected the first head of the National Federation of Settlements, a position she held until 1935. Settlements were the tips of an iceberg of reform activities during this period. Drawing on the sociological studies they helped to create at the same time they were creating "social work," settlement house workers devoted themselves to improving the physical and mental health of the working-class population. They attempted to rid city dwellers of unsanitary housing, poisonous sewage, contaminated water, high infant mortality, adulterated food, smoke-laden air, juvenile crime, and overcrowded tenements. They gave classes in many subjects, including the English language and American civics, and they provided the space and means for a host of recreational activities, from debate to dance, athletics to theater. Addams made a point of celebrating immigrant cultures, including women's traditional work. Most obvious in this huge range of issues was an emphasis on the concerns of women and children.[6]

The frustrations of attempts to ameliorate living and working conditions of poor working women and men led Addams and her fellow workers into municipal and then national politics. The settlement house workers were the "spearheads of reform." They wished to establish that government's function included the protection of the public's health and welfare. Facing nitty-gritty machine politics in Chicago, they led the middle-class effort to transform it, to open up those clogged channels to the scientific-mindedness of progressivism. Hull House generated leaders, such as Florence Kelley and Grace Abbott, who would go on to head government agencies of inspection and reform. Addams, therefore was vitally important in connecting the scientized but traditional separate-sphere idea of "social housekeeping" with politics. She was a vice president of the National American Woman Suffrage Association from 1911 to 1914. In 1912 she seconded Theodore Roosevelt's nomination as the presidential candidate of the breakaway Progressive party, which, committed to the same goals as Hull House, would, Addams said, "appeal to women, and seek to draw upon the great reservoir of their moral energy so long undesired and unutilized in practical politics. . . ."[7]

Hull House was a meeting place for intellectuals and leaders of all sorts, a seedbed for social work and sociology, and a place where socialism was seriously debated. In the aftermath of the Haymarket riot of 1887, in which violence broke out at a labor rally, Hull House gained a reputation for radicalism because it sponsored speakers across the whole political spectrum. Addams was influenced by Marxism but in the end drew back because of the ideological rigidity of the Chicago socialists. She was rooted in American political traditions of free speech and a belief in "the slow march of human progress." Her conviction "that social arrangements can be transformed through man's conscious and deliberate effort" ran counter, she said, to a "crude interpretation of class conflict" which, to Chicago socialists, was "the test of the faith."[8] In her view of American democratic possibilities, Addams inherited Lincoln's political beliefs. The second chapter of her autobiography is entitled "The Influence of Lincoln," an influence intertwined in her imagination with the influence of her father. To immigrants she "held up Lincoln for their admiration as the greatest American" in a way that spoke to their heritage and to her own. "I invariably pointed out his marvelous ability to retain and utilize past experiences." In asserting that those experiences were of "the common people," Lincoln cleared the title to "our democracy," which was America's most "valuable contribution" to "the moral life of the world." Addams's terms combined Lincoln's views with what she, like the majority of suffragists and reformers at this time, saw as women's special contribution to public life.[9]

Of course, Lincoln had directed the enormous expansion of the federal government during the Civil War, although it had contracted afterwards. Addams held fast to her belief in the free-enterprise system but she, too, advocated the expansion of the powers of the federal government, in effect to prevent class war.[10] Using the expansion of government to clean up the abuses of capitalism can be seen as the application to the public sphere of domestic values, virtue, harmony, and caring, with which women and the "woman's sphere" had been invested. This is what is meant by "social housekeeping."

Her outspoken leadership of the peace movement in World War I brought Addams up against the clear limits of women's activity in the public sphere. In a notorious speech in 1915, Addams suggested that young soldiers on both sides were mutinying against war; many, she said, had to be doped up to make bayonet charges. Instantly her reputation was reversed. She was called "a silly, vain, impertinent old maid. . . . Her dabbling in politics, her suffrage activity and her ill-advised methods of working for peace have materially lowered her in the esteem of her former admirers." Thereafter Addams carefully identified herself as a "Corn Mother," an archetypal figure of a provider, and simply raised supplies of food for wartime refugees.[11]

Out-of-step in the matter of war, she was also out-of-step in peacetime popular culture. Although she regained her reputation, Addams remained a "Victorian lady" and was no longer a "role model for college women."[12]

Jane Addams never married and never had children. Her family relationships were those she established first with Ellen Gates Stars and then with Mary Rozet Smith. In this she resembled a large proportion of college women of their generation[13] who thought of motherhood and public individuality as mutually exclusive alternatives. This was another facet of the culture's belief in a doctrine of separate spheres, the public, dominated by men, the private, inhabited by women with children, the idolized mothers.

Middle- and upper-class women who moved into public life did so by claiming that they were expanding the domestic sphere rather than leaving it. It was precisely on the grounds that "society" beyond the home—men's world—was in such desperate need of the qualities associated with the home and its most constant inhabitant—mother—that from early in the nineteenth century women claimed public roles as charity workers, reformers, teachers, nurses, and eventually, doctors and social workers. Social housekeeping was squared with "the ideology of mother." The apparently widespread adherence to such an ideology after the industrial revolution, by men as well as by women, can be explained in part perhaps as the psychological effect of the experience of children spending increasing hours and years at home with middle- and upper-class women, themselves increasingly isolated at home, their meaningful work confined to childrearing.

Whatever its origins, maternal ideology came to stand for American feminism's "only abiding culture" in a context of pervasive sexual prejudice, antifeminism, and the deep divisions of religion and immigration, as well as class.[14] Of course, there was a profound limitation built into the doctrine of separate spheres because it was held to rest on "nature." Women's capacities, it was asserted time and again, were determined by their reproductive organs. We shall see how this governed the diagnoses of women's illnesses. The male sphere was never held to be determined by nature in that way. Men could transcend nature; this was the rationale for their claim to command women.

The conflict between motherhood and public life was one of several conflicts caused women by the identification of female with private, and male with public. A second lay in the relations between fathers and daughters. At least that is what Addams's own words suggest. In approaching such a difficult subject, the historian must be as careful with the evidence as in the case of any other subject. So, the following history rests squarely on what Addams herself chose to tell. It is a story of which everyone has a particular and historical version, since everyone has a psychic life dependent on childhood, the challenge of growing up. Women's versions have had to take into account the force of sexual prejudice and the variability of resources available to combat it. Success here, as everywhere, depends on consciousness.

Addams wrote a dozen books. Her niece, Anna Marcet Haldeman-Julius describes the scrupulousness with which she did so. Addams "had a compulsion to find exactly the right word and she needed to write, re-write, and write again. This often involved considerable transposition. The mechanical device by which she accomplished this most efficiently, and which she taught me, was that of cutting paragraphs or sentences out of one page of her manuscript and pinning them as inserts in their shifted sequence on another page. This gave her books that flowing spontaneity which is so often the rich reward of thought and toil."[15] Her most famous book was *Twenty Years at Hull House with Autobiographical Notes* (1910), the major text for the rest of this essay. That Addams made it both autobiographical and nonautobiographical, as well as that she wrote it with so much care should be borne in mind.

A significant portion of *Twenty Years* explaining the motive and rationale for the creation of settlement houses is Addams's diagnosis of the mysterious illness from which she suffered between 1881 and 1889, when she founded Hull House. To her, that illness was enormously important, not the least because she thought it one which millions of women shared. She linked it to her ambivalent relationship with her father and suggested the limitations of daughters' identifying with fathers and doing their parents' will. She described how she came to enjoy a multitude of roles—writer, administrator, fundraiser, and politician. But, she showed how she found the "ideology of mother" to be of particular value. By 1910 Addams was clearly identified as a social mother, a reputation she was usually careful to foster. The *Los Angeles Times* called her "a woman who has ever mothered humanity, though herself unwed."[16]

The early death of Addams's mother, Sarah Weber Addams, left Jane's father as the formative influence on her. "I centered upon him all that careful imitation which a little girl ordinarily gives to her mother's ways and habits. My mother had died when I was a baby and my father's second marriage did not occur until my eighth year."[17] While her primary emphasis here is obviously on imitation of her father, we should note in this passage Addams's recognition of conventional sexual identification (daughters with mothers) and the contrast between "My mother" and the exclusion of her father's second wife, Anna Haldeman, Jane's stepmother. Sarah Weber Addams's obituary suggests a general similarity between her reputation and that of her daughter: "Mrs. Addams will be missed everywhere, at home, in society, in the church, in all places where good is to be done and suffering relieved."[18] Sarah Addams had led the kind of life idealized by those moralists so alarmed by the frivolity and ill-health of later generations of young women. According to Allen Davis, Addams's mother

> supervised the operation of what was virtually a domestic factory; she also did a great portion of the actual work herself. The household produced its own soap, lard, candles, rugs, quilts and stockings; it preserved fruits and vegetables, salted meats, baked bread, and prepared meats for as many as twenty farm and mill hands in addition to the family.[19]

As Jane Addams would find herself acting as a midwife to the poor immigrant peasants of Chicago, so Sarah Addams, forty-nine years old and nine months pregnant, had gone one Friday years earlier, "in the best traditions of the rural village to the aid of another woman in labor. The doctor was out on another call and Sarah took complete charge." She "overexerted" herself, and became deathly sick.[20]

After going blind, having convulsions, being delivered of a dead infant, and falling unconscious for long periods, Sarah Addams died the following Wednesday. Jane Addams's uncle, George Weber, described Jane's reactions to her dying mother. Sarah Addams had lain "unconscious until Sunday about 11 o'clock. The first we noticed of any consciousness was when their little daughter Jenny [Jane Addams] cried with a loud shriek. Sarah raised up in bed, but oh the wild look she had! she soon sunk back again."[21] Seventy years later, Addams recalled this episode from her early childhood for her nephew, James Weber Linn, who was writing her biography, Addams insisted that she remembered one of her mother's responses to her as her mother lay dying:

> She remembered being aware that her mother was in the ground-floor bedroom of the house; pounding on the door with her fist, and hearing her mother say, 'Let her in, she is only a baby herself.' As she [Jane Addams] declared, "No one ever told me this, and it is impossible that I could have invented it."[22]

Addams's own declaration about this scene shows the importance to her of that maternal caring and of her remembering it.

After Sarah Addams's death, Jane's eldest sister Mary, "her mother's replica," managed the Addams household. Jane is believed to have said to Mary's son, James Linn, that Mary was "so far forgetting of herself in others that by them she became unforgettable."[23] It remained the same kind of household as it had been under Sarah Addams and must have been full of memories of her. Jane became especially attached to her old sister Martha, and must have experienced a second maternal deprivation on Martha's death when Jane was six. Naturally Jane then apprehended the loss of her mother's replica: "my horrible dream every night would be Mary's death and no one to love me."[24] Mary provided her with maternal continuity, as it were, until it was disrupted by John Addams's marriage in 1868 to Anna Haldeman, when Jane was eight. At the same time, Mary moved away first to the college at Rockford, then to marry John Linn. The household also changed in character from what it had been under Sarah Addams and her daughters, that is, from a "domestic factory" along traditional lines to as close to a "center of culture and art" as Anna Haldeman Addams could make it.[25]

Jane Addams resisted going to Rockford Female Seminary. In 1877 the seventeen-year-old Addams had visited Smith College (which had opened two years earlier), passed the entrance examination, and had been admitted, but John Addams had insisted she go to Rockford to which he had sent Jane's elder sisters. Addams published an account of this conflict with her father in *Twenty Years:*

> As my three older sisters had already attended the seminary at Rockford, of which my father was trustee, without any question I entered there at seventeen. . . . I was very ambitious to go to Smith College, although I well knew that my father's theory in regard to the education of his daughters implied a school as near at home as possible, to be followed by travel abroad in lieu of the wider advantages which an eastern college is supposed to afford. . . . I was greatly disappointed at the moment of starting to humdrum Rockford.[26]

The passions on each side of this conflict are unmistakable. On one side Jane Addams was "very ambitious" and then "greatly disappointed." On the other side was the immovable, indeed, the unchallengeable will of her father. For years his feelings had been elaborated into a rigid "theory" regarding female education which required daughters to stay as close to parental supervision as possible. Such parental supervision would have been supplemented, in both his eyes and his daughters', by his authority as a Rockford trustee. Obviously,

John Addams lacked institutional authority at the college his daughter preferred: his parental supervision would also have been curtailed had she gone to faraway Smith. Although it was slowly changing, Rockford, like other female seminaries, emphasized "accomplishments" and morality for young ladies being shaped for marriage. Smith, with its contemporaries Vassar, Wells, Elmira, and Wellesley, was founded in part as criticism of the inequalities offered "females" by the seminary. The colleges would offer women an education equal to that offered men.

The trouble was that if John Addams believed that after her seminary education his daughter should follow the traditional role of domestic women, he had also "passed on to her his own driving sense of ambition" and social responsibility.[27] Addams tells us in *Twenty Years* how he had paid her "as a little girl, five cents a 'Life' for each Plutarch hero I could intelligently report to him, and twenty-five cents for every volume of Irving's *Life of Washington*." He supplied her with masculine models and she had reciprocated by modeling herself after him. John Addams conveyed to her his reverence for Lincoln, his ally and friend in Illinois politics, and she responded by always associating Lincoln "with the tenderest thoughts of my father." Addams's identification with her father included her "consuming ambition" to have hands shaped, like his, by milling: "This sincere tribute of imitation, which affection offers its adored subject, had later, I hope, subtler manifestations, but certainly these first ones were altogether genuine. In this case, too, I doubtless contributed my share to that stream of admiration which our generation so generously poured forth for the self-made man." From the vantage point of 1910, when she wrote this, Addams reaches back to locate her particular experience in a broad social context, that of laissez-faire. But how could a daughter become a self-made man?[28]

At Rockford, Addams became a friend and inspiration to teachers as well as fellow students. The latter looked to her for advice and leadership and her teachers regarded her as at least their equal. This is clear in the letters they continued to write her after she left Rockford. They all expected her to act on the ambition she had expressed, to study medicine and live with the poor, in spite of the physical weakness and pains to which they knew she was vulnerable. They were vulnerable to them too. In *Twenty Years*, Addams tells us that "long before the end of my school days [at Rockford] it was quite settled in my mind that I would study medicine. . . ." Because Rockford did not yet grant degrees, she planned to take a B.A. from Smith before going to medical school. She had never given up the ambition her father had blocked when she was seventeen. But she became sick immediately before leaving Rockford in 1881. She must have anticipated the opposition to her future plans that she knew she would meet at home. Her graduating essay, entitled "Cassandra," embodied the conflict. While it was optimistic about the future of the "contemporary woman," Addams wrote it was her tragic-fate "always to be in the right and always to be disbelieved and rejected."[29]

Addams presents the conflict to her public a second time in *Twenty Years*, but on this occasion it is generalized to the typical female graduate. Nonetheless, its context makes it clear that such a conflict had occurred in her own life and that Addams intended this to be understood. That context is Addams's explanation for her post-college illness and cure, amounting to what Addams calls "The Subjective Necessity for Social Settlements."[30] It was the amplification of the personal diagnosis she had made of her sickness in a previous chapter, "The Snare of Preparation." She says of what she presents as the typically frustrated graduate facing her parents on her return from college: "She is besotted with innocent little ambitions, and does not understand this apparent waste of herself, this elaborate preparation if no work is provided for her." She is prepared by her parents to expect a life devoted to "the good of the whole" and then, she implies, is confined to a cultivation of "the good of the ego."

> Parents are often inconsistent: they deliberately expose their daughters to knowledge of the distress in the world; they send them to hear missionary addresses on famines in India and China; they agitate together over a forgotten region of East London. . . . from babyhood the altruistic tendencies of these daughters are persistently cultivated. They are taught to be self-forgetting and self-sacrificing, to consider the good of the whole before the good of the ego. But when all this information and culture show results, when the daughter comes back from college and begins to recognize her social claim to the "submerged tenth," and to evince a disposition to fulfill it, the family claim is strenuously asserted. . . .[31]

Addam's disposition when she left college had been "to study medicine and 'live with the poor.' " It was her father who, in her words, had opened up to her in childhood "the great world of moral enterprise and serious undertaking," a sense of the genuine relationship which may exist between men who share large hopes and like desires, even though they differ in nationality, language, and creed; that those things count for absolutely nothing between groups of men who are trying to abolish slavery in America or to throw off Hapsburg oppression in Italy." It was her father, she is telling her readers in the meticulously constructed *Twenty Years*, who had been "inconsistent."[32]

Addams had published another description of this parent-daughter conflict eight years earlier, as chapter two of *Democracy and Social Ethics* (1902), "Filial Relations." Here she pointed out that modern education had finally recognized woman "apart from family or society claims. . . ." This quality allowed women potentially to identify with the individualism claimed by men, even with the self-making Addams believed her father epitomized. Modern education she said, gave woman "the training which for many years has been deemed successful for highly developing a man's individuality and freeing his powers for independent action." But when she returned home from college she found that her parents assumed "that the daughter is solely an inspiration and refinement to the family itself and its own immediate circle, that her delicacy and polish are but outward symbols of her father's protection and prosperity. . . . She was fitted to grace the fireside and to add lustre to that social circle which her parents selected for her." The educated woman had to struggle against the family's, above all the father's, definition of her as "a family possession." The struggle was between this "family claim" and the "social claim" to "act her part as a citizen of the world." Addams said that most daughters "repress" the social claim in the face of the concrete and strenuous assertion of the family claim. Each one "quietly submits," but not without a continual feeling of having been "wronged." It was in this same chapter, "Filial Relations," that Addams presented most dramatically her insight into a father's attempt to limit a daughter: "It was new to him that his daughter should be moved by a principle obtained outside himself, which even his imagination could not follow; that she had caught the notion of an existence in which her relation as a daughter played but a part."[33]

The family claim was asserted, Addams said, by "parents." While I am suggesting that Jane Addams's veneration of her father was to prove the chief obstacle to her attainment of independence, we should not ignore the woman she faced at her father's side on her return from college. John Addams's second wife is absent from Jane Addams's autobiography. Anna Haldeman Addams's letters to her stepdaughter show her to have been anxious, petty, and demanding in her attempt to fulfill the rich woman's cultured and decorative role and to have Jane Addams fulfill it as well. Jane Addams's using her education to add "lustre" to her father's social circle would have been simply augmenting the role Anna Haldeman Addams played for her husband. Addams's eventual repudiation of the cultured role exemplified by her stepmother would entail the rejection of marriage in general, and marriage to Anna Haldeman Addams's beloved youngest son George in particular. He had hoped to marry Jane as his brother Harry had married Jane's sister, Alice, after she had completed her education at Rockford.[34]

So each member of the Addams family who went on a combined business and pleasure trip to northern Wisconsin in August after Jane's return home from Rockford in 1881 had considerable interest in her future. They were John, Jane, Anna, and George. This common concern and the preceding struggle over Jane's "Smith plan" suggests that the Wisconsin trip could have been in part a reassertion of family purpose, one of those minimally conciliative group ventures whose aim is in fact to reinforce the decision of the strongest members or the largest number. George may well have courted his stepsister—he was to "press his affections" the following spring and summer after the intervening trauma—while John and Anna could have believed that Jane was too weak to go to college and would settle down to adorn her father's home while George was finishing his education, as her sister had done before marrying Harry.[35]

But if she was to appear to defer to her father's wishes during this summer (as she had done already in 1877 by attending Rockford), Addams had decided to enter the Woman's Medical College in Philadelphia for the 1881 winter term. Giving up Smith (as she had done by July) to go directly to medical school was only a telescoping of plans she had described to a friend at Rockford. We do not know whether or not Addams had told her father during the summer that she still planned on going to medical school. In any case, on August 17, 1881, after a strenuous day on the mining property in which he was considering investing, John Addams died in Green Bay, Wisconsin, of "inflammation of the bowels." How now could Jane reconcile herself with her father? How could she betray him by responding to the social claim?[36]

Addams sent letters and telegrams telling friends and relatives the news. Their replies show us how powerful a psychological presence he was in his daughter's life: "I remember how affectionately you used to speak of him—and the time when we came home together, how happy you looked when you saw him waiting outside"; "the poignancy of your grief arises from many causes, principally from the fact that your heart and life were wrapped up in your Pa"; "by a word you spoke at one time I know your father's life transfused itself through yours. . . ." These observations testify to the profound difficulty Addams would have in arriving at some sense of herself independent of the identification with him.[37]

Four months after her father's death, her Rockford teacher and friend, Sarah Blaisdell, wrote to the still deeply grieving Addams, referring to the influence of John Addams's principles on Jane Addams's "own character," and reinforcing this attempt to get Addams to distinguish herself from her father by criticizing him, albeit very subtly. She said that a father can act as "a wall of defence" for a young girl, "but when he is gone she stands out in her own person to meet the responsibilities of life." A wall around someone can be as much a prison as a defense. But when Jane Addams received this prescient letter she had been in medical school for three months, since the term had started on October 6. She had gone in spite of physical weakness and "vertebrae" problems that had persisted through the summer.[38]

Addams went to Philadelphia as part of a family group, this circumstance representing more of a compromise (perhaps literally negotiated by the parties) between "family" and "social" claims than her solo attendance at Smith would have represented. Harry Haldeman attended a third session of the Medical Department of the University of Pennsylvania, while Alice matriculated with Jane at the Woman's Medical College of Pennsylvania. His session began October 17, theirs October 6.[39] Anna Haldeman Addams came with them. Given the vicissitudes in Addams's health, her father's recent death, and the struggle over her future, one can see the family's logic in making this a group venture, whether one construes it as support or pressure. Addams had become sick enough by the middle of December 1881 to be placed under the supervision of a doctor.[40] Her apparent problem was exhaustion, which she was soon to call "nervous." Addams had, in Sarah Blaisdell's December 24 paraphrase of Addams's own description, "lost . . . physical vigor," having "taxed it . . . very severely both in study and in doing for others and at their suggestion." She had depleted her "original stock" of vigor. The "doing for others" must have referred in part to Addams's attempts to comply with her stepmother's demands that she play the lady with and for her accompanying family, as well as with the demands made by her fellow medical students. Nonetheless, Addams had written to a Rockford friend before the end of the year that her "physical strength" was returning; perhaps her medical treatment at that time was working. She passed the first year's examination in March. But then she relapsed.[41]

The condition, which, Addams tells us, forced her into "Mitchell's hospital" in the spring of 1882, was a "development of the spinal difficulty which had shadowed me from childhood." Later she would say that "development" (in 1882) was "a nervous affliction which compelled me to abandon my studies."[42] Her use of the word *nervous* reflected nineteenth-century belief. Although doctors and students of physiology had not yet fully mapped or understood the nervous system, they believed it was only a matter of time before all disorders of function would be explained as diseases of the nervous system. Nerves, they thought, provided the key to understanding the relations between functional and organic disorders, between mind and body. Physical, organic disease could give rise to what the twentieth century calls psychological disorders by way of the nerves; conversely, psychological disease could give rise to physical disorders by way of the nerves. The physical treatment of mysterious functional or psychological problems was thus easily justified.

Addams provides our first lead into the tangled question of the somatic dimensions to her illness in the period between leaving Rockford in 1881 and founding Hull House in 1889. When she tells us in *Twenty Years* that her spinal difficulty originated in childhood, she is referring the reader back to the chapter "Earliest Impressions," which mentions her "crooked back" and her "disability of the curved spine." She later said that her spinal curvature resulted "from an illness at the age of four." While there are several childhood illnesses that can have this result, her biographers are probably correct in ascribing Addams's crooked back to tuberculosis of the spine.[43] Significantly, in *Twenty Years* Addams does not tell us when or how it was believed her disease originated, progressed, or was treated in her childhood. Instead she explains the effects of the disability on her childhood sense of herself, just as she did with the "development of the spinal difficulty" in her twenties.

Addams first refers to her spine in her account of a childhood dream. The contexts she presents to her readers for this account are "the theory that our genuine impulses may be connected with our childish experiences," the belief that all of her impressions of childhood were "connected with my father," and the organizing principle of stringing "these first memories on [the] single cord of the connection" with her father because he "was so distinctly the dominant influence. . . ." It is tempting to point out the connection that the ambiguous word *cord* suggests between Addams's sense of herself as a child and of her father who provided her with a central sense of self, standing back of her moral values as well as becoming so much of an authoritative burden as to crook her back. Yet the dream "exhibits" Addams's own childhood sense of significance to the world, to society. "I dreamed night after night that everyone in the world was dead excepting myself, and that upon me rested the responsibility for making a wagon wheel. . . . no human being was within sight. They had all gone around the edge of the hill to the village cemetery, and I alone remained alive in the deserted world." A page earlier she had described the dread she had of dying while in a state of sin (specifically of having told a lie) and therefore going to hell, which was combined with the fear that her father, "representing the entire adult world which I had basely deceived," should "himself die before I had time to tell him." (We can see that such a circumstance had happened on the fatal 1881 trip to Wisconsin, between the childhood dream and Addams's adult recording of it.) The wagon-wheel dream was, then, in part a realization of this fear; and both fear and dream may well have reflected Addams's apprehension of final abandonment by her father, already having experienced her mother's death. It also registered the sheer power of her father as moral judge and bridge (or wall) to the adult world. It also may well have represented her wish (fulfilled by 1910 when she published this description) to stand alone, free particularly of that dominant/dominating figure. Her account then goes on to juxtapose the figure of herself as a child, weak by way of "delicacy," size, sex, age, and deformity, with the figure of the powerful, skilled, adult, male blacksmith. The juxtaposition foreshadows the contrast for which it serves as introduction or "doorway" to Addams matching herself against the man and workplace she found even more powerful, that is, against her father, his intellectual and political skills and his workplace in public life. That matching in turn served as the doorway for Addams' entry into public life.[44]

Her second reference in *Twenty Years* to her spinal deformity in childhood is part of her invidious comparison of herself—an "ugly, pigeon-toed little girl, whose crooked back obliged her to walk with her head held very much on one side"—to her powerful, physically imposing father, a comparison she invited in a sentence beginning "My great veneration and pride in my father. . . ." The paragraph goes on to conflate the memories of several days "doubtless occurring in two or three different years" when the "Union Sunday School of the village was visited by strangers." Their presence allowed Addams to dramatize the vast difference she felt existed between herself and her father, who taught the large Bible class. She "could not endure the thought that 'strange people' should know that my handsome father owned this homely little girl." She describes this attempt as an example of her "doglike affection." It seems to be self-abasement; conversely, the elevation of the venerated, "fine," "imposing," "dignified," paternal, religious teacher, "rising high above all the others" in the church, is to almost godlike eminence. But she corrects this child's eye view even as she gives it, writing with the hindsight of someone who has successfully overcome too strong an identification with her father. The tone of the whole description is humorous. She calls that "doglike affection" "grotesque." And everybody knows the truth of "the ugly duckling" to which Addams compared herself in the same passage—the duck turns out to have been a cygnet (and can thus disassociate itself from its "parents"), a creature that would grow into a big beautiful swan.[45]

In sum, while it was Addams herself who pointed out to her readers how her illness "shadowed" her from childhood, both of the references to her spinal difficulty present (1) the striking physical contrast between her filial, female self and a powerful adult male, above all, her father; and (2) the certainty that by 1910 when she presents this past contrast, she has outgrown it and overcome the inequality.

She concluded her discussion of her deformity in childhood by describing how her father ridiculed the notion that he shared her feeling about her "personal appearance . . . [that] thrust itself as an incongruity into my father's life." Lifting his "high and shining silk hat" to her on a main street, he had made her "an imposing bow." This parodied both of their statures. Addams is showing her readers that she had let John Addams overshadow her; his figure with its "shining" hat had come between her and the sun, stunting her growth. Part of her "difficulty" had been her contrast of herself to her father and her having internalized his judgment of her.

Of course there were other factors influencing the nature of her sickness, such as the fact that she had suffered from Pott's disease (spinal tuberculosis); the social expectation that the strain of education would lead to sickness in women; and the widespread belief that a major focus for such sickness was the spine. The autobiographical sentence in 1910 leading back to the childhood origin and meaning of her "spinal difficulty" in 1860 also leads into "Mitchell's hospital" in the late spring of 1882. To the famous neurologist and self-proclaimed woman-expert, S. Weir Mitchell, Addams's case must have looked exactly like that of hundreds of cases of nervous exhaustion accompanied by spinal difficulties. Mitchell believed that spinal problems in young women were usually symptoms of a disorder of the entire nervous system and therefore susceptible to Mitchell's special source of wealth and claim to fame, his "rest treatment." He and his contemporaries were primed to address such female patients through hostile and devaluative stereotypes. Instead of the person we know Jane Addams, for one, to have been in 1882, talented, torn, idealistic, frustrated, pained, ambitious, and depressed, this doctor was prepared to see her as, in his words, "a creature" "with a back."[46]

This is not the place to describe or examine Mitchell's "rest treatment," save to mention (for later reference) that it included fattening the patient, in part by a diet of milk. It is fair to characterize the treatment as an attempt to impose Mitchell's conventional, literally paternalistic view of woman's role onto his patients by infantilizing and reeducating them.[47] In the very short run it seems to have been effective in restoring Addams's physical strength and in bringing her up from the "breakdown" so that she could at least move about, write letters, plan travel, and honor social obligations. Sarah Anderson's letters to Addams in April and June 1882 confirm that the therapy was aimed at her gaining strength. They show that Anderson and, in all likelihood Addams, agreed with convention and with Mitchell that such an aim had to be at the expense of study and that study itself had been debilitating to her. Anderson advised Addams to take a restorative trip to the seashore should she not have "made good progress" by the end of June, advice consistent with the frequent practice of Mitchell's patients following the rest treatment. In July Addams did visit Nantucket in her pursuit of "strength" and "color." At the end of August Sarah Blaisdell wrote Addams a letter that illustrated and reinforced the widespread apprehension that a woman's health was vulnerable to education, even though Blaisdell, a college teacher, was committed to education and wanted Addams to go on. As might be expected, ambition and apprehension emerged as a typical syndrome in the college women of this period.[48]

Addams's weakness, nervousness, and spinal problems, including backache, lassitude, melancholy, and "general crookedness" of temper, and all of her therapies—the rest treatment, travel to the seashore, experimental surgery, recumbency on an orthopractic couch to which she was strapped, and her wearing of a mechanical support,— were the common experiences of thousands of women of her class, a fact that would become a major concern of Addams. The symptoms became a major concern because the therapies failed her. They failed her and the large proportion of women with cognate disorders because they were offered from a particular set of social and sexual assumptions that were in fact a fundamental cause of the symptoms. Doctors' diagnoses of women's spinal problems and nervous disorders generally provide evidence of large-scale social change perceived in the lives of middle- and upper-class women, in contrast to the lives led by their grandmothers. Most spinal experts agreed with Dr. Charles Fayette Taylor's proposition that women's spinal difficulties were causes or symptoms of what he called a "lack of power." He also called general muscular weakness "delicacy" in the book describing his therapeutic couch, probably similar to the one to which Addams was strapped. The irony and appropriateness of such diagnoses becomes apparent from a feminist perspective. Women were supposed to lack power, lack energy, in contrast to men.[49]

Addams's account in *Twenty Years* of her own diagnosis and treatment gives short shrift to the kinds of explanations that had dominated her doctors' diagnoses. In *Democracy and Social Ethics* (1902)

Addams had challenged Mitchell directly, opposing active, emancipating work to passive, confining rest. The educated, repressed, and therefore, frustrated young woman

> looks out into the world, longing that some demand be made upon her powers, for they are too untrained to furnish an initiative. When her health gives way under this strain, as it often does, her physician invariably advises a rest. But to be put to bed and fed milk is not what she requires. What she needs is simple health-giving activity, which, involving the use of all her faculties, shall be a response to all the claims which she so keenly feels.

By "claims," of course, she refers to the "social claim" of meaningful work beyond the home, in contrast to the "family claim" that Mitchell, like her father, had attempted to enforce. She now explains the sickness she had experienced to have been the result of conflict. The woman graduate who defers to her parents' wishes "either hides her hurt, and splendid reserves of enthusiasm and capacity go to waste, or her zeal and emotions are turned inward, and the result is an unhappy woman, whose heart is consumed by vain regrets and desires." To it Addams adds an account of the physiological effects of such conflict (not of weak nerves nor of spinal curvature), the effects of which were precisely the ones she had suffered on leaving Rockford:

> the situation is not even so simple as a conflict between her affections and her intellectual convictions, although even that is tumultuous enough, also the emotional nature is divided against itself. The social claim is a demand upon the emotions as well as upon the intellect, and in ignoring it she represses not only her convictions but lowers her springs of vitality. Her life is full of contradictions.[50]

In the same chapter of *Twenty Years*, Addams broadened her diagnosis to include the whole "first generation of college women." While she has shown us it is rooted in her own experience of conflict leading to nervous exhaustion, lack of energy, deep nervous depression, spiritual struggle, a sense of failure, clutching at the heart, despair, resentment, paralysis of will, and disgust with herself, her diagnosis from now on (and she frequently returned to it in books and articles) would always be projected onto a larger social canvas, from the first generation of college women to middle-class women to all women and to young people in general. Addams assumed the symbolic value of her diagnosis and cure, and in doing so followed her characteristic pattern of dealing with her own pain by seeing it as something that connected her with others. In *The Spirit of Youth and the City Streets* (1909), where Addams pointed out the frustration of poor and largely immigrant urban youth—not simply of educated, middle-class women—she wrote, "We allow a great deal of this precious stuff—this Welt-Schmerz of which each generation has need—not only to go unutilized, but to work havoc among the young people themselves."[51]

Addams goes on to summarize the diagnosis and anticipate the therapy she elaborated in "The Subjective Necessity for Social Settlements."

> I gradually reached a conviction that the first generation of college women had taken their learning too quickly, had departed too suddenly from the active emotional life led by their grandmothers and great-grandmothers; that the contemporary education of young women had developed too exclusively the power of acquiring knowledge and of merely receiving impressions; that somewhere in the process of "being educated" they had lost that simple and almost automatic response to the human appeal, that old healthful reaction resulting in activity from the mere presence of suffering or of helplessness; that they are so sheltered and pampered they have no chance even to make "the great refusal."

This generation of woman, she went on to say, was "smothered and sickened with advantages."[52]

This romantic view of the lives of previous generations of women had a great deal in common with those authorities on women's health from whom I am concerned to distinguish Addams. In regard to generations, to sex, and to explanatory models, the view was a cliché of her era. Doctors frequently compared sickly young women with their healthy forebears. The most salient and, from the point of view of the overwhelmingly male analysts, most appalling symptom of what one of them called this "physical decline of American women," was the declining birth rate. Women, they said, were unable or unwilling to bear babies in the numbers they knew their ancestresses had. Unwillingness was as much an expression of sickness as incapacity, since such an attitude had to be the expression of an enfeebled constitution: "healthy women were willing mothers." Most unwilling of all were those rich and leisured enough to attend college; the birth rate of female graduates was especially low. Attendance at college and decrease in fertility were explained as cause and effect. At the crucial stage of sexual development, it was argued, young women's energies were being absorbed by their brains instead of going to the development of their sexual organs. The higher education of women, a key goal of feminists, was contributing to what Theodore Roosevelt would call "race suicide."[53]

This was the context for the half-century-long debate over the effects of the higher education of women on society. It was also the context for the concern of Addams, her classmates, and her teachers over the effects of study on women's health. Addams's founding of Hull House and her description in *Twenty Years* of the process whereby she came to do it must be seen as a contribution to this debate. Addams agreed that the outcome of higher education was to make "girls" sick by cutting them off from a part of themselves she characterized as more fundamental than mere thought. But unlike medical orthodoxy, Addams did not say that women's meaningful connection with life should be submersion in traditional motherhood. In Addams's view, the more fundamental part of women consisted of an emotion (comprising zeal, enthusiasm, capacities) that she called "social sentiment" to be "utilized" in "social" work. Addams's answer to nervous disorders among women, including "nervous exhaustion," was the expression of self in meaningful work rather than the repression of self in the interests of "society." This is how Starr had explained Addams's conception of settlements during the time they were looking for a house in Chicago:

> Jane's idea which she puts very much to the front and on no account will give up is that it is more for the benefit of the people who do it than for the other class. She has worked that out of her own experience and ill health. She discovered that when recovering from her spinal trouble that she could take care of children, actually lift them up and not feel worse but better for being with them. While an effort to see people and be up to things used her up completely. . . . Nervous people do not crave rest but activity of a certain kind.

Drumming up support for Hull House in the spring of 1889, Addams told a Chicago club woman that Hull House would be "a place for invalid girls to go and help the poor."[54]

Addams was not alone in arguing that meaningful work could be a cure for the nervous disorders that her own case illustrated. For example, Ann Preston, an early dean and guiding spirit in the founding of the Pennsylvania Woman's Medical College, was deeply pained that young, educated women led "wasted, suffering, unsatisfied lives." Like Addams, Preston diverged from orthodox therapy by recommending against medication in favor of putting "to ennobling uses the powers of faculties which are the glorious birth-right of humanity." The answer to those women's sickness was work. "You know," she told her students, "that quiet, interesting, imperative work—work for hand and for mind—is essential to [such women's] health."[55] But Addams's version of this discovery was, in my view, of much greater moment than Preston's for three reasons. Addams opened up a myriad of new kinds of healthy, satisfying work for women, all based on Hull House. She established herself as a national symbol of such work for women, whatever the class limitations of her symbolism. And, most important, she showed in *Twenty Years* precisely how she had struggled from sickness to health by way of her own analysis and how others could do it as well.

If Addams saw a correspondence between her own depression and the wretchedness of the poor, she found health in those whom she called "the most vital part of humanity." Addams found that the humanity in them corresponded to the humanity she was eventually able to find in herself. The crucial connection here for my argument is that Addams saw those resources, outside as well as inside herself, as maternal. It was in this diagnosis written so soon after her founding of Hull House (in "The Subjective Necessity for Social Settlements") that Addams characterized the uneducated, unshriveled, live, vital, cooperative, emotional, and healthful resources she had in common with working people as "the great mother breasts of our common humanity."[56]

This maternal metaphor is repeated in different forms throughout Addams's writings. She personified art, religion, and modern industry as mothers, and referred to life as "she." Memory, she wrote in 1916, was "the Mother of the Muses . . . that Protean Mother. . . ." Her explanation for the dynamic of the peace movement was nearly the same.

> There are . . . strenuous forces at work reaching down to impulses and experiences as primitive and profound as are those of struggle itself. That "ancient kindliness which sat beside the cradle of the race," and which is ever ready to assert itself against ambition and greed and the desire for achievement, is manifesting itself now with unusual force, and for the first time presents international aspects.[57]

The same image had existed very powerfully in Addams's imagination in 1879 when her chief concern was religion. (So her reaching back to a primal mother represented three great passions of Addams' life—religion, the settlement movement, and peace.) In 1879 she wrote to Starr:

> As a general rule I regard [the Deity] with indifference, think of the Jewish faith just as I do of Mohammadism or any other system of religion. Lately it seems to me that I am getting back to all of it— superior to it, I almost feel. Back to a great Primal Cause; not Nature exactly, but a fostering mother, a necessity brooding and watching over all things, above every human passion & yet not passive, the mystery of creation. I make a botch trying to describe it & yet the idea has been lots of comfort to me lately . . . you see I am not so unsettled,

as I resettle so often, but my creed is everyone be sincere and don't fuss. I began with an honest desire to say something in myself which is intangible—'impale a man on the personal pronoun.'—I give you my blessing my dear. . . .[58]

In 1879, she was unable to base her "I" on her father because she was female (impaled, it can be suggested, by having ambitions only men could have). Yet there are clues in this letter, and in the maternal references just quoted, to the "settlement" she would eventually find, that is, to a sense of self not utterly based on her father. Again the idiom of the age, this time conceptualizing selves in terms of "the childhood of the race," held a very personal meaning for its heroine, whose mother had died when she was two years and four months old. Her depiction of her sense of a primal mother is both literally tangible (cradle, breast) and a depiction of feelings (kindliness, comfort, brooding, watching, godlike power, mysteries of creation) that together give the sense of an infant's intimate experience of its mother or rather the experience that Jenny Addams had until her mother's traumatic death. To reach this sense Addams had to move back even more systematically, more consciously, than she did in 1879 ("it seems to me I am getting back to all of it . . . Back . . .") to describe something "in myself which is tangible." Back to before she felt burdened—by that appalling sense of loss represented by the wagon-wheel dream, before perhaps she came to depend on her father so much and to learn from him the burden-bearing of social responsibility, and more to my point here, before her spinal tuberculosis at four, before she had a crooked back at all, back, in short, to health. . . . She was reaching back to her mother. The "subjective necessity which led to the founding of Hull House," that is to Addams's own "motherhood," incorporated, she said in *Twenty Years*, "the impulse beating at the very source of our lives. . . ." Addams's commitment to her kind of maternity and her position as the mother of mothers was rooted in her childhood. She would cure herself by discovering something that she believed had been there all along and which existed in clear contrast to the values she associated with her father.[59]

So it was that Addams criticized competition and advocated co-operation. She shared such views with her fellow progressives, male and female, who emphasized cooperation for the good of the whole social organism, and with those corporate leaders who were tending increasingly toward "rationalization" of the economy and against wasteful competition. But such views coincided with Addams's own very individual experience. She said it was maternity and woman's other roles in family life that held society together, even if she also maintained, quite consistently, that male adherence to Victorian domestic ideals was important. She celebrated women as specialists in cooperation. She held that good "mothers, through their sympathy and adaptability, substitute keen present interests and activity for solemn warnings and restraint, self-expression for repression. Their vigorous family life allies itself by a dozen bonds to the educational, the industrial and the recreational organizations of the modern city. . . ." Parents', especially mothers' "wonderful devotion to the child seems at times in the midst of our stupid social and industrial arrangements, all that keeps society human, the touch of nature which unites it, as it was that same devotion which first lifted it out of the swamp of bestiality."[60] Those most responsible for "stupid social industrial arrangements" were men. She pitted the new, ameliorative, cooperative ethic (rooted in the "great mother breasts of our common humanity") against the male ethic of laissez-faire. Her "settlement" had several connotations, especially in the light of the "Primal Cause" letter to Starr, and stood in opposition to the dominant male ideology.

> A Settlement is above all . . . a spot to which those who have a passion for the equalization of human joys and opportunities are early attracted. It is this type of mind which is in itself so often obnoxious to the man of conquering business faculty, to whom the practical world of affairs seems so supremely rational that he would never vote to change the type of it even if he could.

In *Twenty Years*, Addams described the opposition of large glass companies and other manufacturers to child labor legislation in Illinois. While she acknowledged the attraction to the glass manufacturers of saving money by employing cheap, child labor, Addams devoted more time in her account to the psychological motives of the men involved, believers in "untrammeled energy and 'early start' " as "generators of success." A child labor law ran "counter to the instinct and tradition, almost to the very religion of the manufacturers of the state, who were for the most part self-made men."[61] Again personal history fuses with sexual and political ideology to emphasize the full meaning of Addams's cure of herself. Her characterization of the opposition echoed the opposition of her father to her fulfillment in a broad social role. He had been a "pioneer" in Illinois, a miller, banker, land speculator, investor in railroads, and president of an insurance company. Addams herself had described him as a representative "self-made man" in the same book now criticizing the values of the type he epitomized. These values can be contrasted with "the wonderful devotion" of her dying mother's concern for her baby.

In sum, in reaching out to independence, to a new role, Addams had to traverse the psychic reality that her father was both a bridge and a wall. Her traversal was marked by sickness and cure. While I am describing a contrast in Addams's view between the values represented by her father, and those she associated with her mother, I do not want to suggest she simply jettisoned the former. In her *A New Conscience and an Ancient Evil*, Addams said it "is better to overcome the dangers in this newer and freer life, which modern industry had opened to women, than it is to attempt to retreat into the domestic industry of the past." She wanted to recover "*something* [my emphasis] of the . . . sanctity and meaning" of such women's work.[62] The reaching back was a psychical one, not a literal one, coexisting with, indeed supporting, the host of new roles sponsored by Hull House. Those roles incorporated the skills and values Addams had learned from her father, most obviously the political, Lincolnesque ones. Her history led Addams to explore ways for women to reconcile Lincoln's liberalism with maternal ideology. Soon after *Twenty Years* was published, a Boston newspaper called Addams "that mother Emancipator from Illinois."[63] She had found a way of continuing to share her father's values without crippling herself.

Notes

[1]James Weber Linn, *Jane Addams: A Biography* (New York: Appleton-Century, 1935), p. 6.

[2]Linn, *Addams*, p. 32.

[3]Jane Addams, *Twenty Years at Hull House with Autobiographical Notes* (New York: Signet, 1960 [1910]), p. 59.

[4]Jane Addams to Alice Haldeman, 14 June 1888, Jane Addams Memorial Collection, University of Illinois, Chicago; Anne Firor Scott, "Jane Addams," *Notable American Women*, 3 vols. (Cambridge, MA: Belknap Press, 1971), 1:16–22; 22.

[5]Allen F. Davis, *American Heroine: The Life and Legend of Jane Addams* (New York: Oxford University Press, 1973), p. 92. I am deeply indebted to this splendid biography—as my frequent citations indicate.

[6]The best sources for Hull House's activities are Addams's own writings, especially *Twenty Years*. For a very helpful and brief recent account, see Nancy Woloch, *Women and the American Experience* (New York: Alfred Knopf, 1984), ch. 11.

[7]Davis, *Spearheads for Reform: The Social Settlements and the Progressive Movement, 1890–1914* (New York: Oxford University Press, 1907); Addams, *The Second Twenty Years at Hull House* (New York: Macmillan, 1930), pp. 33–34.

[8]Addams, *Twenty Years*, pp. 137–39.

[9]Addams, *Twenty Years*, pp. 42, 45.

[10]Davis, *American Heroine*, p. 287.

[11]Davis, *American Heroine*, pp. 226–29.

[12]Davis, *American Heroine*, pp. 277–78. See Donald B. Meyer, *Sex and Power: The Rise of Women in America, Russia, Sweden and Italy* (Middletown, CT: Wesleyan University Press, 1988), pp. 354–62.

[13]Davis, *American Heroine*, pp. 85–91.

[14]Donald B. Meyer, "Capitalism and Feminism in Italy, Sweden and the United States 1870–1970," American Historical Association Annual Meeting, San Francisco, 1978. This anticipated Meyer, *Sex and Power*, pp. 311–30.

[15]Anna Marcet Haldeman-Julius, "Jane Addams as I Knew Her," *The Reviewers Library* 7 (1936), 3–30; 30.

[16]Quoted in Davis, *American Heroine*, p. 250.

[17]Addams, *Twenty Years*, p. 25.

[18]Quoted in Linn, *Addams*, pp. 22–23.

[19]Davis, *American Heroine*, p. 5.

[20]Addams, *Twenty Years*, p. 88; Davis, *American Heroine*, p. 5.

[21]George Weber to Elizabeth and Enoch Rieff, 17 Jan. 1863, Jane Addams Correspondence, Swarthmore College Peace Collection (hereafter cited as SCPC). I am very grateful to Ann Gordon for drawing my attention to this letter.

[22]Linn, *Addams*, p. 25. Addams collaborated with Linn in writing this biography to a significant extent; he tells us in the preface that "my aunt read over and annotated the first draft of the first eight chapters of this book, talked over the next three, and agreed upon the proportion of the remainder." It is reasonable to assume that many of the unacknowledged quotations in the book are Addams's own commentary on the past events.

[23]Linn, *Addams*, p. 25.

[24]Addams to Alice Haldeman, 20 Aug. 1890, quoted in Davis, *American Heroine*, p. 6.

[25]Davis, *American Heroine*, p. 6.

[26]Addams, *Twenty Years*, p. 46.

[27]Davis, *American Heroine*, p. 9. Davis has emphasized the contradictory messages John Addams gave his daughter and his account of Addams's sickness and her "Creative Solution" is consistent with mine (*American Heroine*, ch. III). We have both been influenced by Meyer's pathbreaking *The Positive Thinkers* (Garden City, New York: Doubleday, 1965), ch. 3.

[28]Addams, *Twenty Years*, pp. 48–49; 38; 26.

[29]Addams, *Twenty Years*, 57.

[30]Addams, *Twenty Years*, ch. 6. This was a paper she had given in 1892, only three years after the founding of Hull House.

[31]Addams, *Twenty Years*, pp. 93–94.

[32]Addams, *Twenty Years*, pp. 57; 31–2.

[33]Addams, *Democracy and Social Ethics* (New York: Macmillan, 1902), pp. 83; 85; 96. The last reference is to Lear's relation with Cordelia.

[34]Linn, *Addams*, p. 30.

[35]Linn, *Addams*, p. 65; Davis, *American Heroine*, p. 29.

[36]Linn, *Addams*, p. 68; Mary B. Down to Addams, 23 May 1880, SCPC; Davis, *American Heroine*, p. 26.

[37]L. D. Cummings to Addams, 20 August 1881; J. M. Linn to Addams, 26 Aug. 1881; C. A. Potter to Addams, 20 Aug. 1881, SCPC.

[38]Sarah Blaisdell to Addams, 24 Dec. 1881, SCPC; Women's Medical College of Pennsylvania, "Announcement," 1881–82; Sarah Anderson to Addams, 11 Sept. 1881, SCPC.

[39]University of Pennsylvania Archives, 1866–84: Med. Matrics. Book, UPC 2.7 # 17); Women's Medical College of Matriculates, 1881–82, Archives and Special Collections on Women in Medicine, Florence A. Moore Library of Medicine, Medical (WMC) College of Pennsylvania.

[40]Davis, *American Heroine*, p. 27; Sarah Blaisdell to Addams, 24 Dec. 1881, SCPC.

[41]Davis, *American Heroine*, p. 78; Emma Briggs to Addams, 30 Dec. 1881, SCPC.

[42]Addams, *Twenty Years*, p. 60; A. L. Bowen, "The World Is Better That This Woman Lived," *New Age Illustrated* 11 (1927), 84–87; 84.

[43]Addams, *Twenty Years*, pp. 22–23; Bowen, "This Woman," p. 27; John Farrell, *Beloved Lady: A History of Jane Addams' Ideas on Reform and Peace* (Baltimore, MD: Johns Hopkins University Press, 1967), p. 40; Davis, *American Heroine*, p. 6. For a more detailed account of this issue and other aspects of this article, see Barker-Benfield, " 'Mother Emancipator': The Meaning of Jane Addams' Sickness and Cure," *Journal of Family History* 4 (1979), 395–420.

[44]Addams, *Twenty Years*, pp. 19; 21.

[45]Addams, *Twenty Years*, pp. 23–24.

[46]Silas Weir Mitchell, "The Annual Oration," *Transactions Medical and Chirurgical Faculty of Maryland* (1877), 51–68; 63–64.

[47]Barker-Benfield, "S. Weir Mitchell and the 'Woman Question': Gender, Therapy and Social History," *Quarterly Journal of Ideology* 5:3 (1981), 25–37.

[48]Anderson to Addams, 27 Apr. 1881, SCPC; Harrington to Addams, 25 July 1882, SCPC; Blaisdell to Addams, 29 Aug. 1881, SCPC.

[49]Barker-Benfield, " 'Mother Emancipator,' " pp. 26–28.

[50]Addams, *Democracy and Social Ethics*, p. 87.

[51]Addams, *The Spirit of Youth and the City Streets* (New York: Macmillan, 1909), pp. 146–47.

[52]Addams, *Twenty Years*, p. 64.

[53]James Reed, *From Private Vice to Public Virtue: The Birth Control Movement and American Society Since 1930* (New York: Basic Books, 1977), p. 28.

[54]Starr to Mary Blaisdell, 23 Feb. 1889, Smith Collection, Smith College, Northampton, Mass.; Addams quoted in Davis, *American Heroine*, p. 64.

[55]Preston quoted in Guilielma Fell Alsop, *History of the Women's Medical College, Philadelphia, Pennsylvania, 1850–1950* (Philadelphia: J. B. Lippincott, 1950), 76–77.

[56]Addams, *Twenty Years*, p. 93.

[57]Addams, *The Long Road of Woman's Memory* (New York: Macmillan, 1916 [1907]), p. 8.

[58]Addams to Starr, 11 Aug. 1879, in Christopher Lasch, ed., *The Social Thought of Jane Addams* (Indianapolis: Bobbs-Merrill, 1965), pp. 3–4.

[59]Addams, *Twenty Years*, p. 98.

[60]Addams, *Spirit of Youth*, pp. 47, 33.

[61]Addams, *Twenty Years*, p. 153.

[62]Addams, *A New Conscience and an Ancient Evil* (New York: Macmillan, 1912), p. 92; Addams, *Twenty Years*, p. 175.

[63]*Boston American*, 15 Feb. 1911, quoted in Davis, *American Heroine*, p. 164.

Ida Wells-Barnett

(1862–1931)

Paula Giddings

Ida Bell Wells was born to slave parents in the Deep South in the middle of the Civil War. She attended a freedpeople's school, Rust College, in her hometown of Holly Springs, Mississippi, before she began teaching school at the age of sixteen.

In 1892, Wells started what would become a lifelong anti-lynching campaign. Because of her outspoken views she was forced to leave the South; she moved to New York, where she supported herself as a journalist and lecturer. As a tireless crusader against racial violence, she crisscrossed the North and made two successful tours of England on behalf of her anti-lynching campaign. After marrying Chicago lawyer and journalist Ferdinand Barnett, in 1895, Wells-Barnett curtailed her travels, but not her commitment to equal justice for blacks. In same year as her marriage, she published A Red Record, *a detailed indictment of lynching in the South. She participated in the Niagara Movement, which was founded by W. E. B. Du Bois to promote direct action for fighting discrimination; she was also a founding member of the National Association for the Advancement of Colored People, but broke with the organization when she felt it was too timid in its approach to ending racism. Wells-Barnett believed that the only way for African-Americans to achieve equality was to come to consciousness through direct action, just as she had. In Chicago, Wells-Barnett was an active supporter of women's rights as well. She organized several women's clubs and in 1913, she founded the first suffrage club for black women in Illinois. Throughout her long career as an activist, whether working within the black women's club movement or serving on a protest delegation to the president of the United States, Wells-Barnett was an example of how one person's challenge to racism and sexism could un-*

dermine the powerful forces which sought to preserve these institutions.

As the journalist who led the nation's first antilynching campaign from Memphis in 1892, Ida Bell Wells entered the reform period at the height of her influence. Her investigative reporting aroused public opinion and resulted in the decline of lynching. Her antilynching campaign was also a catalyst for the formation of the National Association of Colored Women (NACW) in 1896, whose programs to promote women's suffrage and self-help became a model for those of the Urban League and the National Association for the Advancement of Colored People (NAACP). Wells was also a founder of the NAACP, a pioneering suffragist, and a political and community activist in Chicago.[1]

When Ida Wells was born in Holly Springs, Mississippi, on July 16, 1862, neither Blacks nor women enjoyed the rights of full citizenship. African-Americans were discriminated against in the North and enslaved in the South. Neither they, nor women of any class or color, had the constitutional right to vote. But Ida Wells would grow up in a country on the threshold of change. Before she was a year old, President Abraham Lincoln issued the Emancipation Proclamation freeing slaves in Mississippi and other Southern states that were fighting the Union. Before she was three, Robert E. Lee, general-in-chief of the Confederate armies, surrendered in Appomattox, Virginia, ending the Civil War. And by the time she was five, Black freedmen in Mississippi were poised to vote for the first time in the election of 1867. In that year, the young Ida may well have learned her first political lesson at her father's knee.

Her father, James Wells, was undoubtedly aware that the rights conferred on him and other Black men by the Republican Reconstructionists would be contested. In Mississippi, Black men made up the majority of the voter registration rolls and White supremacist Democrats, vanquished in war, would not willingly absorb another defeat at the polls. At first the Democrats planned to merely boycott the election of 1867, then thought better of it. It would be more effective, they concluded, to manipulate the Black vote; intimidate freedmen into voting for the Democratic ticket. Black men may have had the right to vote, they noted, but most were still dependent on their White employers.

This was true of Ida's father who worked as a carpenter for Old Man Bolling, the leading contractor in Holly Springs. Wells, the son of his Tippah County slaveowner, had been apprenticed to the Bolling plantation in Holly Springs as a slave. It was there where he met and married his wife, Elizabeth Warrenton, who worked as a cook. After the Civil War, the couple elected to remain on the Bolling plantation, where Ida, the first of their eight children, was born, and where James Wells now worked for wages. Still, the freedman refused Bollings' entreaties to vote for the Democratic ticket; and when Wells returned from the polls, he found his shop locked. Whether he anticipated the reaction of his employer is not known, but Ida recalled that her father, without a word to anyone, returned to town, bought a new set of tools, and made arrangements for the family to rent another house nearby. Now he would work as he voted: for himself.

Such a strike for independence, however, must have been fraught with anxiety. One of Ida Wells's earliest memories was of her mother nervously pacing the floor when her father was out to late-night political meetings. Ida also recalled the almost palpable fear that encircled the words "Ku Klux Klan" even before she knew what they meant. But she would also witness what could come of determination, grassroots mobilization, and the courage of conviction. By the 1870s, Mississippi freedmen had put together some of the most powerful Black political organizations in the country. In that decade Black men held both of its U.S. Senate seats, and within the state, they held the offices of lieutenant-governor, secretary of state, speaker of the house and superintendent of education. For Ida Wells, Black power was not an abstract notion. Hiram Revels, who had filled Jefferson Davis's unexpired U.S. Senate seat when he became "President of the Confederacy," lived near her family. And the secretary of state, a former slave named James Hill, was one of her father's closest friends.

Such political strength, it might have been further learned, was rooted in the community and family life that the former slaves were shaping for themselves. Black citizens of Holly Springs supported institutions and participated in organizations that cohered their small community. James Wells was a member of the Black Masonic order, a fraternal and benevolent organization founded in 1787, and a trustee of Shaw University (later named Rust College) that had been built by the Freedmen's Bureau in 1866. Both Ida and her mother attended the college and Hiram Revels, in addition to his duties as an elder of the AME Church in Holly Springs, taught at Shaw part-time.

For Ida's parents, as for so many freed men and women in this period, the meaning of emancipation was reflected in their personal as well as public lives. Although James and Elizabeth Wells were married as slaves, one of their first acts as free persons was to remarry as citizens. For Elizabeth Wells, especially, the autonomy to organize one's own family life was a cherished value. Born in Virginia and separated from her parents and ten siblings when sold to a Mississippi slavetrader, she spent much of her time writing letters of inquiry to find her family.

For her own children—who belonged to the first generation of African-Americans that would live more of their life in freedom than in slavery—discipline was regarded as prelude to achievement. Under the especially watchful eyes of her mother, all of the siblings were expected to "Go to school and learn all that we could," Ida Wells recalled. And in addition to homework, all were assigned specific household tasks. For Ida, the latter seemed to include, happily, reading the newspaper to her father and a circle of admiring friends. And of course, each Sunday found Elizabeth's well-scrubbed brood in church. In 1877, she won the church prize for Sunday school attendance. It all added up to what Ida Wells described as a "butterfly existence." But in the following year, when Ida reached the age of sixteen, her existence became grounded in harsh reality.

Much of the talk heard in Holly Springs during the summer of 1878—the summer that Ida went to Tippah County to visit her Grandmother Peggy—was about the yellow fever epidemic that was raging through Memphis, Tennessee. Although Memphis was only fifty miles north of Holly Springs, there was, in the beginning, no cause for alarm. If the proper precautions were taken, the epidemic would stop short of Holly Springs. And even if the fever did penetrate the Mississippi community, Ida's father, it was assumed, would evacuate the family to Tippah County, some six miles away. But all of the assumptions proved wrong.

For some reason, the mayor of Holly Springs did not quarantine the town, allowing sojourners—and with them the fever—to come through it at will. So many people became ill so quickly, a crisis situation soon developed. The town's courthouse had to be quickly made into a makeshift hospital. James Wells found himself overwhelmed by requests to make caskets for the burgeoning number of dead. When he passed through the courthouse on the way to his carpentry shop, he would often stop to pray with the dying or calm the delirium of a feverish patient.

Elizabeth Wells was the first to be struck by the fever. When she became sick, her husband stayed home to nurse her but fell ill himself. James Wells died—twenty-four hours before Elizabeth did. Neighbors sent news to Ida in Tippah County, who, against the advice of health officials and her grandmother, planned to return home immediately. Alone, she took a freight train bound for Holly Springs.

She arrived to find a household in mourning and confusion. Not only her parents but her youngest brother, nine-month-old Stanley, had perished in the epidemic. Two of her five remaining siblings were in bed with the fever; and all showed symptoms of the disease save her sister Eugenia, who, previously crippled with a spinal disease, seemed immune. Two days later, Ida herself would experience its daunting chills. But all would survive, and recover. When the crisis subsided, Wells was visited by her father's Masonic brothers and their wives to discuss the future of the orphaned family.

After some discussion, it was decided by the adults that the children should be divided between them. Her younger sisters, five-year-old Annie and two-year-old Lily, would live with separate couples. The two boys, James and George, aged eleven and nine respectively would be apprenticed to two different men. No one wanted fourteen-year-old Eugenia, a paralytic whose spine was bent nearly double. She would be sent to an institution. And finally, sixteen-year-old Ida was considered old enough to fend for herself.

She was also old enough to think for herself. And what came to mind was that her parents "would turn over in their graves," if the family were separated. Her mother, Ida remembered, spent much of her time trying to find her own siblings. So the fierce sense of independence that would characterize Ida Wells throughout her life was demonstrated in her response. She would keep her family and take care of her brothers and sisters herself, Ida Wells told the assembled adults. What she needed from them was help in finding a teaching position so that she could support the family. The family friends were skeptical, but did find Ida a job in a rural school six miles out of Holly Springs. And so in the space of a tragic summer, Ida Wells exchanged her "happy, lighthearted" childhood for the full-blown responsibility of a single parent. Each week, the sixteen-year-old traveled to the one-room schoolhouse by mule, and returned on the weekends to tend to the washing, ironing, and other needs of her young family. The exhausting routine lasted until an aunt who had been widowed by the epidemic and had three children of her own invited Ida, Lily, and Annie to live with her in Memphis. Another aunt was able to care for Eugenia, and arranged for Ida's brothers to work on the family farm. Once in Memphis, Ida found another teaching position in nearby Woodstock, Tennessee, and attended classes at Fisk University with an eye toward passing the examination to teach in the city school system of Memphis.

Memphis was only fifty miles away from Holly Springs, but for Ida Wells, it must have felt like another world. A financial center of the South, and the seat of the nation's cotton exchange, Memphis was a veritable metropolis. There was a vibrant press, both Black and White, filled with commentary about the racial and political situation. There were theaters, lyceums that featured lectures and readings; and eligible young men who found her pretty.

For Ida, who was self-conscious about not having read books by Black authors, the lyceum was especially attractive. It featured the reading of the *Evening Star,* which she described as "a spicy journal containing literary notes, poetry, criticism and news items." And although she professed to having none of the "literary graces," her contributions to the meetings must have been appreciated, because when the editor of the publication accepted another position, Wells was asked to take his place.

She was less successful in her social life. Perhaps due to her harsh experiences, she had a sullenness about her that underlied a serious nature and a complete lack of social skills. Although she had several suitors, for example, the relationships bristled with anxiety and ambivalence. "I blush to think I allowed [a suitor] to caress me, that he would dare to take such liberties and yet not make a declaration," reads an entry in the diary that she kept upon arriving in Memphis. Yet her pride and independent spirit precluded her playing the role of coquette: "I will not begin at this late date by doing that which my soul abhors, sugaring men, weak, deceitful creatures, with flattery to retain them as escorts," she promised. In any case, although Wells wished "for the society of gentlemen," she was not interested in marriage. Her reasons were not clearly spelled out, but the responsibility of rearing her siblings couldn't have been far from her mind. As a result of her mercurial temper, and tendency to set unrealistic standards for herself and others Ida Wells had few friends and suffered an "almost complete isolation from [her] fellow beings on account of lack of congeniality," as she wrote.

Nevertheless Wells did long for a "lasting friendship such as I have read about." When she met Mary Church, a member of a wealthy political family who was on the verge of her own activist career, Wells hoped that she had found such a friend. Mary Church was "the first woman of my age I've met who is similarly inspired with the same hopes and ambitions," Wells observed. The two women, whose lives would periodically intersect, did share a seriousness of purpose. For Ida, that purpose would become unmistakably clear by 1884.

On May 4 of that year, Ida Wells boarded the Chesapeake & Ohio Railway for the short trip between Woodstock, where she was teaching, and Memphis. As was her custom, she took a seat in the first-class "ladies car." But customs were changing. As early as 1875, Tennessee led other states in passing segregation statutes, known as Jim Crow laws. In 1877, Republican President Rutherford B. Hayes removed federal troops from the South and with them, the protection of Blacks and their newly won rights. But the meanest blow was struck by the United States Supreme Court in 1883, when it ruled that the Civil Rights Acts of 1875 were unconstitutional. Now Blacks throughout the South could be effectively banned from public accommodations including hotels, theaters, barber shops, and restaurants. Trains were also increasingly a target. As Wells knew, there had "been efforts all over the South to draw the color line on the railroads."

The Supreme Court decision was vehemently attacked by the Black press, which was in its full vigor by the 1880s. Wells had agreed with an 1883 editorial in the *New York Age* by one of the country's most militant and widely read journalists, T. Thomas Fortune: Blacks should resist such segregation, he wrote, even "if they were beaten or killed" for it. On May 4, Fortune's advice, so boldly offered from the North, would be taken quite literally by Wells in Memphis when a conductor ordered her to leave the ladies car for the second-class smoker's section. She refused, then braced her feet against the seat in front of her. When the conductor reached for Wells, she bit him. At that point, the conductor called on the aid of two more train workers to assist him. After the ensuing tussle, the three of them managed to push Wells off of the train—to the standing applause of the White passengers. Twenty-two years old, humiliated and angry, her dress torn in the melee, Wells vowed to take the railway and segregation to court.

At first, the railway attempted to bribe her to drop the case—an offer that Wells disdainfully refused. Despite the worsening racial climate, there were still remnants of Reconstruction in the Tennessee courts; the presiding judge on the case turned out to be an ex-Union soldier from Minnesota. He ruled in Wells's favor and awarded her $500 in damages.

Wells was ecstatic. Even the insulting Christmas day headline in the *Memphis Daily Appeal*—"A Darky Damsel Obtains a Verdict for Damages"—did not dampen the victory. Nor did she pay much attention to the railway's angry promise to appeal. For now, Wells had struck a blow for the race in her way, as her father had in his. But though she hardly realized it at the time, the most important result of the suit would not be its impact on civil rights, but on her journalistic career. After winning the case, Wells was asked to write about it by the editor of the *Living Way,* a Baptist weekly.

She eagerly accepted the invitation and continued to write about other issues and Wells soon realized that journalism tapped something deeply within her. It was the "outlet through which to express the real me" as she wrote in her autobiography. What emerged in her articles was a style and perspective that would make her one of the most widely read journalists of her time. Critical of high-toned intellectuals who seemed to have lost touch with the common folk, Wells consciously wrote in "a plain common-sense way on the things that concerned our people," and never used a "word with two syllables where one would do." It was a successful approach. Before long, her articles, signed with the pen name Iola, were picked up in the leading papers of the day, such as the *New York Age*, the *Detroit Plaindealer*, and the *Washington Bee*, among others of the nearly two hundred Black weeklies being published in this period.

By 1886, Wells was beginning to feel a new sense of well-being in Memphis with her Aunt Fannie and two sisters. She felt, as she confided in her diary, that she "was just beginning to live." She was licensed by the Memphis City school system, where the pay and working conditions were vastly better than that of her previous positions. More important, Wells had found a sense of fulfillment in her budding journalistic career. But in the summer of that year, when Wells visited her Aunt Fannie in California she would be forced to make another emotional decision that would mark a turning point in her life.

Her aunt Fannie had taken Annie and Lily with her to visit Visalia, California, the year before and in the summer of 1886, Wells had the chance to visit them by extending an excursion trip to Missouri, sponsored by the National Education Association. When Wells arrived in Visalia she learned, to her surprise, that her aunt had decided to settle there and wanted Wells and her sisters to remain with her. Aunt Fannie had even found a teaching position for Wells—in a poorly equipped, one-room school. Wells, of course, felt indebted to her aunt who had taken in her family, and so reluctantly agreed to sell her return ticket. But she regretted her decision immediately. Wells loved her life in cosmopolitan Memphis, and Visalia, a small town with less than a dozen Black families, seemed like a step backward. When Wells told her aunt that she wanted to return to Memphis, Fannie angrily responded that Wells would have to take her two sisters with her, making the return fare beyond Wells's grasp. The proud Wells became so desperate that she wrote Robert Church, Mary Church's father, to lend her $150, since he was "the only man of my race I knew could lend me that much money and wait for me to repay it." He sent her the money, but the crisis was not over yet. Her sister Annie, who had become close to her California cousins, also protested their return to Memphis. Painfully, after assurances that her aunt would rear Annie "as her own," Wells made the decision to return to Memphis with only her younger sister, Lily.

Wells had scarcely recovered from that emotional ordeal when she received more bad news. In April 1887, the Tennessee Supreme

Court issued its ruling on the Chesapeake & Ohio's appeal of her case. It found that Wells's intent had been to "harass, not to obtain a comfortable seat for the short ride," and thus the earlier lower-court decision was reversed. Wells was devastated. "I had hoped such great things from my suit for my people generally," she wrote in her diary. "I have firmly believed all along that the law was on our side and would, when we appealed to it, give us justice. I feel shorn of that belief, and utterly discouraged," she continued, "and just now if it were possible would gather my race in my arms and fly away with them."

Although at the time Wells understood the importance of the case, she would not be conscious of its true significance until years later. For when she filed her suit, she became the first African-American to challenge the 1883 Supreme Court decision in a state court. So, the case was larger than the Jim Crow policies of a railroad, or the humiliation of a second-class seat; she had stirred a congealing pattern of White supremacy and her last obstacle was the courts. Now with the full complicity of the law, the South's counterrevolution could continue. And as early as by 1889, Henry W. Grady, part-owner of the *Atlanta Constitution*—the largest newspaper in the South— confidently pronounced: "The negro as a political force has dropped out of serious consideration."

"This morning I stand face to face with twenty-five years of my life," wrote a despondent Ida Wells in her diary on her birthday in 1887, ". . . within the last ten, I have suffered more, learned more, lost more than I ever expect to again. . . ." Despite all that had happened to her over the last decade, she blamed herself for not taking full advantage of the opportunities offered her, and was determined to do better—especially in her journalistic pursuits.

So although she was still teaching, when she was offered a position on the weekly *Free Speech and Headlight,* Wells readily accepted—on the condition that she be allowed to purchase a one-third interest in the paper with the two male owners. The men agreed, and with the assurance of her editorial independence, Wells's muckraking style quickly surfaced. She took a leading Black minister to task for adulterous behavior, then threatened to expose the entire Baptist ministers' alliance when they tried to pressure her to desist. She lampooned powerful politicians. She took leaders, such as the educator Booker T. Washington, to task for for criticizing Blacks in the White press. Even one of her partners—a minister whose congregation purchased five hundred copies of the *Free Speech* each week—was not immune. He sold his interest in the paper after one of her editorials criticized him for using the paper as a bully pulpit in matters concerning his congregation. However, her employer, the Memphis city school system, proved to be more recalcitrant. When she wrote an 1889 editorial charging White board members with sexually exploiting Black female teachers, Wells was fired. Her response was characteristically unrepentant. "I had taken a chance in the interest of the children of the race and lost out," she said unapologetically. "But I thought it was right to strike a blow against a glaring evil and I did not regret it."

Teaching had bored Wells anyway. Now she could devote full time to the paper, and canvass for subscriptions throughout the Mississippi valley. Wells showed herself to be as adept at selling as she was at writing. Within a year, she increased the paper's circulation enough so that she began earning almost the same income she had as a teacher. More important, she also received the acknowledgment of her colleagues, and was elected in 1889 as the first female secretary of the National Afro-American Press Association. Noting the event, T. Thomas Fortune, describing her as "girlish looking in physique with sharp regular features, penetrating eyes, firm set thin lips, and a sweet voice," proclaimed that she had "become famous as one of the few of our women who handles a goose quill with diamond point as handily as any of us men." "If Iola was a man," he averred, "she would be a humming Independent in politics. She has plenty of nerve; she is smart as a steel trap, and she has no sympathy with humbug."

Even Fortune, however, who in the following year organized the National Afro-American League as a militant voice of protest, would not know to what extent his observations of the "Princess of the Press" as she was now known, would be proved.

In 1892, Ida Wells was selling subscriptions in Natchez, Mississippi, when she heard the news: on March 9, her friend Thomas Moss and two of his business partners, Calvin McDowell and Henry Stewart, had been taken from their jail cells, put on a train, and lynched a mile outside of Memphis. The news of any lynching would have been disturbing, but that one of the victims was Thomas Moss made it take on the proportion of a personal tragedy. Since she had first met him at the offices of the *Free Speech*—where he delivered the mail and often brought newsbreaking information to her— Moss had become one of Wells's few close friends. She was the godmother of his daughter Maurine and also close to Moss's wife Betty, who was pregnant with their second child.

Wells knew that the only thing that Tommie, as she called him, was "guilty" of was co-owning a grocery store that took away business from a White competitor. The White proprietor had instigated a chain of events that had reached a climax when the Black men shot three Whites who had come to raze the black men's grocery store. Not content that Moss, Stewart, and McDowell were jailed on trumped-up charges, a group of Whites dragged them out of their cells and killed them.

Wells returned from Natchez to a stunned community. Despite the evidences of increasing racism, commercial Memphis—conscious of its image—still had been able to function in relative racial harmony. But now the bloodtides had reached it, too. In lurid detail, the White press described how McDowell's fingers had been shot off when he tried to grab one of the abductor's guns, and how his eyes had been gouged out. Moss, the papers said, pleaded for his life for the sake of his family and unborn child. His last words, the papers said, were "Tell my people to go West—there is no justice for them here." The details of the reports were clear evidence that the perpetrators were known—but no efforts were made to punish them. "I have no power to describe the feelings of horror that possessed every member of the race in Memphis when the truth dawned upon us that protection of the law was not ours," she wrote. Angry and determined, looked to as a leader of the community, Wells launched the antilynching campaign that has been characterized by some as the beginning of the modern civil rights movement. The array of strategies she used as its leader foreshadowed those that would be used in the decades to come.

Since her community was no longer protected by law, one of the first things Wells urged was armed self-defense. "A Winchester rifle should have a place of honor in every home," she counseled in an editorial. Wells herself began wearing a pistol, vowing to "sell my life as dearly as possible." Then, honoring Moss's last words, she urged Memphis Blacks to emigrate West, and went to the newly opened Oklahoma territory so that she could report back on the conditions there. Within two months, Wells reported that six thousand Blacks followed Moss's advice. The White business community watched in horror as their Black clientele abandoned the city. Whole families left—by wagon if they could not afford the train fare; ministers took entire congregations. Those that remained were urged by Wells to boycott the Memphis trolley cars. The boycott was so effective that owners of the company came to see Wells and begged that she desist. The company, they pleaded, was teetering on the edge of bankruptcy.

But other strategies that Wells employed reflected her conviction that the issue was larger than the death of her friend Moss, or increasing racial violence in Memphis. The incidence of lynchings of Blacks had been increasing throughout the South, with—as had happened in Memphis—impunity. The rationale that stilled protest against the mob violence was the Black men were being lynched for the onerous crime of raping White women. Widely accepted at the time was the idea that Black men, free from the constraints of slavery—

and surrounded by Black women who themselves were immoral—
found pure White womanhood irrestible.

But rape was not even an issue in the Memphis lynching. Perhaps
it was not the real motive elsewhere either. Culling newspaper reports, going to the scene of lynchings, and interviewing eyewit-
nesses, Wells meticulously documented the circumstances that had
led to 728 lynchings over the preceding decade. Only a third of the
lynching victims, she found, were even accused of rape, much less
guilty of it. There were interracial liaisons, however, but virtually all
were at the instigation or consent of the White women themselves.
The true victims of rape, Wells knew, were Black women who were
sexually exploited by White men without "reproof from church,
state, or press." Yet the lynch rope was reserved for Blacks like Moss,
who competed economically with Whites. White resentment was
the motive behind the rape charge, concluded Wells, because Blacks
were no longer their "servants," "playthings" or their "source of
income."

On May 21, 1892, Ida Wells wrote the editorial that would banish
her from the South. "Nobody in this section of the country believed
the threadbare lie that Negro men rape white women," it said in
part. "If southern white men are not careful . . . a conclusion will be
reached which will be very damaging to the moral reputation of
their women." Before the editorial appeared, Wells left Memphis to
accept a long-standing invitation to go to Philadelphia and then New
York, where she was met by T. Thomas Fortune. He promptly informed her that it would not be possible for her to return home in
the foreseeable future. The editorial had so incensed White Mem-
phisonians, he said, they had burned the *Free Speech* office down,
her co-owner had been chased out of town within an inch of his life,
and there were threats to lynch Wells herself. There were guards
posted at the railway station in the event of her return. "Now that
you are here," Fortune told her, "I'm afraid that you'll have to stay."
It didn't take long for Wells to settle down and take advantage of her
circumstances. Exchanging her subscription list for some of the paper's stock, Wells began publishing her investigative findings in the
New York Age. "Having lost my paper, had a price put on my life,
and been made an exile from home for hinting at the truth, I felt that
I owed it to myself and to my race to tell the whole truth now that I
was where I could do so freely," Wells determined.

For the next three years, Wells continued to write about lynching
and tirelessly campaigned throughout the country with the passion
of a woman who believed that she was "God's instrument" to do
that work. In 1893, she was invited to speak in the British Isles,
where she was particularly anxious to galvanize the opinion of the

English, who had an abolitionist tradition that influenced American opinion, and were the major importer of American cotton. After her first trip, cut short to attend the World Columbian Exposition in Chicago, she pledged to return.

The Exposition, a cultural event celebrating the four-hundredth anniversary of Columbus' discovery of America featured the contributions of peoples in the Western world, but African-Americans, as a group, were denied representation. Consequently, Wells, editor Garland Penn, reformer Frederick Douglass, and Ferdinand Barnett, publisher of the Black Chicago weekly, the *Conservator*, co-authored and distributed an eighty-one-page booklet that stressed Blacks' achievements and denounced their exclusion from the Exposition. Her association with Barnett, whom she had met previously, turned out to be a particularly meaningful one: they fell in love. Little wonder. He was handsome and distinguished, and important for Wells, shared the same political temperament while complimenting her personal one. Barnett brought levity to her seriousness, a level-headedness to her prickly temper. And as a widower with two children of his own and a mother who organized the household, the dreaded pressure of domestic responsibility falling on Wells was lessened. They set a marriage date for June 27, 1895, in Chicago—after Wells's return from her six-month second tour of England.

It was this second trip to the British Isles that was the more fruitful one, largely because Frances Willard, president of the powerful Women's Christian Temperance Union (WCTU) was also there to provide an effective foil. The English had remained incredulous of Wells's charges that even American liberals, such as Willard, were accomplices to mob violence. But on this trip, Wells brought along a newspaper article that quoted the WCTU president stirring up fears against Black men in an effort to further women's suffrage in the South. The vitriolic response of Willard, and the "liberal" American press that picked up the story, actually served to verify Wells's claims. As a result, prominent figures such as the Archbishop of Canterbury and the Duke of Argyll, rallied to her cause, and formed the British Anti-Lynching Committee. This development in turn spurred the support of American liberals such as Hull House reformer Jane Addams, labor leader Samuel Gompers, editor of the popular *Century* magazine, Richard Gilder—and even, eventually, Frances Willard.

Of course, Wells's campaign also reverberated among Black activists, especially women who were already in the process of forming clubs that focused on women's suffrage and community self-help. In 1892, women from New York City and other parts of the East Coast had sponsored a tribute to Wells and raised funds to publish her investigative findings. Following the tribute there was discussion of forming a national organization. "Ida Wells was creating so much interest in her crusade against lynching, it was a good time to carry out the club's idea," pronounced the Boston-based magazine the *Woman's Era.* The urgency behind the idea was underscored by events at the Columbian Exposition, and by a scurrilous article by the president of the Missouri Press Association that questioned Wells's morality and that of Black women in general. By 1896, the National Association of Colored Women (NACW) was formed, headed by Wells's friend Mary Church Terrell, who was now married and living in Washington, D.C.

In 1896, Ida B. Wells-Barnett was asked by the Illinois Women's Central Committee to campaign for Republican presidential candidate William McKinley. By that year, her campaign had gained her international notoriety and her muckraking journalism on behalf of African-Americans made her a valiant symbol of the nascent Progressive Era. The country was now poised to relieve the poor, expose injustice, and check the exploitive power of industrialists—increasingly seen as "robber barons"—who were monopolizing the nation's newly generated wealth. The nature of Wells's crusade had made much of the nation look differently at not only lynching and those that committed it, but the plight of African-Americans victimized by racial exploitation. Since her campaign, the number of recorded lynchings decreased; Memphis would not report another lynching for twenty years.

But the invitation to stump the state for the Republicans forced Wells-Barnett to weigh domestic considerations against her political ones. Now she was not only a relative newly-wed, but a mother of her first child, Charles. Nevertheless, Wells handled the situation deftly. The Committee, she told them, would have to provide a nurse at each stop. They agreed, and as Wells-Barnett wrote in her autobiography, "I honestly believe that I am the only woman in the United States who ever traveled throughout the country with a nursing baby to make political speeches."

However, when Charles was soon followed by another child, Herman, in 1897, then Ida B. Wells, Jr. in 1901 and Alfreda in 1904, she *was* forced to intermittently "retire" to take care of the children. This caused the suffragist Susan B. Anthony, who never married, to once remark disparagingly that because of Wells-Barnett's "divided duty" agitation seemed "practically to have ceased." But Wells-Barnett did not seem particularly conflicted about it, in part because Ferdinand, politically active himself as the first Black assistant state's attorney in Chicago's Cook County, supported her in both roles. He urged her to continue her activism, despite the complaints of some Black male

leaders that she always "jumped ahead of them." And, once ambivalent about domestic responsibilities, to her own surprise, she came to
believe that motherhood was "one of the most glorious advantages in
the development of [one's] own womanhood."

But these years were "divisive" for Wells-Barnett in another way.
All of her experiences as an effective activist had taught her that
confrontation, mobilizing the Black community, and refusing to compromise were effective strategies. Consequently, Wells-Barnett continued to speak out against the continuing racial violence, now also
prevalent in the North, as well as against the federal administrations,
including McKinley's, that failed to act against it. In the wake of the
Springfield, Illinois, race riots of 1909 during which two Blacks were
lynched within a half-mile of Abraham Lincoln's former home, she
organized the Negro Fellowship League, a settlement house and employment center for indigent Blacks. She founded the league, she said,
because "Our race had not yet perfected an organization which was
prepared to take hold of the situation."

In a city where other ethnic groups were consolidating their political power, Wells-Barnett organized the Alpha Suffrage Club in 1913—
the first of its kind for Black women in the state—to respond to the
granting of limited suffrage for women (the right to vote in presidential elections) in Illinois. The club was also instrumental in the
election of Chicago's first Black alderman, Oscar DePriest. And
Wells-Barnett defiantly refused to march in the rear of the historic
1913 women's suffrage demonstration in Washington, D.C., despite
the entreaties of its White organizers for her not to offend the Southern participants.

But as would become increasingly clear to Wells-Barnett, the exi-
gencies of the reform era stressed gradualism and compromise rather
than confrontation, interracial consensus in lieu of grass-roots mobilization. This was evidenced, in part, by the rise of the conservative
Booker T. Washington in 1895 after his Atlanta Exposition speech
that stressed the need for industrial training rather than political and
social equality for blacks, and by the emergence of the NAACP in
1909 and the National Urban League in 1911.

Washington's formula was especially welcomed by the White establishment. The extraordinary influence of the Tuskegee president
was derived from his role as adviser to presidents McKinley, Theodore Roosevelt, and William Taft, and as the beneficiary of industrialists, such as Andrew Carnegie who gave Tuskegee $600,000 in 1904.
The power of the "Washington Machine" soon extended to virtual
control of the Black press and of progressive organizations that were
created to advocate political equality for Blacks—organizations that
had in the past touted Wells-Barnett's leadership.

Wells-Barnett felt the shadow of Washington at least as early as 1899, when she gave an impassioned speech before Thomas Fortune's once-militant Afro-American League. She spoke heatedly about the Wilmington, North Carolina, riots earlier that year, during which eleven Blacks were killed with impunity. But her condemnation of both Washington and McKinley for failing to call for punishment of the guilty Whites offended more than it incited. By this time, a good portion of the League was made up of Blacks who owed their political appointments to the President, to Washington, or both men.

As Washington's power grew stronger, Wells-Barnett, perhaps the leader who was the most impolitic about confronting him, grew more isolated—even from Black activist women. Despite her role in the organization of the NACW, for example, she was hissed from the floor at a 1909 meeting when she attempted to wrest control of its publication from the editor, Margaret Murray Washington, wife of the Tuskegee president. The publication, Wells-Barnett was reminded, was subsidized by Tuskegee.

Wells-Barnett found little respite in the NAACP, founded in 1909 allegedly to provide a counterweight to Washington's power and policies. The founders were primarily made up of White liberals, such as Jane Addams and Oswald Garrison Villard (grandson of the abolitionist William Lloyd Garrison) who had actually issued the call for its formation. It was clear to Wells-Barnett that the organization would be too conservative for her liking when in its first meeting, it failed to pass a resolution calling for the passage of an antilynching bill that had been introduced in Congress in 1902. Writing of the meeting, W. E. B. Du Bois, the only Black officer of the organization, described a woman, undoubtedly Wells-Barnett, who "leapt to her feet and passionately cried, 'They are betraying us again—those White friends of ours.' "

She probably felt no better about the NAACP when Du Bois and Villard selected Jane Addams to head its first branch in Chicago—probably at the behest of Sears and Roebuck magnate Julius Rosenwald, who promised to help capitalize it. Rosenwald, an active member of Tuskegee's board, was known to like Addams—he also provided funds for the operation of her settlement, Hull House—and dislike Wells-Barnett. Rosenwald's largesse also helped, subsequently, to finance the Chicago branch of the interracial National Urban League, which soon put Wells-Barnett's settlement house out of business. She had reason to believe that the national organization "was brought to Chicago to supplant the activities of the Negro Fellowship League."

Cast adrift from the major racial reform organizations of her times,

Ida Wells-Barnett remained undeterred. And as the economic gains of Blacks achieved in the World War I years melted away into racial violence, her convictions—and activism—only intensified. Branded as one of the most dangerous radicals in America by the Secret Service, she defied its threat, in 1917, to charge her with treason for protesting the execution of Black soldiers in Texas who had killed civilians in self-defense. In 1918 and 1919, she investigated race riots in East St. Louis and Chicago that had claimed seventy-eight deaths—and for which Blacks were wrongly held responsible. And in 1922, at age sixty, Wells-Barnett decided that she had to return to the South that had banished her thirty years before. What drew her there was a racial incident known as the Arkansas Massacre.

It was an apt description of the attack by armed Whites—some from bordering states—to break up a meeting of Black sharecroppers from Elaine, Arkansas, attempting to form a union. But it was the Black men who were tried and imprisoned: sixty-seven were given long prison terms, twelve were slated to be executed. While their case languished, there were reports of the men being tortured with electric prods. However, despite several attempts to gain access to the garrisoned men, to hear their side of the story, no one but family members were able to get inside the prison to see them.

From Chicago, Wells-Barnett had been writing about the case in the *Chicago Defender,* and decided that the time had come to get a first-hand report. She traveled to Arkansas, under cover, and upon her arrival, got in touch with family members of the prisoners. Posing as a cousin to one of the men, she got into the prison and gathered the details about what had happened. Then she did what she could do best: arouse public opinion to a pitch by publishing her findings. Within a year, the Supreme Court ruled that the sharecroppers had not had a fair trial, and subsequently, all of the prisoners were set free.

Her final "campaign"—launched in 1930, a year before her death from uremia, a kidney ailment—was less dramatic and successful, but vintage Wells-Barnett. She ran, unsuccessfully, for a state senate seat as an independent. But Wells-Barnett could count victories of the past and the future. In the same year Texan Jesse Daniel Ames formed the all-white Association of Southern Women to Prevent Lynching. This organization, in turn, became an important ally to the NAACP, which would launch its most vigorous antilynching campaign in 1935 for the passage of the Wagner-Costigan antilynching bill in Congress. Although the bill was never able to pass the Southern-dominated Senate, it galvanized public opinion and, ironically, catapulted Walter White, the NAACP executive director, into national prominence.

By the time she died, the status of Ida B. Wells as a national leader and symbol of the Reform era had diminished. Clearly, one reason was that her belief in Black-led, direct action and grassroots mobilization set her apart from the other leaders of racial reform. After all, she had learned to distrust the legal system, the focus of the NAACP's activities, because it had proved to be a fickle ally for Blacks. And her experience had taught her that meaningful concessions were gained by agitation and mobilization of the Black community, not by compromise or aquiescence to the White industrial order. Wells-Barnett believed in working with Whites, as she had with the Republican committee, with the interracial clubs to which she belonged, and even with the Negro Fellowship League for which she sought assistance from White political and business leaders in Chicago. But she had less faith in the fidelity of White liberals than did some of her counterparts, and believed that Blacks should lead organizations created to advance racial equality.

But her alienation from virtually all reform leaders, Black and White, male and female, was also partially self-inflicted. She seemed to lack even the most fundamental interpersonal skills, making disagreements flare into deep and permanent hostility. In her autobiography, Wells-Barnett admitted that she often failed to control her temper; and the tone of the book suggests a woman who was so critical of others that she appears to be a perennial malcontent. And certainly a shortcoming in her leadership abilities is evidenced in the fact that throughout her life, she was unable to sustain a relationship to any organization, save those that she led herself. Nevertheless, it can be argued that her vision as a leader, if realized, would have made African-Americans less dependent on White largesse in the ensuing decades.

It also can be argued that few leaders of the Progressive era had a greater impact on national perceptions, or catalyzed more reform activity, than Ida Wells-Barnett. Her investigative journalism revealed the base motives behind mob violence. And by revealing the truth about lynching, she also laid bare the racism and sexism behind it. Her campaign galvanized Black feminists as well as White, and was the precursor of the modern civil rights movement to follow.

Notes

[1]The primary source of information on Ida B. Wells-Barnett's life is *Crusade for Justice: The Autobiography of Ida B. Wells* (Chicago: University of Chicago Press, 1970) edited by her daughter, Alfreda Duster. Her diary can be found among the Ida B. Wells papers at the University of Chicago, and excerpts are reprinted in Dorothy Sterling's *We Are Your Sisters: Black Women of the Nineteenth Century* (New York: W. W. Norton, 1984). There are additional writings of Wells in *On Lynching* (New York: Arno Press, 1969), which is a reprinted collection of three pamphlets: *Southern Horrors, A Red Record,* and *Mob Rule in New Orleans;* also in *Black Women in White America: A Documentary History* (New York: Vintage Books, 1973); ed. Gerda Lerner, and in Bettina Aptheker, ed., *Lynching and Rape: An Exchange of Views* (Occasional Paper no. 25, American Institute for Marxist Studies, 1977). Useful secondary sources include Charles Flint Kellogg, *NAACP: A History of the National Association for Colored People, 1909–1920* (Baltimore: Johns Hopkins University Press); Arvarh Harrington, *History of the Chicago Urban League* (Urbana: University of Illinois Press, 1966); Allan H. Spear, *Black Chicago: The Making of a Black Ghetto* (Chicago: University of Chicago Press, 1967); and John Hope Franklin and August Meier eds., *Black Leaders of the Twentieth Century* (Urbana: University of Illinois Press, 1982), which includes biographical essays on Ida Wells, T. Thomas Fortune, W. E. B. Du Bois and Booker T. Washington, among others.

PART VI

The Transition to Modernity

By 1900 the great American industrial machine was geared for the mass production of consumer goods. The conditions inviting reform remained, but their context was gradually changing. In 1890, the average work week in manufacturing was 60 hours long; by 1910 it was 51 hours. Although these averages hide wide variations and continuing exploitation, more and more families could participate in consumerism as men's wages improved and were augmented by the wages of women and children. Significantly, too, single working-class women found ways to pursue the pleasures of a growing consumer culture.

The increase of life expectancy by six years between 1900 and 1920 was connected with the decline in deaths from diptheria, typhoid, and influenza. The flush toilet and sewage treatment facilities contributed to this decline. Such factors, along with the limitation of family size, had a significant impact on domestic environments. Traditionally strenuous domestic demands on women's work at home were mitigated by the availability of processed foods and much more ready-made clothing, although these items were being produced by women who were among the most exploited of industrial wage-earners.

A host of similarly mass-produced items and mass-marketed goods permitted new levels of self-expression. For example, although young department-store saleswomen worked for low pay and long hours, they could also be exponents of style. Additionally, more and more young people could read at higher levels, as the enrollments in high schools grew from 203,000 in 1890 to 2.3 million in 1920. The new service-sector jobs, as well as mass advertising and certain forms of mass entertainment, required new levels of literacy. And if on the one hand, the decline in the hours of work was in large part the result of a mechanization that deprived some workers of traditional skills, on the other, it also permitted the enormous expansion of leisure activities. Like fashionable clothing and literacy, these were avenues for self-expression.

Leisure, too, became big business. There were 10 million bicycles in America by 1900. Bicycling was one of a number of activities which encouraged women to wear less cumbersome and constrictive clothing that allowed more physical activity. Furthermore, the anxiety over the effects of concentrated study on young women's brains led to their widespread participation in college athletics such as basketball, rowing, and swimming, with a consequent enhancement of their sense of strength and physical freedom. Whether young women went to college or not, they could attend circuses, vaudeville, musical comedy, and ocean resorts in increasing numbers, again suggesting new ways to imagine selfhood. Commerce responded to working women's demands in these respects. Dance halls became very significant sites for working-class women's "cheap amusements," including the expression of sexual desire although women also ran sexual risks in enjoying themselves there. And after 1900, the movies were established as one of America's greatest dream machines encouraging even married women to extend their pleasures outside the home.

In the 1920s, women surged into business and the professions. They entered coeducational colleges in far greater numbers than ever before. There they would enjoy a very different cultural environment than that of their pre-war predecessors in women's colleges: their circumstances were part of a new "youth culture" that was fostering new ways for young women and men to enjoy themselves in each other's company and drawing on the possibilities for self-conception in clothing, cosmetics, cars, movies, radio, and music. While it included a renewed emphasis on marriage and motherhood, in contrast to the doubts raised by previous generations over the compatibility of marriage and college education, it also fostered greater acceptance of female desire and the ideal of greater sexual equality in marriage. This youth culture extended from the middle to the working class, both groups exposed regularly to the powerful influence of the movies.

The rise of a consumer culture, then, had special meanings for the great mass of American women, in their homes, in that women's work was made easier, but also in opening up a public life based on pleasure, not reform. This dimension of consumerism has often been neglected in favor of the negative aspect—making women mere sex objects—which was also a tendency. In any case, the pursuit of pleasure was sanctioned by the most powerful voices in American society, those of big business. Access to such pleasure was immediately attractive to all classes. By the end of the nineteenth century, isolated farm households had been linked to the consumer culture by the mail-order houses, Montgomery Ward and Sears Roebuck, through their catalogs and the new Rural Free Delivery Service. In the cities, the daughters of the "new immigration" were just as eager as rural women to join a "consumption community." After the trauma of uprooting themselves, immigrant families were reconstituted in some cases to become stronger than had been possible under the disintegrative effects of impoverishment in their land of origin. Family ties played a key role in easing the transition of the millions of immigrants, who flooded into America in their greatest numbers in the years immediately prior to World War I.

Among other things, trade unionist Rose Schneiderman's story symbolizes the fact that different traditions of gender relations have responded to the American tradition of domesticity in different ways. Schneiderman's generation of Eastern European Jews had been preceded by the German Jews of the 1840s who, by the 1890s, had become Americanized enough to become leading contributors to that "new world" of "social feminism," prominent in suffragism and in many aspects of reform. Many immigrant women carried with them deeply conservative attitudes toward gender; others yearned to escape patriarchal traditions by coming to the United States. Immigrant Italian women limited their births, but still focused their lives on their families. Americanization provided women opportunities for literacy and (after 1920) for voting participation, as well as for work and pleasure outside the home. Immigrant wives could look to the laws and customs of the new country for protection from beatings within their families. Settlement houses could be the sites for a sympathetic and respectful acknowledgment of Old World cultures as well as what must be seen as the necessary education into the traditions of the new. At the same time, the middle-class female reformers' temperance crusade, eventually leading to Prohibition, was at odds with the festive traditions of immigrant cultures. This symbolizes the powerful tensions in American life, generated by the contrasts between cultures.

Immigrant families, then, consolidated for the future. Eventually they became more prosperous than would be possible in their countries of origin for decades. But along with the families of native-born, white Americans migrating to the cities in record numbers, immigrant families faced a more rapid shifting of their traditional functions. Formerly, children had learned skills at home. There, too, family members had entertained themselves in a variety of ways. Now children went to school, and as they grew older, to dance halls and movie houses. Young women formed peer groups by way of the paid workforce, as well as in schools and college. Families saw their daughters joining a national consumer culture that generated vastly new role models.

The outbreak of World War I in 1914 temporarily halted the massive influx of immigration. Amidst jingoistic hatreds left by the war, including the "red scare" that Crystal Eastman faced, conservative groups of white Anglo-Saxon Protestants made a last stand. The Emergency Quota Act was passed in 1921, aimed at restricting the new immigration from southern and eastern Europe, in favor of the old immigration from the north and west. The restrictions were made still more effective by the National Origins Act of 1924. Big business had adequate supplies of labor, which it kept cheap by systematic union-busting; thus, it no longer resisted the nativist campaign as it had done in earlier decades, when it had looked to immigration for cheap labor. Immigrant cultures were no longer being invigorated by fresh infusions from the old countries and now they were exposed to the full force of consumer culture. The result was to accelerate Americanization. From a political and reform point of view, the 1920s were intensely conservative, whatever the liberalizing juices unleashed by consumerism's triumphs.

Conservative forces were also provoked by a particular migration within the United States. Poor African-Americans from rural areas met far more enduring and pervasive discrimination when they migrated to northern cities than their contemporary immigrants who came from outside the nation's borders. African-Americans had begun significant migration to the north in the 1880s as whites intensified their economic and political oppression in the rural south. In southern states, African-Americans were systematically purged from any participation in the political system in the wake of the defeat of Populism. Moreover, temporary employment opportunities of World War I greatly increased black migration to northern cities. Detroit's black population, for example, increased 300 percent between 1910 and 1920, and it more than doubled in the next ten years. But if black people moved away from the constant threat and reality of southern lynchings, their mass migration to the north often provoked northern whites to riot against them. In violence following the murder of a black person swimming at a whites-only beach in Chicago on a hot July day in 1919, thirty-eight people, black and white, were killed.

Expanding ghettoes were to be powerful centers for the generating of African-American culture. In the 1920s, jazz emerged as "a major art form" celebrated in mainstream popular culture. Among the creators and performers of jazz were a series of magnificent women singers, including Bessie Smith, and later, Billie Holiday. Jazz was rooted in generations of African-American experience. It fearlessly expressed pain and sexuality, injustice and transcendence. Jazz would be the chief wellspring for that twentieth-century popular American music upon which each generation would draw to define itself. The ability to do so was fostered in the 1920s by radio and recordings.

Harlem, in New York City, was the site of an outpouring of many other forms of African-American self-expression, in addition to music. They ranged from painting to poetry and fiction (shaped by the same cultural traditions as music) and from social science to the separatist politics of Marcus Garvey. This outpouring has become known as the Harlem Renaissance. The poets included Claude McKay, of whom Crystal Eastman was a friend, and Langston Hughes. One of the greatest of the Harlem Renaissance's writers was Zora Neale Hurston. Trained as an anthropologist, Hurston celebrated the uniqueness of African-American culture, insisted on a woman's ability and right to participate fully in it, and demonstrated its integrity in the face of racism.

The creation of a national consumer culture; the massive immigration of new immigrants into the cities; and the intensification of racist politics, south and north, formed the context for suffragism's final push during the second decade of the twentieth century. The Nineteenth Amendment to the Constitution, finally passed in 1920, declared that the "right of citizens of the United States to vote shall not be denied or abridged . . . on account of sex." Originating in the social reforms of the 1820s and 1830s, women's suffrage was the culmination of the first women's movement in which suffragists identified themselves as a distinct, collective interest. It formally connected women to public life in a culture where political participation was fundamental in ideology and in practice. It symbolized sexual equality, although it did not achieve it. The winning of suffrage had taken nearly a "century of struggle." Suffragists only achieved a critical mass of support in the second decade of the twentieth century. The heritage of "separate-sphere" domesticity and of social science converged with the political goals of progressivism. During the two decades after the Civil War, suffragists had split acrimoniously over the granting of the vote to black males. One of the two suffrage associations, the National Woman Suffrage Association, pressed for a national amendment, while the American Woman Suffrage Association continued its state-by-state strategy. But of the 480 state campaigns between 1870 and 1910, only 17 resulted in state referenda and suffragists won in only 2 of those, Wyoming and Colorado. In 1890 the two associations merged as the National American Woman Suffrage Association (NAWSA). It was infused with new life in 1907 when Elizabeth Cady Stanton's daughter, Harriet Stanton Blatch, and a younger generation of suffragists reached out to a broader constituency and initiated more dramatic tactics. Rose Schneiderman's career illustrates that working-class women participated in the suffrage campaign. Alice Paul, schooled in the English suffrage movement, became a suffrage leader in America and led still more militant protests. In 1913 she and her followers broke away to form the Congressional Union, which became the National Woman's Party in 1916. It took a hard line against the Democrats in power under President Woodrow Wilson, which distinguished it from NAWSA, which tried to stand above party politics.

When the United States entered the first World War against Germany and its allies in 1917, more militant suffragists compared Wilson to the German Kaiser. They dramatized the contradiction of President Wilson's war goal, asking how America could be "saving the world for democracy," while half of all Americans were denied the vote. They chained themselves to the White House fence and when they were arrested they went on hunger strikes in prison. The media made them martyrs and this advance guard of radicals made the more numerous and less militant NAWSA seem the lesser of two evils to the male establishment. Both Democrats and Republicans embraced women's suffrage and Wilson reversed his opposition to it.

At another level, less radical suffragists had worked hard since the turn of the century to show it was in either of the two major parties' interests to support women's suffrage. Suffragists shared common ground with progressives generally, including the goal of political "reform." For example, mainstream politics were still deeply racist. To make themselves more acceptable to those men who could grant them the ballot, some white suffragists used racist tactics. They emphasized the "superiority" of educated white women to illiterate African-Americans and non-English-speaking and illiterate immigrant males.

Suffragists also emphasized the conventionality of their beliefs about gender roles. They argued that women would bring the special gender qualities to bear on public life. They presented women as "social housekeepers" for the public sphere. Then, during the war, the majority of suffragists patriotically threw themselves into the war effort, demonstrating their loyalty to the same imperatives as men. Suffragists argued that women's wartime work, in factories and near the battlefields as medical volunteers, in addition to various charitable efforts on behalf of the troops, further demonstrated women's qualifications for the vote.

By contrast, a number of women socialists and pacifists, including Jane Addams and Crystal Eastman were made outcasts by their opposition to the war. Another was Emma Goldman, who had come to the United States from Russia to find freedom from traditional patriarchy in the form of a marriage arranged by her father. Always individualistic, her politics were those of an anarchist. She was a magnificent public speaker. Her topics ranged from the evils of capitalism to advocacy of birth control. Repeatedly imprisoned and finally deported from the United States to Russia in 1919 during the "red scare," Goldman became deeply critical of the emerging totalitarianism there. She died in Canada on a trip to raise money to fight General Francisco Franco, the fascist usurper in Spain. A lifelong feminist, Goldman distinguished herself from most of her contemporary American feminists by her open expression of sexual appetite. Goldman criticized her fellow feminists for their "narrow Puritanical vision" which sought to banish "man, as a disturber and doubtful character, out of their emotional life."

The directions that feminists had taken in order to win the vote had been disquieting to several of their leaders. Those directions included capitalizing on racial and class prejudices. They also included repressing the issue of sex. But tapping Victorian roots, separately nourished in domesticity and deeply suspicious of the association of male power with sexuality, a significant proportion of female college graduates and social feminists found public life and conventional family lives mutually exclusive. Some chose homosocial relationships. Others hoped to establish a single, sexual standard for heterosexual relations. They saw sexual puritanism and even celibacy as necessary strategies in women's historical conflict with men. Hence suffragists succeeded in winning women the vote but left aside the issue of sexual freedom. This powerful element in the dominant, middle-class feminist tradition put it at odds with a freer, more sexual popular culture.

By the 1920s, much of feminism was, in a crucial sense, anachronistic. This is why it languished. Charlotte Perkins Gilman was contemptuous of "the newly freed" women's giving in to a sexuality that Gilman could only see as "masculine," as women mastered "birth control" and acquired "experience." It was in the 1920s that contraception finally became a respectable subject of discussion. While quite effective techniques had been known for at least a century, social beliefs—especially religious ones—had inhibited their dissemination. In 1921 Margaret Sanger set up the American Birth Control League in Brooklyn, New York, through which the new secular authorities on such matters, doctors and social workers, were persuaded to give their expert imprimatur to birth control. But users had their own reasons, too. Gilman, Addams, and others of their generation were deeply conscious of the gulf between themselves and younger women over the issue of sex and style, a gulf that showed itself within feminism, as the story of Crystal Eastman illustrates. She, like many of her generation, attempted to combine career and family. On the other hand, Alice Paul sustained the traditional asceticism of feminism and Rose Schneiderman devoted herself to reform rather than family.

While differing sharply in personal and sexual styles, Paul and Eastman jointly campaigned in the 1920s on behalf of the full equality of the sexes. Paul's party introduced the Equal Rights Amendment in 1923. It opposed "protective legislation" on the grounds that it assumed women needed protection, that is, that women were naturally weaker than men. Their opponents, among

them Rose Schneiderman, preferred to maintain reform legislation defending female workers, whatever its rationale. They saw
this as especially important because of big business' successful
anti-labor campaign of the 1920s. Protective legislation's effects
were ambiguous; the laws went largely unenforced and were used
frequently to exclude women from certain jobs. This was one of
many struggles splitting feminism in the 1920s, a decade which
for some symbolized the end of the old feminism and the beginnings of the new.

Rose Schneiderman
(1882–1972)

Annelise Orleck

Rose Schneiderman was born in Saven, Poland, in 1882 to a close-knit Orthodox Jewish family. In 1890 the family came to New York City. Poverty forced Schneiderman to enter the paid work force at thirteen, first as a saleswoman and then as a capmaker. By 1904 she was the first woman to be elected to the general executive board of an American labor union, the United Cloth Hat and Cap Makers Union. Schneiderman then became a vice president of the New York Women's Trade Union League (WTUL) in 1906 and its chief organizer in 1908. She helped organize the great uprising of New York shirtwaist makers in 1909–1910, and between 1914 and 1916 was the general organizer for the International Ladies' Garment Workers Union. In 1911 she helped found the Wage Earner's League for Woman Suffrage and in 1917 she was elected president of the Industrial Section of the New York Woman Suffrage Party, the working-class wing of the party. Schneiderman was elected president of the New York WTUL in 1917 and president of the National WTUL in 1926, retaining both positions until her retirement in 1949. In 1933 President Roosevelt appointed her the only woman on his National Labor Advisory Board. From 1937 until 1945 Schneiderman served as secretary of labor for the state of New York. She retired in 1949, after which she wrote her memoirs, made radio speeches, and appeared at various union functions. She lived alone in New York City until 1969, when declining health forced her to enter a nursing home. She died in 1972 at age ninety.

Rose Schneiderman always liked to remind people that she was "a redhead." In speeches and writings she used her hair color as a symbol of her fiery personality. So did her detractors, who called her, among other things, "the Red Rose of Anarchy." Only four feet nine inches tall, the diminutive immigrant Jew from Poland had an uncanny ability to cut to the heart of an issue. That quality won her both lifelong friends and enemies. For nearly half a century, from 1905 through the early 1950s, Schneiderman stirred crowds with her words. Speaking on street corners, soapboxes, lecture platforms, and, during the 1930s, over the radio, the militant trade unionist and women's rights advocate could move even those who were prepared to dislike her. New York City patrol officer John Kelly was one unlikely convert. During the spring of 1911 he decided to attend a memorial for victims of the Triangle Shirtwaist Company fire, at which Rose Schneiderman was to be the featured speaker. He did not expect to hear anything he liked from ". . . one of them foreigners. But she herself can make you weep," he commented afterward. "She is the finest speaker I ever heard." A year later, when Schneiderman toured Ohio to build support for a statewide woman suffrage referendum, a local suffragist wrote to a friend that she was amazed by Schneiderman's affect on crowds. "We have had splendid speakers here before, but not one who impressed the people as she did. Strong men sat with tears rolling down their faces. Her pathos and earnestness held the audiences spellbound."[1]

From the time she was first introduced to socialism as an eighteen-year-old capmaker at the turn of the twentieth century, to her retirement in 1949, Rose Schneiderman committed herself to improving the conditions of working-class women's lives in the United States. Despite only four years of formal schooling in the United States, Rose Schneiderman moved to the forefront of the American labor and woman suffrage movements. She became a friend and adviser to progressive Democrats including Al Smith, Eleanor and Franklin Roosevelt, and eventually won the presidency of both the New York and National Women's Trade Union Leagues, to a seat as the only woman on Franklin Roosevelt's Labor Advisory Board, and to a seven-year term as secretary of labor for the state of New York. She organized tens of thousands of working women into unions and convinced them of the importance of getting the vote. She promoted the organization of housewives into a nationwide network of neighborhood consumer organizations. She lobbied effectively for maximum hour, minimum wage, maternity, disability, and unemployment insurance legislation that affected millions of women. When she died in 1972, a *New York Times* editorial summed up her life and work this way: "A tiny red haired bundle of social dynamite, Rose Schneiderman did more to upgrade the dignity and living standards of working women than any other American."[2]

Acclaimed as she was, Rose Schneiderman was not without her critics. Her pragmatic focus sometimes made her seem conservative to radical feminists, such as the leaders of the National Woman's Party, who had broken with the National American Woman Suffrage Association to take more direct action in securing the vote. She was a passionate advocate of women's rights; and yet, for decades she fought bitterly against a proposed Equal Rights Amendment to the federal Constitution, which would ban sex discrimination, because she feared that it would nullify hard-won legislation protecting female workers. She was sharply criticized for this stance by activists in the National Woman's Party, who accused her of ignoring the needs of American women. Schneiderman was also chastised by communists, during the twenties and thirties, for her work with upper-class women and her service to the state and federal administrations of Franklin Roosevelt. She did not flinch under either attack. She had a single goal in mind, to aid American working-class women, and she pursued that goal with the combined pragmatism and passion that were the hallmarks of her long career.

But a lifetime of standing her ground had its costs. Fewer than a dozen people attended Rose Schneiderman's funeral. Her oldest friend, Pauline Newman, was shocked. "I thought I'd find a lot of people who knew her and for whom she worked all her life," she recalled sadly. "I could not believe it, you know?" In part the small turnout was due to the fact that Schneiderman had no children and had outlived many of her contemporaries. But it was also a reflection of the fact that her life and work did not always meet with approval from the media, the Democratic party, or even the men with whom she worked in the labor movement. Male colleagues praised her often for her contributions to the cause of labor, but they also resented her for her insistence that the American labor movement address women's needs and make full use of women's talents. They appeared with her at union functions where they cheered the solidarity of men and women in the labor movement, but they were not comfortable with this Jewish woman who never married, who chose to live a public life when women were expected to devote themselves exclusively to home and family.[3]

Schneiderman's own writings and her repeated refusals to reveal any details about her private life to reporters or, after her retirement, to historians, reflect a deep ambivalence about the private costs of her public life. By all accounts her personal life seems to have been a rich one. Still she was torn, as she put it in a letter to Pauline Newman, by a "yearning, yearning for warmth and tenderness."

Like many of her contemporaries, Schneiderman had absorbed the belief that women who chose a public career had to be willing to forgo ". . . the fulfillment of love." She was aware of what she lacked. "I am," she wrote to Newman at age thirty-five, "used to going without the things most wanted." A lifetime of activism brought Schneiderman excitement, fulfillment, and a measure of fame, but it also left her open to criticism. She did not mind battling those who attacked her for her politics. It was harder having to deal with those who would not accept her personal choices. An immigrant, working-class woman challenging the limitations that American society imposed on people of her ethnicity, her class, and her sex risked giving up the comfort of being socially acceptable. Though it did not stop her from fighting, Schneiderman was never able to resolve to her own satisfaction the tension between cherishing difference and demanding equality. She felt the strain of that tension throughout her life.[4]

Rose Schneiderman's early life was in many ways typical of her generation of Eastern European Jewish immigrants. She was born in Saven, Poland, in 1882, a time when the thousand-year-old traditions of Eastern European Jewry were cracking apart. Political repression combined with economic dislocation as the Russian empire industrialized rapidly and suddenly, leaving Jewish craftspeople and artisans unable to compete. Tens of thousands migrated to the cities hoping to find work in one of Russia's new garment factories.

There Jewish young people came into contact for the first time with a wide range of secular ideas. Young men and women who socialized, worked, and studied together in Kiev, Odessa, Vilna, and Warsaw began to see traditional Jewish religious life as old-fashioned, narrow, and provincial. Typical of that provincialism, many Jewish intellectuals argued, was the belief that women did not need to be, indeed should not be, educated. The intellectual, political, and artistic ferment of the cities soon reached small Jewish towns like Saven. As in the cities, study groups sprang up, composed of equal numbers of men and women. Some traditionalist parents still sought to prevent their daughters from receiving any education, religious or secular, but others, like Deborah Schneiderman, perhaps taking a vicarious pleasure in it, encouraged their daughters to learn as much as they could.

"I started going to Hebrew school when I was four," Rose Schneiderman later recalled. "Though it was somewhat unusual for girls to study . . . Mother was determined that I learn Hebrew so I could read and understand the prayers recited at home and in the synagogue." When the family moved from the small town of Saven to the city of Khelm they sent Rose to a public school where she learned to read, write, and speak Russian. Though Schneiderman would later express embarrassment at her limited education, perhaps because so many of the American women she worked with had college degrees, her reading knowledge of Hebrew and Russian made her an educated woman by comparison with her mother's generation of small-town Jewish women.[5]

In 1890, Rose Schneiderman, her mother, and brothers left Poland for New York City, where Rose's father Samuel waited for them, having gone on ahead to find work and living quarters for his family. Part of a mass migration that brought 1.25 million Jews from Russia and Poland to the United States between 1881 and 1914, the Schneidermans settled on the Lower East Side of Manhattan, in a crowded, dirty ghetto that was also a center of trade union and socialist activity. Like thousands of other new Jewish immigrants, Samuel found work there in the burgeoning garment trade.

Less than two years later, Samuel Schneiderman died of the flu, leaving thirty-year-old Deborah with the prospect of providing for three small children and a baby soon to be born. Like many Eastern European Jewish women, Deborah Schneiderman was accustomed to earning money to help support her family. In Poland, she had supplemented the small income Samuel derived from his tailoring business by doing a little bit of everything. She sewed for neighbors, baked ritual breads and cakes for local weddings, treated the sick with homemade herbal medicines, and tended bar in a nearby saloon when the proprietor was too drunk to do it herself. Now in New York she did what the majority of immigrant women of all ethnicities did during the early twentieth century when they needed to enhance the family income: Deborah took in boarders.[6]

For a while after Samuel Schneiderman's sudden death, the family had no income besides the daily basket of food provided by United Hebrew Charities. Deborah Schneiderman was forced to send six-year-old Harry to the Hebrew Orphan Asylum. The arrival of a boarder fresh from Poland temporarily postponed further breakup of the family.

> After father died, we rented out the living room of our apartment to a young man, a tailor who worked at home, and we kept the bedroom and the kitchen. As long as he stayed we were able to pay the rent of $7.00 a month.[7]

For a year, while Deborah Schneiderman worked to supplement the boarder's contribution, Rose stayed home from school to care for the baby. But when her mother lost her outside job, Rose was sent to live for a year in a Jewish orphanage. Deborah Schneiderman found another job lining capes and slowly saved enough money to rent a room in the home of a family on Norfolk Street where she brought her two daughters, Rose and Jane, to live with her.

When the family again was faced with starvation after Deborah Schneiderman lost this new job, thirteen-year-old Rose decided to leave school. Fearful of what would happen to her on the factory floor, Deborah insisted Rose instead take a job in a department store where she might get to know "a higher class of people" who could help her escape the Lower East Side. The United Hebrew Charities, an organization staffed by middle- and upper-class German Jewish women who had helped the young family through many crises, got Rose her first job. For three years she was the sole support of her family, until her mother took a job as superintendent of their Lower East Side tenement.

Schneiderman enjoyed her three years as a shop girl. She particularly appreciated the camaraderie of the saleswomen. However, she could not earn enough at the store to support her family. The family moved to a tenement on Sulfolk Street where her mother got a job as Superintendent. Though her mother's labor cleaning the outhouses, halls, and stairways of their building entitled them to free rental, Rose's salary was all they had to buy food and clothing. When she started she was paid $2.25 for a sixty-four-hour week, out of which she had to subtract the cost of laundering her uniform. During the Christmas season the shopwomen worked an eighty-four-hour week, without any compensation for overtime. After three years on the job, she was only earning $2.75 per week and she found out that one female supervisor, a fourteen-year veteran, was paid just $7.00 per week. "I decided I couldn't possibly wait fourteen years, as Martha had, and so must find another job," Schneiderman later recalled. She decided to look for work in a garment factory.[8]

When a neighbor offered to teach her to line caps, Rose jumped at the chance. In 1898, she was hired by Fox and Lederer, where she began at $6.00 per week. Out of that she had to pay for her own thirty-dollar sewing machine and thread, for lunches and transportation. Still, she felt confident that the move would pay off. She hoped to work her way up to a more skilled position in the trade. Then Rose was introduced to the principles of trade unionism by a young coworker, Bessie Braut.

> Bessie was an unusual person. Her beautiful eyes shone out of a badly pockmarked face and the effect was startling. An outspoken anarchist she made a strong impression on us. She wasted no time in giving us the facts of life—that the men in our trade belonged to a union and were, therefore, able to better their conditions. She added

pointedly that it would be a good thing for the lining-makers to join a union along with the trimmers, who were all women.[9]

Schneiderman agreed to join with Braut, Bessie Mannis, and other lining-makers in requesting a charter from the United Cloth Hat and Cap Makers Union (UCHCU). The young women were told to enroll twenty-five women working in different factories. Schneiderman and her comrades stationed themselves at factory doors and, with membership blanks in hand, approached women workers as they were ending their shifts. Within a few days they had enough signatures to win a charter for Local 23 of the UCHCU, and Schneiderman was elected secretary. In her new position, Schneiderman met with women workers at the end of each shift to hear their problems, then attempted to intervene with management on their behalf. She was elected to the Central Labor Union of New York. By 1904 Schneiderman was involved in a strike against a runaway shop* in New Jersey, during which she addressed a crowd of workers for the first time. Schneiderman found that she enjoyed organizing, but her mother was disturbed by Schneiderman's penchant for public speaking. She warned Rose that if she continued along this path she would never marry: Men did not want a woman with a big mouth.

At the 1904 convention of the United Cloth and Cap Makers Union, Rose Schneiderman was elected to the general executive board, the first woman to achieve an executive position in the American labor movement. During the winter of 1904–1905, the capmakers were faced with an attempt by owners to open up union shops to nonunion workers. In response, the largely immigrant Cap Makers Union struck. The strike would be a turning point for Schneiderman, for her role in the strike brought her to the attention of the infant Women's Trade Union League (WTUL), an organization of progressive middle-class women founded in 1903 to help working women organize themselves into trade unions. Although Schneiderman had misgivings about the group because she "could not believe that men and women who were not wage earners themselves understood the problems that workers faced," the favorable publicity that the WTUL won for the strikers moved her to become a member. By the end of March 1905 Schneiderman was elected to the executive board of the New York WTUL. It was a position she would hold for the next forty-five years.[10]

Schneiderman's entrance into the New York WTUL was an important turning point not only in her career, but for the fledgling organi-

---

Runaway shop was the name given to manufacturing businesses that relocated outside of major cities to avoid paying union wages.

zation. Despite a genuine commitment on the part of the organization's officers to organizing working women into unions, the WTUL had credibility problems among workers. Although the WTUL was proud that it had representatives from most of New York's major unions on its executive board, union members rarely attended. The league's work and emphasis was dominated by upper-class women who described themselves as "allies" of the working class. Although the league would, as years went on, come to have an increasingly working-class leadership and tone, its primary financial support always came from very wealthy women rather than from the unions.[11] It was a contradiction that Schneiderman was never able to resolve.

Friendships with middle-class and wealthy women in the league deeply influenced young working women, making them aware of the possibility of women's solidarity across class lines. But, while they derived tremendous emotional nourishment from these alliances, Schneiderman, Pauline Newman, and Irish shirtmaker Leonora O'Reilly never lost sight of the ways in which their class background distinguished them from the league's wealthier members. Sisterhood was exhilarating but, outside the WTUL, their lives were starkly different and their political agendas diverged. The progressive reformers who dominated the league were committed to helping working-class women organize but they were also concerned with steering them away from radical influences. Schneiderman, Newman, and O'Reilly, on the other hand, were active members of the Socialist party. Caught between the indifference or outright hostility of men in the labor movement and the well-meaning but often patronizing benevolence of upper-class women, working-class members of the league struggled to insure that their own voices would not be lost.

This political and social tension heightened working women's emotional dependence upon one another. Schneiderman, Newman, O'Reilly and other working-class league organizers formed deep bonds. When heart disease and an invalid mother bound O'Reilly for years to her home in Brooklyn, Newman and Schneiderman visited her every Saturday and, when they weren't in New York, wrote weekly. Letters among the three are filled with political advice, affectionate banter, and perhaps most important, with expressions of gratitude for the friendship of other activist working-class women. In the midst of all the turbulence of union organizers' lives, they needed to know that there were at least a few people with whom they could relax and just be themselves.[12]

With the appointment of Schneiderman as organizer, the New York WTUL initiated a new policy—listening to workers. Previously, league women had approached organizing as social reformers might, focusing on the most exploited workers. The results were discouraging. By the end of 1906, league leaders decided only to respond to requests for aid from workers already trying to organize. The garment trades seemed a fertile field for testing this strategy, but many of the workers were Jewish immigrants and the league had no Yiddish-speaking organizers. Eloquent as she was, Irish garment worker Leonora O'Reilly could only organize English speakers. Schneiderman provided a vital link between the WTUL and the Jewish female workers of the Lower East Side. In 1906, hoping to improve the crediblity of the WTUL within the labor movement, the New York League elected Rose Schneiderman vice president.[13]

Schneiderman organized feverishly for the next three years. Though fear and hunger made it slow going at first, female workers in New York suddenly began to express their anger through strikes, surprising male garment union organizers who had tended to ignore them. "It was not unusual for unorganized workers to walk out without having any direct union affiliation," Schneiderman later wrote about that restless season.[14]

In April 1907 a group of women's underwear makers at the Milgrim shop on Grand Street staged a spontaneous walkout to protest speedups, wage cuts, and the requirement that employees pay for thread. Schneiderman came in to guide the strike, setting up picket lines and arranging for a committee of strike leaders to negotiate with the owner. The strikers won almost all of their demands, including the establishment of a permanent grievance committee to negotiate future problems. Schneiderman believed that the Milgrim strike reflected a growing sense of group consciousness among young women workers on the East Side. She later remembered

> the young Russian woman who was the leader of the group . . . told me how different things had been in her shop before the strike. The women looked upon each other as enemies because one might get a better bundle of work done than the other. But now, since they had organized and had fought together, there was a kinship among them.[15]

Schneiderman sought to build on such successes. Every day she and her fresh converts mounted soapboxes on crowded street corners, calling to other women to join their union. It was an effective strategy that took full advantage of the speaking skills of the East Side organizers. Fearful that manufacturers were attempting to stir up antagonism among Jewish, Italian, and American workers, organizers conducted street meetings in Yiddish, Italian, and English. Their campaign succeeded beyond their expectations.[16]

In November 1909 New York's shirtwaist and dressmakers, the

vast majority of them immigrant women under age twenty-five, walked off their jobs in a general strike. As chief organizer for the New York WTUL, Schneiderman attended countless workers' meetings, spoke to crowds, and walked the picket lines. The tender age and courage of the young strikers during that long winter of 1909–1910 in the face of hunger, cold, police brutality, and attacks by hired company guards won them support from an unexpected source. In December 1909 some of New York's wealthiest women, including suffragists Alva Belmont and Anne Morgan, daughter of financier J. P. Morgan, decided to join the young strikers on the picket lines to prevent further violence. These wealthy women were able to generate positive press coverage for the strikers, and contributions for their strike fund. The active proselytizing of suffragists on the picket lines also brought masses of working women into the woman suffrage movement for the first time, marking a turning point in working-class women's struggle for improved conditions.

During the next decade working-class women would fight on two battlefields: for both political and economic rights. Between 1909 and 1916, women workers struck across the Northeast and Midwest. The 1909 shirtwaist "uprising" in New York was echoed by women's strikes in Philadelphia; Brooklyn; Boston; Chicago; Cleveland; Muscatine, Iowa; Kalamazoo, Michigan; Lawrence, Massachusetts; and Paterson, New Jersey. Schneiderman was involved in a number of those strikes as organizer, speaker, or mediator. But the strike that most deeply involved her was the 1913 general strike of underwear and lingerie makers in Brooklyn and Manhattan. Thirty-five thousand young women, many of them little more than children, poured onto picket lines and captured the attention of such leading progressives as former President Theodore Roosevelt and Wisconsin Senator Robert La Follette. After nearly five years of intensive organizing, Schneiderman had pulled together young women from a wide variety of ethnic backgrounds and proved that they could stick together through a bitter struggle. Once again progressives were moved by the eloquence and determination of the young female workers. The strike, which received national press coverage, heightened pressure for state regulation of the conditions under which women and children worked.

The militance displayed by immigrant female workers exacerbated class and ethnic tensions within the WTUL. Almost as soon as the 1909 shirtwaist strike ended, upper-class members of the league's executive board had begun to argue that too much attention was being paid to immigrant workers, particularly to Jewish women. Schneiderman fought hard to keep the league from withdrawing its support for Jewish workers. She was hurt and angered when league secretary Helen Marot, a socialist and someone Schneiderman had considered a good friend, lashed out at Jewish organizers: "We have . . . realized for several years that the Russian Jew had little sense of administration and we have been used to . . . their depending solely on their emotions and not on constructive work." In response, Schneiderman handed in her resignation, which the league refused to accept because she was in the middle of organizing the white-goods workers. After the strike, she decided to run for president of the New York League. She might have been willing to accept her loss to American organizer Melinda Scott had she not been informed by Newman and O'Reilly that upper-class league members had lobbied secretly for her defeat. The trade union women were all behind her, Newman assured Schneiderman shortly after the election. Schneiderman lost, she wrote, "because [she was] a Socialist, a Jewess and one interested in suffrage."[17]

This time when Schneiderman resigned, the league let her go. From 1914–1916, she worked as general organizer for the International Ladies Garment Workers Union (ILGWU), traveling throughout the Midwest and New England. Frustrated by the union leadership's lack of support for her efforts at organizing women, Schneiderman resigned from her position with the ILGWU after only two years. In a vote that reflected how much they wanted her back, the New York WTUL elected Schneiderman president in 1917. She returned to New York to take over the league and also to replace her ailing friend Leonora O'Reilly as president of the Industrial Section of the New York Woman Suffrage Party (WSP).[18]

Increasingly through the decade that followed the 1909 "uprising," Schneiderman had come to focus on the vote as a key weapon in the struggle to empower working-class women. Drawn to suffrage as early as 1907, when she became the most popular speaker for Harriot Stanton Blatch's Equality League of Self Supporting Women, Schneiderman had in 1911 helped to found the first suffrage organization composed primarily of industrial workers—the Wage Earner's League For Woman Suffrage. The Wage Earner's League reached out not only to working women but to the wives and mothers of workers by pointing out ways women could use the vote to improve conditions in their homes and communities.[19]

In 1912 the Wage Earner's League and the Collegiate Equal Suffrage League called a mass meeting to protest the New York state legislature's failure to pass a resolution endorsing woman suffrage. The working-class suffrage movement showcased the best speakers it had in New York to answer the "sentimentality of New York Senators," with the "common sense of working women." On the night of April 22, 1912, the Great Hall of the People in Cooper Union, where in 1909 the waistmakers had met, was once again filled with cheering women.

Rising to her full height of four foot nine, Schneiderman imitated the New York senator who claimed, "Get women into the arena of politics with its alliances and distressing contests—the delicacy is gone, the charm is gone, and you emasculize women." Schneiderman the pragmatist had no patience for such romanticized nonsense. She immediately won cheers with an open question.

> What does all this talk about becoming mannish signify? I wonder if it will add to my height when I get the vote. I might work for it all the harder if it did. It is just too ridiculous, this talk of becoming less womanly, just as if a woman could be anything else except a woman.

Schneiderman believed that men and women had different talents and values. However, she was deeply offended by a double standard of femininity that required working women to be strong and sexless in the factory, helpless and modest outside it.

> It seems to me that the working woman ought to wake up to the truth of her situation; all this talk about women's charm does not mean working women. Working women are expected to work and produce their kind so that they too may work until they die of some industrial disease.

Whatever benefits upper-class women derive from the men who admire their feminine charms, Schneiderman told her audience bluntly, will never accrue to the working women.

> Senators and legislators are not blind to the horrible conditions around them. . . . It does not speak well for the intelligence of our Senators to come out with statements about women losing their charm and attractiveness. . . . Women in the laundries . . . stand thirteen hours or fourteen hours in terrible steam and heat with their hands in hot starch. Surely these women won't lose any more of their beauty and charm by putting a ballot in a ballot box once a year than they are likely to lose standing in . . . laundries all year round.[20]

Schneiderman continued her suffrage activism through the 1910s, touring Ohio for the National American Woman Suffrage Association, heading up the WTUL Suffrage Committee and finally leading the Industrial Section of the New York WSP. When women won the vote in New York in 1917, Schneiderman made regular trips to the state capital in Albany, to lobby for passage of bills granting a forty-eight-hour week for New York working women, and a minimum wage. The latter, she argued, would benefit working men as well as women in insuring that employers would not replace male workers with lower paid female workers.

Schneiderman wanted to make sure, now that New York women had the vote, that they used it. In 1918 she led a group of working women in a neighborhood campaign to defeat several New York state legislators who had been particularly hostile to wage, hours, and working conditions legislation. Schneiderman, with her powerful voice, spoke from the back of a horsedrawn truck as it moved slowly up and down the streets of each legislator's district. The campaigns were relatively successful. Four antilabor legislators were defeated; two of them replaced by women who strongly supported legislation regulating workplace conditions.[21]

In 1919 Schneiderman was nominated, along with former shoe worker Mary Anderson, to serve as the only women in the trade union delegation to the Paris Peace Conference. While in Paris, Schneiderman commenced a long friendship with British Labour party leader Margaret Bondfield, who would later become England's first female minister of labor. Excited by their own friendship, and their late night conversations, the two women began to plan for an international conference of working women. It was held in Washington, D.C., in November of 1919, the first in a series of such conferences and the beginning of a new era in working women's politics— an era of internationalism, during which the ideas and aims of activist working women in the United States and in Europe would be shaped by regular communication across the Atlantic.

Schneiderman's international experience was an important consideration when, in May 1920, the newly formed New York State Labor party nominated Schneiderman for the U.S. Senate. Although Schneiderman never expected to win, the seriousness with which her campaign was treated by the press reflects the power of labor as a force in New York state politics at the end of the First World War. The *New York Times* reported her nomination on page two. The domestic goals of Schneiderman's campaign for the Senate are also worth noting because they highlight Schneiderman's increasing emphasis on government intervention. Just as the Wage Earner's League for Woman Suffrage had called for legislation protecting the worker both in the workplace and in the home, so in her campaign for the Senate Schneiderman suggested that government must become involved in all aspects of workers' lives. Her broad platform also called for the use of public monies to pay for construction of nonprofit housing for workers, improved neighborhood schools, publicly owned utilities and food markets, and for state-funded health and unemployment insurance for all Americans.[22]

During the 1920s, the labor movement was severely weakened by conservative backlash. Government repression following World War I and the Russian Revolution, and internecine struggles between communists, socialists, and progressives racked the unions. As a result Schneiderman and other female labor leaders began to focus increasingly on women's concerns outside the workplace. Rose Schneiderman believed that one of the most important things she could do for working-class women was combat their sense of inferiority.

In order to enrich the lives of women laborers and to cultivate a younger generation of leaders, Schneiderman and ILGWU colleagues Fania Cohn and Pauline Newman helped design a series of education courses geared specifically to working women. As early as 1915, Schneiderman, Newman, and Cohn had collaborated with a young Barnard professor named Juliet Poyntz to establish an education program for the ILGWU dressmakers who had struck in 1909. The largely young, immigrant women of ILGWU's Local 25 responded enthusiastically to classes in economics, history, labor law, art and music appreciation, and public speaking. That program was so successful that the union established a worker-education department to coordinate courses for workers across the country. In 1920 Schneiderman and Cohn were approached by the president of Bryn Mawr College, M. Carey Thomas, and asked to help design a special summer school there for women workers. The Bryn Mawr Summer School for Women Workers became the model for several others that followed, including the Hudson Shore School which lasted until 1952. In 1923, the New York WTUL also established a school of its own that grew in the range of its offerings and in the size of its classes through the 1940s. These schools for female workers were based on an idea shared by Cohn and Schneiderman that the greatest obstacle working-class women faced was their own lack of confidence.[23]

The second front on which Schneiderman and her colleagues battled working-class women's sense of inferiority, was literally the homefront. In an era when the costs of food, rent, and clothing were quickly climbing higher than many housewives could afford, Schneiderman knew that this sector of the working class was ripe for organization. Immigrant housewives on the Lower East Side had rioted numerous times between 1902 and 1917, boycotting butchers and bakers who would not bring their prices down, smashing store windows and pouring kerosene on the stock of any business owner who would not close to honor their boycotts. During the 1920s and 1930s, Schneiderman sought to organize housewives into permanent organizations that would parallel workers' trade unions and allow them to inject the larger concerns of home and neighborhood into the working-class movement.

In 1922, Schneiderman and Grace Klueg, wife of a Brooklyn Navy Yard worker and president of the Women's Auxiliary of the International Association of Machinists, established the Housewives Industrial League to organize wives of workers from a variety of trades. The two women hoped to build up existing women's union auxiliaries into a broad-based, militant movement. Supplementing their organizing drives by lobbying the government, Schneiderman and the leadership of the WTUL called for federal investigation into the status of non–wage-earning women—their labor conditions in the home, housing conditions, and health. Such an investigation, they believed, would also lay the groundwork for an organization of domestic workers. Domestic workers, then as now, were difficult to organize because they were scattered across every city and nearly impossible to protect legally because of the problem of enforcing labor laws in private homes. Schneiderman wanted the labor movement and the government to recognize the home as a workplace. It was a radical concept then as it is now.[24]

In June 1928, after six years of agitating and educating in communities across the country, Schneiderman and ILGWU Education Secretary Fania Cohn convened the First Women's Auxiliary Conference. Held at the garment workers' cooperatively owned resort, Unity House, it was attended by delegates from women's auxiliaries across the country. Their goal was to set priorities and plan strategies for an organized movement of working-class housewives, regionally based, but national in its scope. In her welcome to the delegates, Schneiderman stressed the need for community-based action. Lose your timidity, she chided. Stop clinging to ideas about women's inferiority. The mother's role in her children's education should not be restricted to the home. Mother's committees should demand a voice in shaping the curricula in public schools. Run for local school boards or make sure that pro-labor people get on them. Women have power as consumers, she told them. Exercise it. Set up cooperative buying arrangements to keep prices down. Set up cooperative child care so that mothers in the communities have the time to become active in community-based organizations. Learn to lobby for legislation that affects working-class women, Schneiderman told them. "It is time," she concluded, "the women's auxiliaries become something more than agencies for sick benefits, relief work and tea parties."[25]

They did. In the decade that followed the Unity House Conference, women's union auxiliaries responded to the challenges issued by Schneiderman, Cohn, and Klueg. The 1930s saw a radicalization of women's union auxiliaries across the United States, particularly in coal, steel, and automobile towns where one major employer's outright ownership or domination of local housing, banks, and food stores meant that women were directly oppressed by management, just as their husbands were. From the coal and steel towns of western Pennsylvania and southern Illinois to the automobile towns of northern Michigan, from New York City to Los Angeles, women's union auxiliaries aided working men and women's strikes, formed and guarded soup kitchens, walked picket lines, and fought with police. Participation in such activities broadened their political horizons; by the end of the decade they were demanding not only a just price for food but also education, child care, and a greater say in the running of their lives and their children's lives.

Following Schneiderman's advice, women's councils and auxiliaries also gathered information about food prices, utility rates, and school curricula in their neighborhoods and used that information both to build grass-roots organizations and to lobby for social legislation. They were so effective in gathering and disseminating information about the quality of life in their respective communities that, in 1941, when Franklin Roosevelt was facing pressure to cut social programs to appropriate money for the war effort, Eleanor Roosevelt called on the housewives' groups to provide information to the president and his advisers.[26] Eleanor Roosevelt was an old friend of the WTUL.

Twenty years earlier Eleanor Roosevelt's interest in women's politics had drawn her into a circle of women deeply committed to social welfare legislation. By 1921, Roosevelt had thrown herself into Women's Trade Union League work with all her characteristic passion. Rose Schneiderman became a regular guest at the scrambled-egg suppers that Roosevelt liked to cook for friends and, through her Roosevelt came into contact for the first time with the world of the immigrant working class. Both her friendship with Schneiderman and Roosevelt's interest in working-class women deepened quickly.[27]

Using her considerable influence with Democratic party leaders, including Governor Al Smith, Roosevelt did much to sensitize the Democratic party in New York State to the needs of women workers. As an important step in her own political career, Roosevelt became a lobbyist for the Joint Legislative Conference (JCL), a consortium of New York women's organizations founded by the WTUL to promote social legislation, including child-labor laws, minimum-wage and maximum-hour laws, unemployment insurance, and old-age pensions. By the mid-1920s Roosevelt had became one of the most effective and indefatigable lobbyists in the Joint Legislative Conference. Another of the JLC's most persuasive lobbyists was Rose Schneiderman. She and Roosevelt taught each other a great deal.

Schneiderman knew, from personal experience, that labor laws were far more than abstract policies defining government's relationship with workers. Women's and children's lives depended on them. Ever since 1911, when hazardous conditions had resulted in a fire at the Triangle Shirtwaist Factory that killed 146 young women, Schneiderman had been a passionate advocate of legislation regulating workplace conditions. Organization was a painfully slow process; legislation was comparatively easy and far more efficient. Over her quarter century as an organizer, Schneiderman was personally involved in organizing strikes that affected, at most, several hundred thousand women workers. The legislation that she lobbied for from 1917 to 1949 ultimately affected millions of female workers and established the model for fair labor legislation that would affect millions of male workers. Schneiderman's success as a lobbyist exhilarated her, and by the late 1920s, the former socialist had become a committed supporter of the Democratic party.

Schneiderman's attraction to the Democratic party had more than a little bit to do with her growing affection for Eleanor and Franklin Roosevelt. Rose Schneiderman's forty-year friendship with Eleanor Roosevelt, and her twenty-five-year friendship with Franklin, had a profound impact on her. It also deeply affected the Roosevelts. Although there was none of the intimacy between Schneiderman and FDR that she shared with Eleanor Roosevelt, FDR spent a good deal of time with Schneiderman, particularly during the 1920s.

Eleanor Roosevelt first invited Schneiderman and her companion Maud Swartz, the outgoing president of the Women's Trade Union League, to Campobello in 1925 and to Hyde Park in 1926. Franklin Roosevelt was so attracted by their forcefulness and clarity that they became frequent guests. The young, aristocratic politician would talk for hours with the two trade unionists. Frances Perkins, Franklin Roosevelt's secretary of labor, later commented that FDR's ideas about government's proper relationship to labor were crystallized and fleshed out during those conversations: "Relying on the knowledge he had gained from these girls," Perkins concluded, "he appeared to have a real understanding of the trade-union movement." The two unionists gave him a theoretical framework for the policies he later developed as governor and then as president.[28]

In 1933, President Roosevelt appointed Rose Schneiderman to the National Recovery Administration's Labor Advisory Board. The task of the board was to establish codes for each industry, setting minimum wages, maximum hours, and price controls for finished goods. Schneiderman was the only woman on the twelve-person board and as a result was expected to supervise all codes affecting female workers. To keep up with her new responsibilities Schneiderman took a leave of absence from the WTUL and temporarily relocated to Washington. There she was drawn into the New Deal women's political network headed by Eleanor Roosevelt and including Frances Perkins (secretary of labor), Mary Anderson (director of the Labor Department Women's Bureau), Molly Dewson (director of the Women's Division of the Democratic National Committee), and many others. It was an exciting time for Schneiderman: as she said, it was "the most exhilarating and inspiring of my life."

These women, many of whom had come to know, respect, and love each other over long years of struggling together in the suffrage movement and the movement for social legislation, now were in position to inject their ideas about government's social responsibilities into the New Deal. To participate in the shaping of a new state structure was a remarkable experience for all of them, but for none so much as for the immigrant whose formal schooling had ended when she was thirteen years old.[29]

In 1937 Rose Schneiderman was appointed secretary of labor for the state of New York. In Albany, as in Washington, Schneiderman's closest colleagues were also her closest friends. Longtime friend Nell Swartz (no relation to Maud) worked with Schneiderman on the state compensation board. Frieda Miller, the companion for many years of Schneiderman's closest friend Pauline Newman, served as director of the New York State Labor Department Women's Bureau and in 1941 became industrial commissioner for New York State. Newman herself represented the ILGWU and the WTUL on a great many of the investigative boards convened by the New York State Labor Department. Outsiders in an almost exclusively male political preserve, these four, along with National WTUL Secretary Elizabeth Christman, formed their own political network. They had regular dinners at Nell Swartz's house, held serious discussions about political strategy, and, when there was nothing more they could do, the five friends played poker.[30]

When American soldiers returned home at the end of the Second World War, Schneiderman resigned her post in the New York State Labor Department and turned her attention to the problem of how to preserve the gains female workers had made while working to support the war effort. As Schneiderman well knew, most women could not afford to leave the work force at the end of the war. Rather than shifting them back into unskilled industrial and low-paid clerical jobs, Schneiderman argued, the government should provide training programs that would allow women to maintain their newly won position as skilled laborers.

She and the WTUL also fought for a comparable-worth bill in New York State which they hoped would establish a model for other states. An equal-pay law was meaningless, she argued on the radio and in front of the New York State Factory Investigating Commission in 1947, because employers could simply continue arguing that the jobs they hired men to do were worth more than the jobs they hired women to do. There must, she insisted, be some objective criteria for establishing the worth of all jobs in a factory. Few American employers were ready for such an idea. Many have still not accepted it.[31]

In April 1949, at sixty-seven, Rose Schneiderman surprised everyone who knew her by announcing her retirement. Eleanor Roosevelt and the Women's Trade Union League hosted a testimonial luncheon attended by many of the leading lights of the American labor movement. Letters and telegrams poured in from around the country expressing a mixture of sadness at her departure from public life and pleasure that she would finally have time to rest. Over the next decade, Schneiderman continued to attend league meetings, appeared from time to time at union functions, made a few radio speeches, protested the activities of the House Committee on Un-American Activities, and worked on her memoirs.

As she faded into old age, so the organization that she had championed for fifty years also faded away. The National Women's Trade Union League closed its doors in 1950 and the New York WTUL voted to dissolve itself in 1955. The women who had run it and funded it since the first decade of the century were now all old, some had died, and few young women workers seemed to care about the league. The leadership of the newly united, predominantly male AFL-CIO had little interest in lending financial support to an organization they had long viewed as a nuisance. Male union leaders had never, Schneiderman noted, "realized how important it was to have an organization like the League to interpret trade unionism to women. . . ." Through the conservative 1950s and early 1960s it seemed as though much of Schneiderman's work might die with her.

But the 1960s saw a resurgence both of militant labor activism and of a nationwide women's movement. In 1969 a group of female trade unionists founded the Coalition of Labor Union Women (CLUW). The CLUW was in many ways the grandchild of the Women's Trade Union League. A generation had been skipped, but once again women in the labor movement were asserting their rights, and they paid homage to those who had come before them—Schneiderman, Newman, and others.

Though, in her old age, Schneiderman liked to portray herself as mild-mannered and nonthreatening, many of her ideas seemed radical even in the late 1980s. Long before the most recent wave of feminist activism began, Schneiderman was attacking sexual segregation in the workplace, trying to unionize not only industrial women but also white-collar and domestic workers, calling for state regulation not only of factory and office working conditions, but also of working conditions in the home. She organized housewives on a community basis to fight for fair rents and food prices, better housing and public education. She argued for comparable-worth laws, government-funded child care, and maternity insurance. And always, she reminded audiences that "the woman worker must have bread but she must have roses too." For more than half a century, Rose Schneiderman organized women to fight not just for economic independence, but also for the right to have meaning and beauty in their lives. She died in 1972, just as a new women's movement was growing in the United States. But many of her ideas and dreams were taken up by that movement and they are still being debated in classrooms, courtrooms, and congressional chambers today. Those ideas and dreams, as much as the government protections that most American workers now take for granted, are the legacy of Rose Schneiderman.

Notes

[1]For a fuller treatment of Rose Schneiderman's life see Annelise Orleck, "Common Sense and a Little Fire: Working Class Women's Activism in the Twentieth Century U.S." (Ph.D. diss., New York University, 1989). During the Red Scare of 1919–1920, New York State Senator Thaddeus Sweet was the first public official to call Schneiderman "Red Rose." The name stuck. In 1940, Schneiderman's lawyer Dorothy Kenyon mounted a libel suit against William Wirt who had called Schneiderman "The Red Rose of Anarchy" in print; see Dorothy Kenyon to RS, 6 March, 1940. The testimony of the police officer is recounted in Margaret Dreier Robins to RS, 14 June, 1943; Schneiderman's suffrage speaking tour in M. Sherwood to Harriet Taylor Upton, 15 July, 1912; Rose Schneiderman Papers, Reel 3082, Tamiment Library, New York City.

[2]*New York Times,* 14 August, 1972.

[3]Pauline Newman interviewed by Barbara Wertheimer, November 1976, Pauline Newman Papers, Schlesinger Library, Cambridge, MA.

[4]Rose Schneiderman to Pauline Newman, 11 August 1917; Pauline Newman Papers, Box 1.

[5]Rose Schneiderman with Lucy Goldthwaite, *All for One* (New York: Paul S. Eriksson, 1967), pp. 10–22.

[6]Schneiderman, *All for One,* pp. 11–15.

[7]Schneiderman, *All for One,* p. 29.

[8]Schneiderman, *All for One,* pp. 35–47.

[9]Schneiderman, *All for One,* p. 48.

[10]Schneiderman, *All for One,* p. 77; Minutes of the New York WTUL Executive Board, 24 February and 24 March, 1905, Reel 3044, Tamiment Library, NYC.

[11]Minutes of the New York WTUL Executive Board, 24 February, 24 March, 5 May, 25 August, 24 September, 26 October 1905; 25 January, February, 29 March, 26 April, 28 June, 1 August, 12 September, 22 November, 20 December, 1906; 28 February, 24 April, 27 June, 25 July, 22 August, 26 September, 26 November, 1907; 28 January, 1908; NYWTUL Papers; Schneiderman, *All for One,* p. 83.

[12]See letters among Schneiderman, Newman, and O'Reilly in the Leonora O'Reilly Papers, Reels 3075–76, Tamiment Library, New York City, and the Rose Schneiderman Papers Reel 3082 and File 18A; and the Pauline M. Newman Papers, Box 1.

[13]Minutes of the Executive Board NYWTUL, 24 February 1905–1 February 1909, NYWTUL Papers.

[14]Schneiderman, *All for One,* p. 84.

[15]Schneiderman, *All for One,* p. 86.

[16]Schneiderman, *All for One,* pp. 84–88; Minutes of the New York WTUL Executive Board, 21 May, 1 June, 25 August, 27 October, 1908; 24 August, 15 September 1909. NYWTUL Papers.

[17]Minutes of the NYWTUL Executive Board, Secretary's Report, 15 February, 27 April 1911. NYWTUL Papers; PMN to RS, n.d., Rose Schneiderman Papers.

[18]Schneiderman, *All for One,* pp. 110–117; RS to Benjamin Schlesinger 6 February 1916; RS to Abe Baroff 1 December 1916, Schneiderman Papers; RS to PMN 6 February 1916; RS to PMN 6 August 1917, Newman Papers.

[19]See Ellen Carol Dubois, "Working Women, Class Relations and Suffrage Militance: Harriot Stanton Blatch and the New York Woman Suffrage Movement, 1894–1909," *Journal Of American History* (June 1987); also "Miss Rose Schneiderman, Gifted Young Lecturer," Leaflet of the American Suffragettes, n.d. Rose Schneiderman Papers; see also Papers of the Wage Earner's League for Woman Suffrage in the Leonora O'Reilly Papers, Reel 3080.

[20]"Senators vs. Working Women," handbill for the April 22 meeting, and *Senators Vs. Working Women,* pamphlet, both by the Wage Earner's League for Woman Suffrage, included in the O'Reilly Papers.

[21]Rose Schneiderman. "WTUL Legislative Efforts," typescript for a radio speech, June 1955, Schneiderman Papers, Reel 3083; see also Nancy Cott, *The Grounding of Modern Feminism* (New Haven: Yale University Press, 1988), p. 105.

[22]*New York Times,* 31 May 1920; RS to Margaret Dreier Robins, 10 March 1919, Schneiderman Papers; Schneiderman, *All for One,* pp. 146–148; Cott, *The Grounding of Modern Feminism,* p. 65.

[23] Annual Reports of the New York Women's Trade Union League, 1922–1955, Papers of the WTUL, Reels 3045–3048, Tamiment Library. See also Alice Kessler-Harris "Problems of Coalition Building: Women and Trade Unions in the 1920's," in Ruth Milkman, ed., *Women, Work and Protest* (London: Routledge, Kegan & Paul, 1985); Schneiderman, *All for One*, pp. 157–163.

[24] Proceedings of the Ninth Biennial NWTUL Conference, held in New York, 1924.

[25] Summary of Speeches, Women's Auxiliary Conference Unity House, Forest Park, PA, 30 June–1 July, 1928, Mary Van Kleeck Papers, Sophia Smith Collection, Northampton, MA.

[26] *New York Times*, 26 October 1941.

[27] See Joseph P. Lash, *Eleanor and Franklin* (New York: Signet, 1971); Schneiderman, *All for One*, pp. 150–153, 156–157, 175–184; *New York Times*, 3 June, 8 June 1929.

[28] Swartz, who worked briefly as a proofreader, was a member of the typographical union, but, although she came from a family of modest means in Ireland, she had some extremely wealthy relatives in the United States. This distinguished her from Schneiderman, who had absolutely no money in her family. See Frances Perkins, *The Roosevelt I Knew* (New York: Vintage Press, 1946), pp. 32–33. See also Lash, *Eleanor and Franklin*, p. 380; Schneiderman, *All for One*, pp. 177–180 (both cite Perkins). After FDR became governor of New York in 1928 he kept up a steady if sketchy correspondence with Schneiderman. He appointed her to represent the state in the International Association of Public Employment Services, and to serve on committees dealing with prison labor and workers' compensation. FDR to RS, 11 January, 17 September 1929; 12 May, 2 August 1930; 12 October, 1932; RS to FDR, 16 March, 18 November, 1932; Schneiderman Papers.

[29] *New York Times* 20 June 1933; Rose Schneiderman Papers, Reel 3083, Part I, Frames 450–661 and Part II, Frames 221–232; Susan Ware, *Beyond Suffrage: Women and the New Deal* (Cambridge, MA: Harvard University Press, 1981).

[30] Interview with Elizabeth Berger, 15 December 1987. (Berger was adopted as an infant by Frieda Miller and raised by Miller and Newman); Schneiderman, *All for One*, pp. 121–130.

[31] New York WTUL Annual Reports 1930–1950, Reels 3046–3048, Tamiment Library, New York City; Radio Speech, "Women's Role in Labor Legislation," 1955, Rose Schneiderman Papers, Reel 3083; *New York Times*, 16 March, 20 September 1936; 4 March, 14 March, 12 April, 13 May, 20 May 1937; 8 January 1939; 28 October 1943; 28 January 1945.

Crystal Eastman
(1881–1928)

Blanche Wiesen Cook

Crystal Eastman was born on June 25, 1881, in Marlborough, Massachusetts. She graduated with a B.A. from Vassar in 1903, an M.A. in sociology from Columbia in 1904, and, in 1907, an LL.B. from New York University Law School. She was appointed member and secretary of the New York State Employer's Liability Commission from 1909 to 1911. In 1910 she published Work Accidents and the Law, *a book that contributed to the passage of worker-safety laws. In 1914 she helped found the Congressional Union, along with Alice Paul and Lucy Burns. She was chairperson of the New York branch of the Woman's Peace Party and on the executive committee of the American Union Against Militarism (AUAM), organizations formed to protest the United States' entrance into World War I. In 1917, Eastman was a founder of the Civil Liberties Bureau, a committee of the AUAM established to defend conscientious objectors to the draft. In March 1918, she began coediting the socialist publication* The Liberator *with her brother Max, a position she held until 1922. Throughout her life she wrote on a wide range of feminist and socialist issues. In 1916 she divorced her first husband and married English pacifist Walter Fuller, with whom Crystal Eastman had two children, Jeffrey and Annis. In England with her husband for most of the years 1921–1927, she wrote regularly for* Time and Tide, *a radical feminist journal. She returned to the United States in 1927 where she died on July 8, 1928.*

For full citations to this essay, readers should consult the introduction to *Crystal Eastman on Women and Revolution* by Blanche Wiesen Cook (New York: Oxford University Press, 1978) from which this essay is adapted.

To lean on and be protected by a man, Crystal Eastman wrote, is not the same as standing on your own two feet. Patriarchal protection of workers is not the same as workers' control. Equal rights for all; work for all; peace and justice and equal opportunity; the end to privilege as well as poverty—those are very radical demands. They were Crystal Eastman's demands, and it is no accident that her work has for so long remained unknown—along with her joy in life and enthusiasm for people. The neglect and disappearance of Crystal Eastman's work is partly explained by the fact that history tends to bury what it seeks to reject. There was little room for the writings of a militant feminist who was also a socialist in the annals of America as it went from Red Scare to Depression to Cold War and back again.

Surely, Crystal Eastman would not have been so lost to history if she had been more conventional. It is perhaps more comfortable to picture a woman of her views tragic in exile, rather than undaunted at the speaker's platform in Rome, Budapest, Paris, London. It would have been simpler if she had not also socialized with Charlie Chaplin, titled nobility, black intellectuals, and government officials; and when she partied with women she dressed entirely for herself and their company with a flamboyance for which she become noted. For women to dress for themselves and each other was really unfathomable. How was history to appraise the militant feminist wing of the international "smart set"? How could history appraise the life of a tough woman lawyer who was not only a feminist, but a mother and socialist?

There was nothing simple about her work, her political vision, or the nature of her personal relationships. Her vision demanded radical, profound, and absolute changes. Crystal Eastman's ideas were heretical and dangerous. Her life by its very example embodied a threat to customary order. "Freedom is a large word," she wrote in 1920. It demanded a large struggle, a long battle. She committed the entire range and intensity of her energy and spirit to that struggle.

Crystal Eastman loved life and was generally surrounded by friends. Protected and fortified by the support of women and men who shared her ideals and battled beside her, she was free and bold. Her close friend Jeannette Lowe said that "you wouldn't believe her freedom—she was entirely free, open, full of joy in life." Her brother Max wrote that "she poured magnetic streams of generous love around her all the time" and boldly plunged into new experiences. Roger Baldwin, who worked closely with her during World War I in the American Union Against Militarism and the Civil Liberties Bureau which they jointly created, remembered Crystal as "a natural leader: outspoken (often tactless), determined, charming, beautiful, courageous. . . ." She spoke in a deep and musical voice and could be entirely captivating as she dashed about the country on behalf of suffrage or peace or to organize against an injustice. Her sincerity was absolute and she frequently grew red with anger. She was impulsive and passionate and once consulted Dr. A. A. Brill, the first Freudian psychoanalyst to practice in America, to bring her intense "libido down."

Crystal Eastman was a woman-identified woman. She neither sought male approval for her activities nor courted male protection. While she delighted in the company of women, she enjoyed male alliances whenever she found them genuine. She worked with and loved easily many women and men who were her friends and comrades. She was also determined. Hazel Hunkins Hallinan, the suffragist organizer who knew Crystal best when she lived in England, recalled that she was "very realistic but not very docile. We used to call her a 'tigress' because she was so vital and aggressive."

Crystal Eastman spent most of her childhood in Glenora, a small town on the shore of Seneca Lake in New York. The daughter of suffragist parents, both of whom were ordained Congregational ministers, she claimed feminism as her birthright. Toward the end of her life Crystal wrote that "the story of my background is the story of my mother." Her mother, Annis Ford Eastman, was "the most noted minister of her time," an inspiring orator who found new ideas from Santayana to Freud "dangerously fascinating." She encouraged Crystal and her two brothers, Max and Anstice, always to be independent in thought and vigorous in action. (A third brother, the oldest son, Morgan, died of scarlet fever in 1884. Crystal had scarlet fever at the same time and it marked her health throughout her life.)

When Crystal was fifteen, her mother organized a summer symposium at which Crystal read a paper called "Woman." She dedicated the rest of her life to the fulfillment of the theme of that paper: Women "must have work of their own . . . because the only way to be happy is to have an absorbing interest in life which is not bound up with any particular person. No woman who allows husband and children to absorb her whole time and interest is safe against disaster."

Although Crystal Eastman hated the traditional institutionalization of marriage and "homemaking," she believed that most women shared "the normal desire to be mothers." An early advocate of birth control, she wrote in 1918: "Feminists are not nuns. That should be established." Although she ultimately married twice, she did not marry until she was almost thirty. Both she and her brother Max remained single until after their mother's death. And all their friends apparently believed that Crystal and Max really loved each other above all. In his autobiography, *Love and Revolution*, Max wrote: "As a boy ... I used to announce that I would never marry any girl but my sister."

During her junior year at Vassar in 1902 Crystal wrote in her journal that men were typically "clever, powerful, selfish and animal"— except for her brother Max. Should she ever marry a man he would have to have Max's qualities: "I don't believe there is a feeling in the world too refined and imagined for him to appreciate." Crystal thought her brother might not like it, but it was "the highest compliment you can pay a man to say that he has the fineness of feeling and sympathy of a woman. . . . All mothers ought to cultivate it in their boys."

Many of Crystal's later writings reflect her high sense of gender injustice—bolstered not only by public law but everywhere propped up by cultural attitudes. Throughout her life, homemaking—the notion that women's mission was to provide a comfortable home for men who shared no similar responsibility—symbolized women's servility, women's bondage. To end that bondage, women as well as men needed to be educated and involved with their own life's work; and both women and men needed to function efficiently in the home.

On the other hand, Crystal Eastman insisted, women who wanted to work at home—or needed to work at home—should be paid for their labor. What is today referred to as "wages for housework" she called a "Motherhood Endowment." In "Now We Can Begin," she wrote that the only way for women "at least in a capitalist society" to achieve "real economic independence" was for the political government to recognize and subsidize housework as skilled labor.

From 1903 to 1911 Crystal Eastman lived among people who shared her views. A settlement house worker while studying for her M.A. in sociology at Columbia (1904) and for a law degree at New York University (1907), she lived in and became a leading member of the new feminist and radical community just then emerging in Greenwich Village. She lived with suffragists who were her close friends from Vassar or law school, notably Madeleine Doty, Inez Milholland, and Ida Rauh. Eventually Ida Rauh married Eastman's brother Max.

Comfortable in many worlds, Crystal Eastman moved with ease among artists, social workers, poets, anarchists, socialists, and progressive reformers. It was a time of experiment and change, and she was committed to both. Appalled by poverty and its senseless waste, she was a socialist by nature and conviction. Her concern for the poor, nurtured by her mother from childhood, and her anguish over brutal economic conditions intensified during this period.

In 1907 Crystal graduated from law school; she was second in her class and had a particular interest in labor law. When her good friend Paul U. Kellogg, then editor of the social-work magazine *Charities and the Commons,* organized the celebrated *Pittsburgh Survey* for the Russell Sage Foundation, an institution that supports social service research, he invited Crystal to join the staff. She remained in Pittsburgh for over a year to complete the first in-depth sociological investigation of industrial accidents ever made. This work catapulted her to prominence, and in June 1909 Governor Charles Evans Hughes appointed her New York's first woman commissioner, the only woman among fourteen members of the Employer's Liability Commission. As secretary of that prestigious commission, she drafted New York State's first workers' compensation law, which was soon used as a model by many other states.

She believed that industrial accidents happen almost inevitably because of organized neglect of workers' safety. Her goal was to shift the burden of guilt or blame from victim to industry and its management and to adopt, as almost every "civilized country except the United States" already had, the principle of workers' compensation. Industry's refusal to secure the safety and health of its workers remains today a primary labor issue. Unfortunately, corporations now often prefer to pay insurance fees rather than make the necessary capital investments to secure safe working conditions. But in 1910 when the loss of a leg or an eye or a life generally resulted in no compensation to the worker or the worker's family, Crystal Eastman's book *Work Accidents and the Law* resulted in a major progressive reform, although she herself considered the new legislation a minimal compromise.

The contribution Crystal Eastman made to labor law and industrial safety was internationally acclaimed. Moreover, her work in Pittsburgh and New York, and later Washington, confirmed her radical vision and clarified her understanding of economics. She began to identify herself as a socialist. In 1911 she wrote "Three Essentials for Accident Prevention," in which she referred to the Triangle Shirtwaist Company fire, in which 140 women locked into the room that was their "sweatshop" perished. When healthy women and men die because of preventable disasters, she wrote, we do not want to hear about "relief funds." "What we want is to start a revolution." Nothing short of revolution would finally end "this unnecessary killing and injuring of workers in the course of industry." Revolutionary change began, she wrote, by collecting the information necessary to prevent economic disaster and human suffering.

Suffrage was for Crystal Eastman a primary enthusiasm, and she expected the men in her life to be suffragists. She introduced her brother Max to political and social issues and, in 1909, encouraged him to organize the Men's League for Woman Suffrage. But the vote represented only a part of the power denied to women that Crystal Eastman believed women needed to reclaim.

Tall, almost six feet tall, athletic and robust herself, Crystal Eastman sought to extend the contours of women's strength and women's sphere far beyond suffrage. With Annette Kellerman, a champion swimmer and diver from Australia who was then in New York to entertain Broadway audiences with her aquatic skills, she attempted to work out a program for the physical "regeneration of the female sex."

To promote her vision of women's power, Crystal Eastman spoke before large audiences on "women's right to physical equality with men." Journalist Freda Kirchwey recalled that Eastman pictured a utopia of athletes, with women "unhampered by preconceived ideas of what was fit or proper or possible for their sex to achieve." Eastman believed that "when women were expected to be agile, they became agile; when they were expected to be brave, they developed courage; when they had to endure, their endurance broke all records." According to Kirchwey, who was at this time still a student at Barnard, as Crystal Eastman "stood there, herself an embodiment of tall, easy strength and valor, her words took on amazing life. . . ."

From adolescence onward Crystal Eastman was aware that fashion served to confine and limit women's ability to move freely. In matters of style, from short hair and short skirts to her insistence on wearing bathing suits without the customary stockings and skirt, her guiding principle was the achievement of greater and easier activity. Freedom involved discarding antique and unnecessary encumbrances. She never rode sidesaddle, and careened about her hometown "on a man's saddle in fluttering vast brown bloomers" that shocked polite Glenora society. When her neighbors complained to her father about her swimming clothes, she received her family's support. Although her father never said a word to her, she believed that he was "startled and embarrassed to see his only daughter in a man's bathing suit with bare brown legs for all the world to see. I think it shocked him to his dying day." But "he would not want to swim in a skirt and stockings. Why then should I?"

In 1911, shortly after her mother died, Crystal Eastman married a ruggedly handsome insurance salesman named Wallace Benedict ("Bennie"). Although she made it clear to her friends and family, including Max, that she was physically and romantically excited by Bennie, they remained puzzled by her decision actually to marry him. Nevertheless, Bennie believed in and supported her work, and according to Max, he was full of "admiring passion." But the marriage was burdened by the need to move to Bennie's home in Milwaukee, which for Eastman resulted in periods of deep melancholy. Within two years she returned to New York, and in 1916 married Walter Fuller. Crystal Eastman's time in Milwaukee was devoted largely to the suffrage campaign.

In 1911, Wisconsin was the only large industrial state east of the Mississippi where a suffrage referendum was pending. The entire suffrage movement focused on Wisconsin, and Crystal Eastman served as the campaign manager and chaired the Political Equality League, which directed all activities in and out of the state. When it was over, she attributed the suffrage defeat in Wisconsin to the dominating power of the brewery industry and its ability to pressure a variety of dependent industries: "There are whole cities of 20,000 . . . where not a single businessman dares to let his wife come out for suffrage . . . because practically every man's business is dependent . . . on the good will of the big breweries. . . ." The big corporations, she explained, generally "put their business . . . ahead of democracy, justice, simple human right."

In 1913, as a delegate to the Seventh Congress of the International Woman Suffrage Alliance at Budapest, Eastman met with the women who were soon to become the leaders of the movement for international peace: Hungary's Rosika Schwimmer, Holland's first woman physician, Dr. Aletta Jacobs, and English suffragist Emmeline Pethick-Lawrence. As soon as the European war was declared Crystal Eastman limited or suspended all other concerns to organize American sentiment against the war, against America's participation in the war, and against militarism generally. She feared that if the United States entered the European war all recently achieved reforms, such as her own efforts to improve and enforce industrial health and safety standards, would be ended. She regarded the European war as a war of colonial ambition and believed that because all wars were organized for efficient international murder, they inevitably threatened to destroy those interests that most concerned people: labor legislation, public health care, decent housing, the movement for new parks and playgrounds, and all democratic institutions or, as she wrote, "such beginnings of democracy as we have in America."

The international woman's movement, already organized on behalf of suffrage and allied with the major movements for economic and social change, seemed to Crystal Eastman to be ideally suited to become the major force behind a new, bold, and vigorous international peace movement.

In November 1914, Crystal Eastman called together the first meeting of the Woman's Peace Party (WPP) of New York City and invited

Emmeline Pethick-Lawrence to speak. A militant suffragist who had been imprisoned in Holloway gaol and brutally force-fed, Pethick-Lawrence maintained that there was "no life worth living, but a fighting life." It was time, she said, for the peace movement to learn from the women's movement. The established peace societies were "passive and negative," and it was time for women to be angry, "active and militant." Active and militant throughout the war, the Woman's Peace Party of New York, over which Crystal Eastman presided until 1919, differed dramatically in method and style from two other organizations she helped to create: the national Woman's Peace Party and the American Union Against Militarism.

To mobilize women for peace throughout the United States, Eastman persuaded Emmeline Pethick-Lawrence to go to Chicago and meet with Jane Addams. As a result, Jane Addams called a national conference of women's organizations in Chicago in January 1915 to found the national Woman's Peace Party, today called the Women's International League for Peace and Freedom. Also in 1914, Eastman met with Lillian Wald, the director of the Nurse's Settlement and the Visiting Home Nurse Service, Paul Kellogg, Rabbi Stephen Wise, Oswald Garrison Villard, the publisher of the *Nation*, Jane Addams, and others at Wald's Henry Street Settlement in New York to organize what was originally called the Anti-Preparedness Committee. Lillian Wald became the president of this organization, soon to be renamed the American Union Against Militarism (AUAM), and Crystal Eastman its executive director. The AUAM published anti-militarist analyses, lobbied in Washington against preparedness and conscription, and campaigned against U.S. imperialism in Latin America and the Caribbean.

The social reformers within the union believed that their testimony before congressional committees and their private meetings with President Wilson and his advisers (many of whom were personal friends or at least professional associates) were sufficient to make a difference in the forming of public policy. Their Washington lobbyist, Charles T. Hallinan, was well known and highly regarded. In the beginning their activities were analytic, educational, discreet, supportive of what they believed was the president's real desire: to keep the United States neutral. Crystal Eastman's ability as an administrator, the clarity of purpose she maintained during moments of high tension, enabled her not only to function effectively as the executive officer of the AUAM, but to persuade Lillian Wald and Paul Kellogg of the need to broaden the committee's vision and purpose, to expand and intensify its range of activities.

In November 1915 she launched a dramatic "Truth About Preparedness Campaign." Supported by both the AUAM and the Woman's

Peace Part of New York, the campaign emphasized that economic profiteering was behind the industrialists' propaganda for military increases. Crystal Eastman identified the economic interests of the members of such pro-war organizations as the Army League and the Navy League and called for a public investigation of America's defenses "to root out the graft and inefficiency" and to insist on the nationalization of the defense industries.

To counter Theodore Roosevelt's claim that the United States had "a puny little egg-shell of a navy," the AUAM's literature revealed the size and scope of the world's third largest fleet. When the AUAM's lobby failed and Wilson adopted a preparedness package that included a force of 400,000 trained "citizen soldiers," the antipreparedness activities intensified. The "Truth About Preparedness Campaign" held mass meetings in the largest halls of countless cities. AUAM speakers addressed thousands of people and "won hundreds of columns of publicity from an unwilling press." The AUAM grew from "a small emergency committee of fifteen members to an organization of 6,000 members with local committees in 22 cities. It conducted a national press bureau which served 1,601 papers—including labor and farm weeklies and regular dailies."

Under the auspices of the less restrained Woman's Peace Party of New York, Eastman organized public debates and forums between businessmen associated with the Navy League and antimilitarists. The leadership of New York's WPP was comprised largely of Eastman's closest friends—suffragists, socialists, militant feminists. Although there were many differences among them in age, affluence, and position, to the press and the general public they seemed all to wear bobbed hair, believe in "free love," and belong to New York's "Bohemia." The WPP of New York was dominated by women like Margaret Lane, Anne Herendeen, Freda Kirchwey, Katherine Anthony, Madeleine Doty, Marie Jennie Howe, Agnes Brown Leach. They were members of Heterodoxy, an extraordinary luncheon club that met on Saturday afternoons for over twenty years to discuss women, literature, and politics. They stood on street corners and handed out birth-control literature. They helped organize strike committees and were occasionally arrested. They were rude to authority and careless about adverse publicity. Booing and hissing the business advocates of preparedness became a regular feature of their public meetings. When their meetings were broken up by violent patriots, frequently in uniform, the WPP was criticized in the press despite the fact that the women were the victims of the violence. Such publicity created additional difficulties for Eastman in her work with the AUAM leadership.

But Crystal Eastman believed that the activities of both organizations were necessary for success. She was convinced that lobbying by respectable and influential progressive Americans such as Lillian Wald, Paul Kellogg, Amos Pinchot, and Jane Addams had not yet been rendered meaningless. She remained optimistic that democratic control of foreign policy might still play a role in presidential policies. Aware that the private lobbying of the AUAM without sustained public protest and as much publicity as possible would be futile, she supported entirely the more radical efforts of the WPP of New York. In addition, she believed that the international nature of the woman's peace movement was "unique and priceless" and urged women to "stand by it and strengthen it no matter what other peace organizations we may identify ourselves with."

Lillian Wald and Jane Addams shared Crystal Eastman's convictions and agreed with many of her political analyses. Their disagreements involved issues of emphasis, style. While Lillian Wald remained on the executive board of the New York party and Jane Addams maintained cordial relations with Crystal Eastman, the social reformers were unwilling to engage in certain kinds of public protest and opposed Eastman's more confrontational tactics.

Tensions over Crystal Eastman's flamboyant political methods and unconventional life persisted throughout the war. One example was a popular "War Against War" exhibit which drew crowds of five to ten thousand New Yorkers a day for several months. British pacifist Walter Fuller helped the WPP of New York erect this graphic exhibit, which featured a huge metallic dragon representing the war machine of Wall Street, vivid cartoons, colorful posters, and a series of militant speakers. The exhibit was costly and well publicized, and its spirited sense of protest became a major focus of contention.

Also at this, time Eastman divorced Bennie and married Walter Fuller, with whom she had been living. While such living arrangements would rarely be considered objectionable today, Eastman's private activities gave rise to additional criticism from her associates. Her good friends, however, delighted in her new happiness. Roger Baldwin recalled that Walter Fuller was "extremely witty and totally pacifist and worked hard to make Crystal laugh—and, you know, Crystal loved to laugh."

Others were not at all amused by his wit, especially as represented in the "War Against War" exhibit. Mabel Hyde Kittredge, a patron of causes associated with the Henry Street Settlement and later president of the national Woman's Peace Party, resigned in protest over the tone of the exhibit. She complained that the New York branch "made fun" of the munitions-makers and "ridiculed" certain American interests. Others complained that "the sentiments expressed" at the New York meetings were "very extreme and dangerous."

Crystal Eastman's conviction that public activity and private lobbying could have a real impact on presidential policy was bolstered by the union's success regarding Mexico in the summer of 1916. A massive publicity campaign to avert war in Mexico resulted in an "unofficial commission" of three Mexican and three U.S. antimilitarists that met through June and July at El Paso. Organized by Eastman, this effort at private mediation was supported by the American Federation of Labor, whose officials met with officials of sixty Mexican labor unions in "the most effective effort ever made by the workers of two countries to avoid war." On July 6, 1916, Crystal Eastman and her associates held a press conference in Washington with three Mexican delegates and issued a press release which compared the Mexican Revolution to the French Revolution and analyzed the issues which jeopardized Mexican-American relations, notably the fact that 75 percent of Mexico's national wealth was controlled by foreign capital, mostly North American. The AUAM feared that United States policy in Mexico would impose a "suzerainty from the Rio Grande to Panama," creating "a suspicious and embittered South America."

Crystal Eastman criticized the United States' entire Latin American policy, beginning with the Monroe Doctrine. Why not, she asked, substitute a truly "democratic union of American republics," so that the United States may "rid itself of the temptation to establish profitable protectorates" where anti-American attitudes were "growing and perhaps warranted."

Wilson's response to the union's activity was to appoint a Joint High Commission on Mexico to mediate differences, and war was averted. In "Suggestions to the AUAM for 1916–1917," Eastman wrote that "we must make the most of our Mexican experience. We must make it known to everybody that people acting directly—not through their governments or diplomats or armies—stopped that war, and can stop all wars if enough of them will act together and act quickly."

But 1916 was an election year, and the victory for peace in Mexico was the final victory for the antimilitarists. The AUAM campaigned for Wilson despite the fact that Justice Charles Evans Hughes, the Republican candidate, had been a progressive governor and had worked closely with Crystal Eastman, whom he had appointed to her post as commissioner, and with Lillian Wald—who had faith in his profound interest in protecting the "ordinary people." But Republican Hughes did not promise peace. He promised suffrage. Most of Crystal Eastman's closest friends in the radical suffrage movement supported Hughes, and campaigned vigorously against Wilson, who refused to endorse the suffrage amendment.

The year 1916 was a tense and bitter time for the suffragist women who led the United States peace forces. It foreshadowed the dilemma feminists faced over the Equal Rights Amendment during the 1920s. While there was no correct position, there were priorities. In 1916 suffragists against the war had to vote for one or the other: Hughes, who seemed to promise suffrage with war, or Wilson, who promised peace without suffrage.

Several months before the election, in June 1916, Crystal Eastman gave a rousing and enthusiastic speech at the "Suffrage First" luncheon of Alice Paul's National Woman's Party convention. Nevertheless, all the AUAM's election efforts endorsed Wilson. From the beginning one of the members of the executive committee of the Congressional Union (reorganized in 1916 as the National Woman's Party), Eastman now seemed to support the candidate some of her closest comrades—Doris Stevens, Alice Paul, Lavinia Dock, Inez Milholland—were picketing and jeering. It seemed incomprehensible.

One of Inez Milholland's last speeches before her sudden death during a lecture tour through the western states seemed specifically aimed at her friend Crystal Eastman: "Do not let anyone convince you that there is any more important issue in the country today than votes for women. . . . There are people who honestly believe— HONESTLY BELIEVE! . . . that there are more important issues before the country than suffrage. . . . Now I do not know what you feel about such a point of view . . . but it makes me mad. . . . We must say, 'Women First.' "

Personal divisions and anguish among the suffragists aroused by the election evaporated quickly, however. In December 1916 Crystal Eastman and Jane Addams testified on behalf of the national Woman's Peace Party before the House Judiciary Committee to endorse the federal amendment for women's suffrage. Moreover, Paul's National Woman's Party opposed the war with consistent vigor; and when it became clear that Wilson had betrayed the antimilitarists, the pages of the *Suffragist,* the official paper of the National Women's Party, rallied to their support.

Contradictions in political life are commonplace. In this case the intensity of profound friendships transcended them. And Inez Milholland's sudden death transcended the election of 1916. Eastman arranged the largest and last memorial service for the beloved Amazon who had given her life to the suffrage movement. The *Suffragist* reported that Crystal Eastman "expressed the feeling of all these personal friends when she said, 'Here we are today, the representatives of so many great movements—and we all claim Inez Milholland. This is very wonderful to me; it simply means that her whole aspiration was for fuller liberty.' "

On behalf of her own aspiration for liberty, Crystal Eastman worked sixteen to twenty hours a day in the months prior to the declaration of war in April 1917. With only a few weeks off following the birth of her first child, Jeffrey Fuller, Eastman campaigned tirelessly. In "War and Peace" she wrote that the radical peace movement had three major emphases: to stop the war in Europe, to organize the world for peace at the close of the war, and to defend democracy against the subtle dangers of militarism. Stimulated "by the self-interest of capitalists, imperialists, and war traders, but supported by . . . thousands who call themselves democrats," the people needed to be demystified about alleged benefits of military conscription and service. "We must make this great democracy know," she wrote, "that military training is bad for the bodies and minds and souls of boys; that free minds, and souls undrilled to obedience are vital to the life of democracy."

As the United States hurtled toward war, Crystal Eastman's continued commitment to civil liberties in wartime and her support for *Four Lights*, the newsletter of New York's WPP, created additional tensions within the AUAM leadership. First issued on January 27, 1917, *Four Lights* became the subject of the first serious antagonism between Eastman and Jane Addams (in her capacity as president of the national WPP) and Lillian Wald. Modeled on the *Masses* (a radical magazine edited by Max Eastman) in format and style, *Four Lights* was gay, impulsive, and entirely disrespectful of authority. Although each issue was independently edited, Crystal Eastman was directly responsible for its tone, and it was the official paper of the organization over which she presided. There was little doubt in the minds of WPP conservatives that Crystal Eastman was no longer a sound ally.

Four Lights gave them little choice. It devoted an entire issue, "The Sister Susie Number" to criticizing such women as Lucia Ames Mead, chair of the WPP's Boston branch, which abandoned its former position to assist in war relief work. Some WPP branches, complained the editors of *Four Lights*, spent the entire war knitting socks. Even Jane Addams and Lillian Wald, opposed to conscription in principle, administered registration programs in their settlement houses. In addition, Lillian Wald chaired the Council of National Defense's Committee on Public Health and Child Welfare, while Jane Addams volunteered to work for Herbert Hoover's Food Administration. As far as *Four Lights* was concerned Hoover had revealed "the cloven hoof of the military dictator," and without mentioning Addams by name, it editorialized that "Hoover Helpers" were those women "who accept their position beside the garbage cans as they have always accepted what God and man has put upon them to endure. . . ."

In its first editorial *Four Lights* promised to be "the voice of the young, uncompromising peace movement in America, whose aims are daring and immediate." Above all, *Four Lights* opposed the mounting tyranny and wartime violence that quickly followed the United States' declaration of war. Within three months after the United States entered the war *Four Lights* editorialized against one of the greatest wartime outrages, the race riot in East St. Louis in which scores of black people were beaten, lynched, burned, and drowned:

> Six weeks have passed since the East St. Louis riots and no public word of rebuke, no demand for the punishment of the offenders, has come from our Chief Executive. These American Negroes have died under more horrible conditions than any noncombatants who were sunk by German submarines. But to our President their death does not merit consideration.
>
> Our young men who don their khaki are thus taught that, as they go out to battle under the flag of the United States, they may outdo Belgian atrocities without rebuke if their enemy be of a darker race. And those who guard our land at home have learned that black men and women and little children may safely be mutilated and shot and burned while they stand idly by.

Moreover, *Four Lights* announced on March 24, 1917, in a dramatic banner headline that it hailed "the Russian Revolution with mad glad joy." It pledged itself to the cause of international democracy and claimed that all nations "must be democratized before a federated world can be achieved." It accused the United States of "busily forging weapons to menace the spirit of freedom struggling to life in an exhausted Europe."

Lillian Wald, Paul Kellogg, Oswald Garrison Villard, Jane Addams, and the other social reformers on the board of the AUAM did not disagree theoretically with Crystal Eastman's position. They endorsed her June 15, 1917, press release that announced that once the United States entered the war the AUAM sought victory "in harmony with the principles outlined by the Revolutionary government of Russia, namely, No forcible annexations, No punitive indemnities, Free development of Nationalities." They disapproved, however, of her forthright public style and the order of her priorities. They particularly disapproved of the AUAM's new committee, the Civil Liberties Bureau, founded by Crystal Eastman, Roger Baldwin, and Norman Thomas.

Wald and Kellogg, for example, did not want to be identified with an "anti-war agitation." They sought to influence the future peace negotiations in the interests of international democracy and federation after the war. Crystal Eastman insisted that the Civil Liberties Bureau represented a "democracy first" movement.

Lillan Wald wrote Crystal Eastman on August 28, 1917, that the AUAM had been accepted by the public as "a group of reflective liberals." It was dignified and respectable. Eastman's enthusiasm for organizations like the Civil Liberties Bureau and the newly organized People's Council represented "impulsive radicalism." Wald wrote that Crystal Eastman's new activities demanded either her resignation or Wald's. It "would be lacking in sincerity for us not to be perfectly frank with each other."

For Eastman, Baldwin, and Thomas the Civil Liberties Bureau was the inevitable development of all their convictions. On July 2, 1917, Crystal Eastman issued a press release to introduce the new bureau: "It is the tendency even of the most 'democratic' of governments embarked upon the most 'idealistic of wars' to sacrifice everything for complete military efficiency. To combat this tendency where it threatens free speech, free press, freedom of assembly, and freedom of conscience—the essentials of liberty and the heritage of all past wars worth fighting—that is the first function of the AUAM today. . . . To maintain something over here that will be worth coming back to when the weary war is over. . . ."

By November 1917 Crystal Eastman's activism and her associates in the Woman's Peace Party of New York, combined with the activities of the Civil Liberties Bureau, ended the once-powerful alliance the AUAM had represented. Of her own resignation and the AUAM's disintegration Lillian Wald wrote in her 1934 autobiography, *Windows on Henry Street:* "The fire and imagination of the Secretary, Crystal Eastman, were often impatient of more sober councils."

An extensive correspondence between Lucia Ames Mead, Jane Addams, and Emily Greene Balch reveals that despite Eastman's formidable efforts throughout the war, the national WPP hierarchy attempted to prevent her from attending the Second International Congress of Women in 1919. Supported only by Balch, others argued that Eastman's "extreme" radicalism and her "casual sex life" would confuse their mission and increase their difficulties.

To continue their public works on behalf of the poor, the social workers depended on the contributions of private financiers and government largesse. They placed a high value on cautious and respectable behavior, and feared to lose the kind of public approval Crystal Eastman never sought. Her openness threatened the closeted self-protectiveness of her critics.

During the postwar Red Scare when all social progress was suspended the attitude of the social reformers seemed justified. But it did not protect them. Their respectability was illusory. When Jane Addams, for example, denounced the food blockade and insisted that the "United States should not allow women and children of any nation to starve," she was vilified as a traitor. Like Crystal Eastman, she was followed by the FBI and assorted secret agents. During the 1920s both their names appeared on all the lists of "dangerous Reds," enemies of America. The states' rejection of the child labor amendment, portrayed as part of a massive communist plot, symbolizes the collapse of progressive reform. While the nominal respectability of social reformers availed them very little, the inability of progressives to work together during the postwar period strengthened the militarist and antidemocratic forces they had so vigorously opposed.

Crystal Eastman's last activity as president of New York's WPP was to organize the First Feminist Congress in the United States, held on March 1, 1919. In her opening statement, she examined the status of women in this self-congratulatory center of "freedom and democracy." Citing dismal statistics, including the fact that four-fifths of the women in America were "still denied the elementary political right of voting," she enumerated the essential changes required before women could be independent. She did not mean to catalog the restrictive laws and repressive social customs that burdened women in a spirit of "bitterness," and she fully recognized "the fact that women by their passivity have made these things possible." Her one goal for this First Feminist Congress was to "see the birth of a new spirit of humane and intelligent self-interest . . . which will lead women to declare: 'WE WILL NOT WAIT FOR THE SOCIAL REVOLUTION TO BRING US THE FREEDOM WE SHOULD HAVE WON IN THE 19TH CENTURY.'"

Throughout the postwar years, Eastman's entire effort involved feminism and the "social revolution," by which she meant socialism. As a feminist she had no illusions about the marginality of feminist principles among the male-dominated socialist parties in the United States and Europe. Her own position, expressed vigorously in "Now We Can Begin," was entirely clear.

> Many feminists are socialists, many are communists. . . . But the true feminist, no matter how far to the left she may be in the revolutionary movement, sees the woman's battle as distinct in its objects and different in its methods from the workers' battle for industrial freedom. She knows, of course, that the vast majority of women as well as men are without property, and are of necessity bread and

butter slaves under a system of society which allows the very sources of life to be privately owned by a few, and she counts herself a loyal soldier in the working-class army that is marching to over-throw that system. But as a feminist she also knows that the whole of woman's slavery is not summed up in the profit system, not her complete emancipation assured by the downfall of capitalism. . . .

If we should graduate into communism to-morrow . . . man's attitude to his wife would not be changed.

Her socialist position, as expressed in *The Liberator*, which she co-owned and coedited with Max from March 1918 until they both resigned in 1922, was equally clear. Crystal Eastman had been radicalized by her wartime experiences. Many of her closest friends had been imprisoned and abused because they sought the most rudimentary political power—the vote—by exercising the most basic rights of free speech and assembly. The abolition of civil liberties in wartime revealed the fragile nature of bourgeois rights even in a country that boasted fiercely of its democratic heritage. The Espionage Act of 1917 and the Sedition Act of May 1918 altered forever the nature of American freedom. Those laws rendered all Crystal Eastman's wartime activity illegal and resulted in the removal of all radical publications from the mails, including *Four Lights* and the *Masses,* as well as the imprisonment of countless dissenters, including her brother and Roger Baldwin. During the postwar Red Scare thousands of Americans were imprisoned or deported—anarchists, socialists, labor leaders, conscientious objectors.

War, the counterrevolutionary mobilization, and the secret Allied intervention in the Soviet Union (which was reported in the United States only in *The Liberator*) served to convince her that the only way to "restore liberty" was "to destroy the capitalist system." "The world's future," *The Liberator* editorialized in February 1919, "shall not be the League of Business Politicians at Versailles, but the New International, the League of the Working Classes of the World."

In March 1919 Crystal Eastman became the first American journalist to visit communist Hungary. Her report from Hungary is as valuable for its information as it is for her feelings regarding the inevitable conflicts and contradictions such situations present to "pacifist revolutionaries." There was, she concluded, nothing simple about the dilemma of force. On the other hand, the activities of the invading British, American, and Japanese armies and Admiral Kolchak's "monarchist forces" helped resolve the conflict. The military invasion, intent on destroying all revolutionary movements, suspended Crystal Eastman's pacifism.

The Liberator was the only monthly in the United States to publish information about socialist movements throughout the world, as well as news about the Allied intervention in Russia. In May 1919, for example, *The Liberator* published the startling news that "Japan has made an offer to England" to send troops to join the Allied intervention in Russia "and bear the expenses of the expedition alone—if she receives a mandate for Indo-China."

Filled with some of the most significant poetry and literature of the postwar period, this "journal of Revolutionary Progress" had an impact that reached far beyond the United States. Italian communist theorist Antonio Gramsci depended on it for international information, "so tight and bristling was the blockade around the Bolsheviks." *The Liberator* published John Reed and Louise Bryant from Russia, a regular column of international news by Alexander Trachtenberg (the founder of International publishers), Bertrand Russell's "Democracy and Freedom," the works of associate editor Floyd Dell, contributions by Helen Keller, Norman Thomas, Roger Baldwin, Lenin and Dorothy Day, and the poetry of Claude McKay.

McKay's poetry had never been accepted by the *Masses*, which had sent him "so sorry" rejections. But when Crystal Eastman read his work in *Pearson's*, a literary journal, she invited him to call at *The Liberator* office. One of the leading black poets of the Harlem Renaissance, McKay was still working on the railroads, writing poems on the trains whenever he had spare time. He wrote: "The moment I saw her and heard her voice I liked Crystal Eastman. I think she was the most beautiful white woman I ever knew. . . . Her beauty was not so much of her features . . . but in her magnificent presence. Her form was something after the pattern of a splendid draft horse and she had a way of holding her head like a large bird poised in a listening attitude." Their lifelong friendship began during that first meeting, and Claude McKay became associate editor of *The Liberator*.

After the war, Crystal Eastman with her husband and son lived communally with her brother Max, their childhood friend Ruth Pickering—who had also graduated from Vassar and was soon to marry Amos Pinchot—the actress Florence Deshon, and Eugen Boissevan—who commanded "a whole fleet of merchant ships" and had married first Inez Milholland and then Edna St. Vincent Millay. Crystal Eastman had engineered this "delightful half-way family" in 1918 to promote companionship and economy. With two houses and a collective courtyard and kitchen, they shared a comfortable communal space in Greenwich Village and also spent weekends and summers together in Croton-on-Hudson with, among others, Boardman Robinson, Margaret and Winthrop D. Lane, Floyd Dell, and—until they left for Russia—John Reed and Louise Bryant.

The communal harmony and pastoral happiness of those years were short-lived. From 1907 to 1921 Crystal Eastman's capacity for work was intense and varied. Before the war her paying jobs, whether as a social investigator or government appointee, occupied only part of her working day. Political activities and organizations occupied far more time. Like all "workaholics," Eastman thrived on work. It energized her and increased her strength. When she was not working she became morose and melancholic. Yet between 1911 and 1921 Crystal Eastman's physical constitution broke down several times. Her blood pressure was frequently and dangerously high, and she had a bad heart. Above all, there was nephritis. Diagnosed late and little understood then, it is now known to be a slowly consuming and painful kidney condition.

With complete disregard for her physical well-being, Crystal Eastman did not slow down until the birth of her second child, Annis, two months prematurely. At the insistence of doctors, she removed herself from the management of *The Liberator,* became a contributing editor, and agreed to rest while writing a book on feminism and taking more personal care of herself and her daughter.

Hospital and medical expenses and the loss of her full-time *Liberator* salary devastated the Eastman-Fuller household. In the spring of 1922, when Annis was three months old, Walter Fuller left for England to look for a better job. Evidently Fuller felt confined in their marriage, which was financially crushed by debts. On April 14, Crystal wrote that she was "so lonely it makes a sick feeling in my solar plexus . . . I hope you will come back." To encourage her husband's return she arranged with Kellogg to offer Fuller a job on the *Survey Graphic.* It entailed more money, and Crystal Eastman believed that he "could work with Paul—he is sensitive and whimsical and humorous. And they have money in sight to run the *Survey Graphic* for three years—just about as long as you like a job to last. . . ." But Fuller refused the offer.

In a subsequent letter dated June 27, Eastman discussed the possibilities of joining Walter in England as soon as she could raise sufficient funds and he could afford the company of his family. She wrote: "Don't worry about harsh words. Have I said any? If I have they certainly can be forgotten now. I knew you had to run away. That you couldn't even send me a line to say so and say you were sorry will forever be incomprehensible to me. But then four-fifths of you is a closed book to me and four-fifths of me is a closed book to you,—and yet we love each other a great deal. Don't we?"

"Marriage Under Two Roofs," written for *Cosmopolitan* magazine, largely for money, was not written largely as spoof. Crystal and her husband lived for years not only under two separate roofs, but in two separate countries. From 1922 to 1927 she and her children traveled back and forth between England and the United States with commuter regularity. Often she spent her summer vacations in the south of France with Jeannette Lowe and their children. Walter might visit occasionally. Very much like "Marriage Under Two Roofs."

Wherever Crystal Eastman spent her time during these years, her life consisted of a continual battle to find meaningful work, to help organize the Anglo-American women's movement on behalf of equal rights, and to ignore the physicians, and several medical quacks, who all agreed on one thing: Crystal Eastman needed rest. She hated to rest, she hated inactivity, and she hated to be without a steady job. Her inability to find work, the fact that she was actually barred from the kind of work she sought, was the hardest for her to comprehend. Today we are more familiar with the facts and effects of political blacklists. But Crystal Eastman, attorney, social investigator, noted orator and author, could not understand why a militant feminist, antimilitarist, and socialist could not between 1922 and 1928 find regular employment. She could not understand it even when old friends like Paul Kellogg told her specifically that there were "practical difficulties in making a fresh start which it does no good to minimize." The United States, wrote Kellogg in a letter, "is not as tolerant as England; we still have a lot of beating up of bugaboos, and you will get a touch of that in any public work . . . and your various espousals—such as the Woman's Party—would not help in some of the few quarters where industrial research is still carried on, etc." Throughout the last years of her life, Crystal's only income was derived from her two houses, in Croton and Greenwich Village, when she rented them, and from feminist articles contracted by the militant wing of the Anglo-American women's movement, notably Alice Paul's journal *Equal Rights*, and Lady Rhonnda's *Time and Tide*.

During the 1920s the contradictions between radicalism and reform, within the context of both socialism and feminism, were vividly apparent in the divisions of the women's movement. For twenty years social reformers like Jane Addams and Florence Kelley had championed protective legislation for women and children. To the extent that Crystal worked for protective legislation for workers, she too had been identified with that reform movement. She regarded protective laws as cruelly discriminatory when they regulated working conditions for women only.

In 1908 Jane Addams and Florence Kelley had rejoiced in a Supreme Court decision that established the principle of protective legislation for women. *Muller v. Oregon* introduced "sociological jurisprudence" into constitutional law. Florence Kelley and Josephine Goldmark had hired Louis D. Brandeis to defend a protective law that established a ten-hour day for women laundry workers. The first of the famous "Brandeis briefs," it demonstrated the physical inferiority of women, their need for protection—and the benefits for the human race should women's toil be specifically restricted by the state. Yes, declared the unanimous Court: "Woman's physical structure, and the performance of maternal functions . . . justify special legislation restricting or qualifying the conditions under which she should be permitted to toil." These restrictions were "not imposed solely for her benefit, but also largely for the benefit of all."

This was the principle that protectionist reformers sought to defend against erosion by the Equal Rights Amendment. When the National Woman's Party introduced this amendment in July 1923, at the seventy-fifth anniversary convention of the Seneca Falls equal rights meeting of 1848, the feminists and the women reformers became irreconcilably divided. *Muller v. Oregon* classed women with minors, and rested its decision on women's biological "inferiority," their potential maternity, and "natural dependence" on men. It represented everything Crystal Eastman had opposed since her first speech called "Woman."

Since she was fifteen Crystal had considered arguments of women's physical inferiority male myths created to keep women untutored, unpaid, and unhappy at home. Now, with all Europe moving toward socialism, working women were urged to return home. It was believed that without patriarchal order there would be anarchy. The working class required stability. Women needed protection. Protection would preserve the home, and the entire human race. All the men in unions seemed to agree.

During World War I women in large numbers had moved into numerous industries and professions from which they had previously been barred. With war's end a great effort to dismiss them emerged. In Cleveland, for example, 150 women streetcar conductors were dismissed after the men struck to eliminate women from the job because there was no longer a "manpower shortage." In Detroit white male conductors petitioned for the dismissal of women and black workers because their contract promised "women and Negroes could be employed only in an emergency, and the emergency was over." By 1919 protective laws forbidding night work were used as a pretext for dismissing women workers from lucrative, interesting, and sought-after jobs.

Nevertheless, Florence Kelley, Jane Addams, Dr. Alice Hamilton—all the friends of labor—opposed the equal rights movement because they did not want to lose hard-won protective laws. Organized labor women may have favored equality—but equality with protection; and they opted for protection first. Given the cruel hours and life-threatening conditions, most working women and their allies believed that it was absurd to abandon specific protective laws for the principle of equality that seemed both abstract and farfetched. Crystal Eastman's support for equal rights represented a socialist feminist tradition that has only recently begun to reemerge. As a socialist in the 1920s she was virtually alone among her allies in the National Woman's Party and its British counterpart, Lady Rhonnda's Six Point Group.

For Crystal Eastman protection was humanitarianism in the interests of "family welfare." It had nothing to do with the needs or rights or aspirations of women. It represented reformism at its worst. It served everywhere to bar women from well-paid jobs that men were eager to keep for themselves. Protective legislation protected male unionists who feared female competition and capitalist power, which used intra-class competition between women and men just as it used ethnic and racial differences: to block real workers' unity, the necessary sense of connectedness that might stimulate a real workers' movement.

Crystal Eastman's commitment to equal rights was not an abstract enthusiasm. With a rare empathy for all women, and an ability to imagine herself in each humiliating or repressive situation, her outrage was as specific as it was theoretical. In "Women, Rights and Privileges," she wrote that "this sudden concern for the health of women when they set out to earn their living in competition with men seems a little suspicious. . . . What working-class mother of small children ever had nine hours consecutive rest? . . . What traditional union husband ever felt that it was his concern to see that she should have?"

By 1927, Crystal Eastman became desperate for challenging work. Besides, she never actually liked England very well. She loathed the climate and longed for the American seasons—the heat of the sun and the snow. She was neither well nor happy. In January she wrote to Paul Kellogg that she had decided, with finality, to return home. "I am rich in health and strength now. . . . Three lazy months at Antibes . . . have given me back myself." And, she wrote, she "was simply crazy to work. England holds nothing for me. . . . I have tried for two years to get a job—research, organizing, editorial, speaking, anything." She returned to the United States with a temporary position organizing the *Nation's* tenth anniversary celebration. Walter was to join her when she secured more permanent work. But in September 1927 Walter Fuller died of a stroke, and within ten months Crystal Eastman too was dead.

The last months of Crystal Eastman's life were given over to hard work and her final battle, to heal "this good for nothing body of mine." Ravaged by nephritis which was never properly diagnosed or treated, she blamed herself for her headaches, her loss of energy. On October 11, 1927, she wrote to Cynthia Fuller, Walter's sister: "I am fighting so hard not to drown and to get my health and hold on to it, so that I'll be equal to supporting the children and making a happy home for them."

Crystal Eastman was forty-seven years old when she died. Her last thoughts were of her children and all the work she had left undone. Many friends offered to adopt the children; Agnes Brown Leach and Henry Goddard Leach did so. Agnes Brown Leach had been among the most consistent supporters of the American Union Against Militarism, treasurer of the New York branch of the Woman's Peace Party, and a member of the executive committee of the National Woman's Party.

Crystal Eastman was mourned by many. Claude McKay believed that Crystal Eastman joined "in her personality that daring freedom of thought and action—all that was fundamentally fine, noble and genuine in American democracy." She was, he wrote, "a great-hearted woman whose life was big with primitive and exceptional gestures. She never wrote that Book of Woman which was imprinted on her mind. She was poor, and fettered with a family. She had a grand idea for a group of us to go off to write in some quiet corner of the world, where living was cheap and easy. But it couldn't be realized. And so life was cheated of one contribution about women that no other woman could write."

Crystal Eastman's contemporaries considered her "a great leader." In Freda Kirchwey's memorial in the *Nation* she wrote that when Crystal Eastman "spoke to people—whether it was to a small committee or a swarming crowd—hearts beat faster and nerves tightened as she talked. She was simple, direct, dramatic. Force poured from her strong body and her rich voice, and people followed where she led. . . . In her personal as in her public life her enthusiasm and strength were spent without thought; she had no pride or sense of her own power. . . . Her strength . . . her rich and compelling personality— these she threw with reckless vigor into every cause that promised a finer life to the world. She spent herself wholly, and died—too young."

Alice Paul

(1885–1977)

Christine A. Lunardini

Born into a Quaker family in Moorestown, New Jersey, Alice Paul was reared in the intellectual tradition of her parents, William and Tacie Parry Paul. She attended Swarthmore College, and after graduation went to the New York School of Philanthropy (a school of social work) in 1905 on a fellowship from the College Settlement Association. For the next few years she was a social worker; during this time she cultivated her interest in women's rights. While active as a caseworker in the settlement house crusade in England from 1906 to 1909, she became involved in the suffrage movement. Paul was arrested for her suffrage agitation and endured force-feeding for almost a month during one hunger strike. Paul received a Ph.D. in sociology from the University of Pennsylvania in 1912 before launching into her full-time suffrage career. In 1914 she cofounded the Congressional Union for Women's Suffrage—a breakaway group from the National American Woman Suffrage Association. She led pickets at the White House and was sentenced to prison for suffrage protests. Paul founded the National Woman's Party in 1916 and was a pivotal factor in women securing passage of the Nineteenth Amendment in 1920. In 1923 she introduced the Equal Rights Amendment (ERA) and became a lifelong advocate for feminist reform, working in Europe as well as the United States. By 1944 the ERA was a plank within the American presidential campaigns of both major parties. Paul continued her fight for women's rights from National Woman's Party headquarters in Washington, but declining health forced her to relocate in 1972 to the Connecticut countryside. Paul promoted the cause for women from her wheelchair until she suffered a stroke in 1974. Paul died in her hometown of Moorestown, New Jersey, in 1977.

An article appearing in *Everybody's* magazine in July 1916 attempted to uncover the real Alice Paul amidst the myriad contradictory descriptions of her that made the rounds of both suffrage and political circles. With more than a touch of exasperated surrender, the author concluded that, "There is no Alice Paul. There is suffrage. She leads by being . . . her cause."[1] Most contemporary journalists assigned to cover Paul were baffled by her and often tried to make her more—or less—than human: "I tried to imagine Alice Paul married," one such writer confided to her readers, "and I almost succeeded when I heard she was taking dancing lessons last Spring."[2] To associate Paul with the ordinary events of middle-class life, however, was beyond the writer's ability. She went on to predict that Paul would follow the fiery road to revolution. To this journalist and many of her contemporaries, Paul's political activities and the ordinary events of life were clearly contradictory, if not mutually exclusive. That Paul should prove to be such an elusive subject was not surprising; she was not a mainstream suffragist. By the time Alice Paul arrived on the scene in 1912, the American suffrage movement had reached a virtual standstill—it had lost the urgency and excitement that Susan B. Anthony and Elizabeth Cady Stanton had generated in the decades following the Civil War. Since Stanton and Anthony's retirement from suffrage, the National American Woman Suffrage Association (NAWSA) had relinquished almost entirely any effort to secure a federal women's suffrage amendment, preferring instead to focus on the state level. NAWSA's new president, Anna Howard Shaw, was a fiery speaker but a lackluster leader. During her presidency of NAWSA, which was the only national suffrage organization in operation at this time, the suffrage movement became mired at the state and local level, settling into the low-keyed, plodding pace that characterized it until 1913. As late as 1912, there were only nine full-suffrage states in the entire country.[3] Alice Paul's arrival on the scene marked a sharp departure from this type of suffrage activity, and a return to a more radical approach.

From the time that she took over the reins of NAWSA's Congressional Committee in 1913, Paul made it clear that her objective would be to secure a federal amendment to the Constitution that would give women the vote with, in a manner of speaking, one stroke of pen. Paul borrowed liberally from the English suffrage movement, making publicity and high visibility the vehicles for educating an uninformed public. When NAWSA objected to her tactics, she broke away from that organization, forming first the Congressional Union in 1914, and then the National Woman's Party (NWP) in 1916. While NAWSA always sought to include on their membership roles women who would not necessarily play an active part in the suffrage battle, Paul wanted only those women who were prepared to lend not only their names, but their time and effort as well. Consequently, her organization never numbered more than fifty thousand members, compared to NAWSA's membership, which numbered in the hundreds of thousands.

The Woman's Party activists possessed many of the same characteristics as their counterparts in NAWSA. But they tended to be a bit younger, somewhat better educated, more career-oriented, less apt to be married, and more cosmopolitan than the NAWSA women. Most of them were from the ranks of the middle class, and in many ways they were typical of middle-class women of their generation. The critical factor that distinguished the women that joined NAWSA and the women that joined the Woman's Party was their brand of feminism. For both groups, suffrage was the issue around which they rallied. For the Woman's Party, however, militancy was the chief weapon. Picketing the White House and Congress both in time of peace and war, the Woman's Party members were fully prepared to risk social status, family approbation, and personal freedom in order to achieve their goal. NAWSA members, on the other hand, chose to adhere to the more traditional, socially acceptable, and much more conservative approach of using gentle persuasion.

Paul herself contrasted sharply with the entrenched suffrage leadership, being at once more aggressive and more willing to employ tactics considered radical in order to achieve her goal of a federal amendment. Paul was idolized and idealized by her suffrage followers, but she often appeared paradoxical. She was alternately described as "exceedingly charitable . . . and patient," and "cold, austere, and a little remote."[4] She elicited both profound and unquestioning loyalty from her coworkers and intense distrust and skepticism from her adversaries. More than one observer described her single-mindedness as "fanaticism." Outraged by Paul's campaign against the Democratic party in the summer of 1914 and its attendant publicity, Mrs. Medill McCormick, a NAWSA officer, described Paul as an "anaemic fanatic, well-intentioned and conscientious . . . but almost unbalanced because of her physical condition." McCormick was referring to Paul's frail appearance, which she attributed to Alice's alleged refusal to spend more than thirty cents a day on food. This, in McCormick's view, demonstrated Paul's instability and characterized her attitude towards suffrage: "She will be a *martyr* whether there is the slightest excuse for it in this country or not, and I am really convinced that she will die for the cause, but," McCormick added disparagingly, "it will be because of her 30 [cent] meals."[5]

Paul's followers were as lavish in their praise of her as her detractors were in their criticism. "I know of no modern leader with whom to compare her," said one admiring political observer. "I think she must possess many of the same qualities that Lenin does . . . cool, practical, rational. . . . And if she has demanded the ultimate of her followers, she has given it herself."[6] Maud Younger, the "millionaire waitress" from California, the founder and president of the waitresses' union in San Francisco and a skilled organizer, could not say enough about Paul's executive abilities: "She has in the first place, a devotion to the cause which is absolutely self-sacrificing. She has an indomitable will. . . . She has a clear, penetrating, analytic mind which cleaves straight to the heart of things. . . . She is a genius for organization, both in the mass and in detail."[7] In a similar vein, Lucy Burns, Paul's second-in-command, noted: "Her great assets, I should say, are her power, with a single leap of the imagination, to make plans on a national scale, and a supplementary power to see that it is done down to the last postage stamp."[8]

In substance, both views of Paul are accurate, although not necessarily in their particulars. The complexities of her personality revealed in such divergent views can be better understood in the context of her background and upbringing. Born on January 11, 1885, in the small Quaker community of Moorestown, New Jersey, nine miles east of Philadelphia, Alice was the oldest child of William M. and Tacie Parry Paul. Her family tree included, on her mother's side, William Penn, and on her father's side, the Winthrops of Massachusetts.[9] The first Paul to settle in New Jersey had fled England due to religious and political conflicts with the Crown.[10] Alice's father was a successful businessperson who served as president of the bank that he helped to found, the Burlington County Trust Company. He also held directorships on the boards of several local companies, invested in several profitable real estate ventures, and owned a working farm. Alice's mother was the daughter of one of the founders of Swarthmore College in Pennsylvania. Indeed, Tacie Parry would have been among the first women to graduate from Swarthmore had she not left in her senior year to marry William Paul. Alice eventually followed in her mother's footsteps, first attending a Quaker school in Moorestown, and then enrolling at Swarthmore, where she earned a degree. Both of the elder Pauls were active and devout Quakers and subscribed to traditional Quaker beliefs, including that of equality between the sexes.[11] Quakers have always been heavily represented in social justice movements. It is not surprising, then, that Quaker women were so heavily represented in the ranks of American suffragists. Their participation in public affairs at a time when most women did not engage in controversial activities stemmed in large part from the greater role that women had in the Quaker religion than women had in most other religions. Lucretia Mott, a prominent

Quaker, was one of the original organizers of the American suffrage movement at its founding in 1848, when she, along with Elizabeth Cady Stanton, called women to meet at Seneca Falls, New York, and issued the women's Declaration of Sentiments.

In addition to Alice, the Pauls had three other children: William, Jr., Helen, and Parry Haines Paul. Alice Paul's relationship with her parents was apparently good, although not very well documented. She was sixteen years old when her father died suddenly of pneumonia, but her recollections of his death were vague and she could say only that, "I just remember that life went on."[12] We do know, however, what William Paul thought of his oldest daughter, as revealed in a magazine article published in 1916. An interviewer, seeking hometown opinion regarding Paul's militant suffrage activity, asked Tacie Paul what she thought about her daughter. "Well," she sighed, "I remember that Mr. Paul used to say that whenever there was anything hard and disagreeable to do, 'I bank on Alice.' "[13] Although both William and Tacie Paul were suffrage advocates, the article implied that Tacie Paul did not quite understand her daughter's militant activities. Tacie Paul's attitude towards militancy may have been influenced by Alice Paul's uncle, Donald Paul. When William Paul died so suddenly, his wife and family, although well off financially, depended upon Donald for advice and guidance on money matters. Like many middle-class women, Tacie Paul had little knowledge of family finances and neither the experience nor the confidence necessary to take over when faced with the disaster of her husband's death. The circumstances of having the family finances taken over by an uncle did not affect Alice directly since she had already left home for college. But she was aware of her mother's new dependence and it influenced her own determination to be independent and self-sufficient.[14] In any case, her uncle did not approve of Alice's suffrage activity, and Tacie Paul may have withheld public approval in the magazine article in order to maintain harmony within the family.[15] Despite Tacie Paul's ambivalence regarding Alice's suffrage activities, and her reluctance to offend her brother-in-law, she nevertheless supported her daughter financially, which allowed Alice to devote full time to suffrage.[16]

The elder Pauls raised their children in an atmosphere of discipline, achievement, and service. In keeping with Quaker teaching, neither music nor dancing was encouraged as part of the younger Pauls' childhood experiences. The children knew that their Irish maids went off to dances but assumed that only "a sort of common people" engaged in such behavior.[17] Instead of music and dance, Paul's recreational activities centered on sports, especially tennis. Suffrage coworker Mabel Vernon, a year ahead of Paul at Swarthmore, remembered her as a shy, sports-minded young woman. In contrast to Paul's frail and sickly pallor that later caused much concern and comment, Vernon recalled Paul's healthy and vigorous appearance as a college student.[18]

Paul read voraciously, especially in the classics, and she haunted the local Friends library as a youth. She read every line written by Charles Dickens "over and over again."[19] Dickens's social commentary undoubtedly helped to shape her own sense of justice. Her suffrage coworker, Anne Martin, confided that one of the sacrifices that Paul made during the suffrage campaign was to stay away from Washington bookstores, to keep no books in her rooms, and not to read anything not specifically related to suffrage. She feared that any indulgence in reading for pleasure might tempt her to give less than 100 percent to the suffrage cause.[20]

At Swarthmore, Paul initially chose to major in biology. She did so not because she especially liked biology or the sciences, but because of a personal conviction that she would carry with her into adulthood. Opportunities for new adventure, to learn new things, had to be grasped immediately. To stick with the things she believed she already knew—English and Latin, for example—meant passing up an opportunity to engage in something about which she knew nothing. Biology was a new adventure, an unknown quantity, a challenge to be met.[21] Later on, this conviction would manifest itself in other ways as well. She was not a particularly introspective person. Paul always professed to believe that the past was past and ought not to be dwelt upon. As a result, she more often than not refused to talk about her past experiences, particularly when she believed that doing so would make her and not suffrage the focus of public attention.

Her commitment to biology was superficial at best, for she never really considered pursuing a career in the sciences. Paul's first introduction to political science and economics came only in her senior year when Swarthmore hired Professor Robert Brooks to teach those subjects. Paul was immediately attracted to both disciplines and did so well that Brooks recommended her for a College Settlement Association fellowship at the New York School of Philanthropy (later Columbia University School of Social Work).[22]

Paul spent several years after her graduation from Swarthmore in the study and practice of social work. After she completed her year at the New York School of Philanthropy, she earned a master's degree in sociology at the University of Pennsylvania in 1907, with minor fields in political science and economics. (Although she was no stranger to the problems women faced because of their legal status in an unequal society, she had not yet exhibited publicly a concern for the issue of equal suffrage. Paul had already begun research on the project that would become her doctoral dissertation, "Towards Equality," an examination of women's legal status in Pennsylvania.) Her familiarity with suffrage, however, reached back to her childhood. One of her earliest memories was accompanying her mother to suffrage meetings at the home of a neigboring Quaker family in Moorestown.[23]

Paul interrupted her graduate work at the University of Pennsylvania to accept a second fellowship to study social work in Woodbridge, England, the central training school for Quakers. As with biology, Paul's commitment to social work was not all-consuming. She arrived in England in the fall of 1907 with the belief that she was only marking time. "I knew in a very short time that I was never going to be a social worker, because I could see that social workers were not doing much good in the world. . . . You knew you couldn't *change* the situation by social work."[24]

It was while she was in England, however that Paul found the cause that integrated and brought into focus her family heritage, her service-oriented Quaker education, and her interest in economics, political science, and the status of women. Christabel Pankhurst, the English suffragist, was invited to speak at the University of Birmingham, where Paul was fulfilling the academic requirements of her fellowship. Suffrage at that time was even less popular than it was respectable. The Pankhursts, Christabel, her mother Emmeline, and her sister Sylvia, founders of the Women's Social and Political Union (WSPU), were avowed radicals who employed militant tactics to achieve their goals. Christabel Pankhurst's appearance at Birmingham incited the usually proper students to rowdy behavior. She was shouted down and the embarrassed Birmingham administration was forced summarily to cancel her talk. The reaction to Pankhurst's appearance both angered and surprised Paul. She had not encountered any opposition to suffrage at the meetings she had attended as a child. Now, as a young adult, it shocked her that people would react so violently to the idea. For Paul, such resistance was both foolish and ill-informed, and she left the auditorium thinking that even though her fellow students were so-intolerant, the suffragettes "had anyway one heart and soul convert . . . that was myself."[25]

When Paul finished her year at Woodbridge, a representative of the Charity Organization Society of London invited her to become a caseworker in the working-class district of Dalston. By now she was determined to throw in her lot with the Pankhurst group; thus, she accepted the caseworker position because it placed her where she wanted to be. In the fall of 1908, she participated in her first suffrage parade and began an association with the WSPU that would last for two years. During that time she became thoroughly versed in the strategy and tactics of confrontational suffragism. Paul's participation in subsequent parades and demonstrations led to her arrest and imprisonment on several occasions over the next year on charges of disturbing the peace and disorderly conduct. Along with her English comrades, she took part in hunger strikes to protest against the British government's treatment of the suffrage prisoners.[26] It was a profoundly formative period in her political awakening for, prior to this time, Paul had evinced little interest in political activism. Indeed, aside from the meetings she had attended with her mother, and despite her academic interest in inequality, Paul had not been sufficiently inspired by the American suffrage movement to join any suffrage organizations at home.

While in Europe, Paul met only one other American active with the WSPU—Lucy Burns, a woman of Irish descent born in Brooklyn. Burns graduated from Vassar and then went on to Yale to do graduate work in languages at a time when women were not highly regarded by their male colleagues on that campus. She left Yale, returning to Brooklyn to teach English at Erasmus High School. In 1906, much to the dismay of her Erasmus students, she resigned her teaching position to study languages in Europe. Burns went first to the University of Berlin (1906–1908), and then to the University of Bonn (1908–1909). But Burns, much like Alice Paul, felt she was drifting along with no particular focus to her life. While she was vacationing in England, she met the Pankhursts and discovered her intense interest in the suffrage movement. By 1909, she had transferred to Oxford with the intention of pursuing her Ph.D., but by that time her only real concern was suffrage.[27] From 1909 to 1912, Burns worked with the WSPU as an organizer, primarily in Edinburgh. She, too, gained invaluable experience that would later serve the American suffrage cause well.

Alice Paul first met Lucy Burns at a London police station where both were waiting to be processed after having been arrested for demonstrating. Paul, noticing the tiny American flag pinned to Burns's lapel, maneuvered her way through the crowded station house and introduced herself. They found an empty tabletop and perched there, exchanging stories of their English experiences and talking about their hopes for the American women's movement.[28] The two became fast friends and worked closely together on their return to the United States.

In both style and appearance, Alice Paul and Lucy Burns provided a striking contrast to one another. Burns, much the better diplomat of the two, possessed a quicker wit and a readier sense of humor. She was spontaneous, outspoken, and laughed easily. Paul, on the other hand, was irrepressibly shy. Paul was reserved, soft-spoken, and appeared to be much more businesslike. Lucy Burns, with her red hair, sturdy build, and rugged Irish features, seemed equal to any task. Alice Paul was slight of build and almost timid-looking. She suffered periodic bouts of ill-health which, on several occasions, required hospitalization. Many of her later health problems stemmed from the hunger strikes in which she participated as a suffrage prisoner.[29] Mabel Vernon recalled how shocked she was the first time she saw Paul after the latter's return from England. Paul appeared on the verge of collapse. The painful and dangerous forced-feedings administered by British prison officials left her weak, pale, and underweight.[30] To even casual observers, the toll extracted for standing on principle was a harsh one. The experience also helped to shape the careless eating habits that later prompted Mrs. Medill McCormick to predict that Paul would become a self-made martyr. Nothing could have been further from the truth; Paul was much too pragmatic to choose martyrdom. She approached risky situations with a healthy degree of trepidation and never thought of herself as especially brave. When Emmeline Pankhurst asked her, in the spring of 1909, to take part in a demonstration against Herbert Asquith, the British prime minister, that would almost certainly lead to arrest and imprisonment, Paul recalled later: "I remember hesitating the longest time and writing the letter [accepting the invitation] and not being able to get up enough courage to post it, and going up and walking around the post office, wondering whether I dare put it in."[31]

But Lucy Burns was impressed with Paul's courage, as well as her "extraordinary mind . . . and remarkable executive ability." She thought the frail-looking Quaker had two serious disabilities that would hamper her effectiveness in a grueling political campaign: her apparent ill-health and a "lack of knowledge about human nature." Burns later acknowledged that "I was wrong in both."[32] Paul herself always believed that Burns possessed far greater courage than she, pointing out that Lucy Burns never hesitated to risk possible arrest on the picket lines, both in England and in the United States, despite Burns's phobic fear of rats and other animal life that inhabited the damp, dark prison cells.[33]

Paul and Burns worked so well together that observers often attributed to them one mind and spirit. One suffragist, when asked to describe the differences between the two, found more similarities than differences in their beliefs and attitudes. However, she was able to detect differences in temperament: "Both saw the situation exactly as it was, but they went at the problems with different methods. Alice Paul had a more acute sense of justice, Lucy Burns a more bitter sense of injustice. Lucy Burns would become angry because the President or the people did not do this or that. Alice Paul never expected anything of them."[34]

After her imprisonment in Hallowell Jail in 1910, Paul returned to the United States from England and resumed graduate study at the University of Pennsylvania. Burns, however, remained in Europe to organize for the WSPU, thus the two were not united again until 1912, when they joined forces to do suffrage work in America.

At NAWSA's annual convention in 1912, Alice Paul, along with Lucy Burns, petitioned for and was granted permission to take over NAWSA's Congressional Committee. The Congressional Committee was, theoretically, established to lobby for suffrage on the federal level, that is, to lobby for a women's suffrage amendment to the United States Constitution. In fact, NAWSA in this period focused its efforts almost exclusively on the states, with the goal of securing changes to each individual state constitution. Other than lip service, very little attention was paid to the idea of securing a federal amendment.

When Paul assumed leadership of NAWSA's Congressional Committee, most people who noticed such things would not have predicted the effect she was about to have, either on the suffrage movement or on the people who worked with her. Alice Paul possessed many of the same social and educational characteristics of other women suffragists. Her marital and professional status, while somewhat unusual, could not be viewed as extraordinary. She never married, but neither did many of her contemporaries. She collected a string of degrees that eventually included two law degrees and a Ph.D., but there were others as versatile. Yet Paul was an extraordinary personality, perhaps the single truly charismatic figure in the twentieth-century suffrage movement. Certainly she was the force that powered the militant suffrage movement. She successfully mobilized both impatient New Suffragists—the mostly younger generation of American women determined to secure their rights even if it required more militant tactics to do so—and the discontented Old Suffragists—women who had been engaged in the suffrage movement for years who were generally older and more conservative, but who were beginning to despair of ever realizing their goal by following the strategy employed by NAWSA. To the new suffragists, Paul represented the force that made them willing to take uncommon risks, including imprisonment and possible estrangement from families, friends, and peers.

When Max Weber wrote *The Sociology of Religion* in 1922, he might have used Alice Paul as his model in developing the concept of the charismatic leader. Such a person, Weber concluded, challenged the established order in ways both constructive and destructive, established boundaries by drawing on legitimacy from sources within herself or himself, and disregarded public opinion.[35] This certainly applied to Paul. When faced with a law or a convention that, if observed, would have nullified a particular plan of action, Paul usually just commented on the "absurdity" of the existing situation and proceeded to do exactly as she pleased.[36] When public opinion turned against her, as it did at various times, for example, during a suffrage parade in 1913 and again in 1917 when she picketed the White House while the country was at war, she either ignored the opposition or turned it to her own advantage. Publicity was one of the major tactics Paul employed. She did not desire nor incite the crowds to turn riotous during the suffrage parade of 1913, but when they did she exploited the resulting publicity to the benefit of both her organization and the suffrage movement in general.[37] In similar fashion, attacks on the White House picketers by hostile crowds during the First World War generated publicity that sometimes rivaled the war news for front-page coverage in the nations' newspapers.[38] For Paul, with her keen understanding of the media, publicity was the event.

In attempting to explain Paul, historians have often dismissed her as either well-meaning but harmlessly misguided, or as fanatical and dangerously misguided—in either case harmful to the suffrage movement. At best, she is given minimal credit for advancing suffrage.[39] Others have gone so far as to label her pathological—a personality who appealed only to persons on the fringes of the suffrage movement.[40] In a very limited sense, this explanation of Paul may be understandable. Contemporaries who responded to her were alienated from society to the extent that they willingly followed a leader who advocated what were considered extreme, radical tactics. Attempts by women to improve their status in society and to secure their rights more often than not have been criticized by those who held power and wished to maintain the status quo. Aggressive action, militancy, and perceived radicalism on the part of women have been even more severely criticized and condemned. Aggression, when attributed to women, has always been and remains to a large extent, a negative trait. But, as S. N. Eisenstadt, in his commentary on Weber's work, observed, "The search for meaning, consistency, order is not always something extraordinary, something which exists only . . . among pathological personalities, but also in all stable situations . . . focused within some specific parts of the social structure and of an individual's life space."[41]

American society in the early twentieth century often produced disorientation and alienation for women, particularly for middle-class women who had the desire, the means, the motivation, and the opportunity to be actively involved in pursuing equal rights. Their response to Alice Paul was a manifestation of their own search for balance and equality in a world they perceived to be disorderly. And Paul herself was motivated not by an unrealistic obsession that could justly be interpreted as pathological, but by a logically deduced expectation of equality for both sexes. Her charismatic appeal made her more effective in pursuing that goal, and a continually modernizing industrial society provided her with a constituency more receptive to her message.

Paul, although she professed to be unaware of her power or the source of it, nevertheless used her unfailing ability to motivate people to do things they did not necessarily want to do.[42] "I cannot say that I personally like to do the things that Alice Paul set us to do," wrote one less-than-enthusiastic worker, "But . . . I helped to picket the White House, to keep the fires burning near suffrage headquarters, and to pester congressmen and senators and did my little best to swell all sorts of parades and demonstrations."[43] More commonly, however, the women who worked in Paul's organization did so with great enthusiasm and were more than willing to follow Paul's instructions to the letter.

She may not have understood fully the source of her power, but Paul despite her protests to the contrary was aware of it and more important, she used it effectively. One suffrage volunteer vividly recalled how newcomers to the organization met Alice Paul for the first time. Those women who wanted to work for Paul were assigned tasks about the headquarters, but not specifically told which job they were being trained for or what precisely would be expected of them. Throughout their internship, Paul would receive reports on the volunteer's performance and potential from her coworkers. "And then Miss Paul sent for you," one such intern reported. "I will never forget that first interview. Miss Paul sat at a desk in a room seemingly completely dark except for a small desk lamp. . . . I felt she deliberately created an atmosphere of the tough executive. There was no subtlety about her. Direct, blunt, she asked why I wanted to do this. She wanted to probe sufficiently without wasting time, to discover if I had any weaknesses and to what extent she and the movement could depend on me."[44] This woman, like most others, left the meeting with a sense of deep commitment not only to suffrage but to Alice Paul as well. Not only was she determined not to let suffrage down, but she was even more determined not to let Alice Paul down.

Paul was more concerned about enthusiasm for the movement than she was with an individual's specific talents.[45] Ardent feminism and unwavering adherence to Paul's vision and goals were the criteria for acceptance in those whom she entrusted responsibility. Class, social standing, education, or experience did not particularly concern her. Thus, although her organization, like most suffrage groups, was largely white and middle-class, dedication to feminism and not an elite status was the common bond.[46] At the same time, Paul harbored many of the same biases and prejudices associated with her elite, white, upper-middle-class milieu. Clearly, she was much more comfortable with people of her own background and status. She could speak with no self-consciousness of her desire to find a quiet secluded home where there were still "some American people left."[47] While she claimed long-standing friendships with both African-Americans and Jews, at the same time she had a reputation for particularly noticeable prejudices against both groups.[48] She was, in short, neither better nor worse than the society in which she lived.

Whatever the degree of her racism, Paul's relationship with African-Americans often had less to do with an established racial policy—either articulated or unarticulated—than it did with her perception at the moment of how her organization might be affected. Thus her actions were not always predictable. In 1913, one of her coworkers, Elsie Hill, then in charge of the College Suffrage League's contingent in the Washington suffrage parade, informed Paul that several delegations of white marchers contested the inclusion of representatives from Howard University, one of the nation's most prestigious black universities at that time. These white marchers, Hill reported, were threatening to boycott the parade if the black women were allowed to participate. In 1913, Paul could easily have resolved the problem by refusing the black women a place in the line of march, without fear of creating a larger problem. Racism, both openly virulent and covert, prevailed throughout the country. Theodore Roosevelt, the Progressive party candidate in the election of 1912, conducted a "Lily White" campaign in order to secure southern votes. And the newly elected Wilson administration inaugurated a policy of racial segregation in federal government agencies within months of taking over the Oval Office.[49] Like professional politicians, most suffrage leaders perceived a danger in alienating white legislators, voters, and real or potential supporters of their cause. The social climate that encouraged and fostered discriminatory behavior also dictated that, with few exceptions, African-Americans were not asked to attend or to speak at suffrage meetings in most sections of the country.[50] For these reasons then, Paul could have appeased the white marchers by disallowing the Howard women to march. Instead, she refused to pull them from the parade. And, to protect them from possible harrassment or worse, Paul ordered that they march between two groups of male participants. This solution apparently mollified the white complainers and ensured the safety of the black women.[51]

Ironically, long after the Nineteenth Amendment was ratified, when the objections of white potential suffrage supporters towards the inclusion of blacks would have carried much less weight, Paul took a less charitable stand. The event was the post-ratification meeting of the National Woman's Party, the political party founded by Alice Paul in 1916. The convention was billed as an opportunity to discuss issues facing women in the post-ratification era, as well as an opportunity to set the agenda for the NWP. For Paul personally, her goal was to bid farewell to her party in an atmosphere free of dissension and discord—Paul had announced that she was retiring from the NWP after the convention. A number of minority groups requested time to speak at the convention, including a coalition of black women's clubs, one of which was the National Association of Colored Women. In this case, Paul decided almost petulantly that "these people" were "harassing" her and that they were "spoilers."[52] She allowed the African-American women to speak, but she did not give them a prominent place, nor did she give them more than a few minutes to address the convention.

These decisions were arbitrarily made. Paul certainly possessed her own prejudices, but she did not attempt actively to enforce a policy as such, regarding either race or class. Rather, she utilized a pragmatic approach that offered solutions dependent upon her perception of the moment. Her own racism, of course, had to influence her perceptions. Sometimes her decisions coincided with the prevailing social mores; often they did not. But they were always made, she believed, with an eye on the long-range goal.

Paul was not an easy person to know. Her public persona was that of a professional organizer, an astute politician, a forceful leader. Her private persona was enigmatic at best. At a time when most women were "other directed," Paul apparently had made the ego-identity shift to an individualistic ethic necessary for development as a strong individual.[53] Never introspective, Paul applied her abilities to the task at hand with a cool measuredness and without emotionalism. Her intellectualism and purposefulness made her seem aloof, coldly efficient, and abrupt to the point of rudeness and insensitivity. Frequently, however, what was interpreted as insensitivity was really absentmindedness. When it was pointed out to her that a volunteer worker had left in anger because Paul had not adequately appreciated the woman's efforts, Paul made a point to express gratitude to other workers and even went so far as to apologize for uncommitted transgressions.[54]

Despite her refusal to dwell on adversity or obstacles, Paul was not immune to attacks leveled against both her and her organization. She never forgot an incident in 1914, just after she had embarked on her first anti–Democratic party campaign. She went to Mississippi to attend a conference with NAWSA and other suffrage groups. But rather than enjoy the camaraderie of her fellow suffragists, Paul was shunned by the other delegates. The profound sense of isolation that she experienced was still with her sixty years later. "I remember going down in the morning for breakfast, and here were all these people from all the different states in the Union, and I remember not one human being spoke to me. I just felt *such* an outcast, and for a long time we were regarded in that way."[55]

Although she had many devoted admirers and loyal coworkers and friends, Paul had few intimate, long-term relationships. Most of her close friends were women who worked with her in the American and international women's movements. Although she never married, she certainly had no conflicts with the institution of marriage.[56] Her closest friend throughout her long career was Elsie Hill, a Connecticut congressperson's daughter who came to work for Paul in 1913. They were immediately drawn to one another and worked together almost constantly from then on. Much later, after the deaths of Elsie's husband and Alice's sister Helen, with whom Alice had made her home in the 1940s, the two friends moved in together and continued working on women's issues until Elsie's death in the late 1960s.[57]

Recent scholarship suggests that some relationships between women reformers and activists during this period were also sexual relationships. There is no evidence to date that suggests that this was true of Paul's relationship with Hill. The lack of such evidence is not, in and of itself, enough to conclude that Paul did not engage in sexual relationships with women friends (or men, for that matter).[58] But in her private life, Paul was as conservative as she was radical in her public life. She never hesitated to censor coworkers or to monitor their behavior about even the pettiest matters. She refused, for example, to allow her workers to smoke in the main floor offices of the suffrage headquarters. Moreover, she prohibited smoking in the upstairs secluded rooms on occasions when important visitors were scheduled to be in the building.[59] On more substantive issues, such as birth control, abortion, and divorce, party workers clearly understood that they were not to express their own personal opinions. Paul went so far as to chastise members for making statements that she had not personally authorized.[60] Other issues took a back seat to suffrage, for Paul adamantly insisted that the organization stick to its single-issue framework. In many instances, this strategic and tactical stance was reinforced by her personal conservatism and sense of morality which, for example, prompted her to express disdain for persons who advocated the right to sexual preference.[61] There is no evidence, therefore no reason, to suggest that her private conduct contradicted her public statements.

The contours of Paul's private life suggest that she monitored her own actions as relentlessly as she governed her coworkers—surely a strange practice for an advocate of women's freedom. Her followers, however much they may have chafed under her tight rein, did not view her as arrogant, presumptive, or unfaithful to their cause—at least not until after suffrage had been passed and new political lines had to be drawn in the women's movement. Regardless of how her public image changed over time, Paul always maintained a larger vision, one that transcended her own conservatism: "I think if we get freedom for women, then they are probably going to do a lot of things that I wish they wouldn't do; but it seems to me that isn't our business to say what they should do with it. It is our business to see that they are free."[62]

Freedom, for Paul, extended beyond suffrage. Her goal was to remove all legal inequalities from the statute books throughout the country through passage of a federal Equal Rights Amendment (ERA). Such a goal was, and is, profoundly revolutionary in nature. Equal suffrage was the most radical demand of the nineteenth-century women's rights movement because it propelled women into the public sphere.[63] Just so, the struggle for equal rights in the twentieth century demanded a radical redefinition of power relationships, one directed primarily at the public sphere, but that also had important and unavoidable consequences for the private sphere.

But securing support for an Equal Rights Amendment in the 1920s proved to be more difficult than its advocates anticipated. Battle lines very quickly were drawn between those who believed in equality for everyone, with special treatment or special legislation for no one, regardless of sex, and those who believed that protective legislation was necessary for women and children, especially in the workplace. And, since every major women's organization with the exception of the Woman's Party favored protective legislation, it was clear to all by 1925 that the ERA would be at least as difficult to secure as suffrage had been.

Many members of the Woman's Party retired from political activism after suffrage was won, for a variety of reasons. Some were simply exhausted and wanted to resume normal lives again. Others, like Lucy Burns, were both tired and a little bitter towards those who had sat out the suffrage movement. "I don't want to do anything more," Burns announced. "I think we have done all this for women, and we have sacrificed everything we possessed for them, and now let them . . . fight for it. I am not going to fight anymore."[64] For a while, there was some doubt regarding the role Alice Paul would play in activist politics. After the suffrage amendment was ratified, one of her goals was to get a law degree, which she did. But she could no more disassociate herself from seeking justice and equality for women than she could take up needlepoint as a full-time occupation. As one Washington reporter later observed, "Every other woman in Washington I can imagine without a cause. . . . Even over teacups I think of [Paul] as a political force, a will bound to express itself politically."[65]

Paul continued to express her will politically. After launching the National Woman's Party on the ERA road, she went to Europe and helped to found the World Woman's Party. She had always voiced discontent over the exclusion of women from participating in the League of Nations. For over a decade, until the start of World War II, Paul stayed in Europe, lobbying the League of Nations and working to involve women in international politics. When she returned from Europe, Paul threw herself back into the American ERA campaign. She was also instrumental in having a reference to sex equality included in the preamble to the United Nations Charter.[66]

After more than a decade in Europe, Paul found many changes in the National Woman's Party. It was still dedicated to promoting the ERA and had accomplished a great deal in the intervening years by persuading almost every major women's organization to support the ERA. But not everyone was happy to see Paul return to Washington and the national headquarters. Many believed she was trying to pick up where she had left off and that it was an unfair usurpation of power since she had chosen to spend so much of her time in Europe. In the late 1940s, a power struggle for control of the Woman's Party took placed amidst unfounded accusations that Paul had misused organization funds. Throughout the remainder of her life, however, Paul remained a leader of the National Woman's Party and active in the causes near and dear to her heart. In 1968 and 1969, already nearing her eighty-fifth birthday, Paul was on the front lines in the antiwar marches, and she continued to lobby for the ERA until a stroke in 1974 incapacited her. Alice Paul died on July 10, 1977, believing that the ERA, then three states short of ratification, would very soon be the law of the land. That was not to be, but Alice Paul will always be associated with equal rights. Late in her life, assessing her own career, Paul concluded, "The thing I think that was the most useful thing I ever did was having a part in getting the vote for all women."[67]

Notes

[1]Anne Herendeen, "What the Hometown Thinks of Alice Paul," *Everybody's* (July 1916), pp. 1127–1128.

[2]Ernestine Evans, "Women in the Washington Scene," *Century Magazine* (Sept. 1923), pp. 507–517.

[3]Full suffrage states as of November 1912 were Wyoming (1890; territory, 1869) Colorado (1893) Utah and Idaho (1896), Washington (1910), California (1911), and Oregon, Arizona and Kansas (1912).

[4]Inez Haynes Irwin, *The Story of the Woman's Party* (New York: Harcourt, Brace, 1921), pp. 14–16.

[5]Mrs. Medill McCormick to Harriet Vittam, 31 July 1914, Papers of the National American Woman Suffrage Association, the Library of Congress (hereafter cited as NAWSA Papers). The emphasis in the quotation is McCormick's.

[6]Doris Stevens, *Jailed For Freedom* (New York: Boni & Liveright, 1920), p. 17.

[7]Maud Younger, quoted in Inez Haynes Irwin, *Up Hill with Banners Flying* (Penobscot, ME: Traversity Press, 1964), pp. 15–16.

[8]Lucy Burns, quoted in Ibid., p. 16.

[9]Conversations with Alice Paul: Woman Suffrage and the Equal Rights Amendment, interview by Amelia Frye, 1971–73, Suffragists Oral History Project, Bancroft Library, University of California at Berkeley (1976), pp. 1–5, 279–284 (hereafter cited as Paul Interview).

[10]Ibid., p. 6.

[11]Robert Gallagher, "I Was Arrested Of Course . . . ," *American Heritage* 25 (February 1974), pp. 17–18.

[12]Paul Interview, pp. 7–8.

[13]Herendeen, "What the Hometown Thinks," p. 1128.

[14]Paul Interview, pp. 7–8.

[15]"LMWW" to Alice Paul, 26 October 1914, The Papers of the National Woman's Party, 1913–1920, The Suffrage Years, Library of Congress, Washington, D.C. (hereafter cited as NWP Papers). The letter, from a friend of Paul's who knew the family quite well, reports on a running argument between Paul's uncle and a cousin who supported Paul's activity.

[16]Paul Interview, pp. 67–70.

[17]Ibid., p. 16.

[18]Mabel Vernon to Amelia Frye, "Mabel Vernon, Speaker for Suffrage and Petitioner for Peace," Berkeley Oral History Project, Bancroft Library, University of California, pp. 33–34 (hereafter cited as Vernon Interview).

[19]Paul Interview, p. 16.

[20]Inez Haynes Irwin, *Up Hill with Banners Flying* (Penobscot, ME: Traversity Press, 1964), p. 24.

[21]Paul Interview, p. 17.

[22]Ibid., pp. 17–18.

[23]Ibid., p. 31.

[24]Ibid., p. 20.

[25]Ibid., pp. 31a, 34.

[26]Suffrage Scrapbooks, vol. 1, pp. 80, 95, Sophia Smith Collection, Smith College, Northampton, MA.

[27]"Lucy Burns," *Notable American Women: A Biographical Dictionary,* Edward L. James, et al., eds. (Cambridge, MA, and London: The Belknap Press of Harvard University, 1971–1980), vol. 4, pp. 124–125; also, Irwin, *Up Hill with Banners Flying,* pp. 14–18.

[28]Paul Interview, p. 48.

[29]Irwin, *The Story of the Woman's Party,* p. 16.

[30]Vernon Interview, pp. 35–36.

[31]Paul Interview, p. 47.

[32]Irwin, *The Story of the Woman's Party,* p. 16.

[33]Paul Interview, pp. 225–227; Irwin, *Up Hill with Banners Flying,* p. 18.

[34]Ibid., p. 18.

[35]Max Weber, *The Sociology of Religion* (London: Methuen, 1965), pp. 45–59.

[36]Irwin, *Up Hill with Banners Flying,* p. 26.

[37]See, for example, newspaper coverage in the *New York Times,* 4–6 March 1913.

[38]*New York Times,* 23 June and 7 and 8 July 1917; also *Washington Post,* 23, June 24, 7 July 1917.

[39]See, for example, Aileen Kraditor, *Ideas of the Woman Suffrage Movement, 1890–1920* (New York: Anchor Books, 1970); Eleanor Flexner, *Century of Struggle: The Woman's Rights Movement in the United States* (Cambridge, MA: The Belknap Press of Harvard University, 1975); and Anne Firor Scott and Andrew Scott, eds., *One Half the People: The Fight for Woman Suffrage* (Philadelphia: Lippincott, 1975).

[40]Foremost among historians who apply this interpretation to Paul is William O'Neill, *Everyone Was Brave: The Rise and Fall of Feminism in America* (Chicago: Quadrangle Books, 1969); and *The Woman Movement: Feminism in the United States and England* (Chicago: Quadrangle Books, 1969); and Robert Riegel, *American Feminism* (Lawrence, KS: University of Kansas Press, 1963).

[41]S. N. Eisenstadt, ed., *Max Weber on Charisma and Institution Building* (Chicago: University of Chicago Press, 1968), pp. xxiii–xxvi.

[42]In her interview with Amelia Frye, Paul, on several occasions, expressed wonderment over, for example, the reason why the Pankhursts singled her out of the hundreds of WSPU members and invested responsibility in her. She was inclined to attribute it more to the fact that she was an American

and therefore more noticeable than to the fact that people were drawn to her because of her charismatic personality.

[43]*Biographical Cyclopedia of American Women*, p. 125.

[44]Rebecca Hourwich Reyher to Amelia Frye, "Rebecca Hourwich Reyher: Search and Struggle for Equality and Independence," Suffragists Oral History Project, Bancroft Library, University of California at Berkeley (1977), pp. 45–50 (hereafter cited as Reyher Interview).

[45]Paul Interview, p. 189.

[46]Ibid., pp. 183–189.

[47]Ibid., p. 11.

[48]Vernon Interview, pp. 157–158; Frieda Kirchwey, "Alice Paul Pulls the Strings," *The Nation* (March 1921), p. 332.

[49]Arthur S. Link, "Theodore Roosevelt and the South in 1912," *North Carolina Historical Review* (July 1946), pp. 313–324, and "Correspondence Relating to the Progressive Party's 'Lily White' Policy in 1912," *Journal of Southern History* (November 1944), pp. 480–490; Nancy J. Weiss, "The Negro and the New Freedom: Fighting Wilsonian Segregation," *Political Science Quarterly* (March 1969), pp. 61–79; Christine A. Lunardini, "Standing Firm: William Monroe Trotter's Meetings with Woodrow Wilson, 1913–1914," *Journal of Negro History* (Summer 1979), pp. 244–264.

[50]Rebecca Hourwich Reyher: Search and Struggle for Equality and Independence. Interview conducted by Amelia R. Frye and Fenn Ingersoll, Suffragists Oral History Project, University of California at Berkeley (1971), pp. 61–62.

[51]Paul Interview pp. 132–133.

[52]Kirchwey, "Alice Paul Pulls the Strings," *Nation*, p. 332.

[53]Phyllis Chesler, *Women and Madness* (Garden City, NY: Doubleday, 1972), pp. 299–300.

[54]Irwin, *The Story of the Woman's Party*, pp. 14–15.

[55]Paul Interview, p. 110. The emphasis is Paul's.

[56]Ibid., pp. 267–272.

[56]Ibid., p. 250.

[58]Carroll Smith-Rosenberg, "The Female World of Love and Ritual: The Relations between Women in the Nineteenth-Century America," in Nancy Cott and Elizabeth Pleck, eds., *A Heritage of Her Own* (New York: Simon & Schuster, 1979), pp. 311–342; Blanche Weisen Cook, "Female Support Networks and Political Activism: Lillian Wald, Crystal Eastman, and Emma Goldman," Ibid., pp. 412–444.

[59]Reyher Interview, pp. 65–66.

[60]Dora Lewis to Alice Paul, 14 July 1916; Paul to Lewis, 25 July 1916, NWP Papers.

[61]Paul Interview, pp. 195–196.

[62]Ibid., p. 196.

[63]Ellen Carol DuBois, *Feminism and Suffrage: The Emergence of an Independent Women's Movement in America, 1848–1869* (Ithaca, NY: Cornell University Press, 1978), pp. 15–20.

[64]Paul Interview, p. 257; *Notable American Women*, Vol 4, pp. 124–125.

[65]Ernestine Evans, "Women in the Washington Scene," *Century Magazine*, CVL (September 1923), p. 514.

[66]Ibid., p. 514; *New York Times*, 10 July 1977, p. 42.

[67]Ibid., Paul Interview, p. 42.

PART VII

New Horizons

Following World War I, the business boom in America signaled an era of unprecedented economic speculation. The era was short-lived, however. The stockmarket crash in October 1929 initiated a traumatic shift for all Americans and ushered in the Great Depression. Popular perceptions of women's roles transformed dramatically within a period of a few years. As Americans were thrown into the business of survival and recovery, feminist demands took a backseat to larger economic concerns.

By 1933, over 25 percent of American workers were unemployed. But it was not only the unemployed who feared for their futures: hundreds of thousands of middle-class Americans found wages cut and job "security" threatened. Attitudes toward women's participation in the labor force were affected by these setbacks. Women out in the wage-earning economy—except female heads of household—were branded as barriers to full economic recovery. President Franklin D. Roosevelt's "New Deal," a myriad of platforms and agencies for economic recovery, instituted new government employment programs, many of which included women. Even a feminist leader such as Frances Perkins, who became the first woman to hold a cabinet post when she was appointed Secretary of Labor in 1933, was forced to denounce the "pin-money worker," the housewife who allegedly worked outside the home for petty cash to purchase luxury items.

The National Economy Act of 1933 forced many women out of the civil service by banning both spouses from working for the government. Three-fourths of the spouses who resigned, generally the lower paid of the couple, were women. Members of the League of Women Voters (the post-suffrage heir of the National American Woman Suffrage Association) supported this move: "We of the League are very much for the rights of women, but we are not feminists primarily; we are citizens." But many New Deal feminists, Eleanor Roosevelt among them, condemned this policy.

Public opinion and policy discriminated against women despite feminist opposition. Private businesses tried to keep women from competing with men for positions. The American Federation of Labor (AFL), the largest and most powerful union in its day, declared that married female workers with employed husbands should be banned from employment. Even women's colleges discouraged their graduates from taking paying jobs, trying to renew interest in the nineteenth-century ethic of domestic feminism. Married women were told they should volunteer their labor to do social housekeeping within their communities. Government policy and media campaigns worked well. By 1936, a Gallup poll found that 82 percent of all Americans believed that wives should not work if husbands were employed, and 75 percent of the women polled echoed this sentiment.

The depression affected nearly all aspects of American women's lives. The marriage rate dipped and the birth rate was in long-term decline, with 1933 as the nadir year. Birth control clinics grew during this period, not because of feminist demands, but because of the simple need to limit the number of mouths to be fed in a period of economic deprivation and instability. Feminists tried to push birth control into New Deal programs, but Congress resisted. Finally, reformers were able to win victories in the courts, with the result that doctors could distribute birth control information and devices unless prohibited by state law.

Women's roles in the marketplace changed as well as their family expectations. Rather than being conspicuous consumers of goods, women were expected to become thrifty and enterprising producers for the household. Wives hoped to save their husband's hard-earned cash for those essential goods that could not be provided by female domestic labor. Home industry replaced smart buying in advice columns in women's magazines. Eleanor Roosevelt provided special "White House menus" to spur homemakers into making more nutritious and thrifty meals. Some women transformed this new ideology into more activist roles by forming housewives' associations and women's groups committed to public housing.

Some scholars have found that the only women whose lives did not alter dramatically were the very rich or the very poor. Women in poverty in the South shared lives much like those of their mothers and grandmothers. They worked by their husbands' sides in the fields, tended large families, and were saddled with harsh household labor; they had only outdoor plumbing and primitive fuel supplies. Nevertheless, the depression could and did increase the number of hardships endured by rural families. Perhaps the decline of male status within society gave women the opportunity to demonstrate their enormous reserves of strength, while men crumpled under the weight of economic burdens. Women often held families together. Massive migrations wreaked havoc with family stability when thousands of farmers from the Dust Bowl ("Okies," as they were called) moved westward to California or other more prosperous states. Rural mothers resolutely tried to keep kinfolk fed and clothed and housed despite mighty challenges. Women did not welcome these opportunities, but met them with a courage that enhanced their family roles, a theme exemplified in John Steinbeck's classic novel, *The Grapes of Wrath.*

Another group of poor women who found its lot worsened was factory workers. While the closing of immigration in the 1920s should have created better conditions for industrial workers (by shutting the door on cheaper labor flowing into the marketplace), worse ones prevailed. Women found themselves working for reduced wages. Further, employers introduced the abusive "apprentice system" and hired apprentices (providing them with room and board but no pay) during a speedup, then fired them when orders were met. These and other hardships drove women into increasing labor militance. Women's roles in unionization drives were enhanced, given a boost by the National Industrial Recovery Act of 1933, which specifically guaranteed workers' rights to organize. Although women had been given the cold shoulder by the AFL (mainly craft and other skilled labor unions), they were warmly welcomed into the more accessible Congress of Industrial Organization (CIO) in 1938. The CIO was interested in organizing all workers, including the unskilled, and profited from mass-production industries such as textiles and auto manufacturing. Women were prominent in strike organization, "with babies and banners," walking on picket lines in the 1937 Chicago Republic Steel plant strike and organizing an Emergency Brigade in Flint, Michigan, during strikes at auto factories. By 1940, over 800,000 women were union members, tripling their participation since 1933.

Other groups, noting women's labor activism, began to draw women into their movements. Communist Party organizers were able to promise a greater equality for women within political organizations—something democratic and union leaders were unable to deliver. One woman who joined the Communist Party was Elizabeth Gurley Flynn, who began her activist career as a socialist and joined the International Workers of the World (IWW, known as "the Wobblies") in 1906. Helping organize the 1912 Lawrence, Massachusetts textile strike and the 1913 Paterson, New Jersey strike, she also spearheaded organizing in 1916 at the Mesabi Range in Minnesota. In 1917, Flynn and 168 fellow Wobblies were indicted for violation of the Espionage Act of 1917. Her legal defense activities led her to help found the American Civil Liberties Union in 1920, an organization from which, ironically, she was expelled when she joined the American Communist Party in 1937. She later headed the Party after serving time in jail for dissident activity. Although few women threw themselves so wholeheartedly into Communist activities, Flynn was one of thousands of young women who experimented with radical politics during the Depression decade.

Just as the Depression had given rise to a new ideological ethos for women, so the outbreak of World War II and America's entry into the war in December 1941 introduced yet another reshaping of concepts of ideal womanhood. The national emergency demanded women's mobilization as well as men's. The number of women in the wage-earning force increased by 57 percent during the war. Over 6 million women who had never worked for wages before took jobs, married women's labor force participation doubled, and unions gained 2.2 million women in a matter of four years. Not all of this was achieved without resistance, however. At the outset, most male managers were reluctant to employ women in all aspects of the defense industry, citing, for example, "the lack of adequate toilet facilities" as an excuse for not hiring women. But reservations were abandoned by necessity within the first year of war production. During the war, 60 percent of those polled in a Gallup canvass supported wives working in the war industry. The shift in perception from the Depression ethic was rapid and widespread.

American women, wooed with "Commando Mary" and "Rosie the Riveter" and other propaganda, responded positively to the call. Such campaigns were in no way linked to sexual egalitarianism nor feminism, but women were often exploited despite the fact that they were doing a "man's job." Employers hoped to maintain rigid gender roles despite women's massive participation in the war industries, and despite men and women's working side by side with little differentiation except pay. Although the National War Labor Board mandated equal pay for equal work, the government allowed job classifications which provided *de facto* separate pay scales for men and women. However, women complained little because the wages they received in the war industry were superior to any they might earn in the other sectors of the economy.

Further, the government response to the needs of mothers with federally funded daycare programs was feeble. In 1943 the Lanham Act provided for child care centers, but so few were built that only one in ten defense workers could take advantage of these facilities. Despite its limited effectiveness, this brief experiment served as an example for a future generation: with safe and inexpensive child care support, mothers might be vital contributors to the national economy. The unsolicited opportunities of wartime production offered women the means of balancing household responsibilities and wage-earning roles.

One group of women who had been balancing work and family for centuries, African-American women, improved their status as well. At the outbreak of war, almost three-fourths of African-American women wage-earners were employed as domestic servants. They were virtually excluded from clerical and retail positions outside the black community and they were discriminated against as factory operators. By 1944, this proportion was reduced by one-third as the number of African-American women working in factories grew to nearly 20 percent. This did not, however, represent status or wage equality. Indeed, black women testified that segregation of tasks was common in factories. White women were given jobs that were "cleaner" or "more skilled." Often, however, crunches on the assembly line inadvertently created the breakdown of barriers erected by prejudice. Although this did not signal a change in attitude, it gave African-American women opportunities for service and achievement—as well as disproving racist theories of inferiority.

The media worked to recreate women's images during both the Depression and the war. Government propaganda and advertising were central factors in dictating what roles women would have in the work force, and during the war, in shaping women's self-images: soap ads featured women with blow torches and coveralls and posters highlighted stenographers in uniform as "secretaries of war." A larger role in shaping women's self-images was played by an increasingly powerful medium: American movies. During the 1930s, film audiences included millions of young women seeking role models in the parade of stars. Film magazines and movies themselves refined and shaped star images and the models of womanhood to which many American women aspired.

During the early years of filmmaking, two separate screen images dominated—the virgin and the vamp. Mary Pickford, the most successful female film star of her day, typified the former. She was forced to play the role of a child onscreen until she was well past the age of thirty. Pickford's image was wedded to the American ideal of healthy, wholesome, and, above all, innocent beauty. The first Miss America, Margaret Gorman, chosen at a pageant dreamed up by Atlantic City promoters in the 1920s, bore a striking resemblance to Pickford.

A contrasting screen idol was embodied in the character of the vamp, an image that Theda Bara popularized during the silent film era. Eye makeup created for Bara by Helena Rubenstein was mass marketed, and the connection between movies and fashion flourished. Gloria Swanson, Marlene Dietrich, and Greta Garbo played variations of the vamp. It was no accident that many of these "exotic" roles were portrayed by foreign women imported for American audiences. The screen siren, although alluring, often met with tragic consequences to reinforce the values stamped on the American screen by Pickford and her celluloid descendants. The *femme fatale* character did not empower women in any real sense and nearly all these seductresses pursued a goal similar to that of their virginal sisters in film: a man.

During the 1930s, however, female film stars played a wider range of roles, and many more assertive and independent models emerged. The spunk and savvy demeanors of women played by Irene Dunne, Jean Arthur, and Myrna Loy paved the way for a stronger breed of screen women. Even the stars of comedies were able to create more daring roles: Carole Lombard transformed the "dizzy" blonde into her own intelligent brand of femininity and Claudette Colbert plunged zestfully into sexual banter, often besting her man. Although Jean Harlow may have been exploited as a "sex goddess" (and indeed led a tragic personal life before her premature death at twenty-nine), her screen characters projected more complexity than the one-dimensional women studio publicists tried to portray. Mae West, who by 1935 was earning over $480,000 per year, transformed the image of the sex symbol into much more than Hollywood bargained for when her tough-talking, wise-cracking characters projected power as well as appeal.

West was but one of a generation of women in Hollywood who began to command respect as well as shape ideals for an eager female audience. Others included Rosalind Russell, Bette Davis, Joan Crawford, and Katharine Hepburn. Hepburn was born into a socially prominent family in Connecticut, and her mother was a birth control crusader with Margaret Sanger, the most prominent twentieth century advocate of birth control. Hepburn attended Bryn Mawr before going on the stage in 1928 and began her film career in 1932. Hepburn has won four Academy Awards, but is perhaps best remembered for some of her dozen film collaborations with Spencer Tracy, classics such as *Woman of the Year*, in which she portrayed an outstanding woman journalist, *Pat and Mike*, in which she played a woman athlete, and *Adam's Rib*, where her portrait of a lawyer entangled in a "battle of the sexes" with her husband and courtroom adversary includes one of the most sophisticated treatments of feminism on the screen.

The rapid proliferation of opportunities for women on screen during the 1930s and 1940s reflected changes within society as a whole. Female journalists were gaining prominence and influence, as the careers of Dorothy Thompson, foreign correspondent-columnist, and Dorothy Day, founder of the *Catholic Worker*, demonstrate. Photographers Margaret Bourke-White and Dorothea Lange captured the American public's imagination, as well as bringing national and international events into dramatic visual focus. Mildred Ella (Babe) Didrickson became an Olympic gold medalist before becoming a professional golfer, and African-American Althea Gibson, a tennis star, was treated to a ticker-tape parade in New York City when she returned triumphant from Wimbledon in 1957, having won both the singles and the doubles titles. Female scholars such as anthropologist Margaret Mead and biologist Rachel Carson, whose *Silent Spring* stirred a generation into ecological awareness, began to have a wider impact on society. Artists such as Georgia O'Keeffe may not have garnered the critical attention and wide audience of their male counterparts, but their work would influence the art world and reshape perspectives on cultural aesthetics with the advent of the feminist renaissance in the 1960s.

The women of the generation between the World Wars found themselves caught within several snares. Many fought to fulfill the competing ideals ushered in by each new decade. Some struggled to hold the ground hard won by an earlier generation. Some women saw not a recycling of patterns but innovative and pioneering transformations—changes that might make a permanent difference in women's experiences. During this important era the majority of women looked to new horizons—new role models, images, and opportunities—to have greater control over their own lives and greater influence over the lives of others.

Eleanor Roosevelt
(1884–1962)

William H. Chafe

Eleanor Roosevelt was born October 11, 1884. Educated privately, in her youth she combined an upper-class social whirl with great interest in "social housekeeping," working for the National Consumers' League and at a New York settlement house. She married her cousin, Franklin Delano Roosevelt, in 1905; they had six children between 1906 and 1916. During World War I and the 1920s Eleanor Roosevelt emerged in the public world of reform politics. For the rest of her life she was an important leader in putting the concerns of working-class women, of African-Americans, of the poor, and of the politically oppressed worldwide, onto America's national political agenda. She did so only in part through her relationship with her husband, who was president from 1933 until 1945. While she always had an unprecedently equal working relationship with FDR, Eleanor Roosevelt established a separate living space for herself at Hyde Park, called Val-Kill, in 1926. After FDR's death in 1945, Roosevelt continued to campaign for social justice through her writings, speeches, and as the U.S. delegate to the United Nations. She maintained a deep involvement in the reform wing of the Democratic party until her death on November 7, 1962.

Anna Eleanor Roosevelt was born in New York City on October 11, 1884, the first child and only daughter of Elliott Roosevelt and Anna (Hall) Roosevelt. Descended on both sides from distinguished colonial families active in commerce, banking, and politics, she seemed destined to enjoy all the benefits of class and privilege. Yet by the time she was ten, both her parents had died, as had a younger brother Elliott, leaving her and her second brother Hall the only survivors.

As a youngster, Eleanor experienced emotional rejection almost from the time she could remember. "I was a solemn child," she recalled, "without beauty. I seemed like a little old woman entirely lacking in the spontaneous joy and mirth of youth." Her mother called her "Granny" and, at least in Eleanor's memory, treated her daughter differently than her son, warmly embracing the boy while being only "kindly and indifferent" to her little girl. From most of her family, young Eleanor received the message that she was "very plain," almost ugly, and certainly "old fashioned." When her parents died, she went to live with her grandmother, who was equally without warmth. As Eleanor's cousin Corinne later remarked, "it was the grimmest childhood I had ever known. Who did she have? Nobody."

In fact, Eleanor had one person—her father. "He was the one great love of my life as a child," she later wrote, "and . . . like many children, I have lived a dream life with him." Described by his friends as "charming, impetuous, high-spirited, big-hearted, generous, [and] friendly," Elliott exhibited ease and grace in his social interactions. With Eleanor, he developed an intimacy that seemed almost magical. "As soon as I could talk," she recalled, "I went into his dressing room every morning and chattered to him . . . I even danced with him, intoxicated by the pure joy of motion . . . until he would pick me up and throw me into the air." She dreamed of the time when they would go off together—"always he and I . . . and someday [we] would have a life of our own together."

But Elliott's capacity for ebullient play and love also contained the seeds of self-destruction—alcoholism, irresponsibility, cruelty. He never found an anchor, either in public life or business, to provide stability for himself and his family. Elliott's emotional imbalance quickly produced problems in his marriage and banishment from the household. The last four years of his life were like a roller coaster. Elliott nourished the emotional relationship with Eleanor through letters to "father's own little Nell," writing of "the wonderful long rides . . . through the grand snow-clad forests, over the white hills" that he wanted them to enjoy together. But when his long-awaited visits occurred, they often ended in disaster, as when Elliott left Eleanor with the doorman at New York's Knickerbocker Club, promising to return but going off on a drunken spree instead. The pain of betrayal was exceeded only by Eleanor's depth of love for the man she believed was "the only person who really cared." Looking back later in life for an explanation of her inability to express emotions spontaneously, she concluded that the trauma of her childhood was the main cause. "Something locked me up," she wrote.

After her father's death, an emotional void pervaded Eleanor's life until, at age fourteen, she enrolled in Allenswood, a girls' school outside London presided over by Marie Souvestre, daughter of a well-known French philosopher and radical. At Allenswood, the girl found a circle of warmth and support. "She was beloved by everybody," her cousin remarked. "Saturdays we were allowed a sortie in Putney which has stores where you could buy books, [and] flowers. Young girls had crushes and you left [gifts] in the room with the girl you were idolizing. Eleanor's room every Saturday would be full of flowers because she was so admired." Allenswood also provided educational inspiration. Souvestre passionately embraced unpopular causes, staunchly defending Dreyfus in France and the cause of the Boers in South Africa. "I consider the three years which I spent with her as the beginning of an entirely new outlook on life," Eleanor wrote. Marie Souvestre toured the continent with the girl, confiding in her and expressing the affection that made it possible for Eleanor to flower. Describing her stay at Allenswood as "the happiest years of my life," Eleanor noted that "whatever I have become since had its seeds in those three years of contact with a liberal mind and strong personality." The love and admiration were mutual. "I miss you every day of my life," Souvestre wrote her in 1902.

The imprint of Marie Souvestre was not lost when Eleanor returned to the United States at age seventeen to "come out" in New York society. Even in the rush of parties and dances, she kept her eye on the more serious world of ideas and social service. Souvestre had written her in 1901: "Even when success comes, as I'm sure it will, bear in mind that there are more quiet and enviable joys than to be among the most sought-after women at a ball." Heeding the injunction, Eleanor plunged into settlement-house work and social activism.

Much of Eleanor Roosevelt's subsequent political life can be traced to this early involvement with social reform. At age eighteen she joined the National Consumers' League, headed by Florence Kelley. The league was committed to securing health and safety for workers—especially women—in clothing factories and sweatshops. On visits to these workplaces, Eleanor learned firsthand the misery of the working poor and developed a lifelong commitment to their needs. At the same time, she joined the Junior League and commenced work at the Rivington Street Settlement House, where she taught calisthenics and dancing and witnessed both the deprivation of the poor and the courage of slum dwellers who sought to improve their lot. Eleanor discovered that she preferred social work to debutante parties. More and more, she came to be recognized as a key member of a network of social reformers in New York City.

At the same time, however, Eleanor was secretly planning to marry her cousin Franklin Roosevelt, an event that would be followed by a fifteen-year hiatus in her public activities. Like his godfather (Eleanor's father), Franklin was "a gay cavalier," spontaneous, warm, and gregarious. But unlike Elliott, Franklin also possessed good sense and singleness of purpose. Eleanor saw in him the spark of life that she remembered from her father. After their engagement, she even sent to Franklin a letter signed "little Nell," her father's favorite name for her. Franklin, in turn, saw in Eleanor the discipline that would curb his own instincts toward excess.

After their marriage on March 17, 1905, the young Roosevelts settled in New York City while Franklin finished his law studies at Columbia. Franklin's mother, Sara, had warned Eleanor that she should not continue her work at the settlement house because she might bring home the diseases of the slum, but soon Eleanor was preoccupied with other concerns. Within a year, Anna was born (1906), then the next year James (1907), and two years later Franklin. Although Eleanor cherished her children, it was not a happy time. Sara dominated the household and imposed her will on almost all issues, including the raising of the children. As Eleanor later recalled, her mother-in-law "wanted . . . to hold onto Franklin and his children; she wanted them to grow up as she wished. As it turned out, Franklin's children were more my mother-in-law's children than they were mine." Nor was Sara's possessiveness limited to the children. At the family estate at Hyde Park, she was in total control. At dinner, Franklin sat at one end of the table, his mother at the other, and Eleanor in the middle. Before the fireplace there were two wing chairs, one for the mother, the other for the son. Eleanor was like an uninvited guest.

Fearing that she would hurt Franklin and lose his affection, Eleanor did not rebel. But she did experience a profound sense of inadequacy about her abilities as a wife and mother. Daughter Anna described her mother as unpredictable and inconsistent with the children, sweet one moment, critical and demanding the next. "Mother was always stiff, never relaxed enough to romp . . . Mother loved all mankind, but she did not know how to let her children love her." Eleanor herself recognized the problem. "It did not come naturally to me to understand little children or to enjoy them," she later said. "Playing with children was difficult for me because play had not been an important part of my own childhood." Instead of comforting the children when they experienced pain, she urged upon them an attitude of stoicism and endurance, as if to say that expressing emotion was a sign of bad character. The death of her third child, Franklin, a few months after his birth only reinforced Eleanor's unhappiness and feeling of inadequacy. Three additional children were born in the next six years— Elliott in 1910, Franklin in 1914, and John in 1916. Eleanor was devoted to each, yet motherhood could not be fulfilling in a household ruled by a grandmother who referred to the children as "my children . . . your mother only bore you."

In the years between 1910 and the beginning of World War I, Eleanor Roosevelt's activities revolved more and more around Franklin's growing political career. Elected as the Democratic assemblyman from Dutchess County in 1910, he rapidly became a leader of insurgent anti-Tammany forces in Albany. In 1913 Franklin was appointed assistant secretary of the Navy, and Eleanor, in addition to managing a large household, became expert at hosting the multiple social events required of a subcabinet member, as well as moving the entire household at least twice each year—to Campobello in New Brunswick during the summer, then to Hyde Park and back to Washington. During these years, she fulfilled the many traditionally female social activities expected of her.

America's entry into World War I in 1917 provided the occasion for Eleanor to reassert the public side of her personality. As her biographer Joseph Lash has noted, "the war gave her a reason acceptable to her conscience to free herself of the social duties that she hated, to concentrate less on her household, and to plunge into work that fitted her aptitude." She rose at 5 a.m. to coordinate activities at the Union Station canteen for soldiers on their way to training camps, took charge of Red Cross activities, supervised the knitting rooms at the Navy department, and spoke at patriotic rallies. Her interest in social welfare led to her drive to improve conditions at St. Elizabeth's mental hospital, while her sensitivity to suffering came forth in the visits she paid to wounded soldiers. "[My son] always loved to see you come in," one mother wrote. "You always brought a ray of sunshine."

The war served as a transition for Eleanor's reemergence as a public personality during the 1920s. After Franklin's unsuccessful campaign for the vice-presidency on James Cox's ticket in 1920, the Roosevelts returned to New York where Eleanor became active in the League of Women Voters. At the time of her marriage, she had opposed suffrage, thinking it inconsistent with women's proper role; now, as coordinator of the league's legislative program, she kept track of bills that came before the Albany legislature, drafted laws providing for equal representation for men and women, and worked with Esther Lape and Elizabeth Read on the league's lobbying activities. In 1921 she also joined the Women's Trade Union League—then viewed as "left-leaning"—and found friends there as well as political allies. In addition to working for programs such as the regulation of maximum hours and minimum wages for women, Eleanor helped raise funds for the WTUL headquarters in New York City. Her warm ties to first- and second-generation immigrants like Rose Schneiderman and Maud Swartz highlighted how far Eleanor had moved from the upper-class provincialism of her early years.

When Franklin was paralyzed by polio in 1922, Eleanor's public life expanded still further: she now became her husband's personal representative in the political arena. With the aid of Louis Howe, Franklin's political mentor and her own close friend, Eleanor first mobilized Dutchess County women, then moved on to the state Democratic party, organizing all but five counties by 1924. "Organization," she noted, "is something to which [the men] are always ready to take off their hats." No one did the job better. Leading a delegation to the Democratic convention in 1924, she fought (unsuccessfully) for equal pay legislation, the child labor amendment, and other planks endorsed by women reformers.

By 1928, Eleanor Roosevelt had clearly become a political leader in her own right. Once just a "political wife," she gradually extended that role and used it as a vehicle for asserting her own personality and agenda. In 1928, as head of the national women's campaign for the Democratic party, she made sure that the party appealed to independent voters, to minorities, and to women. She was also instrumental in securing the appointment of Frances Perkins as commissioner of industrial relations in New York after Franklin had been elected governor there. Dictating as many as one hundred letters a day, speaking to countless groups, acting as an advocate of social reform and women's issues, she had become a political personality of the first rank.

Eleanor Roosevelt's talent for combining partisan political activity with devotion to social welfare causes made her the center of an ever-growing female reform network. Her associates included Marion Dickerman and Nancy Cook, former suffragists and Democratic party loyalists; Molly Dewson, a longtime research secretary of the National Consumers League; and Mary Dreier of the Women's Trade Union League. She walked on picket lines with Rose Schneiderman, edited the *Women's Democratic News,* and advised the League of Women Voters on political tactics. Her political sophistication grew. "To many women, and I am one of them," she noted, "it is difficult to care enough [about an issue] to cause disagreement or unpleasant feelings, but I have come to the conclusion that this must be done for a time so we can prove our strength and demand respect for our wishes." By standing up for women in politics, ER provided a model for others to follow. In the process, she also earned the admiring, if grudging, respect of men who recognized a superb organizer when they saw one.

During the 1932 campaign, which led to Franklin's election to the presidency, Eleanor coordinated the activities of the Women's Division of the Democratic National Committee. Working with Mary (Molly) W. Dewson, she mobilized thousands of women precinct workers to carry the party's program to local voters; for example, the women distributed hundreds of thousands of "rainbow fliers," colorful sheets containing facts on the party's approach to various issues. After the election, Molly Dewson took charge of the Women's Division, corresponding daily with Eleanor both about appointing women to office and securing action on issues that would appeal to minorities, women, and such professional groups as educators and social workers. The two friends were instrumental in bringing to Washington an unprecedented number of dynamic women activists. Ellen Woodward, Hilda Worthington Smith, and Florence Kerr all held executives offices in the Works Progress Administration, while Lorena Hickok acted as eyes and ears for WPA director Harry Hopkins as she traveled across the country to observe the impact of the New Deal's relief program. Mary Anderson, director of the Women's Bureau, recalled that women government officials had formerly dined together in a small university club. "Now," she said, "there are so many of them that we need a hall."

Eleanor Roosevelt not only provided the impetus for appointing these women but also offered a forum for transmitting their views and concerns across the country. Soon after she entered the White House, she began a series of regular press conferences to which *only* women reporters were admitted, and where the first lady insisted on making "hard" news as well as providing social tidbits for the "women's page." She introduced such women as Mary McLeod Bethune and Hilda Worthington Smith to talk about their work with the New Deal. These sessions provided new status and prestige for the female press corps and they also underlined the importance of women's issues to the first lady. Her efforts helped create a community of women reporters and government workers. When the all-male Gridiron Club held its annual dinner to spoof the president and his male colleagues, the first lady initiated a Gridiron Widows' Club where the women in Washington could engage in their own satire.

Largely as a result of ER's activities, women achieved a strong voice in the New Deal. The proportion of women appointed as post-masters shot up from 17.6 percent in 1930 to 26 percent between 1932 and 1938. More important, the social welfare policies of the administration reflected a reform perspective that women like Ellen Woodward and Florence Kerr shared with men like Harry Hopkins and Aubrey Williams. When a particularly difficult issue involving women came up, the first lady would invite Molly Dewson to the White House and seat her next to the president, where she could persuade him of her point of view. ER's own political role appears most clearly in her work on the reelection drive of 1936, when she coordinated the efforts of both men and women and used the "educational" approach developed by the Women's Division in 1932 as a major campaign weapon. More than sixty thousand women precinct workers canvassed the electorate, handing out "rainbow fliers" as the party's principal literature. For the first time women received equal representation on the Democratic Platform Committee, an event described by the *New York Times* as "the biggest coup for women in years."

Eleanor Roosevelt's fear that she would have no active role as a presidential wife had been unfounded. She toured the country repeatedly, surveying conditions in the coal mines, visiting relief projects, and speaking out for the human rights of the disadvantaged. Through her newspaper column "My Day," she entered the homes of millions. Her radio programs, her lectures, and her writings communicated to the country her deep compassion for those who suffered. At the White House, in turn, she acted as advocate of the poor and disenfranchised. "No one who ever saw Eleanor Roosevelt sit down facing her husband," Rexford Tugwell wrote, "and holding his eyes firmly, [and saying] to him 'Franklin, I think you should' . . . or, 'Franklin surely you will not' . . . will ever forget the experience. . . . It would be impossible to say how often and to what extent American governmental processes have been turned in a new direction because of her determination." She had become, in the words of columnist Raymond Clapper, a "Cabinet Minister without portfolio—the most influential woman of our times."

But if Eleanor had achieved an unparalleled measure of political influence, it was in place of, rather than because of, an intimate personal relationship with Franklin. In 1932 Eleanor described a perfect couple as one where two people did not even need to tell each other how they felt, but cared so much that a look and the sound of a voice would tell all. Probably at no time after their first few years together did Franklin and Eleanor achieve that degree of intimacy. Not only was Sara still a dominant presence, but Franklin had embarked on his own interests and enthusiasms, often different from Eleanor's. The differences in their temperaments became a permanent barrier that tormented their relationship. He loved to party; she held back and frowned on his willingness to "let go." In a letter to her daughter Anna from Warm Springs in 1934, Eleanor declared that she "always felt like a spoil-sport and policeman here. . . . I'm an idiotic puritan and I wish I had the right kind of sense of humor and could enjoy certain things. At least, thank God, none of you children have inherited that streak in me."

During the years he was assistant secretary of the Navy, Franklin acted more frequently on his fun-loving instincts. "He deserved a good time," Eleanor's cousin Alice Roosevelt acidly noted, "he was married to Eleanor." A frequent companion on Franklin's pleasurable excursions was Lucy Mercer, Eleanor's social secretary. Over time, the relationship between Lucy and Franklin became intimate, particularly during the summers when Eleanor was absent from Campobello. After Franklin was stricken with pneumonia in the fall of 1918, Eleanor discovered letters between Franklin and Lucy describing their affair. Although Franklin refused Eleanor's offer of divorce, and Sara engineered an agreement for them to stay together if Franklin stopped seeing Lucy, their marriage would never again achieve the magical possibility of being "for life, for death," one where a word or look would communicate everything. In the wake of the Mercer affair, James Roosevelt later wrote, his parents "agreed to go on for the sake of appearances, the children and the future, but as business partners, not as husband and wife. . . . After that, father and mother had an armed truce that endured until the day he died."

In the eyes of some, Eleanor Roosevelt's emergence as a public figure seemed a direct consequence of profound anger at her husband's betrayal. Yet Eleanor's activism predated her discovery of the Mercer affair. World War I provided the occasion for expressing long-suppressed talents and energies that could be traced back to her early involvement with the National Consumers' League and the settlement house and were rooted, ultimately, in her relationship with Marie Souvestre. The Lucy Mercer affair, like Franklin's polio, reinforced the move toward public self-assertion, but did not itself cause a transformation.

What the Mercer affair did cause was a gradual reallocation of emotional energy away from Franklin and toward others. Through the polio episode and afterward, Eleanor remained devoted to Franklin's care and career. During the 1920s a warmth of tone and feeling continued in her letters to and about him. Yet gradually their lives became separate. Franklin went off on his houseboat in Florida or to Warm Springs, Georgia, with his secretary Missy LeHand. Eleanor

stayed away, as if intentionally ceding to others any emotional involvement with her husband. She might have been jealous of Missy
(some have said Franklin had "an affair" with her) or even her daughter Anna for easily giving him the fun and enjoyment that was beyond her ability. But a part of her recognized that others must provide what she could not give.

Increasingly, Eleanor appeared to draw on her own family experience when offering advice to others. When a woman wrote her in
1930 about a marital problem, Eleanor replied: "All men who make
successes of their work go through exactly the same kind of thing
which you describe, and their wives, one way or another, have to
adjust themselves. If it is possible to enter into his work in some
way, that is the ideal solution. If not, they must develop something
of their own and if possible make it such a success they will have
something to interest their husbands." In a poignant piece entitled
"On Being Forty-five," which she wrote for *Vogue* in 1930, Eleanor
elaborated:

> Life is a school in which we live all our days, and by middle-age, we
> should know that happiness . . . is never ours by right, but we earn it
> through giving of ourselves. You must have learned self-control. No
> matter how much you care, how much you may feel that if you knew
> certain things you could help, you must not ask questions or offer
> help, you must wait until the confidence is freely given, and you
> must learn to love without criticism. . . . If you have learned these
> things by forty-five, if you have ceased to consider yourself as in any
> way important, but understand well the place that must be filled in
> the family, the role will be easy.

Above all, Eleanor concluded, the forty-five-year-old woman must

> keep an open and speculative mind . . . and [then] she will be ready to
> go out and try new adventures, create new work for others as well as
> herself, and strike deep roots in some community where her presence
> will make a difference in the lives of others. . . . One can no longer be
> interested in one's self, but one is thereby freed for greater interest in
> others and the lives of others become as engrossing as a fairy story of
> our childhood days.

Taking her own advice, Eleanor increasingly transferred the emotional focus of her life away from Franklin. The political network of
women reformers of which she was the center provided intimate
friendship as well as political camaraderie. During the 1920s she
spent one night a week with Esther Lape and Elizabeth Read, reading
books together and talking about common interests. She also became close friends with Women's Trade Union League women like

Rose Schneiderman, inviting them to Hyde Park for picnics. Molly Dewson became an especially close friend, and Eleanor wrote in 1932 that "the nicest thing about politics is lunching with you on Mondays." In a revealing comment made in 1927, Eleanor observed that "more than anything else, politics may serve to guard against the emptiness and loneliness that enter some women's lives after their children have grown."

Many of Eleanor's friendships during the 1920s and 1930s were with women who lived with other women. She had become particularly close to Nancy Cook and Marion Dickerman, who lived together in New York City. In 1926 she moved with them into Val-Kill, a newly constructed cottage at Hyde Park, an event that accurately symbolized her growing detachment from Franklin and his mother. Although she returned to the "Big House" at Hyde Park when Franklin was present, it was never without resentment and regret. She and Dickerman purchased Todhundter, a private school in New York, where Eleanor taught three days a week even after Franklin was elected governor of New York. The three women also jointly managed a furniture crafts factory at Val-Kill. The linen and towels at Val-Kill were monogrammed "EMN," and the three women together constituted as much a "family" for Eleanor during those years as Franklin and her children.

There were always "special" relationships, however, and during the 1930s these acquired an intensity and depth that were new to Eleanor's life. One of these was with her daughter Anna and Anna's new love, John Boettiger, a reporter whom Anna had met during the 1932 presidential campaign. Eleanor shared a special bond with her daughter, different from the one she had with her sons. Although the two women had had a difficult relationship during Anna's adolescence and early adulthood, caused partly by Anna's resentment of her mother's "distance" and preference for other, competing personalities like Louis Howe, the two women rekindled their affection during Anna's romance with John. Eleanor seemed to be re-living her early days with Franklin by investing enormous energy and love in Anna and wanting her daughter to find the kind of happiness she felt she had lost forever with her own husband. "I love Anna so dearly," Eleanor wrote John in 1935, "that I don't need to tell you that my willingness to let her go to you speaks much for my *trust and love* of you" (italics mine). Eleanor became a ready accomplice in the young couple's effort to find time alone together before their respective divorces and wrote constantly of her hopes for their happiness. One poignant letter to Anna on Christmas Eve 1935 speaks with particular power to the emotional ties that had developed between mother and daughter. "The dogs and I have felt sad every time we passed your door," she wrote. "It was hard to decorate the tree or get things distributed without you . . . and if anyone says much I shall weep for I have had a queer feeling in my throat when I thought of you. Anyway I am happy that you and John are together for I know you will be happy, so please give him a hug for me and tell him I am grateful for him and what he means to you for every day of my life."

Perhaps Eleanor's most carefree relationship during these years occurred with Earl Miller, a former state trooper who had been Governor Al Smith's bodyguard and who subsequently provided the same service to the Roosevelt family. He encouraged Eleanor to drive her own car, take up horseback riding again, and develop confidence in her own personality. He was strikingly different from her other friends—tall, handsome, a "man's man." Although they talked about ideas and politics, the relationship was more that of "boon companions." With Earl Miller, Eleanor found a way to escape the pressures of her political and social status. She went frequently to his home for visits, had him stay at Val-Kill or her New York apartment, and accompanied him whenever possible for long walks and late-evening suppers. Although some of her friends disliked his tendency to "manhandle" Eleanor, all understood the importance of the relationship, and Marion Dickerman even said that "Eleanor played with the idea of marriage with Earl." Miller himself denied that the subject had ever been raised. "You don't sleep with someone you call Mrs. Roosevelt," he said. But without question, the two had an extraordinarily close relationship, and James Roosevelt later observed that his mother's tie to Miller "may have been the one real romance in [her] life outside of marriage. . . . She seemed to draw strength from him when he was by her side, and she came to rely on him. . . . Above all, he made her feel like she was a woman."

It was Eleanor Roosevelt's relationship with Lorena Hickok, however, that proved most intense during the 1930s and that subsequently has caused the most controversy. The two women became close during the 1932 campaign, when Hickok was covering the prospective first lady in her role as a reporter for the Associated Press. "That woman is unhappy about something," Hickok noted. Eleanor had not wanted Franklin to become president and feared that life in the White House would destroy her independence and cast her in an empty role as hostess and figurehead. As the two women talked about their respective lives, they developed an intimacy and affection so close that Hickok felt compelled to resign her position as a reporter because she no longer could write "objectively" about the Roosevelts.

Within a short time, the two women were exchanging daily letters and phone calls, the contents of which suggested that each woman was deeply infatuated with the other. "Hick darling," Eleanor wrote on March 6, "how good it was to hear your voice. It was so inadequate to try to tell you what it meant. Jimmy was near and I could not say, *je t'aime et je t'adore* as I long to do but always remember I am saying it and I go to sleep thinking of you and repeating our little saying." The next night, Eleanor was writing again. "All day," she said, "I thought of you, and another birthday I *will* be with you and yet tonight you sounded so far away and formal. Oh! I want to put my arms around you. I ache to hold you close. Your ring is a great comfort. I look at it and think she does love me, or I wouldn't be wearing it!" The two women plotted ways to be together, to steal a few days in the country, to bridge the gap of physical separation that so often stood between them.

> Only eight more days [Hickok wrote]. Twenty-four hours from now it will be only seven more—just a week! I've been trying today to bring back your face—to remember just *how* you looked. . . . Most clearly I remember your eyes, with the kind of teasing smile in them, and the feeling of that soft spot just northeast of the corner of your mouth against my lips. I wonder what we will do when we meet—what we will say when we meet. Well—I'm rather proud of us, aren't you? I think we have done rather well.

Over time, the relationship cooled somewhat under the pressure of Hickok's demands on Eleanor's time and Eleanor's reluctance to give herself totally to her new friend. Hickok was jealous of Eleanor's other friends, even her children. "Darling," Eleanor wrote, "the love one has for one's children is different, and not even Anna could be to me what you are." From Eleanor's point of view, the two were like a married couple whose relationship had to "flower." "Dearest," she wrote, "strong relationships have to grow deep roots. We are growing them now, partly because we are separated. The foliage and the flowers will come somehow, I'm sure of it. . . ." But an impatient Hickok was jealous of Eleanor's other friends and unable to limit the ardor of her affection.

In time, the situation became too much for Eleanor. In an attempt to explain herself to Hickok, she wrote: "I know you often have a feeling for me which for one reason or another I may not return in kind, but I feel I love you just the same and so often we entirely satisfy each other that I feel there is a fundamental basis on which our relationship stands." "Hick" had to understand, Eleanor wrote, "that I love other people the same way or differently, but each one has their place and one cannot compare them." But in the end, Eleanor could not explain herself sufficiently to satisfy Hickok and concluded that she had failed her friend. "Of course dear," she wrote,

"I never meant to hurt you in any way but that is no excuse for having done it. It won't help you any but I'll never do to anyone else what I did to you." However much she might try, Eleanor could not let herself go emotionally. As a result, she said, "I am pulling myself back in all my contacts now. I have always done it with the children, and why I didn't know I couldn't give you (or anyone else who wanted or needed what you did) any real food, I can't now understand. Such cruelty and stupidity is unpardonable when you reach my age. Heaven knows I hope in some small and unimportant ways I have made life a little easier for you, but that doesn't compensate." Although the two women remained close during the 1930s and 1940s and continued to share the "special Christmases" that Eleanor reserved for her most intimate friends like Earl Miller, Nan Cook, and Hickok, the two women never resumed the intensity and ardor of their early relationship.

Many observers have speculated on the sexual significance of Roosevelt's relationship with Hickok. Hickok herself appears to have had numerous lesbian involvements, and the intimacy of her correspondence with Roosevelt has suggested to some that the love the two women shared must, inevitably, have had a sexual component as well. Many of Eleanor's other women friends lived together in what were called, at the time, "Boston marriages," and some of these associates undoubtedly found fulfillment through sexual relationships with other women. In all likelihood, Marie Souvestre was one of these. Nor has speculation about Eleanor's sexual life been limited to women. Her son James believed that she had an affair with Earl Miller, and later in her life some believed that she had sexual relationships with other men.

Although the accuracy of such speculation may ultimately be irrelevant, the preponderance of evidence suggests that Eleanor Roosevelt was unable to express her deep emotional needs in a sexual manner. Her friend Esther Lape has recalled the distaste and repugnance with which Eleanor responded to the issue of homosexuality when they discussed a French novel dealing with the topic in the 1920s. Eleanor herself told her daughter that sex was something to be "borne," not enjoyed. Eleanor's own reference to Hickok having "a feeling for me which for one reason or another I may not return in kind" may be an allusion to a sexual component of Hickok's desire that Roosevelt could not reciprocate. Earl Miller, and other men with whom Eleanor was rumored to have had a sexual relationship, have all denied—persuasively—the truth of such conjecture. Moreover, we must never forget that Eleanor was raised in a Victorian culture that attempted to repress the sexual drive. She tied her daughter's hands to the top bars of her crib in order to prevent her from masturbating. "The indication was clearly," Anna recalled, "that I had had a bad habit which had to be cured and about which one didn't talk!"

All of this conforms to Eleanor's own repeated declarations that she could never "let herself go" or express freely and spontaneously her full emotions. A person who had been raised to believe that self-control was all-important was unlikely to consider sexual expression of love—especially outside of marriage—a real option. She might sublimate her sexual drives and seek fulfillment of them through a series of deeply committed, even passionate, ties to a variety of people. But it is unlikely that she was ever able to fulfill these drives through actual sexual intimacy with those she cared most about. She was imprisoned in the cage of her culture, and her own bitter experiences through childhood and marriage reinforced her impulse toward self-control and repression. Within her world, she used verbal and emotional lovemaking to achieve whatever satisfaction she could. But ultimately, she could not liberate herself from that world. She would give to others as much as she could within the confines of her life, but she could not take from others—or give—in a manner that her culture defined as forbidden.

In this context, it is not surprising that Eleanor Roosevelt derived some of her emotional gratification from public life and by giving herself emotionally even to distant correspondents who somehow sensed her willingness to listen to their needs. Such expression of concern constituted the intersection of her public and private lives. Over and over again she answered pleas for help with either a sensitive letter, an admonition to a federal agency to take action, or even a personal check. When a policeman she knew suffered a paralyzing injury, she helped pay for his treatment, visited him repeatedly and, to encourage his rehabilitation, even asked him to help type a book she was composing about her father. The indigent wrote to her because they knew she cared, and in caring she found an outlet for her own powerful emotional needs.

The same compassion was manifested in Eleanor Roosevelt's advocacy of the oppressed. It was almost as though she could fully express her feelings only by externalizing them through political issues. Visiting the poverty-stricken countryside of West Virginia and hearing about the struggle of Appalachian farmers to reclaim land, she became a champion of the Arthurdale Resettlement Administration Project, devoting her lecture fees as well as influence to help the community regain autonomy. Poor textile workers in the South and garment union members in the North found her equally willing to embrace their cause. She invited their representatives to the White

House and seated them next to the president at dinner so that he might hear of their plight. She and Franklin had worked out a tacit understanding that permitted her to bring the cause of the oppressed to his attention and allowed him, in turn, to use her activism as a means of building alliances with groups to his left. The game had clear rules: Franklin was the politician, Eleanor the agitator, and frequently he refused to act as she wished. But at least the dispossessed had someone advocating their interests.

Largely because of Eleanor Roosevelt, the issue of civil rights for black Americans received a hearing at the White House. Although Roosevelt, like most white Americans, grew up in an environment suffused with racist and nativist attitudes, by the time she reached the White House she was one of the few voices in the administration insisting that racial discrimination had no place in American life. As always, she led by example. At a 1939 Birmingham meeting inaugurating the Southern Conference on Human Welfare, she insisted on placing her chair so that it straddled both the black and white sides of the aisle, thereby confounding local authorities who insisted that segregation must prevail. Her civil rights sympathies became most famous when in 1939 she resigned from the Daughters of the American Revolution after the organization denied Marian Anderson permission to perform at Constitution Hall. Instead, the great black artist sang to seventy-five thousand people from the Lincoln Memorial—an idea moved toward reality owing to support from the first lady.

Roosevelt also acted as behind-the-scenes lobbyist for civil rights legislation. She had an extensive correspondence with Walter White, executive secretary of the NAACP, who wished to secure her support for legislation defining lynching as a federal crime. She immediately accepted the role of intermediary and argued that the president should make such a bill an urgent national priority. She served as the primary advocate for the antilynching bill within the White House, and she and White became fast friends as they worked toward a common objective. When the NAACP sponsored a New York City exhibit of paintings and drawings dealing with lynching, Roosevelt agreed to be a patron and attended the showing along with her secretary. After White House Press Secretary Steve Early protested about White, she responded: "If I were colored, I think I should have about the same obsession [with lynching] that he has." To the president ER communicated her anger that "one could get nothing done." "I'm deeply troubled," she wrote, "by the whole situation, as it seems to me a terrible thing to stand by and let it continue and feel that one cannot speak out as to his feelings."

Although Eleanor lost out in her campaign for Franklin's strong endorsement of an antilynching bill, she continued to speak forthrightly for the cause of civil rights. In June 1939, in an address before the NAACP's annual meeting, she presented the organization's Spingarn Medal to Marian Anderson. A few weeks later, she formally joined the black protest organization.

As the threat of war increased, Roosevelt joined her black friends in arguing that America could not fight racism abroad yet tolerate it at home. Together with Walter White, Aubrey Williams, and others, she pressed the administration to act vigorously to eliminate discrimination in the Armed Forces and defense employment. Although civil rights forces were not satisfied with the administration's actions, especially the enforcement proceedings of the Fair Employment Practices Commission created to forestall A. Philip Randolph's 1941 march on Washington, the positive changes that did occur arose from the alliance of the first lady and civil rights forces. She would not give up the battle, nor would they, despite the national administration's evident reluctance to act.

Roosevelt brought the same fervor to her identification with young people. Fearing that democracy might lose a whole generation because of the depression, she reached out to make contact with the young. Despite warnings from White House aides that her young friends could not be trusted, between 1936 and 1940 she became deeply involved in the activities of the American Student Union and the American Youth Congress, groups committed to a democratic socialist program of massively expanded social-welfare programs. She advanced their point of view in White House circles and invited them to meet the president so that they might have the opportunity to persuade him of their point of view. To those who criticized her naiveté, she responded: "I wonder if it does us much harm. There is nothing as harmful as the knowledge in our hearts that we are afraid to face any group of young people." She was later betrayed by some of her young allies, who insisted on following the Communist party line and denouncing the European war as imperialistic after the Nazi-Soviet Non-Aggression Pact in 1940. Nonetheless, Eleanor Roosevelt continued to believe in the importance of remaining open to dissent. "I have never said anywhere that I would rather see young people sympathetic with communism," she wrote, "But I have said that I would rather see the young people actively at work, even if I considered they were doing things that were a mistake." It was through her contact with the American Student Union that she first met Joseph Lash, a vigorous leader of the anticommunist faction of the student movement, who would later become as close to her as anyone in her life.

With the onset of World War II, the first lady persisted in her efforts for the disadvantaged. When it appeared that women would be left out of the planning and staffing of wartime operations, she insisted that administration officials consult women activists and incorporate roles for women as a major part of their planning. Over and over again, she intervened with war-production agencies as well as the military to advocate fairer treatment for black Americans. After it seemed that many New Deal social-welfare programs would be threatened by war, she acted to protect and preserve measures directed at the young, tenant farmers, and blacks. Increasingly, she devoted herself to the dream of international cooperation, perceiving, more than most, the revolution rising in Africa and Asia, and the dangers posed by the threat of postwar conflict.

When Jewish refugees seeking a haven from Nazi persecution received less than an enthusiastic response from the State Department, it was Eleanor Roosevelt who intervened repeatedly, trying to improve the situation. Parents, wives, or children separated from loved ones always found an ally when they sought help from the first lady. Nowhere was Roosevelt's concern more poignantly expressed than in her visits to wounded veterans in army hospitals overseas. When the world of hot dogs and baseball seemed millions of miles away, suddenly Eleanor Roosevelt would appear, spending time at each bedside, taking names and addresses to write letters home, bringing the cherished message that someone cared.

Perhaps inevitably, given the stresses of the times, the worlds of Franklin and Eleanor became ever more separate in these years. As early as the 1936 reelection campaign, she confessed to feeling "indifferent" about Franklin's chances. "I realize more and more," she wrote Hickok, "that FDR's a great man, and he is nice, but as a person, I'm a stranger, and I don't want to be anything else!" As the war proceeded, Eleanor and Franklin more often became adversaries. He was less able to tolerate Eleanor's advocacy of unpopular causes, or her insistence on calling attention to areas of conflict within the administration. "She was invariably frank in her criticism of him," one of his speechwriters recalled, "[and] sometimes I thought she picked inappropriate times . . . perhaps a social and entertaining dinner." In search of release from the unbearable pressures of the war, Franklin came more and more to rely on the gaiety and laughter of his daughter Anna and other women companions. One of these was Lucy Mercer Rutherfurd, who began to come to White House dinners when Eleanor was away (with Anna's complicity) and who, unbeknownst to Eleanor, was with the president in Warm Springs when he was stricken by a cerebral hemorrhage and died in April 1945.

With great discipline and dignity, Eleanor bore both the pain of Franklin's death and the circumstances surrounding it. Her first concern was to carry forward the policies that she and Franklin had believed in and worked for despite their disagreements. Writing later about her relationship with Franklin, she said: "He might have been happier with a wife who had been completely uncritical. That I was never able to be and he had to find it in some other people. Nevertheless, I think that I sometimes acted as a spur, even though the spurring was not always wanted nor welcome. I was one of those who served his purposes." What she did not say was that Franklin had served her purposes as well. Though the two never retrieved the intimacy of their early relationship, they had created an unparalleled partnership to respond to the needs of a nation in crisis.

Not long after her husband's death, she told an inquiring reporter, "The story is over." But no one who cared so much for so many causes, and was so effective as a leader, could long remain on the sidelines. Twenty years earlier, ER had told her students at Todhunter: "Don't dry up by inaction, but go out and do new things. Learn new things and see new things with your own eyes." Her own instincts, as well as the demands of others, reaffirmed that advice. Over the next decade and a half, Roosevelt remained the most effective woman in American politics. She felt a responsibility not only to carry forward the politics of the New Deal, but also to further causes that frequently had gone beyond New Deal liberalism. In long letters to President Truman, she implored the administration to push forward with civil rights, maintain the Fair Employment Practices Committee, develop a foreign policy able to cope with the needs of other nations, and work toward a world system where atom bombs would cease to be negotiating chips in international relations.

Appropriately, President Truman nominated the former first lady to be one of America's delegates to the United Nations. At the UN, her name became synonymous with the effort to compose a declaration of human rights embodying standards that civilized humankind would accept as sacred and inalienable. For three years, she argued, debated, lobbied, and compromised until finally on December 10, 1948, the document she had fundamentally shaped passed the General Assembly. Delegates rose in a standing ovation to the woman who more than anyone else had come to symbolize the cause of human rights throughout the world. Even those in the United States who had most opposed her nomination to the delegation applauded her efforts. "I want to say that I take back everything I ever said about her," Senator Arthur Vandenberg of Michigan commented, "and believe me, it's been plenty." At times a figure of scorn and ridicule during the New Deal, Roosevelt was now fast becoming a national heroine, even to former enemies.

The cause of world peace quickly became as central to Eleanor

Roosevelt's efforts as anything in which she had engaged before. With the same emotional fervor that had earlier characterized her response to the dispossessed, Roosevelt reached out to the victims of war. "The weight of human misery here in Europe," she said after a visit to Germany and its concentration camps, "is something one can't get out of one's heart." In moving speeches that vividly portrayed the suffering wrought by war, she sought to educate America to its responsibilities in the postwar world. She had driven through England in 1928, she told her audience, noting the names of all the young men who had died during World War I. Now, she had completed the same kind of journey through Germany. "There is a feeling that spreads over the land," she said, "the feel of [a] civilization that of itself might have a hard time coming back." If America wished to avoid such a world, it must avoid isolationism and wake up to the necessity of helping those who had suffered.

Although Roosevelt disagreed profoundly with some of the military aspects of U.S. foreign policy, she supported the broad outlines of America's response to Russia in the developing Cold War. In debates at the UN, she learned quickly that Soviet delegates could be hypocritical, and on more than one occasion she responded to Russian charges of injustice in America by proposing that each country submit to investigation of its social conditions—a suggestion the Soviets refused. When Henry Wallace and other liberal Americans formed the Progressive party in 1947 with a platform of accommodation toward the Soviet Union, Roosevelt demurred. Instead, she spearheaded the drive by other liberals to build Americans for Democratic Action, a group that espoused social reform at home and support of Truman's stance toward Russia.

Through public speeches and her newspaper column, as well as her position at the UN, Roosevelt remained a singular public figure, able to galvanize the attention of millions by her statements. She became one of the staunchest advocates of a Jewish nation in Israel, argued vigorously for civil rights, and spoke forcefully against the witch-hunts of McCarthyism, attacking General Dwight Eisenhower when he failed to defend his friend George Marshall from Senator McCarthy's smears. Although Eisenhower did not reappoint her to the United Nations when he became president in 1953, she continued to work tirelessly through the American Association for the United Nations to mobilize public support for international cooperation. She also gave unstintingly of her time to the election campaigns in 1952 and 1956 of her dear friend Adlai Stevenson, a man who brought to politics a wit and sophistication Roosevelt always admired.

It was the private sphere, though, that remained most precious.

"The people I love," ER worte her friend and physician David Gurewitsch, "mean more to me than all the public things. . . . I only do the public things because there are a few close people whom I love dearly and who matter to me above everything else. There are not so many of them and you are now one of them." Gurewitsch was a constant companion after she met him in 1947. She traveled with him to Europe, mothered him, and depended upon him for devotion and nurturance. Some even thought he was her lover.

The same kind of relationship—perhaps even deeper—existed with Joe Lash, the young man from the American Student Union whom she had met in the late 1930s. Lash, too, became an intimate companion, spending evenings with her in her New York apartment and weeks at a time at Hyde Park. "I love to be with you dear boy," Eleanor wrote. "I never want to be alone when I'm with people I love." She brought him presents, corresponded with him almost daily, and looked forward eagerly to times when they could be together. "Do come up whenever you are free," she wrote Lash. "I'll be at the house soon after six waiting to both kiss and spank you and I would love it if you have nothing else that calls, to have you stay the night. It will be nice to tuck you in and say goodnight on your birthday!" With Lash too, she seemed to find a maternal role that had been absent in her relationship with most of her own children. "A little bit of my heart seems to be with you always Joe," she wrote during the war. Eleanor became deeply involved in Lash's love affair with Trude Pratt, doing all in her power to bring them together, to erase misunderstandings between them, and to make it possible for them to find the happiness in marriage that had eluded her and Franklin. Tragically, her involvement with Lash led to one of the most bizarre and disgraceful episodes of the war. Because of Lash's involvement with the American Student Union, he was suspected of being procommunist and was placed under counterintelligence surveillance during the war. Letters between the two were opened by government agents, and even the first lady's hotel room was bugged when she went to visit Lash. As a result of such surveillance, government spies made the unfounded allegation that she and Lash were having an affair, and Lash—a soldier at the time—was sent to the Far East.

During the last two decades of her life, Eleanor Roosevelt's children remained as much a trial as a comfort, with the possible exception of Anna. After Franklin's death, Eleanor lived at Val-Kill with Malvina Thompson, her secretary, and her son Elliott and his family. Anna and Elliott were both involved in radio and TV programs with their mother, while James and Franklin entered politics in California and New York. Among her children, only John carried out a life totally on his own. More often than not, family gatherings degenerated into bitter arguments. It was the grandchildren who brought joy—the grandchildren, old friends like Lash and Gurewitsch, and new friends like Allard Lowenstein and his young compatriots in the National Student Association, whom Eleanor befriended during the late 1940s and for the rest of her life. With Lowenstein, as with Lash and Gurewitsch, she adopted a maternal role, providing a constant inspiration to another young reformer who would try to transform America through political and social action.

As she entered her seventies, Eleanor Roosevelt was applauded as the first lady of the world. Traveling to India, Japan, and the Soviet Union, she spoke for the best that was in America. Although she did not initially approve of John Kennedy and would have much preferred to see Adlai Stevenson nominated again, she lived to see the spirit of impatience and reform return to Washington. As if to prove that the fire of protest was still alive in herself, in 1962 Roosevelt sponsored hearings in Washington, D.C., where young civil rights workers testified about the judicial and police harassment of black protestors in the South.

It was fitting that Eleanor Roosevelt's last major official office should be to chair President Kennedy's Commission on the Status of Women. More than anyone else of her generation, her life came to exemplify the political expertise and personal autonomy that were abiding themes of the first women's rights movement. Eleanor Roosevelt had not been a militant feminist. Like most social reformers, she publicly rejected the Equal Rights Amendment of the National Woman's Party until the early 1950s, believing that it would jeopardize protective labor legislation for women then on the statute books. Never an enthusiastic supporter of the ERA, neither she nor JFK's commission recommended the amendment. In addition, she accepted the popular argument during the Great Depression that, at least temporarily, some married women would have to leave the labor force in order to give the unemployed a better chance. At times, she also accepted male-oriented definitions of fulfillment. "You are successful," she wrote in a 1931 article, "when your husband feels that he has been a success and that life has been worthwhile."

But on the issue of women's equality, as in so many other areas, Eleanor Roosevelt most often affirmed the inalienable right of the human spirit to grow and seek fulfillment. Brought up amid anti-Semitic and antiblack attitudes, she had transcended her past to become one of the strongest champions of minority rights. Once opposed to suffrage, she grew to exemplify women's aspirations for a full life in politics. Throughout, she demonstrated a capacity for change grounded in a compassion for those who were victims.

There was, in fact, a direct line from Marie Souvestre's advocacy of intellectual independence to Eleanor Roosevelt's involvement in the settlement house, to her subsequent embrace of women's political activism in the 1920s and 1930s, and to her final role as leader of the Commission on the Status of Women. She had personified not only the right of women to act as equals with men in the political sphere, but the passion of social activists to ease pain, alleviate suffering, and affirm solidarity with the unequal and disenfranchised of the world.

On November 7, 1962, Eleanor Roosevelt died at home from a rare form of bone-marrow tuberculosis. Just twenty years earlier, she had written that all individuals must discover for themselves who they are and what they want from life. "You can never really live anyone else's life," she wrote, "not even your child's. The influence you exert is through your own life and what you've become yourself." Despite disappointment and tragedy, Eleanor Roosevelt had followed her own advice and because of it had affected the lives of millions. Although her daughter Anna concluded that Eleanor, throughout her life, suffered from depression, she had surely tried—and often succeeded—through her public advocacy of the oppressed and her private relationships with friends to find some measure of fulfillment and satisfaction.

"What other single human being," Adlai Stevenson asked at Eleanor Roosevelt's memorial service, "has touched and transformed the existence of so many? . . . She walked in the slums and ghettos of the world, not on a tour of inspection . . . but as one who could not feel contentment when others were hungry." Because of her life, millions of others experienced a new sense of possibility. It would be difficult to envision a more enduring or important legacy.

Sources

The Eleanor Roosevelt Papers at the Franklin Delano Roosevelt Library, Hyde Park, New York, represent the most comprehensive collection of material available. Of particular interest are her correspondence with Walter White of the NAACP, material about her family, especially her father, and drafts of articles and lectures. Other relevant collections at Hyde Park are the papers of Mary (Molly) Dewson, Hilda Worthington Smith, and Lorena Hickok; the papers of the Women's Division of the Democratic National Committee; and those of Anna Roosevelt Halstead. Several collections at the Schlesinger Library, Radcliffe College, bear directly on Eleanor Roosevelt's life: see especially the papers of Mary Anderson, Mary Dewson, Mary Dreier, and Ellen Woodward. Of Eleanor Roosevelt's own writings the most valuable are *This I Remember* (New York, 1949); *This Is My Story* (New York, 1937); *Autobiography* (New York, 1961); and *It's Up To the Women* (New York, 1933). She also wrote a monthly column, "If You Ask Me," for the *Ladies Home Journal* from June 1941 to spring 1949 and in *McCall's* after 1949. The best place to begin reading about her is Joseph Lash's excellent two-volume biography, *Eleanor and Franklin* (New York, 1971) and *Eleanor: The Years Alone* (New York, 1972). On Lash's personal relationship with Roosevelt, see *Love, Eleanor: Eleanor Roosevelt and Her Friends* (New York, 1982). Other books that cast light on the Roosevelt family include James Roosevelt, *My Parents: A Differing View* (Chicago, 1976) and Elliott Roosevelt with James Brough, *An Untold Story: The Roosevelts of Hyde Park* (New York, 1973), both of which offer personal views by the Roosevelt children. Even more revealing is Bernard Asbell, ed., *Mother and Daughter: The Letters of Eleanor and Anna Roosevelt* (New York, 1982).

Georgia O'Keeffe
(1887–1986)

Sarah Whitaker Peters

Georgia O'Keeffe, a major figure in the evolution of twentieth-century American art, was born November 15, 1887, on a farm near Sun Prairie, Wisconsin, the second child and first daughter of Francis Calixtus and Ida O'Keeffe. She attended parochial and private schools in Wisconsin, and graduated from the Chatham Episcopal Institute in Virginia (1905–1906). For the next two years, O'Keeffe studied at the Art Institute in Chicago and the Art Student's League in New York. In 1908 she returned to Chicago, where she worked as a freelance commercial artist until 1910. After this, she taught art in public schools and colleges in Texas and South Carolina, until 1914, when she began studying at Teachers College, Columbia University, in New York. In 1916, O'Keeffe met Alfred Stieglitz, the great photographer and advocate of modern art, who exhibited her first abstractions at his gallery, 291. He arranged shows for O'Keeffe nearly every year thereafter until his death in 1946. They began living together in 1918, and married in 1924. From 1916 on, her art was labeled erotic by many critics because of the different ways she unified the female body with the forms of nature. She, however, always denied this interpretation. By O'Keeffe's own account, the men of the inner "Stieglitz" circle did not want her around at first. But when her paintings of Manhattan (traditionally a male artist's preserve) sold well and received a good press, as indeed all her work did from the start, she won their respect as an artist—not a woman *artist. There were large retrospective exhibitions of O'Keeffe's work given at major museums around the country in 1943, 1946, 1960, 1970, and 1988. O'Keeffe published* Some Memories of Drawings *in 1974, consisting of a portfolio of drawings and her own text, and two years later,* Georgia O'Keeffe, *which featured 108 reproductions of her paintings, again with her own text. She died March 6, 1986, in Santa Fe, New Mexico.*

Georgia O'Keeffe has written that her first memory was of the brightness of light, and that she decided at age twelve (when she reached puberty) to become a painter.[1] Intentionally or not, these statements come across as profoundly mythic: metaphors of spiritual transformation and psychological change. O'Keeffe was like that—and so was her art.

Born on November 15, 1887, O'Keeffe grew up in a Wisconsin farm family of Irish, Hungarian, and Dutch descent, the second child of seven. Of her childhood O'Keeffe wrote: "I seem to be one of the few people I know of to have no complaints against my first twelve years."[2] Her mother, Ida Totto O'Keeffe, was a strong believer in education, and the young Georgia was sent to strict Catholic and Episcopal schools in Madison, Wisconsin, and Chatham, Virginia (near where the family moved in 1903). She would always like to learn new things, but she never quite mastered spelling—as her exceptionally intelligent and beautiful letters reveal.

At eighteen O'Keeffe went to study at the highly respected Art Institute of Chicago. There she received a rigorous academic training, drawing from casts and the human figure. In 1907, with the traditional (for women) idea of teaching in mind, she went to New York to work in oil, pastel, and watercolor at the Art Students League. Foremost among her instructors was the dedicated and flamboyant American impressionist William Merritt Chase, of whom she wrote: "There was something fresh and energetic and fierce and exacting about him that made him fun."[3] She learned much about the techniques of painting from Chase—and she was awarded first prize by him for a naturalistic still life.

During that same New York winter of 1908, O'Keeffe saw the historic first exhibitions in America of French artists Auguste Rodin and Henri Matisse at the avant-garde Little Galleries of the Photo-Secession, known as 291 from its location at 291 Fifth Avenue, which was directed by Alfred Stieglitz, the internationally famous photographer. For Stieglitz, the name "Photo-Secession" meant seceding from the accepted idea of what then constituted a photograph. Further, he was almost alone in believing that a photograph could have the significance of art. By 1912, he would be on the lookout for painting and sculpture that had also "seceded" from the accepted ways of making art. In a word, abstraction. But O'Keeffe was not yet ready to "see" radical European modernism. (Few in 1908 were.) Nor was she ready to listen to Stieglitz's enlightened, nonstop talk about it at 291. Although she had wanted to return to the League for another year of study, her parents had fallen upon hard times and she felt it necessary to find paid work instead.

For the next four years O'Keeffe gave up painting—the act, if not the dream. She returned to Chicago, where she could stay with relatives, and became a free-lance commercial artist. O'Keeffe has said very little about this humbling, hard-working artistic apprenticeship. We know only that she drew lace and embroidery advertisements, at two different fashion houses, for newspapers under deadline. Long an important center for arts and crafts in America, Chicago was still making outstanding contributions to the international art nouveau movement (the graphic designer Will H. Bradley and architect Louis Sullivan come to mind) during the years O'Keeffe studied and worked there. And it is quite certain that the infinite variety of art nouveau she saw in this city taught her first hand that line, color, and form have powers independent of subject matter—a crucial preparation, however unconscious, for her breakthrough abstractions of 1915.

Although O'Keeffe was not happy in her job, she kept at it resolutely for two years until a bad case of measles seriously affected her eyesight. Sent home to Virginia to recuperate, discouraged and at loose ends, she taught art for a time at her old school. In the summer of 1912, recovered at last, she registered rather indifferently for a drawing course at the University of Virginia. There, to her surprise, she became converted for life to the anti-academic composition theories of Arthur Wesley Dow. The timing seems to have been perfect, for Dow's unorthodox methods of art education—richly saturated with late nineteenth-century symbolist notions of correspondence (analogy), "visual music," and synesthesia (the overlap between the senses)—finally mustered her own latent creativity.

Dow had constructed his teaching system, or "synthesis," on the two-dimensional principles of Japanese picture making: harmoniously spaced linear design instead of descriptive analysis, and abstract arrangements of dark and light patterns (*notan*) instead of illusionistic effects of light and shadow (chiaroscuro). As O'Keeffe was later to describe it, "filling space in a beautiful way." For the next six years she taught the design exercises laid out in Dow's famous book *Composition* at schools and colleges in Virginia, South Carolina, and Texas. During this long, and sometimes frustrating, process she herself learned much about simplifying nature forms to their essence as shapes.

O'Keeffe was teaching in Amarillo, Texas, at the time of the scandalous 1913 Armory Show in New York, so she never saw it. Billed as "The International Exhibition of Modern Art," this large-scale presentation of the extremes of French fauvism and cubism was to reform—and transform—the direction of American art: how it was taught, how it was exhibited, and how it was collected.

As Barbara Novak has pointed out in her important study, *Ameri-*

can Painting of the Nineteenth Century, the qualities of form and modes of procedure most commonly denoted as "American," from the 1700s on, were nearly always a combination of indigenous (folk) styles, and transformations of European traditions. Novak also isolated several traits that can be called "national," since they reappeared in new contexts throughout the nineteenth century. These are: the preservation of literal fact, the unique relation of object to idea, a preoccupation with *things,* and a strong folk art tradition— which may actually have helped to restrain American artists from taking up the more decorative extremes of each successive European style.[4] Theodore Stebbins, in his recent survey of this early material, *A New World: Masterpieces of American Painting 1760–1910,* holds that the roots of a distinctly American culture were set right after the War of 1812, when writers such as Washington Irving, James Fenimore Cooper, and William Cullen Bryant identified American art with the American land—and thus set the stage for the rise of the Hudson River school of native landscape painters.[5]

As O'Keeffe's own formation demonstrates, would-be artists in America were trained along the unadventurous lines of the European academies. To exhibit and sell work, one had to paint in the academic mode. The first rebellion against this rigidly enforced rule was the so-called Ash Can school of painters, which included Robert Henri, John Sloan, William Glackens, and George Bellows. During the first decade of the twentieth century, these artists banded together in New York to paint the life they saw around them: young women drying their hair on a roof top, boxers in the ring, women shopping, and an election night in Herald Square. But if their subject matter was "modern," their styles were not—compared to what Stieglitz was showing at 291. Aware of this, the Association of American Painters and Sculptors, formed in 1911, began to make plans for an invitational exhibition of contemporary American art, one that would include some of the early native abstractionists already being extolled by Stieglitz. But the association had considerable difficulty in getting the show off the ground. Finally, Arthur B. Davies (who was well acquainted with the Paris avant-garde) stepped in as a fund-raiser. He also revamped the original plans—changing them to include some of the most extreme and celebrated European modernists. In the end, about 1,300 sculptures, paintings, and drawings were gathered together, mostly by Davies and the painter Walt Kuhn, for the opening on February 17, 1913. Although three-quarters of these works were by Americans, it was the contemporary Europeans who stole the show—*and* the headlines. Twenty-five-year-old Marcel Duchamps's cubist work *Nude Descending the Staircase No. 2* (1912) caused the most commotion: It was gleefully described as

"the staircase descending a nude," and "explosion in a shingle factory." Former President Theodore Roosevelt attended, and warned
against the European "lunatic fringe." (He thought the Duchamp
looked like a Navajo blanket.) The *New York Times* called the exhibition "pathological." Other art critics labeled Kandinsky, Matisse,
Picasso, and Brancusi as "lunatics" and "depravers." Nevertheless,
the Armory Show, which traveled to Chicago and Boston, was seen
by nearly 300,000 people.[6] Although it offered a flawed and incom-
plete picture of early modernist abstraction (the Italian futurists
were completely ignored), collectors began almost immediately to
collect it, and galleries other than Stieglitz's sprang up to show it.
Encouraged and inspired, a small number of gifted American artists
increasingly took up the advanced European challenge, inventing
their own color abstractions, and their own variations on cubism.
Although Georgia O'Keeffe did not know it in 1913, she too would
ride this new wave of public and private interest in abstract art.

O'Keeffe returned to New York the fall of 1914 to study for six
months with Dow himself at Columbia University's Teachers College. She was painting hard again (Dow rated her as exceptionally
talented), and she went often to 291, where she saw important
exhibitions of Picasso, Braque, Picabia, and the American abstract
watercolorist John Marin. By now she was taking a direct personal
notice of modern art—and of Stieglitz as well. Shortly after leaving
the city to teach in South Carolina, she wrote her Columbia colleague Anita Pollitzer that "I believe I would rather have Stieglitz
like something—anything I had done—than anyone else I know
of."[7]

Actually, she had become increasingly dissatisfied with her own
drawings and paintings—finding them stylistically derivative and,
worse, reflective of other people's sensibilities. She was then twenty-
eight, and she wanted to express *herself.* She resolved suddenly to
start from scratch—jettisoning all the years of hard-won instruction.
As she was to describe this turning point seven years later: "I have
things in my head that are not like what anyone has taught me—
shapes and ideas so near to me—so natural to my way of being and
thinking that it hadn't occurred to me [before] to put them down.
[And] I decided to . . . accept as true my own thinking."[8] Beginning
with pastels and watercolors first and then stripping down from color
to black and white, she spread large sheets of sketch paper on the
floor, and with charcoal sticks, tried to put down in abstract shapes, as
exactly as she could, the essence of her emotions. It was not easy. Her
letters to Pollitzer tell of having too much inside herself for the
"marks" she was transcribing, erasing, changing, throwing away and
re-transcribing. She wrote, too, of disgust and elation, of cramps in her

head, hands, and feet. Sometimes she called what she was doing a "fool's game." The worst was that she couldn't find words for the images that were beginning, mysteriously, to satisfy her. What was she saying with them anyway? She hoped and believed that what she had expressed was "a woman's feeling." In dire need of feedback, she sent several batches of these drawings to Pollitzer who wrote right back, saying, "They spoke to me, I swear they did . . . you ought to cry because you're so happy."[9] On January 1, 1916, Pollitzer, on her own initiative, took O'Keeffe's three-month-old venture into abstraction to Stieglitz at 291. To his experienced eye, these gender-based expressions of self looked like something that had never been done before. "Finally, a woman on paper," is what he would always remember himself as saying. A seeker of the "new," and determined to recognize and foster an indigenous American art, Stieglitz exhibited ten of O'Keeffe's drawings at 291 that May, to immediate public and critical interest. In 1917, he gave her a one-person show, which included the rhapsodic Texas landscape watercolors that are now considered to be among her finest achievements.

It has long been observed that behind her later flowers, stars, sky-scrapers, trees, Penitente crosses, animal bones, hills, and clouds lurk the same organic geometries on which her first abstractions were based: specifically the ovoid, the vertical stalk, the spiral, the seed pod, the tendril, and the arabesque. O'Keeffe admitted as much: "I always say that my work was never as good as it was in the beginning. You may wander around a bit, but your work doesn't change much."[10] Yet, typically, she never said how or why she came to choose the basic language of her forms, and she would not acknowledge their often-remarked uterine, phallic, and esoteric overtones—*or* their thinly disguised art nouveau origins (all of the early drawings carry specific references to plant forms and wave motifs).

Promised financial support by Stieglitz, O'Keeffe moved to New York to paint full time in 1918. About him she has said in retrospect: "He gave a flight to the spirit and faith in their own way to more people—particularly young people—than anyone I have ever known."[11] Although Stieglitz was a generation older than she (he was exactly her mother's age), the two artists married in 1924, and he exhibited her work almost yearly until his death in 1946. From her first show at 291, O'Keeffe was presented to the art world as a native, naive American genius—one who had developed "without the help of the city of Paris," but this was far from the whole story. While true that O'Keeffe never studied in Europe (as had Stieglitz and all the other artists of his circle), she had, by the time of her 1915 abstractions, read (twice) Kandinsky's extremely influential 1912 essay *Concerning the Spiritual in Art*—the bible, so to speak, of early modernist abstraction. And she had obviously learned much from his theories about how to loosen color from line and make it "sing," as her Texas watercolors of 1917–1918 demonstrate. Apparently O'Keeffe was also familiar with Picabia's infamous—and incendiary—1913 statement: "I improvise my pictures as a musician improvises music. . . . Creating a picture without models is art."[12] (Her *Evening Star* and *Light Coming in on the Plains* series are cases in point.) Further, she had long kept up with the important art periodicals of her time, and was well read in contemporary politics, literature, and history. The letters to Pollitzer chart her keen reactions to books like Synge's *Riders to the Sea,* H. G. Wells' *Tono Bungay,* Chekhov's *Sea Gull,* Hardy's *Jude the Obscure,* Randolph Bourne's *Life and Youth,* and Floyd Dell's *Women as World Builders.* She was a subscriber to the doctrinaire journal *The Masses.* She also played the violin and tried her hand at poetry. But if O'Keeffe was never culturally naive, there is little question that Stieglitz changed her life. And he greatly influenced her art—even as she did his. A belief they both shared was that, in Stieglitz's words, "Woman feels the World differently than Man feels it. . . . The Woman receives the World through her Womb. That is the seat of her deepest feelings. Mind comes second."[13] This idea (so specious by present-day standards) may in fact be at the bottom of all her marvelous visual metaphors on the "womb," ranging from barns and shells to fruit and skyscrapers.

Between 1917 and 1937 O'Keeffe posed frequently for Stieglitz's camera. This wide-ranging, composite portrait of her many "Selves" (over 300 prints) remains one of his greatest contributions to the history of photography. Early on, by diverse means, he tried deliberately to link her with favorite artists who had already caused revolutionary change in painting—particularly Rodin, Whistler, and Matisse. The 1918 print of her shown on p. 517 was almost certainly based upon Whistler's famous *Symphony in White, No. 1: The White Girl* (1862). Stieglitz has altered and amended his nineteenth-century source, but tells a similar visual truth. There is, to begin with, the resonance of the familiar name *The White Girl.* It was the highest form of approbation for Stieglitz to call someone, or some thing, "white," and of O'Keeffe, he said, "Georgia is a wonder . . . if ever there was a whiteness she is that."[14] Further, it must also have occurred to Stieglitz that Whistler's famous subject for this painting, Jo Hiffernan, was his model and mistress—even as O'Keeffe was then his. In a real sense this photograph is a triadic portrait, for it would seem quite certain that Stieglitz not only intended to link O'Keeffe with Whistler through his most famous painting, but with himself as well, in ways that are at once intimate, politic, and artistic.

Courtesy, Museum of Fine Arts, Boston; Gift of Alfred Stieglitz, 1924

Stieglitz's exhibitions over the years of selections from this unique portrait helped to create the public personality of Georgia O'Keeffe that we know today: A preternaturally wise, sublimely self-confident, free-and-independent "priestess," who dared to paint "the very essence of womanhood"—as the writers of the first Freudian generation liked to put it. But she thought of herself very differently, and found the strictly sexual interpretations of her work (mostly by male critics) untrue, embarrassing, and extremely hard to live with. They made her feel "invaded," and (protesting, of course, too much) she fought ceaselessly against this reading of her images. (It is not without irony that several women artists in the 1970s—Miriam Schapiro and Judy Chicago among them—took up O'Keeffe's so-called vaginal iconography for specifically feminist intents and purposes.) One of the ways she tried to control matters was never to discuss her sources and intentions. For all her years of fame, O'Keeffe granted few interviews, and made relatively few public statements. Another was to change her style—to become more "objective." That is, to work from the motif instead of putting down what was already in her head.

It was with the intention of becoming more objective in her work that O'Keeffe began to cultivate an aesthetic interest of her own in photography. In a way, this was a logical progression, for she was inexorably drawn into the rich photographic culture of 291—which included such influential figures as Edward Steichen, Paul Strand, and Charles Sheeler—and she often helped Stieglitz with his various professional activities. Early in the 1920s she set about (covertly) isolating elements from the photographic process that could serve this new goal. Chief among them were the crop, the magnified close-up, the enlarged detail, the telephoto, and even such lens malfunctions as halation and flare (random internal reflections in the camera). But she would use them all for abstraction and expression rather than for verisimilitude. The most photo-optic (and perhaps the most metaphysical) of all her works may well be the thirty New York cityscapes she painted between 1925 and 1929. Her *East River from the Shelton* (1927–1928), for example, combines photographic data (halation and a telephoto view) with a spiritual vision of uncommon force and originality.

During their summers and autumns on the Stieglitz family property at Lake George, O'Keeffe and Stieglitz made frequent references to each other's work. Along with many other artists of their time, including Whistler, they were convinced, that all the arts should "aspire to the condition of music." If music, which is essentially non-mimetic could speak directly to the emotions, so also, they reasoned, could abstract painting and photography. Hence such titles as O'Keeffe's *Blue and Green Music* (1919) and Stieglitz's *Clouds in Ten Movements* (1922). As twentieth-century symbolists in the nineteenth-century tradition of poets Charles Baudelaire and Sté-phane Mallarmé, they both believed that the artist should describe the effect an object produces rather than the object itself, should *suggest* rather than say. And whenever one looks at the images Stieglitz and O'Keeffe made, it is helpful to remember two things: First, that the symbolist artist regarded "true reality" as hidden; something that must be found. And second, that the viewer is meant to share with the artist the responsibility for finding it.

O'Keeffe had long been interested in the weather as an influence on and indicator of her emotions. Clouds, the most familiar and potent carriers of weather, are prevalent in her work. As for Stieglitz, he went so far as to describe his 1923 *Songs of the Sky* cloud photographs as "equivalents of my life experience." Many of these photographs hold shape-references to O'Keeffe's paintings, even as her pictures pay countless formal homages to his. In fact, it may be that these cross-references functioned as some sort of secret visual code between O'Keeffe and Stieglitz—especially during the years of their first lyrical happiness. In 1926, Stieglitz tipped his own hand somewhat with this recorded statement:

> Sometimes I've been talking with O'Keeffe. Some men express what they feel by holding a women's hand. But I have wanted to express the more, to express the thing that would bring us still closer. I would look at the sky, for the sky is the freest thing in the world, and I would make a photograph from the clouds and the sky and say to O'Keeffe, "Here is what we were talking about," she would say, "That's incredible, it's impossible."[15]

When their letters to each other are finally published, it may be possible to know more of the gist of these "conversations."

Stieglitz was never an easy, or even faithful, husband.[16] Long after he died, O'Keeffe wrote: "For me he was much more wonderful in his work than as a human being. I believe it was the work that kept me with him—though I loved him as a human being."[17] In addition to the stresses and strains of her marriage, O'Keeffe was becoming increasingly restless in the close and pretty greenness of upstate New York. In the 1926 painting *Lake George Barns*, her feelings of being hemmed in, stifled, imprisoned, are so clear as to be almost palpable. In plain fact, Lake George was not the psychic homeland for her that it was for Stieglitz, and her creative juices seemed to be drying up. She had never gotten over her Texan yen for open spaces, and in the spring of 1929, with Stieglitz's reluctant blessing, she went to Taos, New Mexico. The four months she spent there, with plenty of physical and mental solitude, reinvigorated her art. She was fascinated by the rich traditions of the Pueblo and Hispanic cultures—particularly the adobe buildings, ritualistic dances, and painted wood carvings. But more than anything she loved the light and the landscape. In the desert, "All is God," novelist D. H. Lawrence had written when he lived there, and among the nineteen paintings she did that first liberated summer is one called *The Lawrence Tree*. She described the southwestern light for herself as "the faraway nearby" and never tired of trying to capture it with paint. She thought that the Sangre de Cristo mountains looked like "miles of grey elephants."[18] And they are seen, just so, in the backgrounds of several of her Penitente Black Cross paintings.

When O'Keeffe left New Mexico that August to return to Stieglitz, she had already begun to recognize that she needed him *and* New Mexico. And that because he would never travel there she would have to get along with her "divided self" the best way she could.

After two more summers of separation and hard work (the New York public and critics loved her New Mexico paintings), O'Keeffe accepted a commission to paint a mural for the new Radio City Music Hall. Stieglitz had disapproved of the project from the start (he thought murals a second-rate art form, and that they were beneath what O'Keeffe should be doing), but O'Keeffe considered it to be a new and worthy challenge. A series of technical and contractual difficulties caused the plan to collapse—and after this so did she. Hospitalized for seven weeks with a mental and physical breakdown from an accumulation of stresses, it would be almost two years before she felt like painting again. After this, she (and Stieglitz—who always surrounded himself with people) understood better her intrinsic need for time alone.

In 1940, she bought a house (Ghost Ranch) in New Mexico, but continued to spend six months of the year in New York with Stieglitz. Things were now calmer and happier between them, although Stieglitz had stopped photographing in 1937 because of health problems. A touching glimpse into their lives at this time comes from a letter she wrote to the critic Henry McBride.

> I see Alfred as an old man that I am very fond of—growing older—so that it sometimes shocks and startles me when he looks particularly pale and tired—Aside from my fondness for him personally, I feel that he has been very important to something that has made my world for me—I like it that I can make him feel that I have hold of his hand to steady him as he goes on.[19]

Stieglitz died on July 13, 1946. She buried his ashes secretly at Lake George, writing later, "I put him where he would hear the Lake,"[20] and she never went there again. For the next three years she was completely occupied with settling his estate. He had acquired a vast collection of outstanding American and European art, and she undertook to divide it up so that it could be donated, in his name, to several American museums—among them the Metropolitan Museum of New York and the Art Institute of Chicago.

In 1949 O'Keeffe moved permanently to Abiquiu, New Mexico, where she could lead exactly the life of privacy and work in nature that suited her best. She did not forget Stieglitz, as is evident from a letter written in 1950: "He always seems oddly present here at the ranch—I was always so aware of him here for so many years [for] I wrote to him . . . so many many times."[21] She traveled resolutely to Europe and the Far East. Commenting on her travels, O'Keeffe wrote to a friend in 1953:

> Maybe I am queer that I am so singularly pleased with the life I have in New Mexico. I never even seem to see a dog that looks as fine as mine. . . . I keep wondering how this world would seem to me if I had seen it 40 years ago. . . . I will look at it—and I think I will be pleased to go home."[22]

In her later years, O'Keeffe was given retrospective exhibitions by the Worcester Art Museum (1960), the Amon Carter Museum of Western Art (1966), and the Whitney Museum (1970). In 1971 she lost her central vision and stopped painting, but she soon learned to be a hand potter and worked seriously at it. She also published two books about her art: *Some Memories of Drawings* (1974) and *Georgia O'Keeffe* (1976). In 1979 she wrote the introduction to a catalogue of Stieglitz's photographs of her exhibited at the Metropolitan Museum. She received many of the nation's highest honors and awards, including the Medal of Freedom (1977) and the National Medal of Arts (1985). On March 6, 1986, she died in Santa Fe at age ninety-eight. At her request there was no church service, and her ashes were scattered over the landscape she loved.

Way back in 1945, O'Keeffe may have unwittingly summed up her contribution to American art by what she wrote to James Johnson Sweeney, who was then organizing an exhibition of her work at the Museum of Modern Art in New York:

> I must say to you again that I am very pleased and flattered that you wish to do the show for me. It makes me feel inadequate and wish I were better. Stieglitz['s] efforts for me have often made me feel that way too— . . . For myself I feel no need of the showing. As I sit out here in my dry lonely country I feel even less need for all those things that go with the city. . . . When I say for myself I do not need that showing at the Museum . . . means—I should add that I think that I am one of the few who gives our country any voice of its own—I claim no credit—it is only that I have seen with my own eye and that I couldn't help seeing with my own eye.[23]

It should perhaps be borne in mind that this statement was made well before Jackson Pollock and the abstract expressionists of New York, directly inspired by surrealism's concern for the "unknown within," burst upon (and took over) the world art scene in the 1950s, with their abstraction based upon native American myth, the subconscious and personal gestural techniques.

Georgia O'Keeffe was one of the most autobiographical painters of the twentieth century. She herself admitted, "I find that I have painted my life—things happening in my life—without knowing."[24] But it may take generations before we are able to unlock the meaning of her pictorial forms—not least because critics, historians, and those who look closely always find new questions to ask of great visual images, and time may well put some of her paintings into this perennially radical category. For now, her depicted objects (however abstracted) should probably be read as ideas having to do with body and spirit. As with any major artist, however, no single perspective is possible. This is as true for the feminist viewpoint as for any other.[25] From her own words and actions, O'Keeffe comes across as one who sincerely believed that to separate painting, or music, or literature, into two sexes is to emphasize values in these forms that is *not* art. Hence her determination never to be billed as a "woman artist." She was, nonetheless, acutely aware of the role played by gender in the making of all art—and of her own in particular. She made her position on the issue of feminism very clear in a 1930 debate with Michael Gold, editor of *New Masses*. This remarkably forthcoming statement, elicited under pressure, is as revealing of her intelligence of vocation as anything she ever said publicly.

> I am interested in the oppression of women of all classes . . . though not nearly so definitely and so consistently as I am in the abstractions of painting. But one has affected the other. . . . I have had to go to men as sources in my painting because the past has left us so small an inheritance of woman's painting that has widened life. . . . Before I put a brush to canvas I question, "Is this mine? Is it all intrinsically of myself? Is it influenced by some idea or some photograph of an idea which I have acquired from some man?"
>
> That too implies a social consciousness, a social struggle. I am trying with all my skill to do painting that is all of a woman, as well as all of me. . . . I have no hesitancy in contending that my painting of a flower may be just as much a product of this age as a cartoon about the freedom of women—or the working class—or anything else.[26]

Sixty years later, we can see plainly that O'Keeffe did succeed in making an original art after herself. Her emotionally conceptual images were composed from many human and historical connections, but they gleam with her own rollicking wit, her maverick spirituality, and the doubts, fears, angers, and loves of a lifetime.

Notes

[1]Georgia O'Keeffe, *Georgia O'Keeffe*, (New York, 1976), unpaginated.

[2]O'Keeffe to Mitchell Kennerly, 20 January 1929, *Georgia O'Keeffe: Art and Letters*, Sarah Greenough, et al. (Boston, 1987), no. 41.

[3]O'Keeffe (1976).

[4]Barbara Novak, *American Painting of the Nineteenth Century* (New York, 1979), pp. 15, 55, 59.

[5]Theodore Stebbins, *A New World: Masterpieces of American Painting 1760–1910* (Boston, 1983), pp. 64–65.

[6]For a documented account of this historic exhibition see Milton W. Brown, *The Story of the Armory Show* (New York, 1963).

[7]O'Keeffe to Pollitzer, 11 October 1915, quoted in *A Woman on Paper*, Anita Pollitzer (New York, 1988), p. 24.

[8]Statement by Georgia O'Keeffe in *Alfred Stieglitz Presents One Hundred Pictures by Georgia O'Keeffe*, exhibition catalogue, the Anderson Galleries, 1923.

[9]Pollitzer to O'Keeffe, 1 January 1916, quoted in *The Art & Life of Georgia O'Keeffe*, Jan Garden Castro, (New York, 1985), p. 30.

[10]Quoted in Nessa Forman, "Georgia O'Keeffe and Her Art: Paint What's in Your Head," *Philadelphia Museum Art Bulletin*, 22 October 1971.

[11]*Georgia O'Keeffe: A Portrait by Alfred Stieglitz*, introduction by Georgia O'Keeffe (New York, 1978), unpaginated.

[12]As quoted in Arthur J. Eddy, *Cubists and Post Impressionism* (Chicago, 1914), pp. 96–97. In her correspondence with Pollitzer O'Keeffe cites reading this book.

[13]Quoted in Dorothy Norman, *Alfred Stieglitz : An American Seer* (New York, 1960), pp. 136–138.

[14]Stieglitz to Sherwood Anderson, 18 September 1923, Newberry Library, Chicago. White symbolism was an extremely popular theme in turn-of-the-century literature and painting, appearing often in the writings of Maurice Maeterlinck and Stéphane Mallarmé.

[15]Quoted in Herbert J. Seligmann, *Stieglitz Talking* (New Haven, 1966), p. 56.

[16]For a biography of this brilliant, charismatic man, see Sue Davidson Lowe, *Stieglitz* (New York, 1983). See also Laurie Lisle, *Portrait of an Artist: A Biography of Georgia O'Keeffe* (Albuquerque, New Mexico, 1986), and Roxana Robinson, *Georgia O'Keeffe: A Life* (New York: Harper and Row, 1989).

[17]*Georgia O'Keeffe: A Portrait by Alfred Stieglitz*, (New York, 1978), unpaginted.

[18]O'Keeffe (1976).

[19]O'Keeffe to Henry McBride, early 1940s, *Georgia O'Keeffe: Art and Letters*, no. 94.

[20]O'Keeffe to William Howard Schubart, 8 April 1950, in ibid., no. 103.

[21]O'Keeffe to Margaret Kiscadden, 9 March 1950, ibid, no. 104.

[22]O'Keeffe to William Howard Schubart, 4 January 1953, ibid, no. 112.

[23]O'Keeffe to James Johnson Sweeney, 11 June 1945, ibid, no. 90.

[24]O'Keeffe (1976).

[25]For an excellent summary of the important feminist perspective on art history during the last fifteen years, see Thalia Gouma-Peterson and Patricia Mathews, "The Feminist Critique of Art History," *Art Bulletin*, (September, 1987), pp. 326–357.

[26]O'Keeffe quoted in Gladys Oaks, "Radical Writer and Woman Artist Clash on Propaganda and its Uses," *New York World*, 16 March 1930, Woman's Sections, pp. 1,3.

Margaret Mead

(1901–1978)

Rosalind Rosenberg

Margaret Mead was born on December 16, 1901, in Philadelphia. Her mother, Emily Fogg Mead, was a feminist as well as an academic. After a year at DePauw University in Indiana, Margaret Mead transferred to Barnard College in New York City in 1920. There, her chief mentor was anthropologist Ruth Benedict. Mead earned two degrees at Columbia, an M.A. in psychology (1924) and a Ph.D. in anthropology (1929). She married sociologist Luther Cressman in 1923. Her fieldwork in Samoa in 1925 was the basis for Mead's Coming of Age in Samoa *(1928), a book "about the Samoa and the United States of 1926–1928." From this book and her other works emerge pictures both of Mead as an individual and of the changing facets of American feminism throughout the century. On her return from Samoa, Mead took up an appointment as assistant curator at the American Museum of Natural History of New York in 1926, and had a lifelong affiliation with Columbia. Mead published thirty-nine books and a vast number of articles, as well as making numerous records, tapes, and films. Mead divorced Cressman in 1928 to marry fellow anthropologist Reo Fortune, whom she divorced in 1935. Her third marriage to Gregory Bateson, lasted from 1936 to 1950. Bateson, too, was a famous anthropologist and psychologist. It was with Bateson that Mead had her only child, Mary Catherine Bateson, who published an account of her parents,* With a Daughter's Eye, *in 1984. Mead took a particular interest in world hunger and helped establish UNESCO, the United Nations agency committed to establishing world peace through cultural exchange. She was consulted as an expert on a wide range of issues, particularly in American culture. Her achievements have been widely honored. She died on November 15, 1978.*

Margaret Mead was born in 1901, the year Queen Victoria died, and throughout her life she radiated the confident optimism of the British monarch's final years. She achieved fame, however, not for her Victorian temperament, but for her anti-Victorian career. Working as an anthropologist among the primitive tribes of the South Pacific, Mead blasted the Victorians for their smug confidence in the superiority of Western culture, questioned their settled belief in the rightness of feminine subordination, and criticized their deep reticence about sexuality. For a century, Western governments had employed anthropology to influence and manipulate other cultures. Mead used it to challenge her own.

Mead came by her iconoclasm naturally. Her paternal grandmother had attended college, when fewer than 2 percent of Americans did so, and her parents were both social scientists. Her father, Professor Edward Mead, taught at the Wharton School of Business in Philadelphia, while her mother, Emily Fogg Mead, struggled to complete a Ph.D. in sociology while caring for five children. From the time Margaret was one year old until she was nine, the Meads spent each spring and fall in Hammonton, New Jersey. Margaret's mother selected Hammonton because of its large number of Italians, whom she could study for her dissertation on the acculturation of immigrants, but the small town proved educational for Margaret and her siblings as well. When they complained of the odd behavior of their playmates, Emily tried to make them understand that the neighborhood childred acted as they did, "not because of differences in the color of [their] skin or the shape of [their] heads," but because of "their life experience and the life experience of their ancestors."[1]

Margaret Mead absorbed her mother's critical spirit, but she struggled against her strict feminist principles. Emily Fogg Mead had reached maturity at the turn of the century, as the movement for women's rights was building to a crescendo. The social reform and suffrage movements of those years had captured her imagination and reinforced her sense of outrage at the special difficulties women faced in a male-dominated world. A fervent supporter of the American Association of University Women and the Women's Trade Union League, Emily sought to do her part to create broader opportunities for all women. Her eldest daughter, however, chafed under the private dimension of her mother's feminist commitment. "I wanted to wear a hat with ribbons and fluffy petticoats," Margaret Mead later remembered, "instead of the sensible bloomers that very advanced mothers put on their daughters so they could climb trees." In her moments of thwarted femininity Margaret turned to her paternal grandmother, who lived with the family and who seemed to Margaret less filled with "feminist aggrievement" than her mother.

Premature widowhood had limited Grandmother Mead to only one pregnancy, and Margaret later conceded that "had she borne five children and had little opportunity to use her special gifts and training," she might have taken as stern a view of feminist discipline as did her daughter-in-law. As it was, however, Grandmother Mead condoned the traditional trappings of femininity so long as they did not interfere with her granddaughter's intellectual development.[2]

Margaret could hardly have asked for greater encouragement than she received from her family, but she always regretted the unrelieved seriousness that accompanied it. Her mother had "no gift for play, and very little for pleasure or comfort," Mead later recalled. Her father had even less. He rarely reached toward his children, and when he did he lacked a tender touch. The only time he ever put Margaret's shoes on, the day her brother was born, he forced them onto the wrong feet. Only her grandmother provided the warmth she longed for, and even she could never satisfy Margaret's craving for affection. "I loved the feel of her soft skin," Margaret said years later, "but she never would let me give her an extra kiss."[3]

Not until Mead met Luther Cressman did she find the qualities she so missed in her family. Cressman was demonstrative, funny, and empathetic, all the things her relatives were not. Yet, unlike most of the boys she met as she was growing up, he took education seriously and respected ambition in girls. When he proposed to her in 1919, the year she completed high school and he graduated from Pennsylvania State College, she accepted. They agreed to defer marriage, however, so that he could study for the ministry, and she could go to college.[4]

But suddenly, the prospect of college looked doubtful for Mead. Serious losses in a business venture in the spring of 1919 undermined Edward Mead's commitment to his eldest child's education, and only the determination of Margaret's mother and grandmother stiffened his resolve. In the end, Margaret set off, not for Wellesley, Bryn Mawr, or Chicago, where her mother had studied, but for her father's college, DePauw. She left for Indiana with images of the great openness and freedom that her parents had always taught her the West represented. A year later she returned, bitterly denouncing the anti-intellectualism and antidemocratic atmosphere of an institution dominated by sororities and fraternities. Had her mother's conscientious schooling in the evils of prejudice not already penetrated her consciousness in childhood, the rejection she suffered from the sorority of her choice was enough to persuade her of bigotry's poison. For her sophomore year she transferred to Barnard College, the women's college of Columbia University.[5]

Barnard had always prided itself on its cosmopolitan character, but never more so than in the 1920s when New York City, from Greenwich Village to Harlem, was afire with cultural excitement. At Barnard, Mead had the further advantage of being near Cressman, who was studying at the General Theological Seminary on West Twenty-third Street. At a time when sexual appeal was becoming an increasingly important index of success for college women, having a fiancé relieved Mead from undue worry about her worth as a woman. As she later told a friend, being engaged was "very comfortable, and pleasant; it kept me from worrying about men or dates."[6]

Her popularity with men convincingly demonstrated, Mead spent most of her spare time with Barnard friends with whom she shared an apartment on the edge of campus. They called themselves the Ash Can Cats, which was what a Barnard professor said they looked like after staying up too late at night. Together they cooked, read Freud and Edna St. Vincent Millay, took the Fifth Avenue bus to Greenwich Village, and went constantly to the theater. Mead quickly took charge of the group, bossing them, nurturing them, worrying about their love affairs, and, in turn, being cared for by them. They became her extended family, filling in for the grandmother, parents, and siblings she had left behind and replacing the sorority that had rejected her.[7]

Pleased though she was to have won the approval of this sisterhood, her closest tie at Barnard was not to any other student, but rather to an anthropology instructor fifteen years her senior named Ruth Benedict. A 1909 graduate of Vassar, married, but childless, Benedict was a latecomer to anthropology. After unhappy stints as a charity worker, a high school teacher, and an amateur historian, she had returned to school in 1919, taking a series of lectures on anthropology at the New School for Social Research. Thrilled by the intellectual excitement generated in these classes, she enrolled at Columbia to study with Franz Boas, who at sixty-three was the unchallenged patriarch of American anthropology.[8]

A German Jew, Boas's commitment to egalitarian principles had been forged in his childhood by painful experiences with anti-Semitism, and confirmed in adulthood by American xenophobia.[9] When Benedict arrived at Columbia, Boas had just come through a particularly trying period. His unwillingness to speak out against Germany during World War I had put him in a unpopular position with University President Nicholas Murray Butler, who reduced the Columbia Anthropology Department to one member, Boas, and eliminated undergraduate instruction in anthropology at Columbia. By 1919 only Barnard students had permission to attend his courses.[10]

This clipping of his professional wings bothered Boas very little. He had long been dissatisfied with his Columbia undergraduates. "The quality of the Columbia students is on the whole not as good as I would like to see it," Boas had complained to President Butler. "I think it is largely due to the fact that a large percentage of the Columbia students prepare for professional work, and very few of the better class find time for an isolated subject such as anthropology." Boas much preferred teaching at Barnard, where preprofessionalism seemed less intense. In contrast to his Columbia undergraduates, Boas found that "the Barnard students are interested in the subject, intelligent, and take hold of it in a satisfactory way." With his undergraduate work now confined to Barnard, however, Boas decided that he should have a female assistant to lead discussions in his lecture course and to supervise field trips to the Museum of Natural History. He hired Ruth Benedict.[11]

Having found a purpose in life, Benedict lacked only "a companion in harness," someone who could explore anthropology with her and give her the love that her husband reserved for his medical research. She found that companion in Margaret Mead, who, entering her senior year as a psychology major, elected to take Boas's introductory course in general anthropology.[12]

Awed by Boas's demanding lectures, Mead looked for advice and support to his less intimidating assistant. Shy, beautiful, and dressed indifferently Ruth Benedict captivated the intense senior's attention. "Professor Boas and I have nothing to offer but an opportunity to do what matters," she told Mead in one of their many talks that year. Anthropology mattered, Benedict wrote in 1924, because it sought to resolve a fundamental issue of human life, "how far the forces at work in civilization are cultural, and how far organic or due to heredity." As a brilliant woman living in a society still deeply suspicious of female intelligence, Benedict was obsessed with the nature-nurture question. Primitive cultures seemed to offer a laboratory for exploring the question of how much of human behavior was universal, therefore presumably natural, and how much was socially induced, but year by year these cultures were passing away. "Anthropology had to be done *now*," Mead concluded, as she committed herself to Benedict and to anthropology. "Other things could wait."[13]

Having resolved to become an anthropologist, Mead also decided to marry. Her family did not understand why she was in such a rush. Cressman, who had begun graduate work in sociology at Columbia after completing his divinity studies, worried that they would not have enough to live on as students, but Mead was determined. Ruth Benedict had a husband, most women did. Mead seemed to feel that she ought to have one too. She did not intend, however, to cease being known as Margaret Mead. "I'm going to be famous some day," she declared at the end of a lively argument with her distraught father, "and I'm going to be known by my own name." Mead had her way. On September 2, 1923, she married Cressman in the little Episcopal church in Buckingham, Pennsylvania, where she had been baptized. As Cressman later recalled, she was twenty-one, he was twenty-six, and they were both virgins.[14]

Mead came to anthropology at a point when racism and xenophobia were reaching new heights in America. Still reeling from the most recent influx of immigrants from southern and eastern Europe, many white Americans were confronting African-Americans in large numbers for the first time. With the closing off of immigration during World War I, northern employers found that the only pool of unskilled labor they could still tap was that of blacks caught in southern poverty. Blacks began moving northward, only to be met by ugly race riots and an intensification of both anti-immigrant and anti-black feeling.[15]

Psychological tests conducted by the army during World War I reinforced the general hysteria. The tests purported to prove that recent immigrants and blacks were markedly less intelligent than other Americans. In doing so, they confirmed the biological determinism made popular by Eugenists, scientists who argued that America stood in danger of being swamped by mentally deficient and fecund lesser races. Boas denounced this belief in racial inferiority and sponsored numerous studies that sought to challenge it. One assignment went to Mead, who spent her first year after college earning an M.A. in psychology by studying her former Italian neighbors in Hammonton, New Jersey. Mead found that the longer her subjects had been in America and the more English they spoke at home, the better they did on tests that supposedly measured innate endowment. Her findings persuaded her that intelligence was no fixed quality, but a capacity that could either develop or be crippled, depending upon a person's surroundings.[16]

The year Mead completed her M.A. thesis, Congress virtually cut off immigration from southern and eastern Europe. In this hostile climate Boas believed that there was "a fundamental need for a scientific and detailed investigation of heredity and environmental conditions." The best way to challenge the hereditarians, he decided, would be through a study of adolescence in a culture markedly different from those of Western Europe and the United States, and the best person to do it would be his young student Margaret Mead.[17]

Scholars had been preoccupied with the topic of adolescence for many decades. Psychologist G. Stanley Hall had suggested in his massive study of adolescence in 1904 that the storm and stress of the teenage years stemmed from physiological forces. With the onset of puberty, Hall wrote, "the floodgates of heredity seem opened and . . .

passions and desires spring into vigorous life." Boys as well as girls suffered on the stormy seas of adolescence, but Hall, in common with many scholars of his day, believed that the special demands of girls' maturing reproductive organs made them particularly subject to the physiological dislocations of puberty, especially if they were unwisely subjected to the added strain of higher education. By the 1920s a few psychologists and sociologists were beginning to question Hall's "hereditary floodgates," but because they worked in the same culture, these researchers could only speculate about how much of the rebellion they observed among youths could be avoided. Only by looking at a culture free of Western influence could the issue of the inevitability of adolescent rebelliousness be examined in a fundamentally new way. This is what Boas wanted done.[18]

Mead entered graduate work in anthropology with the intention of working either with immigrant groups in the United States, as her mother had done, or of doing fieldwork among the Amerindians, as Ruth Benedict was doing. But a trip to the British Association for the Advancement of Science in Toronto in the summer of 1924 made the prospect of studying groups that others had already visited seem unexciting. In Toronto, she met professional anthropologists who were working among peoples in Africa and the South Pacific who had never seen an anthropologist before. Everyone talked about "my people," and she felt disadvantaged in having no people of her own.[19]

Mead asked Boas to let her go to the South Pacific; Boas said no. The topic he had in mind for her could be investigated just as well in America as in a region so far away. Besides, the South Pacific was too dangerous, especially for a small, twenty-three-year-old woman. Recounting "a sort of litany of young men who had died or been killed while they were working outside the United States," he insisted that she venture no farther than the American Southwest. Undaunted, Mead appealed to her mentor's egalitarian ideals. "I knew that there was one thing that mattered more to Boas than the direction taken by anthropological research. This was that he should behave like a liberal, democratic man, not a Prussian autocrat." Faced with the charge that he was dealing with a student in an arbitrary manner, and prodded by Ruth Benedict to relent, Boas compromised. If Mead would accept his project of a comparative study of female adolescence, he would support her. She agreed.[20]

For any other woman in the 1920s, the problems Mead faced in dealing with her adviser would have paled before the resistance she would have met from her family. But Mead, unique in so many ways, was especially blessed in her family relations. Trained as social scientists, her parents, as well as her new husband, understood the importance of fieldwork and supported her desire to do something original.

Mead and Cressman discussed the idea of his accompanying her, but Mead's attitude, as Cressman later ruefully recalled, "was that I didn't have the skills or the insights to go there." During the year she spent in the South Pacific, he studied in Europe.[21]

Mead wanted to visit as primitive and remote a people as she could so that the impact of Western influence would be minimized. Initially, she chose the remote Tuamotu Islands, part of French Polynesia, but Boas would not hear of her going there. He insisted that she choose an island to which a ship came regularly at least every three weeks. So she settled on American Samoa, a U.S. protectorate in the South Pacific, where the navy had a base and where her way could be eased by the surgeon general of the United States, a friend of her father-in-law.[22]

Samoa was far from untouched. Congregationalist missionaries from London had been there for over a hundred years, and now missionary schools dotted its islands and a pastor's house graced every village. Despite this Christian influence, however, Samoa remained primitive, and Mead was able to work on one of the most remote islands, the island of Tau, where she lived with the family of the naval officer who ran the dispensary in one of the villages. Each village on Tau was divided into between thirty and forty households whose composition varied from the biological family consisting of parents and children only, to households of fifteen and twenty people who were all related to the head of the household or to his wife by blood, marriage, or adoption. The villagers lived in beehive-shaped houses with floors of coral rubble and walls of perishable woven blinds that were kept rolled up except in bad weather. The villagers were Americanized to the point of attending church and wearing cotton cloth rather than the more traditional bark, but they spoke no English, and in much of their daily life they followed traditional customs, living a mostly self-sufficient existence of fishing and simple agriculture.[23]

Though Mead wanted to study adolescence, she realized that she could not understand the adolescent period without establishing its place within the entire female life cycle. Therefore in the nine months available to her for field work, she complimented her intensive study of fifty girls between the ages of ten and twenty with observations of the preadolescent girls and the grown women of the village.

The infant girl, Mead observed, entered the world without ceremony. Though she slept with her mother as long as she was nursing (two or three years), the principal responsibility for her care rested with an older girl of six or seven, who thereby freed the infant's mother for weaving, gardening, or fishing. Handed carelessly from one person to the next, the infant soon learned not to care "for one person greatly" nor to set "high hopes on any one relationship." At about six the little girl outgrew her guardian and became, in turn, the guardian of some new infant. Baby-tending remained her most important task until puberty, when she was relieved of it to work on the plantation, carry footstuffs down to the village, and learn the more elaborate household skills.[24]

Of girls at adolescence Mead observed, "It may be said with some justice that the worse period of their lives is over. Never again will they be so incessantly at the beck and call of their elders, never again so tyrannized by two-year-old tyrants. All the irritating, detailed routine of housekeeping, which in our civilization is accused of warping the souls and souring the tempers of grown women, is here performed by children under fourteen years of age." The adolescent girl was expected to become proficient in the work that would fall to her as an adult—weaving, planting, fishing. But she was in no hurry about this. "Proficiency would mean more work, and earlier marriage, and marriage is the inevitable to be deferred as long as possible."[25]

The greater freedom of adolescence and the casual attitude toward work and preparation for later responsibilities did much to diffuse any tension that might develop between a child and her parents, but perhaps even more important was the fact that every girl had multiple ties to adults in authority. "Few children live continuously in one household, but are always testing out other possibility residences . . . under the guise of visits. The minute that the mildest annoyance grows up at home, the possibility of flight moderates the discipline and alleviates the child's sense of dependency."[26]

With the onset of puberty came an awakening of interest in the opposite sex, but this new interest constituted no more than a variation of a long-standing sexual awareness. The girls had been masturbating since at least the age of six, had engaged in casual homosexuality, and had frequently witnessed intercourse. While "all expressions of affection are rigorously barred in public," Mead wrote, "the lack of privacy within the houses where mosquito netting marks off purely formal walls about the married couples, and the custom of young lovers using palm groves for their rendezvous makes it inevitable that children should see intercourse, often and between many different people." Sex was viewed as natural, and while there was a formal belief that girls should be virgins at marriage, many were not. With few exceptions, adolescence in Samoa "represented no period of crisis or stress, but was instead an orderly developing of a set of slowly maturing interests and activities."[27]

The United States, Mead concluded, had much to learn about adolescence from the Samoans. First, Americans could greatly minimize the conflicts of adolescence by finding ways of relieving the intense emotional pressure created by their small, tightly knit families. Samoan children could visit friends or relatives if parents became too overbearing; American children could not so easily do so. Remembering the mediating role her grandmother had played in her own childhood household, Margaret found among the Samoans confirmation for her belief that Americans would be much better off if parenting were more widely shared. Children should not be reared by mothers alone, but by a variety of other people as well— including, if necessary, social welfare agencies and psychiatrists.

Americans could further diffuse the emotional intensity of adolescence by adopting the Samoans' openness toward sex. Exposed to the sexual relations of others from early childhood, proficient in masturbation, and likely to have sexual experience before marriage, Samoan girls, Mead believed, did not suffer the intense sexual anxieties so prevalent among American teenagers.

Finally, Mead approved of the Samoan girls' early introduction to work. From earliest childhood, girls labored in a purposeful way, working their way into adult activities. American girls, by contrast, suffered from the sharp discontinuities of childhood play, followed by an education that was cut short by maternal drudgery. What children did as children in America, and especially what females did as children, had nothing to do with what they were to do as adults. The advances made by American women in higher education simply exacerbated the sense of discontinuity in their lives by giving women a sense of choice they later found difficult to exploit. The adolescent girl in America needed to know that her education was leading toward some purposeful end.[28]

Published in 1928 as *Coming of Age in Samoa,* Mead's study of adolescence won an immediate and enthusiastic audience in America. In a country increasingly concerned with the rebelliousness and sexual precocity of the young here was a book with some answers. Rebelliousness was not inevitable. Sex was not bad. Later anthropologists would take Mead to task for much that she said. Some charged that she had downplayed conflict in Samoan society, ignoring the passionate struggle for independence from American political control taking place all around her, exaggerating the degree of sexual freedom, and slighting the competition for rank in Samoan society. In 1969, responding to one particularly impassioned critic, Mead accepted some criticisms and attributed others to regional differences or to changes in Samoan society over time, but she concluded with an important point about perspective. "[T]o the young girl, . . . uninvolved in the rivalries that were related to rank and prestige, moving gently, unhurriedly toward adulthood, the preoccupations of the whole society may have seemed more remote than they would have appeared from any other vantage point. And this is the vantage point from which I saw it."[29]

Mead was a pioneer. In a profession dominated by men, who were interested in the concerns of their male subjects, she set off to study the experience of young women. The lesson that she taught in doing so has proved to be one of the most important of the twentieth century: each society is seen differently by those occupying different positions within it. Men had always looked at societies from the vantage point of chiefs and presidents. In a revolutionary turnabout, Mead advocated placing women at the center of any attempt to understand a culture's character.

On her way back from Samoa, Mead met Reo Fortune, a young New Zealand psychologist, whose work on Sigmund Freud's and W. H. R. River's theories of dreams had won him a fellowship to study in England. "We talked nonstop for six weeks," Mead later recalled, "fitting all that each of us had learned into a new approach to the study of primitive peoples." By the time Mead joined her husband, she found that she had fallen in love with the young New Zealander. Fortune gave her what Cressman could not, a brilliant understanding of the intellectual issues that consumed her and a passionate commitment to anthropological fieldwork. In the 1920s getting a divorce invited scandal, but when Mead reached Marseilles, she told Cressman that she saw no future in their marriage. Within two years she was married to Fortune.[30]

Back in New York Mead went to work as an assistant curator for ethnology at the American Museum of Natural History, taught a class at Columbia, and completed her Ph.D. with a thesis entitled, "An Inquiry into the Question of Cultural Stability in Polynesia" (1929). Though more than qualified for an assistant professorship, she settled for teaching on an adjunct basis at Columbia, while working at the Museum of Natural History. Boas had few academic jobs to distribute to his students, and he assigned those he had on the basis of financial need. Ruth Benedict did not have a full-time position at Columbia until she was divorced from her husband, and the jobs at Barnard always went to unmarried women with no other means of support. Because she was married, Mead could not expect Boas's assistance in finding an academic position, but the curatorship offered her by the Museum of Natural History while she was still in Samoa was more attractive in some ways than an academic appointment. Whereas in a university setting Mead would have had to pick her way through the hostile terrain of a male-dominated institution, in the southwest tower of the museum she was able to build her own fiefdom, one populated almost exclusively by young women chosen for their intelligence and the likelihood that they would move on to their own careers in a few years. These were the foot soldiers in Mead's anthropological army. They organized her field notes, picked up her laundry, and gave her backrubs. Mead achieved unprecedented success in a male world, but from the Ash Can Cats to her south-tower staff, she did so within the protective borders of a devoted female community.[31]

In writing *Coming of Age in Samoa*, Mead suggested that if the crisis of adolescence, with its discontinuities and conflict over goals, could be mitigated, women's lot would be far happier. But the more she talked with Ruth Benedict about the problem of women's nature and role, the more she came to believe that adolescence was simply a particularly dramatic episode in a larger pattern. The problem for American women was not so much the crisis of adolescence, but the absence of real choice in the matter of personal temperament at any stage of their lives. The West, Mead complained, was so accustomed to a thoroughgoing sexual polarity that no one seemed able to conceive of sexual relations without extreme sex differentiation. The pervasiveness of this assumption of sexual polarity found ample demonstration in a widely read feminist work of the 1920s written by Mathilde and Mathis Vaerting. The Vaertings argued that in early matriarchal societies women had dominated men and had shown all of the qualities of aggression that Western men later came to embody. To Mead this understanding of sex was incredibly narrow and culturally biased. So thoroughly did the Vaertings accept the polarization of the sexes that the only alternative to the Western pattern they could imagine was simple role reversal. Surely, Mead thought, there were other ways of patterning sexual behavior than either the one condoned by modern civilization or the flip side of that pattern championed by the Vaertings.[32]

In 1931 Mead traveled with her new husband Reo Fortune to New Guinea to study sexual differences in primitive cultures. They lived among three different peoples, starting with the Arapesh, a group they visited simply because their carriers did not want to transport their equipment all the way to their original destination and dumped it instead in the Arapesh's mountain village. The steep mountains made cultivation extremely difficult, and the possibility of starvation always threatened. Under these harsh conditions, this mountain people had fashioned a simple culture in which the personality and roles of men and women alike were "stylized as parental, cherishing and mildly sexed." For their second group Mead and Fortune journeyed to the cannibalistic region of the Yuat River and studied the Mundugumor, where both the men and the women were fiercely aggressive, highly sexed, and noncherishing toward their children. Finally, they studied the people living on the shore of Tchambuli Lake, where Mead found a surprising reversal of conventional Western roles, the women acting in a brisk, businesslike, and cooperative way and the men behaving in a catty, exhibitionist way, preoccupied with decorative and artistic activities. By the time they had finished with the Tchambuli, Mead had the theme she wanted. Sex was not necessarily as important a basis for behavioral differences as Americans, and indeed most Westerners, believed.[33]

"If those temperamental attitudes which we have traditionally regarded as feminine," wrote Mead, "such as passivity, responsiveness and willingness to cherish children—can so easily be set up as the masculine pattern in one tribe, and in another be outlawed for the majority of women as well as for the majority of men, we no longer have any basis for regarding such aspects of behavior as sex-linked." The sharply contrasting cultural styles of the Arapesh, Mundugumors, and Tchambuli persuaded Mead that "many, if not all of the personality traits which we have called masculine or feminine are as lightly linked to sex as are clothing, the manners and the form of head-dress that a society at a given period assigns to either sex." Human nature, she concluded, was "almost unbelieveably malleable."[34]

Published as *Sex and Temperament*, Mead's study of these three cultures further popularized the environmentalist beliefs of the Boasians. Not all critics accepted Mead's findings, however. Some found it incredible that she could have happened on three such neatly patterned societies. Her own husband and fieldwork partner, in an article entitled the "Arapesh Warrior," later questioned her characterization of the Arapesh as "passive" and "cherishing." Despite these criticisms, Mead believed that her fundamental insight remained unassailable. For anyone willing to look, the world displayed an extraordinary diversity of gender patterning. She found further support for her patterning idea from an English anthropologist who joined Mead and Fortune on the final stage of their research. This was Gregory Bateson, who worked nearby as they studied the Tchambuli. Seeing Gregory often, amid the exhilaration of fieldwork, Mead found herself falling in love once again.[35]

The Mead-Fortune marriage had proved rocky from the start. Mead was brilliant, but she was driven and uncompromising. Fortune was brilliant, but he was cranky and given to emotional outbursts. In the field these qualities did not mix well. The tall, gangly, charming Gregory Bateson seemed to combine Cressman's calm with Fortune's passion for anthropological fieldwork. He also looked like good father material. Mead relished the fame she had won as an anthropologist, but professional success did not make up for the fact that she was childless. Not that she had wanted children at first. Like most career women of her time she had believed that work precluded motherhood. But as she grew older, her views changed. She had her career, but she wanted to be a mother too. Not with Fortune, of course; Fortune would make a terrible father. But Bateson would be perfect.[36]

In 1935, Mead divorced for a second time, and, accompanying Bateson on a new field trip to Bali, began her third marriage. After suffering several miscarriages, she returned to New York in 1939 to have her daughter Mary Catherine Bateson. Gregory Bateson was in England at the time, trying to find a way to be useful to the English who were under attack from Hitler. But pediatrician Benjamin Spock, who would later write *Baby and Child Care,* was there, and Mead arranged for the event to be photographed just as she had photographed innumerable births in the field.[37]

Motherhood changed Mead's life. Drawing on the pattern of her childhood and of the primitive cultures she had studied, she set about creating an extended family to help her raise Cathy. At first she relied on Helen Burrows, an experienced English nanny with a fourteen-year-old child of her own to support. Then, when Cathy was two, the Mead-Batesons moved into the first floor of a Greenwich Village townhouse owned by Lawrence and Mary Frank. Lawrence Frank worked for the Rockefeller Foundation and spent his career holding conferences that brought together anthropologists, sociologists, psychologists, and psychoanalysts to work on various aspects of human development in the 1930s and 1940s. Cathy grew up with the Frank children, under the watchful eye of Mary Frank. Also drawn into the extended family network was Marie Eichelberger, one of Mead's friends from Barnard. "Aunt Marie," as Cathy called her, was a social worker, who served as Mead's general factotum. Throughout their lives together, Eichelberger served as Mead's banker and attorney; she helped her get ready for her field trips; and she helped raise Cathy. There were others, as well, who picked Cathy up after school, and cared for her when her mother was out of town. Mead's colleague Melville Herskovits once said, "You're certainly lucky, Margaret to have all these slaves." "They're not slaves, Mel," Mead replied, "they're people who like to help me." "They're slaves all the same," Herskovits replied.[38]

Mead doubled up on her teaching and cut back on her work at the museum to have more time for her daughter. She hired a maid to clean the apartment, but she made a ritual, when she was in New York, of breakfasting with Cathy each morning and returning home in the evening to prepare their dinner. Bateson contributed little to the complicated arrangements that surrounded Cathy's upbringing. To Mead's sorrow, he slowly drifted away. Unable to keep up with the frenetic pace that she set herself, he became involved with other women who could dote on him. In 1950, Mead and Bateson divorced.[39]

One of the ways in which motherhood changed Mead's life was in her approach to her work. Gradually, maternity came to take center stage in her depiction of gender roles in primitive cultures. The American celebration of family life that followed upon the sacrifices of fifteen years of depression and war reinforced this shift in Mead's thinking, and in 1949 she elaborated on her new sense of maternity's importance in her book *Male and Female*. In her earlier books motherhood had been but an incident in the life cycle, always positively depicted but never having a dominant impact on the culture at large. The power of the Eugenists in the 1920s and the rise of Hitler in the 1930s had made her especially sensitive to the evil uses to which biology could be put, and in her early writings she strove to minimize any suggestion of its importance in human life. By the time she wrote *Male and Female*, however, Mead had begun, tentatively, to discuss the ways in which biology might work dialectically with environmental forces to shape culture. Maternity became the central feature of this dialectic, the one great problem that Mead believed all cultures must confront in organizing gender roles. How, she tried to explain, do societies deal with regularities in the human condition, like pregnancy and childbirth? How do men around the world deal with the fact that they will never bear a child?[40]

While Mead emphasized the need to take maternity into account in explaining the differing ways that cultures pattern gender roles, she scorned the apotheosis of motherhood that was coming to pervade post World War II American society. She objected, in particular, to Ferdinand Lundberg and Marynia Farnham's Freudian inspired bestseller, *Modern Woman: The Lost Sex*. Lundberg and Farnham condemned what they saw as the the neurotic strivings of feminists and called for a return to passive, dependent femininity. Mead had long been interested in psychoanalysis, but she believed that Lundberg and Farnham erred badly in their uncritical acceptance of Freud's belief that "penis envy" lay at the root of the female personality structure. Women suffered not so much from "penis envy," Mead countered, as from envy of the special power and privilege that societies awarded to those who possessed penises. Moreover, any envy that girls might have of the male sex organs (and Mead believed that such envy sometimes did exist) was counterbalanced by the envy little boys often exhibited for the remarkable reproductive organs of the female sex. In contrast to Lundberg and Farnham's tales of penis envy, Mead reported primitive societies in which male ceremonials imitated gestation and childbearing in an obvious display of "womb-envy."[41]

Fourteen years later, Betty Friedan would include Mead in her list of the villainous creators of what she called the "Feminine Mystique," the postwar veneration of domesticated motherhood. Mead resented Friedan's characterization of her as someone caught in a "functional freeze." It was true that she talked in *Male and Female* about the ways in which societies used sexual characteristics to shape gender roles, that she emphasized the positive aspects of maternity, and that she warned of the difficulties society's interconnectedness placed in the way of reform. But her warnings about the difficulties of change stood alongside her warnings of the danger of stasis: "To the extent that either sex is disadvantaged, the whole culture is poorer, and the sex that, superficially, inherits the earth, inherits only a very partial legacy." Moreover, at a time when Friedan, having turned down a graduate fellowship in psychology, was newly married, pregnant, and headed for suburbia, Mead was regretting in *Male and Female* that so few cultures had found a way "to give women a divine discontent that will demand other satisfactions than those of child-bearing."[42]

Mead never called herself a feminist. Feminists were women like her mother whose "feminist aggrievement" made them unhappy about being women, or those like Alice Paul and other supporters of the Equal Rights Amendment who minimized differences in the experiences of men and women and therefore did not reckon with the difficulties those differences posed for comprehensive social reconstruction. "If the women's movement has done any harm," she once told newswoman Barbara Walters, "it's to make it seem as if it all were easy. It *isn't* easy!"[43]

Despite such criticisms as this, by the 1970s many had come to view her as a grandmother of modern feminism. She played that role in her own way, continuing to work until her death in 1978, returning again and again to the South Pacific, maintaining intimate friendships with both men and women, glorying in becoming a grandmother, writing books and articles, and lecturing on the themes that had informed her life's work. She tried to persuade her audiences that understanding the lives of other people could help them understand their own, that a greater ease with sexuality (homosexual as well as heterosexual) could enrich them, that building support networks for the overburdened nuclear family would bring greater well-being for all, and that motherhood and careers could and should go together. Through the 1920s when the Eugenists were railing against immigrants, the 1930s when Hitler was slaughtering the Jews of

Europe, the 1940s and 1950s when psychoanalysts and anticommunists were thundering about the dangers posed by homosexuals, feminists, and career women, Margaret Mead maintained a remarkably steady course. More than any other woman of her generation she forced those around her to think seriously about the ways in which the world could be a more open, more democratic place, a place where women could play a larger role.[44]

Notes

[1]Margaret Mead, *Blackberry Winter: My Earlier Years* (New York: Simon and Schuster, 1970), pp. 23–79; Rosalind Rosenberg, *Beyond Separate Spheres: Intellectual Roots of Modern Feminism* (New Haven: Yale University Press, 1982), pp. 207–213.

[2]Mead, *Blackberry Winter*, pp. 20, 45–54, 61.

[3]Ibid., pp. 26, 35, and 56.

[4]Jane Howard, *Margaret Mead: A Life* (New York: Simon and Schuster, 1984), p. 35.

[5]Mead, *Blackberry Winter*, pp. 93–109.

[6]Howard, *Margaret Mead*, p. 36.

[7]Ibid., pp. 43–50.

[8]Margaret Mead, ed., *An Anthropologist at Work: Writings of Ruth Benedict* (New York: Avon, 1959), pp. 3–11; Judith Schachter Modell, *Ruth Benedict: Patterns of a Life* (Philadelphia: University of Pennsylvania Press, 1983), pp. 1–143.

[9]Rosenberg, *Beyond Separate Spheres*, pp. 165–66.

[10]Ibid., pp. 213–18.

[11]Ibid.

[12]Howard, *Margaret Mead*, pp. 51–59.

[13]Mead, *Blackberry Winter*, pp. 114 and 111–15; Ruth Benedict, "Nature and Nurture," *The Nation* (1924): 118.

[14]Howard, *Margaret Mead*, pp. 60–62.

[15]James R. Green, *The World of the Worker: Labor in the Twentieth Century* (New York: Hill and Wang, 1980), pp. 98–99.

[16]Margaret Mead, "Intelligence Tests of Italian and American Children," Master's Thesis, Columbia University, 1924.

[17]Franz Boas, "The Question of Racial Purity," *American Mercury* 1 (1924): 153.

[18]G. Stanley Hall, *Adolescence: Its Psychology and Its Relations to Physiology, Anthropology, Sociology, Sex, Crime, Religion, and Education* (New York: Appleton, 1904), I:308.

[19]Mead, *Blackberry Winter*, pp. 100, 137, 124.

[20]Ibid., p. 139–40.

[21]Howard, *Margaret Mead*, p. 72.

[22]Mead, *Blackberry Winter*, p. 129.

[23]Margaret Mead, *Coming of Age in Samoa: A Psychological Study of Primitive Youth for Western Civilization* (New York: Morrow, 1928), pp. 266–77.

[24]Ibid., pp. 199, 20, 22, 28.

[24]Ibid., pp. 28, 38.

[26]Ibid., pp. 42, 209, 213.

[27]Ibid., pp. 134–35, 157, 136, 147–50. Mead does not discuss contraception, and it is not clear whether young women tend to be pregnant at marriage.

[28]Ibid., pp. 213–14, 216, 227.

[29]Margaret Mead, *The Social Organization of Manua* (1969 ed; Honolulu, Hawaii: Bishop Museum, 1930), addendum. Mead's best-known critic was Derek Freeman. See his *Margaret Mead and Samoa: The Making and Unmaking of an Anthropological Myth* (Cambridge: Harvard University Press, 1983), pp. 118, 131–140, 226–53.

[30]Mead, *Blackberry Winter*, pp. 167–80.

[31]Howard, *Margaret Mead*, p. 327; Rosenberg, *Beyond Separate Spheres*, pp. 232–33.

[32]For Mead's critique of Mathilde and Mathis Vaerting, *The Dominant Sex: A Study in the Sociology of Sex Differences* (London: Allen and Unwin, 1923), see Margaret Mead, *Sex and Temperament in Three Primitive Societies* (New York: Morrow, 1935), pp. x–xi.

[33]Margaret Mead, *Letters from the Field, 1925–1975* (New York: Harper and Row, 1977), pp. 201–02.

[34]Mead, *Sex and Temperament*, pp. 279–80.

[35]Reo Fortune, "Arapesh Warfare," *American Anthropologist* 41 (1939): 22–41; Mead, *Blackberry Winter*, pp. 227–43. For a more recent evaluation of the Tchambuli see Deborah B. Gewertz, *Sepik River Societies: A Historical Ethnography of the Chambia and Their Neighbors* (New Haven: Yale University, 1983).

[36]Mead, *Blackberry Winter*, pp. 225–26.

[37]Ibid., pp. 227–43, 265–82.

[38]Howard, *Margaret Mead*, pp. 73, 244; Mary Catherine Bateson, *With a Daughter's Eye: A Memoir of Margaret Mead and Gregory Bateson* (New York: William Morrow, 1984), pp. 37–48.

[39]Bateson, *With a Daughter's Eye*, pp. 49–57.

[40]Margaret Mead, *Male and Female: A Study of the Sexes in a Changing World* (New York: Morrow, 1949), p. 160; Virginia Yans-McLaughlin, "Science, Democracy, and Ethics: Mobilizing Culture and Personality for World War II," in George Stocking, ed., *Malinowski, Rivers, Benedict and Others: Essays on Culture and Personality* (Madison: University of Wisconsin Press, 1986), p. 204.

[41]Ferdinand Lundberg and Marynia Farnham, *Modern Woman: The Lost Sex* (New York: Harper and Brothers, 1947), passim; Mead, *Male and Female*, pp. 78–160.

[42]Mead, *Male and Female*, pp. 383, 160; Betty Friedan, "The Functional Freeze, the Feminine Protest, and Margaret Mead" in *The Feminine Mystique* (New York: Norton, 1963), ch. 6; Howard, *Margaret Mead*, p. 363; Marcia Cohen, *The Sisterhood: The True Story of the Women Who Changed the World* (New York: Simon and Schuster, 1988), pp. 62–71.

[43]Howard, *Margaret Mead*, pp. 364–65.

[44]Margaret Mead, "Bisexuality: A New Awareness," and "Women: A House Divided," in Margaret Mead and Rhoda Matraux, *Aspects of the Present* (New York: Morrow, 1980), pp. 57–76, 269–75.

PART VIII

Contemporary Lives

In the 1990s American women's lives are shaped by many transformations initiated immediately following World War II. Peacetime pressures on wives and mothers to return to domestic life and to quit working outside the home failed. Postwar inflation as well as the heightened material expectations of householders (for consumer goods and homeowning, for example) kept women in the wage-earning force. A postwar survey of women war workers indicated that 84 percent of the women who remained in the workforce or found new jobs after being mustered out of wartime industries claimed an economic rationale for their employment. Few were willing to claim personal satisfaction or economic autonomy as a reason for continued employment. Whatever the reason or claims, increasingly, married women without children and record numbers of young unmarried women entered the wage-earning force from the 1940s onward.

While only 20 percent of married women worked in 1950, this grew to 30 percent in 1960, over 40 percent by 1970 and since 1980 clearly the majority of American wives earn wages. This trend persisted through the postwar "baby boom" (1946–1964), when women produced on the average, 2.5 children each in 1960, compared with 1.9 in 1940. Concurrently, the divorce rate doubled from 1940 to 1945, and continued to climb thereafter, only leveling off in the late 1980s. Single mothers also form a sizeable chunk of the female labor force as we entered the 1990s.

While postwar American families shifted in size and composition, the American household underwent an even more dramatic change. Suburbs grew five times faster than cities, and with Veteran's Administration loans and the rise of the "subdivision," such as the Levittown prototype in suburban New York, row after row of homeowners with growing families became the norm within American society. These geographic and demographic factors transformed the lives of middle class women. Given physical isolation in the suburban community and the renewed preoccupation with mothering, chores for suburban mothers seemed to grow exponentially. In but one example, chauffeuring became a major time constraint for women within these "bedroom communities." Cars were turned over to women, but so were all the shopping, domestic and parenting responsibilities—after men were dropped off at the local train depot. Mothers were expected to serve as the primary work force within organizations such as the Parent Teacher Association (PTA), scouting societies (Campfire Girls, Girl Scouts of America, and others) as well as thousands of local voluntary organizations. Women were expected to embody self-sacrificing roles as wives and mothers. As it had in the previous decades, American advertising and media played a key role in trying to transform women's expectations and roles.

Cultural coercion was rampant during this era. Film stars projected roles of wholesome and harmonious domesticity— exemplified by the characters played by Doris Day and Debbie Reynolds. The new medium of television reinforced only maternal stereotypes for women, in programs such as *Father Knows Best* and *Ozzie and Harriet*. By the mid-fifties the majority of women who enrolled in colleges were dropping out before graduation to get married and start a family. Educational institutions increasingly became "husband-hunting grounds"—and even a venerable woman's college like Radcliffe had deans preaching the necessity of preparing students for their roles as wives and mothers. Despite the onslaught of propaganda, even while social scientists preached the positive effects of raising larger families, educated women increasingly manifested discontent with the status quo. These social tensions resulted in what came to be known as "women's dilemma," in reality a problem confronted by both sexes, but addressed in advice literature as a problem specifically for women.

Many psychologists and scholars, especially women in these fields, began to address the widespread disillusionment over traditional sex roles. Arguments and advice blossomed across a wide political spectrum. In 1947 the best-selling *Modern Woman: The Lost Sex* argued that the women's rights movement was a manifestation of women's "deep illness," that feminism "bade women commit suicide as women," that an "independent woman" was a contradiction in terms. Attacks upon women's independence and intellectual development were reinforced by other new "scientific sources." Intelligence Quotient (IQ) studies argued that males and females had measurable, verifiable mental differences, with women's greatest disadvantages showing up in tests of science and math skills—precisely those subjects considered most important to national progress in a politically tense, highly technological era.

Even those scholars skeptical of such scientific data conceded that socialization could produce "role conflict." As sociologist Mirra Komarovsky explained: women involved in culturally approved activities such as service clubs displayed the same traits of agressiveness and competence claimed as "masculine traits" in career women; socialization, not anatomy, determined behavior patterns. These theories gained prominence in the 1970s when psychologists cataloged what they called women's "fear of success." Despite fervent opposition, many women seem to have conquered their fears.

A new generation of women activists had tasted leadership opportunities and earned respect of men and women alike with roles in New Deal programs and wartime movements. Some of these women committed to leadership roles struggled against postwar propaganda and carved out significant careers in local, state and even national politics. Certainly the era marks the emergence of figures such as Clare Booth Luce, who began as an editor at *Vanity Fair*, became a successful playwright (*The Women*) and eventually the American ambassador to Italy, as well as Helen Gahagan Douglas, who started her career on the Broadway stage and went on to become a leading member of the California delegation to the House of Representatives and the Democratic candidate for the U.S. Senate, losing to Richard Nixon in 1946.

African-American women had always feared racism and other roadblocks rather than success; many saw their marginal wartime improvements slip away. Women joined their husbands and brothers in the campaign against segregation and racism. In 1955 Rosa Parks refused to give up her seat on a Montgomery, Alabama, bus. In her wake civil rights activists launched one of the most successful boycott campaigns in the modern era. The Montgomery bus boycott lasted over a year and gave birth to the Southern Christian Leadership Conference (SCLC) and the ascendancy of Martin Luther King, Jr.. Out of this renewed resistance thousands of blacks and whites joined in the crusade against discrimination that included the sit-in campaigns of the student-organized Student Nonviolent Coordinating Committee (SNCC). Hundreds of southern young people and scores of northern college students came South in summertime campaigns to try to register African-Americans to vote. The "Freedom Summer" of 1964 was one of the most dramatic grass-roots campaigns for civil rights ever staged. Ella Baker, Fannie Lou Hamer, and many other outspoken African-American women were in the forefront of this struggle. Hundreds upon thousands of younger women—black and white—participated in the civil rights campaigns in the South during this era. Many encountered sexism within the movement as well as racism outside their organizations.

Women found themselves "pushed off the agenda" within male-dominated political organizations. One such organization was Students for a Democratic Society (SDS), founded in 1962, which embodied the radical struggles of the "sixties" generation. Women were shouted off the stage at mass meetings; their claims on time and attention were subjected to ridicule, shouted down by obscenities. As a result, thousands of young women separated themselves into consciousness-raising (CR) groups and sought to reform society with or without the approval or cooperation of male comrades. This separate activism brought mixed results.

While younger women challenged political movements and formed separate groups, older women as well were re-evaluating their contributions and experiences. Betty Friedan's instantly famous *The Feminine Mystique* (1963) encouraged wives and mothers, and women generally, to examine their lives in light of contemporary developments. The aging of the American population meant that nearly all American women spend most of their mature years in an "empty nest," with children grown and out of the home. Thus, Friedan argued, the socialization of women to unpaid, unspecialized careers only as homemakers and maternal workers stunted women's development as well as rendering them unproductive and unfulfilled for most of their adult lives. Friedan was but one of a score of prominent women who counseled her contemporaries to seek vocations, to make lives outside of the confines of sex-role stereotypes.

President John F. Kennedy was the first Chief Executive to address explicitly questions of gender by establishing a Commission on the Status of Women. He appointed Eleanor Roosevelt to head the group in 1960. Roosevelt and other moderate activists wanted to work within legislative commissions. Betty Friedan, among others, was impatient with these channels. She and younger activists had no time to collect the paperwork demanded by government agencies. Further, many women saw these traditional tactics as stalling techniques developed by the establishment to defuse feminist anger. In an attempt to capture the energy of the moment and bring younger women into the movement, Friedan and her cohorts launched the National Organization for Women (NOW)—a direct-action campaign—in 1966.

These champions of social change witnessed a tidal wave of activist women breaking down barriers of prejudice and discrimination. Legal suits and media tactics loosened the constrictive bonds of gender stereotype. Women began to flood into law, business, and medical schools at an unprecedented rate. In 1972 *Ms.* magazine was launched by Gloria Steinem to give feminism a popular, monthly forum.

A virtual flood of feminist scholarship attracted an increasingly sympathetic readership, including Kate Millet's *Sexual Politics* (1970), Shulamith Firestone's *Dialectic of Sex* (1970), and Robin Morgan's *Sisterhood Is Powerful* (1970). Such writers illustrate the extraordinary vitality, variety, and sheer innovativeness of late twentieth-century feminist thought. In two related ways it was notably distinct from the feminism that culminated in the Nineteenth Amendment. These new feminists were prepared to take up issues of sexuality (both heterosexual and homosexual) in the most explicit and adventurous ways. And second, many women, especially those belonging to the poorest and most exploited cultures, were not persuaded by the white, middle-class tendency to view men's and women's campaigns for justice as fundamentally separate. To Cherrie Moraga, for example, the traditional "women's movement" was "devoid of race, class roots, what you ate at home, the smells in the air." Most lesbians and women of color refused to subsume their interests into a movement preoccupied with only the interests of white heterosexual females. The roots of feminist activism stem in large part from the civil rights struggle where large numbers of white women demonstrated their commitment to racial equality. Furthermore, in the earliest days of feminist organization and activism, lesbian women played a disproportionate role in organizing, staffing, and sustaining the movement. In the past quarter century some mainstream feminists have attempted to incorporate some of these challenges to broaden the base of their movement. Yet some critics have charged the opposite tactic, that American feminist organizations jettison issues which do not appeal to the white, heterosexual, middle-class majority to which the movement increasingly panders.

In contemporary society, women enjoy an unprecedented influence within certain discrete sectors. The majority of bookbuyers continue to be women, and the paperback book market is clearly dominated by the influence of female authors and readers. From the self-help literature (showing feminist influence by way of the pioneering work of the Boston Women's Health Collective which published *Our Bodies, Ourselves* in 1971), to the popularization of sexology (from Masters and Johnson's influential studies to the controversial volumes by Shere Hite), as well as the continuing boom in romance fiction (Harlequin novels hit the 100 million mark in annual sales in 1977 and continue to grow), the female audience is enormous and diverse.

Women increasingly are targeted by advertisers who recognize the growing earning power of women consumers. For example, auto manufacturers realize that the solo female buyer is on the increase and women are more likely to purchase a new car than their male counterpart. Not only are women expanding their range of consumption, but the growth of traditional women's consumer items is staggering. In America today, women contribute to a fiercely competitive billion dollar cosmetics industry, including millions of dollars worth of cosmetic surgery.

The power of this female audience is evident in other media. Women are expected to be the top consumers of "infotainment" news programs and daytime dramas (popularly known as soap operas). Women viewers in the 18–35-year-old range are sought by broadcasters for prime-time programming; this female audience can boost advertising revenues by millions. Today women are contributors to televangelical campaigns by a three-to-one margin. Ironically, many of these televangelists are fundamentalists who condemn "women's lib" as "the devil's work."

Not only women, but feminists have influenced media and the arts during the past quarter century. Female journalists increasingly work their way up the masthead, join "the boys on the bus" (the press corps assigned to political campaigns), and redefine the terms of "hard" and "soft" news. Women in broadcast journalism no longer only decorate weathermaps but also hold prestigious positions as anchors and investigative reporters on television programs. Female performers defy both stereotype and convention—on stage and screen both small and large, as dancers and singers, musicians and composers, stand-up comics, and orchestra conductors. Female novelists inventively refine women's roles within existing literary landscapes, such as Erica Jong, whose characters and language in *Fear of Flying* break down the traditional—and male imposed—boundaries for "women writers." African-American poet, novelist and essayist, Alice Walker writes what she calls "womanist" prose. Besides the celebration of the African-American spirit, both in Walker's *The Color Purple*, and in Toni Morrison's *Beloved*, readers witness the violent impact of racism on black lives.

Contemporary female artists rediscover neglected talents of the past century, such as painter Mary Cassatt and sculptor Harriet Hosmer, while pioneering their own distinctive styles. Contemporary historians have attempted to reclaim women's pasts, as this book illustrates. The training and experience of Judy Chicago (creator of explicitly feminist and collaborative work such as "The Dinner Party" and "The Birth Project") diverges radically from the climb to success taken by painter Helen Frankenthaler. Painters like Frankenthaler resist—like Georgia O'Keeffe before her—the notion that they should be identified as women painters or female artists, and especially object to critical interpretations which analyze art so rigidly in terms of gender.

In addition, during the past three decades, efforts to break down the barriers of gender discrimination have made great progress. Legislative inroads promise permanent change in women's status. First and foremost, Title VII of the Civil Rights Act of 1964 forbade discrimination in employment on the basis of sex. In 1967 the Equal Rights Amendment (ERA) was reintroduced in Congress and almost passed in 1972. That same year the 1972 Education Act forbade institutions of higher learning from discriminating on the basis of sex, threatening to curtail federal funding to those schools and programs that denied women equal access. Affirmative action campaigns were instituted and many employers were required to comply with quotas established to insure women's taking advantage of opportunities.

In 1973 the United States Supreme Court liberalized abortion policy with the *Roe v. Wade* decision that many women believed guaranteed them the right to control their own bodies. Nearly one quarter of a million women joined NOW in its campaign to secure passage of the Equal Rights Amendment; by 1982 thirty-five of the thirty-eight states required for ratification had passed.

Yet the ERA failed to be ratified by the necessary number of states, and the *Roe v. Wade* decision was assaulted by the *Webster v. Missouri* decision in 1989. Women have been prominent in the campaigns to defeat feminist interpretation of the law. Coalitions of fundamentalists and right-wing women have proven increasingly effective. Phyllis Schafly, whose Illinois-based "Eagle Forum" spearheaded the attack on the ERA, drew her strength from the South (in which no state ratified the amendment) and played on the fears of the American public that the ERA would create havoc within society by enforcing "unisex" public bathrooms and drafting women into combat. "Operation Rescue" and other "Pro-Life" activists ironically have borrowed the civil disobedience techniques of the 1960s, as have "Pro-Choice" workers on the barricades outside abortion clinics.

The backlash campaigns against feminism have been strong and, in some ways, successful. Authors such as Midge Decter, in *The New Chastity* (1972), and George Gilder, in *Sexual Suicide* (1973), decried the feminist agenda and identified its defenders as "man-hating, lesbian extremists." Many supporters of political feminism heeded this "lavender herring" and disassociated themselves from "the movement." For example, although many young women readers of *Ms.* embraced feminist principles (equal pay, breaking down sexual prejudice, and even increased toleration for all sexual preferences), the overwhelming majority did not belong to any women's liberation group in 1973. Increasingly, the *New York Times* and other major media labeled young women of the 1980s as the "post-feminist" generation with scarcely a ripple of response.

The real and potential political impact of women was exemplified by Democratic candidate, Walter Mondale's choice of a female running mate, Geraldine Ferraro, in the 1984 presidential campaign. While women were not nominees for the national office in the 1988 election, all candidates were forced to deal with the concerns of women one way or another—even if it meant conservative congressional candidates supporting federally-subsidized daycare and other "family issues."

Women from a variety of political camps have emerged. As yet we are unable to gauge the impact of the appointment of Sandra Day O'Connor to the U.S. Supreme Court by President Ronald Reagan in 1981. Although Sally Ride became the first American woman in space in 1983, her token accomplishment called attention to sexism as much as paved the way for future female astronauts. The same might be said for Barbara McClintock, whose work in genetics earned her the 1983 Nobel Prize in physiology.

Gains must be weighed in the balance of historical context. While the percentage of African-American women wage-earners working as domestics was cut from 30 percent in 1965 to less than 10 percent a decade later, we must remember that immigrant Hispanic women, along with female immigrants recently arrived from southeastern Asia have taken their place. Minority women in the United States face a range of staggering handicaps, including high rates of high school dropout, high rates of teenage pregnancy, high rates of alcoholism and drug use, and patterns of downward economic spirals that plague women of color especially. Although divorce is an unimpeded option for many women today, surveys demonstrate that following marital dissolution, female income drops by over 70 percent while male income increases by over 40 percent.

Today women can find equal representation on the floor of the Democratic National Convention and are approaching equity at the Republican party gatherings, yet less than a handful serve in the Senate, less than twenty in the House of Representatives, and women's showing in governor's mansions and state houses proves equally sparse. For all of the political strides and economic achievements of women during the last quarter century, the overwhelming majority of those underemployed and on welfare rolls (over 80 percent) remain women. Women in the U.S. earn on average less than $20,000 a year and need a college education to earn three-fourths the salary of a male high-school dropout. Further, the average woman continues to earn sixty cents for every dollar earned by a man, a statistic that has remained depressingly stable for nearly two hundred years. However, women's role in the nation's labor force is increasingly significant when predictions indicate that three out of every five new workers will be women.

Perhaps progress cannot merely be measured by weighing women's achievements in terms of men's: status, power, and money. Some women suggest that these measurements reinforce a "penarchy" (the domination of all other groups within society, including poor and minority males, by elite males who use political, economic and sexual control to maintain their status). To weigh women's achievements on these sexist scales perpetuates the stereotype of female inadequacy. Feminists argue that women must not merely measure up to the standards provided by males in power, but struggle to redefine the terms by which all individuals are measured to provide more space and value for alternative scales. Women have not merely entered the work force but are attempting to transform rules of employment as well as the workplace environment. Women have raised gender issues in the workplace, making headway on questions of sexual harassment, parental leave, childcare, care of elderly dependents and other "family issues."

One of the biggest problems facing American women today is the balancing of career and family. Over 60 percent of women with preschool children work outside the home, and the majority of women with infants seek daycare within the first year following birth. In addition to the demand for safe, affordable daycare and other means of lessening the burdens of motherhood, many feminists recognize that fathers should be added to the formula of caretaking. Some feminists like Friedan argue in favor of men participating more actively in parenting and shouldering more domestic responsibilities. This stems from an earlier "male liberation" movement, geared to allowing men to show more emotion and demonstrate nurturing qualities within the home and larger society. Feminists argue that women need not divest themselves completely of these important responsibilities nor shift all the burden onto men, but learn to redistribute more equitably the challenges and burdens of rearing children.

Over the past few decades feminist reformers increasingly have agitated to protect victims of rape and incest, to decrease homophobia and insure equal rights for gay citizens, to prevent child abuse and custody kidnapping, and to heighten awareness of pornographic exploitation and sex-trade violence. Comparable worth campaigns and demands for pay equity challenge women's second-class economic status. At the same time, female workers are in the forefront of many movements to improve productivity and dependability: on-site daycare, increased health benefits, flex-time (workers setting their own hours within a window of daily/weekly scheduling), and many other innovations.

While women struggle within women's movements they also

contribute enormously to peace campaigns throughout the globe, to toxic waste cleanups, to disarmament conferences, to animal rights campaigns, to nuclear power protests, and a range of radical issues. Women also appear in the forefront of anti-abortion violence and pro-Creationist struggles, protests against increased sex education and campaigns promoting quarantines for individuals carrying HIV, the AIDS virus. Sex roles have transformed and propelled women into both feminist and antifeminist camps. Women are free to enter any campaigns they choose, and, as in the past, women will participate on both sides of "women's issues," crusading *with* as well as *against* one another. The impact of these campaigns, the feminist agenda for the twenty-first century, and the meaning of gender for generations to come, remains uncharted.

Helen Gahagan Douglas
(1900–1980)

Ingrid Winther Scobie

Helen Gahagan Douglas was born November 15, 1900, to Lillian Rose Mussen Gahagan and Walter Hamer Gahagan II, a wealthy New York civil engineer. Douglas attended the Berkeley Institute in Brooklyn and the Capon School in Northhampton, Massachusetts, before entering Barnard College in 1920. In 1922 she made her debut on the Broadway stage and abandoned her formal education for a career in the theater as an actor and singer. She married actor Melvyn Douglas in 1931; the couple had two children, Peter (1933) and Mary Helen (1938), plus a son, Gregory, from Melvyn's first marriage. In addition to her film debut in She *(1935), Helen Gahagan Douglas continued her concert appearances and went on a European singing tour in 1937. She turned her energies to politics in 1939, when she was appointed to the State Advisory Committee of the National Youth Authority as well as the National Advisory Committee of the Works Progress Administration. The Douglases' friendship with Franklin and Eleanor Roosevelt drew them increasingly into Democratic party politics. In 1944 Helen Gahagan Douglas won the election in Los Angeles' fourteenth congressional district and was appointed to the House Foreign Affairs Committee. Reelected in 1946 and 1948 by wide margins, her reputation as a leading liberal grew. In 1946 President Harry S Truman appointed her as an alternate delegate to the UN General Assembly. She coauthored the Atomic Energy Act and won numerous plaudits and national attention. In 1950 she lost her race for the United States Senate against her congressional colleague, Richard M. Nixon. In 1951 she moved to New York and maintained her interest in politics, speaking out on disarmament and traveling in Latin America and the Middle East to broaden her political expertise. After Eleanor Roosevelt died in 1962, Douglas published a tribute to her,* The Eleanor Roosevelt We Remember *(1963). President Lyndon B. Johnson appointed her to represent him at the inauguration of the president of Liberia in 1964. That same year she was a delegate at the second Soviet-American Women's Conference sponsored by the Women's International League for Peace and Freedom. Douglas died on June 28, 1980. Her autobiography,* A Full Life, *was published posthumously in 1982.*

W hen Helen Gahagan Douglas died of cancer on June 28, 1980, at age seventy-nine, newspapers across the country reminded readers that in 1950 this actor-turned-politician lost her race against Richard M. Nixon for a United States Senate seat in California in perhaps the most celebrated red-smear campaign of the cold war years. The *Los Angeles Times,* which had virtually shut Douglas out of any significant news coverage during her six-year congressional career from 1944 to 1950, commented that Nixon's campaign "was a model of its kind—innuendo piled on innuendo." The paper cited Douglas's political courage as her most significant contribution to American politics. In a letter to the editor of the *Los Angeles Times,* a prominent San Francisco judge commented that to lose both the noted California writer Carey McWilliams and Douglas in the same week was "a tragic loss for American democracy" and called for "a requiem for the demise of an era." Former member of Congress Jerry Voorhis, himself a political loser to Nixon in 1946, predicted that this "noble" woman would live on as a "symbol of the Gallant American Lady." Tenant-farm worker organizer H. L. Mitchell called Douglas a "sainted person." United States Senators Alan Cranston and Howard Metzenbaum inserted lengthy newspaper obituaries in the *Congressional Record,* adding adulatory remarks of their own. While most obituaries and editorials concentrated on her political career, some also chronicled her accomplishments in theater and opera, noted her uncommon beauty and elegant demeanor, and mentioned her longtime association with Hollywood as the wife of the distinguished actor, Melvyn Douglas.[1]

In 1897, Walter Gahagan, a civil engineer born and raised in Ohio, and his bride Lillian, a teacher who had grown up in Wisconsin, moved to Brooklyn. In the summer of 1900, Lillian, Walter, and their two-year-old twins, Frederick and William, took up temporary residence in Boonton, New Jersey, where Walter had a contract to build a large reservoir. On November 20, Lillian gave birth to Helen, shortly before the family moved back into their Brooklyn home. Two years later, a second girl, Lillian, was born, and the Gahagans moved their growing, active family into an imposing, elegant brownstone house in the city's posh Park Slope area adjacent to Prospect Park and Grand Army Plaza. In 1910, a fifth child, Walter, Jr., added even more bustle to the busy household. Servants eased household work for mother Lillian.

Walter viewed hard work, constant reading, and education as the essentials for a successful life for men and women, but that did not mean to him that women should pursue careers. Lillian also believed in education, as well as exposure to the arts, and a good religious upbringing in the Presbyterian church. Unlike some of her contemporaries, Lillian disagreed with her husband over careers for women, a disagreement which intensified when Walter prohibited her from pursuing a promising singing career in opera. Yet when Helen developed an early interest in the theater, Lillian was as adamant as Walter in opposing it because it was not considered a "proper" profession for a "lady."

Aside from continual friction over her acting ambitions, Helen grew up feeling close to her family. Walter often took the children to his construction sites. Lillian invited musicians to the house to perform. She took the children down the street to the Brooklyn Museum and to the public library on Saturdays. Helen went with her mother to the Metropolitan Opera but did not enjoy it. Helen recalled, "I would be so unhappy sitting through long operas and I'd complain, 'They're all so *fat*, Mother.'" When Helen said she wanted to act, her mother responded, "'Why do you want to be an actress? Why don't you want to be something really worthwhile—a singer?'"[2]

Summers were special times for the Gahagans. They visited family in the Midwest, and when the children became teenagers, the family traveled to Europe. In 1914, Walter bought Cliff Mull, a lovely Victorian house on a hill above Lake Morey near Fairlee, Vermont. After that, the family spent at least part of every summer in Vermont. Even in the last years of her life, Helen found Vermont an escape, a critical source of nourishment, beauty, and repose.

After a summer in the country, it was always a letdown for Helen to return to Brooklyn to begin school. She and her sister attended the Berkeley Institute, a private school in the neighborhood designed to prepare young women for college. Helen's perpetual dislike of school began in kindergarten, when Berkeley dropped her behind a grade because she could not spell, a problem that continued to plague her as an adult. Helen hated both her academic courses as well as the rules outlining proper behavior for "young ladies," and she consistently performed poorly. She much preferred to spend her time making up stories and acting them out. But theater had no place at Berkeley until Helen's freshman year in high school, when Elizabeth Grimball, a drama coach by training, joined the faculty. She quickly realized that this academically rebellious teenager had exceptional acting talent and considerable intelligence. Before long, Helen began starring in plays and participating on the debate team. Helen received excellent grades in Grimball's class, but her marks deteriorated in others. Much to Grimball's dismay, not to mention Helen's, the irate Gahagans pulled their daughter out of Berkeley and sent her to the elite Capon School in Northampton, Massachusetts, which primarily prepared students for admission into Smith College. Against her parents' instructions, Helen immediately involved herself in play productions and did little better academically. She did manage to graduate, but it took a summer of tutoring at Dartmouth for her to pass the entrance examinations for Barnard College in New York, the only school Helen would consider because it was near the theater scene.

Gahagan entered Barnard, the women's college of Columbia University, in the fall of 1920. The college had a strong tradition of dramatic activity, quite unusual for colleges and universities at that time. Wigs and Cues, a student theater organization, provided opportunities for acting and directing. Gahagan also appeared in several off-Broadway productions.

The noted actor Grace George, who had a reputation for finding young actors, saw Gahagan in a performance and insisted that Broadway producer William Brady, George's husband, see Gahagan perform. Brady asked the starry-eyed Gahagan to play the lead role in a Broadway production, *Dreams for Sale,* a new Owen Davis play about to go into rehearsal, and offered her a five-year contract for starring Broadway roles, a most unusual proposal which Helen accepted. Few actors, no matter how talented, stepped directly from any preparatory environment—stock company, drama school, or college theater—into a leading role contract with a New York producer.

The time could not have been more propitious, for the early 1920s marked the beginning of one of the most vibrant decades in the history of American drama. Gahagan's exciting propects, however, enraged her father. Although Brady eventually convinced Walter Gahagan that his daughter was not entering an "improper" profession for women from fine families, Walter deeply regretted his daughter's decision to quit school and found it difficult to accept her acting career.

Despite poor reviews for *Dreams for Sale,* Gahagan caught the critics' attention. In a comment typical of most of his colleagues, the eminent critic Alexander Woollcott called her an "indisputable talent." When the show closed, Gahagan moved on to other starring roles. From her debut, critics compared her style to that of Ethel Barrymore, and rarely failed to mention her uncommon beauty—tall at five feet seven inches, with a regal bearing. Unlike other fledgling stars, Gahagan had financial backing from her family and did not have to worry about supporting herself; she never hesitated, therefore, to turn down a role that did not interest her. In 1925, she left Brady for another veteran producer, George Tyler, whose gentle personality and innovative productions more suited Gahagan. But by 1927 Gahagan was restless with the stage, and under pressure from her mother to develop her singing, she decided to take voice lessons.

Gahagan began instruction with a noted voice coach, Sophia Cehanovska, and eventually immersed herself full time in her lessons. During a tour in Europe in 1929, her repertoire included the lead roles in *Tosca, Aida,* and *Cavalleria Rusticana.* Although she received mixed reviews, Gahagan had visions of auditioning for the Metropolitan Opera and a variety of American engagements. When none of this materialized, she sailed again to Europe in the summer of 1930 with the idea of staying two years.

This plan evaporated several months later when the aging theater legend David Belasco offered Helen the lead role in a new play, *Tonight or Never.* Belasco thought Gahagan ideal to play an opera singer whose agent is convinced she could sing better if she would only have an affair. The agent's predictions prove correct after the diva has a passionate evening with an "unknown gentleman" who turns out to be a Metropolitan Opera scout. With Gahagan's consent, Belasco selected an accomplished actor but a relative newcomer to Broadway, Melvyn Douglas, as the irresistable lover. During the rehearsal period, Gahagan and Douglas fell in love, and in April 1931, near the end of the play's long run, they married.

The couple's lives took an unexpected turn when in May 1931 Hollywood producer Samuel Goldwyn purchased the movie rights to *Tonight or Never* as a vehicle for Gloria Swanson to launch her singing career. The entire cast moved to Hollywood for the filming. The Douglases initially viewed this trip to California as a temporary one, but when movie offers continued to come Melvyn's way, and Helen had some singing and acting opportunities with theaters in San Francisco and Los Angeles, they began to consider California their home. Helen Gahagan Douglas, however, had little luck getting into film; she made only one movie, *She,* with RKO in 1935. The science-fiction fantasy failed at the box office. A radio contract also proved disappointing. The Douglases lives were further complicated by the births of the two children, Peter in 1933 and Mary Helen in 1938.

In the summer of 1937 Gahagan looked forward to a European singing tour culminating with a performance at the Salzburg Festival in Austria. Rather than operatic roles, she sang a solid repertoire of songs including German lieder. Gahagan enjoyed enthusiastic audiences. Despite the tense political situation resulting from the rapid spread of Nazism, no unpleasant incidents occurred until her stay in Salzburg, when a contact of a friend asked her to report on anti-Nazi activity in the United States. Horrified at the request, she canceled a fall engagement with the Vienna Opera and returned home, determined that she and Melvyn should become involved in antifascist activities in Hollywood. They first joined the 5000-member Hollywood Anti-Nazi League.

Helen initially considered her political activity of secondary interest, but after she returned from Europe she had lost much of the drive that had characterized her acting career. Part of the explanation lay in increasingly diminishing opportunities. Chances to sing in the United States had always been limited, and existing European doors were closing fast in 1938 and 1939. Professional theater opportunities on both coasts continued to decline as the depression decade wore on. But another part of the explanation involved Melvyn. By the end of the 1930s, he had become one of Hollywood's highest paid leading men, known for his fine comic timing, his handsome looks, and his ability to play well against Hollywood's female stars. While not all of his films offered him a chance to demonstrate his talent, *Ninotchka* (1939), eliminated any questions about his talent as a screen actor. Although Helen never resented Melvyn's success, she had always felt their careers should be equally successful. With his star rising, and hers on the decline, she was ready to be pulled off in another direction. Within a short time after Helen made her first step into the political foray, she had become a leading figure in the California Democratic party with considerable national visibility. Except for a few minor engagements, Helen neither acted nor sang again until the early 1950s. But she did not set aside her theatrical skills. Her rapid political climb was due in large part to her ability to shift her acting skills from the dramatic to the political stage.

The Douglases' heightened political awareness paralleled the dramatic change in Hollywood's political atmosphere. In the early 1930s, the movie colony had been a center of political indifference, but by 1937, the community had become a hotbed of radical and liberal organizing. Sensitivity to fascism increased throughout the country, although the most intense activity took place in Hollywood and New York City.

Helen Douglas's first serious move into politics began unexpectedly in the fall of 1938. Melvyn, who had become very active in the

Democratic party and other organizations during the previous year, offered the patio of the Douglases' spacious home to a Hollywood group, the John Steinbeck Committee to Aid Migratory Workers, for a meeting. Helen sat in on the meeting and found herself fascinated with the problems being discussed. Her initial curiosity evolved into a commitment to action: She organized a Christmas party for migrant children, attracting thousands. She read extensively, toured migrant camps, and attended government hearings and meetings of concerned citizens. In early 1939, she became the Steinbeck Committee's chair, working hard to publicize the problem, solicit money, and encourage the public to push for labor laws and social security programs that would include migrants. She also urged improvements in housing, health services, and food distribution centers. She listened attentively to experts. Groups sought her out as a speaker. She eventually drew the attention of Washington experts on migrants' problems, including Arthur Goldschmidt, who worked under Secretary of Interior Harold Ickes. Goldschmidt described his first encounter with Douglas: "I found myself subjected to an intense cross-examination—grilling might not be too strong a word. She accepted no vague generalities.... Her questions were not naive;... I came away... enchanted with a sense of wonder at Helen's display of energy—at the physical, emotional and mental drive of this beautiful and glamorous person."[3]

Aubrey Williams, head of the National Youth Authority, also learned about the activities of both Douglases. As he frequently suggested interesting people to Eleanor Roosevelt whom he thought she and FDR would like to meet, he wrote the Roosevelts about the Douglases. He mentioned that Melvyn could be a political asset to FDR for the 1940 campaign and that Helen's information about migrants would be useful to both Roosevelts. Eleanor Roosevelt was quick to respond; she invited the Douglases to dinner and to spend the night at the end of November 1939. The evening proved delightful; the two couples were drawn to each other, and a special friendship, from which both couples stood to benefit, took shape almost immediately.

During the next few days, the Douglases met a large group of high-ranking New Dealers, including Secretary of Labor Frances Perkins and Harold Ickes, who were as eager to rub shoulders with the bright, enthusiastic, and glamorous Hollywood couple as the Douglases were to meet Washington's political elite. The Douglases left Washington exhilarated. The Roosevelts offered them a standing invitation to stay at the White House when politics brought them to Washington, and Eleanor began a practice of visiting and often staying with her new friends on her trips to the West. Neither Douglas hesitated to contact the Roosevelts or the administration members they had met concerning their political activities. The President appointed both Douglases to various White House boards and remained in close touch with what each was doing. In turn, the Douglases devoted increasingly more time to supporting Roosevelt's policies.

When the Douglases returned to Los Angeles, Helen turned her attention to planning the Steinbeck Committee's second Christmas party, a massive gathering that attracted over eight thousand migrant workers. Shortly after the party Helen resigned from the committee because she learned of Communist infiltration into the organization. Before the Soviet-Nazi pact of September 1939, liberals of all persuasions were virtually indistinguishable from each other; they formed a United Front that supported the New Deal and opposed fascism. But after the pact, American Communists began to object to the anti-fascist stands of liberal organizations. The United Front fell apart quickly as non-Communist liberals dropped their membership. After Helen resigned, she wrote her friend Congressman Jerry Voorhis that she found herself in the "absurd position . . . of most liberals today. The Communists call us reactionaries and the reactionaries call us Communists!"[4]

At this juncture, Helen Douglas took her initial steps into the Women's Division of the Democratic party, steps that brought her closer to Eleanor Roosevelt and provided an entry into the power structure of Democratic politics. Douglas continued to lecture about migrants, and gained considerable attention with an article for the February 1940 issue of the *Democratic Digest*, the widely read monthly magazine of the national Women's Division office. She urged state and local governments to respond to migrants' needs, and communities to assimilate the migrant and "recognize him for his true worth—a vital and necessary element in the agriculture structure [and] a human being . . . whose welfare affects the country at large."[5] This article impelled Dorothy McAllister, a national director of the Women's Division, to invite Douglas to speak on migrant labor at the Division's first National Institute of Government in Washington, a conference to educate party women about campaign issues and party organization in preparation for the 1940 fall campaign. Also during the spring Helen and Melvyn arranged for Eleanor Roosevelt to come to California to visit migrant camps.

In July, the Douglases journeyed to Chicago for the party's nominating convention. Melvyn went as a delegate, Helen as an alternate. Two principal candidates surfaced among the delegates for the position of California's Democratic Party Committeewoman: Douglas and Nettie Jones, a longtime party worker, head of the Women's

Division in California, and a conservative. Douglas won, a victory that angered Jones, who legitimately felt resentful that Douglas had none of the traditional credentials required for this position. Douglas's appointment drew national attention.

After the convention, the Douglases plunged into a hectic campaign speaking schedule—Melvyn nationally and Helen throughout California. When Roosevelt took California by a landslide, party officials in Washington singled out the Douglases for their contributions to the victory. Helen's speaking abilities surpassed those of more seasoned politicians, and she had proved that she had the power to draw and hold a crowd no matter the size. Together the Douglases persuaded many Hollywood actors to speak publicly for Roosevelt and to make substantial campaign contributions. After the election, Helen decided to let political activities absorb all her energies. Through state party chair William Malone she gained two additional party positions: vice-chair of the state organization and head of the Women's Division.

During the first few months of 1941, Douglas strengthened the structure of the Women's Division and made new appointments down to the county level. She selected two women to head the counties in northern California while she and an assistant took responsibility for the south. She selected bright, capable, professional women, many of whom had never before been active in the Women's Division. Douglas then turned her attention to the major focus of the national Women's Division office—homefront defense plans and fundraising. She organized, for example, a regional conference held in September 1941 for party women's education. This conference, which included movie stars and national party figures, was a great success.

While the conference demonstrated Douglas's organizational ability, a more significant test of her political acumen lay ahead: the mobilization of California Democratic women for the 1942 election. The national and state picture looked gloomy. The congressional coalition between Republicans and conservative Democrats had continued to grow in strength since the 1936 election. Douglas directed the Women's Division to work outside of the regular party structure because she thought the women would be more effective this way. They wrote and distributed thousands of flyers, registered voters, raised money, and canvassed precincts. In the final election, despite Democratic Governor Culbert Olson's loss to Republican Earl Warren in the gubernatorial race, Democrats won three of six critical districts in Southern California and several other congressional seats. Washington Democrats were delighted with the Southern California victories, particularly since nationally the party had lost 70 of its 318 House seats. Although it is difficult to assess Douglas's role in these victories, many in both California and Washington gave her considerable credit.

Late in 1943, Representative Thomas Ford, a friend and an ardent New Dealer who represented the Fourteenth Congressional District in Los Angeles, suggested that Douglas run for his seat. He had planned to retire in 1944, and he regarded Douglas as an excellent replacement. Douglas found the idea of running somewhat overwhelming, and the dilemma raised questions of how to reorganize her personal life. Melvyn had joined the army and was in India. Peter and Mary Helen were eleven and seven, in need of parental attention. Politically she faced substantial odds. Not only was she a woman but her credentials did not resemble those of other congressional candidates, male or female. She did not live in the Fourteenth District, an ethnically and economically diverse area encompassing the downtown core of Los Angeles, but in the affluent residential hills of the adjacent Fifteenth District. Furthermore, state assemblyman Augustus Hawkins, a black from the district, was a logical successor. He had a distinguished record in his fight for labor and civil rights. During the war years, blacks in the fourteenth had grown to represent 25 percent of the population, and Hawkins had become a powerful voice in the community. But Ford and his political advisers felt Douglas would stand a better chance of winning. Despite Douglas's unfamiliarity with the district's problems, Ford believed the majority of the constituents would identify with her enthusiasm for the New Deal and Roosevelt. Furthermore, as he put it, the "people of the 14th are not going to vote for a Negro, however light-colored he may be."[6] Douglas finally agreed to run.

Hawkins decided not to file, but Loren Miller, a prominent black lawyer in the district, filed, as did several other candidates. Vicious literature began circulating immediately. One flyer reminded voters that Douglas was married to a Jew (Melvyn had a Jewish father) and that she was a Communist. Twelve years of the "communistic Tom Ford" was enough. The *Los Angeles Times* accused her of Communist ties because the Congress of Industrial Organizations (CIO) backed her. A poster from a Democratic opponent pictured Douglas, labeled "Lady Bountiful," coming down out of the hills of the fifteenth district asking a passerby, "Where's the Fourteenth District?" Douglas wrote Eleanor Roosevelt, "Well, I am really in the campaign and I never knew anything could be quite so repulsive."[7]

Douglas conducted an issue-oriented race, championing the New Deal record and emphasizing her confidence in FDR's leadership. Her campaign literature included a supportive statement from the president. In true Women's Division style, she went armed with facts, figures, and simple language, and refused to run down her opponents. While she only hinted that as a member of Congress she would see herself as representing a national constituency, she communicated that what was good for the country was good for the district. She held dozens of meetings in homes to help dissipate some of the hostility from housewives who could not envision a woman in Congress. She knew how to read an audience and could emotionally charge a group by using colorful language, vivid analogies, and large dramatic gestures.

Douglas won the primary despite the nasty opposition. She immediately turned her attention from the exhilaration of her primary victory to the July nominating convention, for which the Democratic National Committee had billed her as the principal woman among the convention speakers. The press played up the decision to include Douglas as a speaker, claiming that the Democrats were trying to compete with the Republicans who had placed the flashy celebrity Clare Booth Luce, a first-term Connecticut congresswoman, in a prominent spot in their June nominating convention. Much to the press's disappointment neither woman had any interest in a "catfight" or a glamour-girl competition.

Douglas began campaigning almost immediately, stressing once again her allegiance to the president who was running for a fourth term. Her Republican opponent, like her Democratic opposition in the primary, conducted a red-baiting campaign, emphasized the fact that she lived outside the district, and pointed out her connections with Hollywood to suggest a lack of qualifications. But Douglas pulled off a victory—barely—that was part of the tide that Roosevelt and California Democrats enjoyed. She won by less than 4,000 votes out of approximately 137,500 cast. Although she gained a majority of the black votes, few black leaders had rallied to her support. Not even the liberal black *California Eagle* which later became her strong advocate did much for her candidacy. Clearly she had a difficult challenge ahead of her to keep her district.

Douglas arrived in Washington early in January 1945. The Democrats controlled Congress, but the combination of conservative Democrats and Republicans formed a majority. Douglas discovered quickly that in order to have any impact as a new member, she would have to play a nontraditional role, and not just because liberal Democrats were in the minority. She was too impatient to wait the necessary length of time dictated by the behavior norms of the House for new members wishing to assume a position of power. She did not want to spend an inordinate amount of time learning the fine points of legislative procedure, realizing that even time did not guarantee power to women. Furthermore, she had a purist's theoretical notion of representative government. She saw political issues in terms of right and wrong. She had faith that government, run by and for the American people, would be improved simply by voters electing legislators who would work for the right programs. This philosophy set her apart from those who believed that legislative success came only with compromise.

Modeling herself after Eleanor Roosevelt, Douglas worked to develop policy for a national and often an international constituency of "ordinary people." She believed the economic interests of the national groups she deemed important, particularly labor and African-Americans, were identical to the key groups in her district. In foreign affairs, she saw herself speaking for every American who wanted peace. What was good for the world, therefore, was good for the country and for the district. She worked hard toward her goals on the floor of Congress, often lecturing her colleagues and inserting articles and speeches in the *Congressional Record.* She took her assignment to the Foreign Affairs Committee seriously. And she spoke before dozens of groups of concerned citizens all over the country, urging them to pressure members of Congress.

The outlines of Douglas's liberal philosophy took shape and matured during her first term, the Seventy-ninth Congress. Initially she had looked to FDR for policy guidelines. After his death in April 1945, her ideals came principally from Truman's Fair Deal program. She developed numerous statements including demands for the creation of a homeland for the Jews, support for the United Nations, a permanent Fair Employment Practices Commission (FEPC), the end of the poll tax, a full employment bill, extension of social security, the building of low-cost housing, the continuation of wartime rent and price controls, additional funds for day-care programs and school lunches, more farm loans, an increase in the minimum wage, support for labor's right to strike, and funding for cancer research. She called the economic need of veterans a national crisis, began a long-term investigation of the problems of water in California's Central Valley, and demanded more attention to the problems of migrant workers. Her principal legislative success was her cosponsorship of the Atomic Energy Act of 1946, a law that placed the development of atomic energy in civilian rather than military hands. Douglas struck out against those who red-baited her with a statement she entitled "My Democratic Credo" in which she explained that the way to keep communism out of the United States was by building a strong economy, controlling inflation, and providing jobs and affordable housing for all Americans.

Douglas's approach to the issue of civil rights illustrates her political style. She was a civil rights proponent in a style reflective of Eleanor Roosevelt. In the upper-class Brooklyn society of her childhood, her Republican family did not mix with blacks, thus Douglas became responsive to blacks only after she entered politics. Eleanor Roosevelt introduced Douglas to black leaders during the war, including Mary McLeod Bethune, head of the National Council of Negro Women (NCNW). In 1942, at the First Lady's request, Douglas called a meeting to discuss employment and housing discrimination problems for African-Americans in Los Angeles. She worked with FEPC investigations in defense industries. Once in Congress, Douglas aligned herself with a small handful of congressional representatives (including the two black representatives, Adam Clayton Powell and William Dawson) who persistently introduced FEPC, antilynching, and anti–poll tax bills despite continual failure to get these bills passed. Douglas not only tried to generate public pressure on Congress to pass civil rights legislation, but she also gave speeches for national and local branches of the National Association for the Advancement of Colored People (NAACP) and helped the NCNW raise funds. Blacks throughout the country recognized her contributions. The Scroll of Honor that she received in 1946 from the NCNW acclaimed her "superb statesmanship" for her first term in Congress.

Douglas's attitude towards civil rights was also politically astute. Her black consituency was an identifiable audience, and she needed to play to it as she looked ahead to the 1946 election. She publicized her civil rights efforts and worked to bring increased services for blacks into her district. She won the primary easily, but the fall campaign proved more challenging. Her Republican opponent, Frederick W. Roberts, a longtime state assemblyman, was black. Red-baiting issues surfaced again. Douglas could not campaign in person because Truman had appointed her to the 1946 General Assembly of the United Nations, an appointment that added to her prestige but kept her out of her district during the fall campaign season. But Douglas's liberal stance on issues in general, her work on behalf of blacks nationally, and her careful cultivation of the black community paid off as black Democratic leaders worked hard for her. While the Republicans enjoyed a landslide victory, gaining control of both the House and the Senate for the first time in sixteen years, Douglas almost doubled her margin from 1944. She was particularly delighted that she won by large majorities in the black precincts. She interpreted this to mean that she had won the confidence of blacks and that they felt their interests would be more effectively served by a white Democrat with a liberal record than by a black Republican.

When the Eightieth Congress opened in January 1947, the Democrats found the political scene in Washington dismal. While Douglas, like all liberals, found it impossible to do much for her supporters, she still played her part in the futile attempts to buck the Republicans. Liberal groups clamored for her attention; she stepped up her speaking schedule in an effort to reduce voter apathy. She considered the problem of inflation and federal funding for low-income housing the most pressing issues. She hired a black secretary from the district, becoming the first white member of Congress to have a black staff person, a move that created quite a stir in Washington.

Douglas also became more outspoken on women's issues, increasingly attacked the House Un-American Activities Committee (HUAC), and took strong positions on foreign policy issues. She urged the extension of social security to cover more women and supported legislation for equal pay for equal work. She opposed Equal Rights Amendment (ERA) efforts, as did all pro-labor legislators who feared that such an amendment would kill hard-earned special interest legislation favoring working women. Her opposition to the House Un-American Activities Committee focused on its mode of investigating, particularly its issuing of certain contempt citations during the committee's investigations into Hollywood in 1947. In foreign affairs, she deviated from Truman in opposing aid to Greece and Turkey in 1947 on the grounds that the aid should come from the United Nations, but she worked strongly for the Marshall Plan, a program for European economic recovery, both in committee, on the floor, and in public gatherings.

By early 1948, Douglas not only had blacks solidly behind her but labor as well. She had worked more closely with labor union leaders during the Eightieth Congress. She had campaigned against the anti-union Taft-Hartley Act of 1947, and her general stand on issues resulted in top ratings from labor unions and liberal magazines including *The Nation* and the *New Republic*. As expected, her Republican opponent in the 1948 election, William Braden, raised red-baiting issues once again, claiming Douglas was part of the left-wing influences in Congress. Braden's literature also played up her Fifteenth Congressional District residence—referring to her as the Hollywood representative who lived in the "hotsy-totsy area of Hollywood" as compared to the "modest home of our good neighbor and friend" Braden who lived in the district. Despite Braden's attacks, Douglas's total vote of approximately 88,000 to Braden's 43,000 surprised even Douglas. She clearly had established a safe congressional seat despite the dirty campaign tactics of her opponents.

In January 1949, at the opening of the Eighty-first Congress, Douglas enjoyed enormous popularity in the eyes of labor, blacks, Jews and other minority groups, and civil libertarians. Many of her supporters agreed with Douglas's somewhat egotistical self-evaluation that she was one of the few and possibly the most conscientious members of Congress. She saw herself as a "people's representative" fighting for America's working class. When Douglas announced late in 1949 that she intended to run for the United States Senate, she found many of her supporters dismayed and concerned. While they believed that she could continue to win her congressional seat, many did not think that she had the statewide political base or the experience to run for the Senate. Further, while her political views suited her district, they did not reflect the majority opinion in the state. But she remained undaunted.

Douglas explained her decision to run on her intense dislike for the aging incumbent, Sheridan Downey, a New Dealer who became progressively more conservative after the war. Douglas particularly opposed Downey's stand on a hotly-debated water rights issue in California. The federal government prohibited use of water from federal dams for any farm larger than 160 acres. Douglas favored this law that protected the small farmer; Downey sided with the corporate farmers who wanted to abolish the limitation. Downey also favored state control of California's offshore oil while Douglas felt that control by the federal government would best protect the average consumer. When Douglas entered the race, she presented herself as representing the lower-middle-income people of California—veterans, small farmers, women, blacks, ethnics and small businesspeople—and Downey as favoring the big farmer, private utilities, oil, and big business.

Although Downey had strong corporate support, Douglas made him nervous. His health was failing as well. At the end of March, he formally withdrew, throwing his support behind Manchester Boddy, the editor of the liberal *Los Angeles Daily News*, who had enthusiastically supported Douglas during her first two terms in the House. Boddy took Douglas and her supporters aback when he not only made clear that he agreed with Downey on the water and oil issues but he also turned to red-baiting as the key to his campaign strategy.

As always before, Douglas campaigned strictly on issues. She cited her support for Truman's Fair Deal program and made clear her role in the refining of foreign policy as a member of the House Foreign Affairs Committee. She stressed that while she opposed HUAC, she hated communism, as she had explained in her "Democratic Credo." Douglas's views cut her off from the major funding sources. The oil industry, big business, and corporate farmers all backed Boddy. Labor unions unanimously stood behind Douglas. She also got considerable help in communities throughout the state from ethnic groups, academics, Jews, farmers, blacks, and liberal women's groups. Eleanor Roosevelt conducted a major fundraising effort in her behalf, and many Hollywood friends offered time and money. Conservative

Democratic women found Douglas's views, particularly her stand against ERA, distasteful.

Douglas won the primary by a comfortable margin—gaining close to 890,000 votes to Boddy's 532,000. Despite Boddy's financial edge and his potentially devastating allegations that Douglas had Communist sympathies, his late entry in the campaign and sudden conservative turnaround after years of gaining a statewide reputation as the well-respected editor of a liberal paper cost him votes. He also did not have Douglas's charismatic appeal as a speaker, nor could he articulate issues clearly. But Douglas's primary victory did not foreshadow success in the fall campaign. She had a formidable Republican opponent in congressional representative Richard M. Nixon, who had won close to 1,060,000 votes in the primary. Nixon knew that if he could take most of Boddy's votes, he could easily beat Douglas.

A member of the House since 1946, a resident of Whittier, a Los Angeles suburb, Nixon had attained significant national visibility as a member of HUAC, particularly in his leadership of the committee's investigation of Alger Hiss and as the co-sponsor of the Mundt-Nixon Communist control bill. Nixon and Douglas, as members of the Southern California congressional delegation, had shared some concerns over nonpartisan issues. But Douglas was revolted by Nixon's HUAC activities and general political stand. Furthermore, in 1946 he had ousted New Dealer Jerry Voorhis, Douglas's close friend and colleague, in a ruthless red-baiting campaign.

Over the summer, Nixon decided that rather than conduct a broad-based issue campaign, he would follow Boddy's lead and concentrate on Douglas's vulnerability on the issue of "red-blooded Americanism." Both domestic and foreign events fed this decision. Americans were up in arms about the so-called fall of China to communism, blaming it on Truman's incompetence. In early 1950 United States Senator Joseph McCarthy embarked on his search for American Communists. McCarthy's "revelations" heightened irrational fears about internal security and resulted in a bipartisan Congress passing the Internal Security Act, even over Truman's veto (with Douglas one of the few voting against the bill). In June 1950 the Korean War began when Americans aided the South Koreans in their struggle against invading Communist troups from North Korea. All these events made Nixon's dubbing of Douglas as the "Pink Lady" an effective device.

Nixon won the election by a margin of 2,200,000 to 1,500,000. Most commentators credited the victory to what they called a vicious campaign. They placed her loss in the category of other leading liberals who also lost in red-baiting races, including Senator

Claude Pepper in the primary and Senators John Carroll, Elbert Thomas, Senate majority leader Scott Lucas, and several other House members in the fall. Setting aside the "dirty campaign" issue for a moment, however, it seems clear that Nixon still had an edge on Douglas. Nixon's position on issues such as taxation, government spending, labor, and farm policy reflected the general sentiment of Californians. Nixon matched Douglas's skill as a speaker; although their styles were different, Nixon could engage a crowd as effectively as his opponent. The Republicans also profited from a substantial financial edge, particularly in the Nixon campaign, and from poor Democratic party organization. Nixon also had the luxury of many "Democrats for Nixon" campaign workers, many of whom had initially backed Downey and Boddy. One of the most effective organizers of this group was George Creel, a prominent member of Woodrow Wilson's administration, who went beyond Nixon in his red-baiting. Finally, Californians had little precedent in electing a woman to statewide or national office.

Douglas remained optimistic even into election night, despite all evidence that her campaign had failed. The numbers of her enthusiastic workers had diminished during the fall. While many viewed her as a more attractive alternative to Nixon, they saw her as a losing candidate and turned away to work for others. Even the numerous Washington luminaries, including Vice-President Alben W. Barkley and cabinet members Charles P. Brannan, J. Howard McGrath, and Oscar Chapman who came to California to support Douglas could not change what seemed a foregone conclusion.

Douglas had mixed feelings about her Senate loss. Winning would have thrust her into a very unusual spot for a political woman, but she also felt relieved. Although her marriage was still intact, the previous eight years had placed a strain on Helen's relationship with Melvyn and their children. Melvyn had spent three years abroad during the war. When he returned, he based himself in Los Angeles, but his work frequently took him away from home for extended periods. The children, after several months with Helen in Washington at the beginning of her first term in Congress, attended boarding school in Los Angeles. In 1950 Helen knew it was critical to reassemble the family. She and Melvyn decided to make New York their home base as Melvyn wanted to leave movie production and return to the theater. Helen also hoped to spend more time in Vermont at the family home in Fairlee.

Once the family settled into a Manhattan apartment, Douglas spent the next thirty years lecturing on college campuses on various current topics, particularly disarmament, and serving on boards of numerous liberal civic and political organizations. She campaigned for presidential, state, and local candidates at the request of the Democratic National Committee and toured as a performer with programs combining singing and poetry reading. In 1973, as the Watergate scandal broke, she found herself once again in the national limelight. Bumper stickers abounded reading "Don't Blame Me, I Voted for Helen Gahagan Douglas." Women's groups suddenly saw her as a role model and asked for advice about how women "make it" in politics. *Ms.* featured her on its front cover. Colleges awarded her honorary degrees. In 1974, she underwent breast cancer surgery but continued to lead an active life. She had spent several years writing her autobiography; it was almost completed when she died in June 1980.

Douglas is remembered by only a handful as a leading Broadway star, and by almost no one as a singer. In Congress, she did not wield significant political power as traditionally defined; but she challenged the male power structure by her insistence on respect for her political style, and she gained that respect. Her passionate appeals for a better America for the average citizen and a peaceful world gave hope to the people she represented—not only those in her own district but around the country—that someone cared. Despite only three terms in Congress, she stood out among her colleagues as an idealist who was willing to take risks, who spoke persuasively and stood for goals that more pragmatic politicians hesitated to embrace, and it is that for which she is recognized. The outpouring of expression at the time of her death suggests that Helen Gahagan Douglas forged a durable legacy of political principle and action.

Notes

I wish to thank the National Endowment for the Humanities, the Eleanor Roosevelt Institute at the Franklin D. Roosevelt Library, and the American Philosophical Society for partial funding for the research and writing of my work on Douglas. A full-scale biographical study is forthcoming in 1991 from Oxford University Press.

[1] *Los Angeles Times*, 1 and 12 July 1980; Claremont *Courier*, 16 July 1980; and H. L. Mitchell, "In Memory of an Early Friend of the Farm Worker" [mimeographed, July 1980].

[2] Helen Gahagan Douglas, "Congresswoman, Actress, and Opera Singer," an oral history conducted in 1973, 1974, and 1976 by Amelia Fry, in Helen Gahagan Douglas Oral History Project, vol. 4, Regional Oral History Project, The Bancroft Library, University of California, Berkeley, 1982, p. 4.

[3] Goldschmidt, Douglas Memorial Service, 2 December 1980, New York City, author's collection of unpublished materials on Douglas.

[4] Douglas to Jerry Voorhis, 12 March 1940, University of Oklahoma, Carl Albert Congressional Research and Studies Center, Helen Gahagan Douglas Collection [HGD Papers], Box 212, Folder 9.

[5] Helen Gahagan, "FSA Aids Migratory Worker," *Democratic Digest* 17 (February 1940), p. 37.

[6] Thomas F. Ford to Douglas, 20 October 1943, HGD Papers, Box 163, Folder 1.

[7] Douglas to Eleanor Roosevelt, 16 March 1944, Franklin D. Roosevelt Library, Anna Eleanor Roosevelt Papers, Box 1756.

Ella Baker

(1903–1986)

Catherine Clinton

Born in Norfolk, Virginia, in 1903, Ella Baker never forgot her roots. Her father Blake was a waiter on the ferry to Washington, while her mother Georgianna was active in the church. When the family moved to Littleton, North Carolina in 1910, they settled on land once owned by Baker's grandparents' former master. Her parents prized education and Baker graduated from Shaw University, a black college in Raleigh, North Carolina, in 1927. She moved to New York City and became a journalist and reformer, participating in local New Deal politics. During the depression Baker became involved in the National Association for the Advancement of Colored People, and served as a field organizer into the 1940s. In the wake of the Montgomery, Alabama, bus boycott, Baker joined the Southern Christian Leadership Conference and became active in radical civil rights politics. She was the political and spiritual midwife for the Student Nonviolent Coordinating Committee and remained an activist until her death at the age of eighty-three.

When four young black men refused to vacate a lunch counter in Greensboro, North Carolina, in February 1960, turning the national spotlight onto segregation, sit-ins sprang up across the South in sympathy with the protest and in solidarity with the cause of racial equality. Some argue the modern civil rights protest movement was born in this heady rush to confrontation; if so, then we must acknowledge that the student movement was midwifed by Ella Baker.

By the spring of 1960 Baker was chafing within the Southern Christian Leadership Conference (SCLC), an organization founded in the wake of the Montogmery, Alabama, bus boycott, which she had joined "temporarily" in 1958. After nearly two years, she was unhappy as executive secretary and sought new directions. Baker enthusiastically embraced the alternative posed by students—youthful crusaders "interested not in being leaders as much as in developing leadership among other people."[1]

Black youth throughout the South were primed for protest in the spring of 1960. Chicago-born Diane Nash went to Howard University in Washington, D.C., before she transferred to Fisk University in Nashville, both black colleges. Segregation—the separation of white and black into two worlds—within American society made her feel "stifled and boxed in." Nash worked to break out by joining the student movement on campus where she met fellow activist Marion Barry. Barry was raised on a Mississippi farm and later moved to Memphis where he graduated from LeMoyne College. While attending graduate school at Fisk, he joined in the student crusade. (Barry would later become mayor of Washington, D.C.) Another politician in the making, John Lewis, was born in a tenant house in Alabama and began his career as a preacher while still in high school. He attended the American Baptist Theological Seminary in Nashville, and befriended other nonviolent activists. John Lawson was a northern-born college graduate who had refused to serve in the Korean War and spent time in prison. Paroled as a Methodist missionary in India for three years, he steeped himself in the philosophy of Mahatma Gandhi. Lawson was an active member of the Fellowship of Reconciliation (FOR), a group dedicated to nonviolent social action for instituting political reform, and became its first southern field secretary. He attended Oberlin College School of Theology before settling at the Vanderbilt School of Theology in 1958. Lawson organized workshops on nonviolence at Vanderbilt in 1959 and spearheaded the movement of 150 sit-in protestors in Nashville during the spring of 1960. These activities, ironically, earned him his expulsion from divinity school. These were but a few of the student activists primed for action in the winter of 1959–60.

Protests required tough self-discipline on the part of these young activists—courtesy and patience were demanded despite trying conditions. All participants were expected to turn the other cheek, never to retaliate despite verbal or physical abuse. The watchwords of this movement were *love* and *nonviolence*. When newspapers across the South erupted with reports of polite, persistent youths disrupting segregated facilities and filling local jails, the civil rights leadership, white segregationists, and lawmakers were all unprepared.

However, one person who responded with foresight and insight was Ella Baker. She knew that Rev. Martin Luther King, Jr., and other activists and ministers of the SCLC were interested in channeling the energy of youth into their own protest program, yet this fiercely energetic and independent woman fought to keep the students disentangled from "parent" organizations. Through Baker's efforts a network of student protestors led to the formation of the Student Nonviolent Coordinating Committee, Freedom Summer (the busing in of hundreds of college students and other civil rights workers in 1964 to register blacks to vote across the South), and one of the most dynamic chapters in the history of the modern civil rights movement.

Baker had recognized something new and exciting in the spontaneous protests in the first months of the new decade, at a time when she was increasingly disenchanted with her role in the SCLC. She had been on the brink of resigning her post when the youth revolution sparked new hope, and a new mission. Her long years of experience led her to believe this was not an opportunity to be missed and she moved rapidly to capitalize on the combustion of activity.

In the first months of 1960, Baker went to two leaders of the SCLC to request funding for a meeting, a Student Leadership Conference, where groups and leaders from across the South might gather. Baker was not concerned with bringing youth in line with the interests of the larger, ministerially dominated movement, yet the eight-hundred dollar donation by the SCLC was their investment in an attempt to maintain interest and, perhaps, exercise control. Apparently many within the leadership believed this financial pledge and Baker's involvement would guarantee SCLC dominance of the youth movement. But they underestimated both college activists' and Baker's commitment to an independent course.

Baker took responsibility for the meeting, using her contacts at her alma mater, Shaw University in Raleigh, North Carolina, to set up a conference on Easter weekend, April 16–18, 1960. Her call for the conference was co-signed by King, but the spirit and content of the message conveyed Baker's concerns. She took pains to insure that students would be featured on the podium, inviting John Lawson, a strong presence in the Nashville contingent, to offer the keynote address. She assured the invitees that the weekend goals were

"TO SHARE experience gained in recent protest demonstrations and TO HELP chart future goals for effective action," hoping to create "a more unified sense of direction for *training and action in Nonviolent Resistance.*" Further, Baker stipulated that the conference should be "youth centered" and those "Adult Freedom Fighters" present were only for "counsel and guidance."[2]

When the conferees gathered at Raleigh, the numbers and representation far exceeded Baker's estimates. Over 300 students attended, and the group was kaleidoscopic in its range and depth, including over 120 black student representatives from fifty-six colleges and high schools from twelve southern states and the District of Columbia. The conference attracted between fifty and sixty representatives from northern colleges and members of thirteen national or northern "observer organizations" (such as the National Student Association, the Students for a Democratic Society, and the National Student Christian Federation). Nearly a dozen southern white students attended. Members of the Congress of Racial Equality (CORE), FOR, and, of course, the SCLC leadership turned up. But the overwhelming majority of attendees were black youths eager to organize struggles, to join the wave of energy sweeping across southern campuses.

When the Southern Christian Leadership Conference funded the meeting, they had assumed that Baker would support their efforts to channel youthful energy into their larger organization. Martin Luther King, Jr. was a rising star within the movement who had begun to attract national attention. Indeed, he was forced to leave the conference early to appear on the nationally televised Sunday news program *Meet the Press.* So when King arrived in Raleigh he called a press conference and outlined his goals for the weekend: establish a permanent organization, pursue a policy of serving time in jail rather than paying fines, become more attuned to Gandhi's philosophy of nonviolent protest, and push the federal government to step in by spreading nonviolent confrontations throughout the South.[3]

King and his followers were distressed that this SCLC agenda was not the preoccupation of debating students; rather, the majority of the students struggled with the political and philosophical questions of building a movement. John Lawson's keynote address eschewed setting specific goals in favor of sharpening group appreciation of the spiritual and moral underpinnings of student protests. Students were not encouraged to become involved because of charismatic leadership or spontaneous whim, rather they were confronted with the serious business of commitment and continuing struggle—a strategy that provided important rewards in the months and years of conflict ahead. Lawson attacked the National Association for the Advancement of Colored People (NAACP) for "fund-raising and court action rather than developing our greatest resource, a people no longer the victims of racial evil who can act in a disciplined manner to implement the constitution."[4] Fellow delegates were concerned with defining the radical ideology with which the group wished to be associated. Almost all disdained the overtures made by established civil rights organizations.

Meanwhile, Ella Baker had reason to fear the plans of SCLC leaders. A reckoning was in the works because Baker had welcomed the student philosophy of "group centered leadership" as refreshing for those who "bore the scars of battle, the frustration and the disillusionment that come when the prophetic leader turns out to have heavy feet of clay."[5] This was a thinly veiled reference to King, among others.

Animosity between the two activists was growing and was apparently based on the simple fact that Ella Baker was unable to conform to the female stereotype envisioned by the conservative black male ministers leading the movement. Andrew Young suggests that this particular feud had to do with King's psychology.

> We had a hard job with domineering women in SCLC because Martin's mother, quiet as she was, was really a strong, domineering force in that family. She was never publicly saying anything, but she ran Daddy King and she ran the church and she ran Martin and so Martin's problems with Ella Baker, for instance, in the early days of the movement were directly related to his need to be free of that strong matriarchal influence.[6]

James Lawson concurred: "Martin had a real problem with having a woman in a high position."[7] King was neither the first, nor the last, of a long line of men with whom Baker would have to do battle. At Raleigh, in April 1960, Baker stood fast and, with the students, won independence.

On the second day of the conference, King, Rev. Ralph Abernathy (an important civil rights activist who would become King's lieutenant and successor), and Rev. Wyatt Walker (the incoming executive director of the SCLC) called a caucus with Baker to which no students were invited. At this meeting the three men, all Baptist ministers, argued that students should organize a "youth group" or a "student arm" of the SCLC. Walker even admitted to Baker that his motives were personal—in an attempt to strengthen the leadership role he was about to assume, he wanted the students "delivered" to his organization. King argued he could influence the Georgia delegation, and Abernathy assumed the Alabama students would follow dutifully Georgia's lead. Walker then argued that he could insure Virginia's cooperation and pull off his coup. Baker, however, resisted the ministers' efforts, and argued that the students should not settle on a structure at this meeting—especially one that suited the "Adult Freedom Fighters" rather than the youth on the front lines. When the ministers pressured her to make a motion to become a part of the SCLC, Baker walked out of the meeting. Her defiance defeated their purposes and the three left town later that night, before the end of the conference.

On April 17, 1960, with Baker's blessing, the students voted against any permanent affiliation with an established group. Ironically, the delegation from Petersburg, Virginia—which Walker thought was in his hip pocket—created the most strenuous opposition to affiliation with the SCLC, so intense that the meeting was forced to stop, sing, and pray.[8] Nevertheless, the students were willing to form a temporary Student Nonviolent Coordinating Committee (SNCC). This group planned to meet every month—"to continue the dialogue"— and Marion Barry was elected chair, a position he resigned in the fall to return to graduate school.

Baker found SNCC exhilarating, and reported in the *Southern Patriot* in May 1960 that "the Student Leadership Conference made it crystal clear that current sit-ins and other demonstrations are concerned with something much bigger than a hamburger or even a giant-sized Coke."[9] (She would later complain that the protests should not be about who got *served* a burger but about who could *afford* a burger in a segregated, racist America.) She applauded the perception that "it is important to keep the movement democratic and to avoid struggles for personal leadership"—especially as a refugee from the ministers' caucus. Finally, she concluded that "Many adults and youth characterized the Raleigh meeting as the greatest or most significant conference of our period."[10]

The group might have become mere footnote to the civil rights movement, if Baker had not continued to nurture it. Eleven SNCC members gathered in Atlanta on May 13 to coordinate efforts. Without money or mailing address, the students gratefully accepted Baker's offer to shelter the organization at the SCLC headquarters, a group with which Baker remained affiliated. Baker recruited Jane Stembridge, a white student from Virginia at the Union Theological Seminary in New York, to run the office. By June, Stembridge and other volunteers produced the *Student Voice*, the SNCC newsletter, full of statements of purpose, solicitation for funds and contributions from black campuses (the young Julian Bond penned a protest poem and sent it from Morehouse College where he was enrolled).

By the end of the summer, Baker officially broke ties with the SCLC and secured SNCC offices provided by a sympathetic donor on Auburn Avenue in Atlanta. She, Stembridge, and Bob Moses, a black

Harvard graduate student recruited by the SCLC for voter registration but who defected upon his arrival in Atlanta, were the unpaid staff that sustained the organization in its first months. The historian Clayborne Carson argues in his study of the organization: "SNCC would probably not have survived its first summer had it not been for the energy and skills of Baker and Stembridge. Whereas SNCC appeared to outsiders and even to many black student leaders to be merely a clearinghouse for the exchange of information about localized protest movements, to the two women it was potentially an organization for expanding the struggle beyond its campus base to include all classes of blacks."[11] And indeed it did accomplish some of these idealistic goals.

What drew the fifty-seven-year-old Baker into an organization staffed and sustained by students? Baker's personal style pulled her into this maelstrom of energy, and her youthful comrades responded enthusiastically. John Lewis, a SNCC veteran, later commented, "She was much older in terms of age, but I think in terms of ideas and philosophy and commitment she was one of the youngest persons in the movement."[12] Her willingness to meet the students on their own terms, without manipulation, taught them to trust her. Her patience through long hours—and in some cases days—of philosophical and political wrangles endeared her to the SNCC rank and file. One SNCC veteran fondly remembered her wearing a surgical mask to protect her against the cloud of smoke filling the room, sitting through endless strategy debates, which Baker had doubtless heard again, and again, and again.[13] But Baker's patience and endurance gave her the strength to impart decades of wisdom to the committed student activists.

Baker was born in Norfolk, Virginia, in 1903 to Georgianna and Blake Baker. Her father was a waiter on a ferry that ran from Norfolk to Washington, a job that kept him from home much of the time. In 1910 the family moved to Littleton, North Carolina, and settled near her maternal grandparents, who had been slaves. After emancipation, Baker's grandfather, a preacher, had settled on the land of his former owner in rural North Carolina, where he built a church. Baker used to be accorded a seat of privilege, placed in a chair next to the pulpit from which her grandfather delivered his sermon. He gathered his family around to form a tightly-knit clan. Baker recalled:

> There was a deep sense of community that prevailed in this little neck of the woods. It wasn't a town, it was just people. And each of them had their twenty-thirty-forty-fifty acre farms. . . . This community had been composed to a large extent by relatives. Over the hill

was my grandfather's sister who was married to my Uncle Carter, and up the grove was another relative who had a place. . . .[14]

This sense of family was accomplished despite the circumstances of slavery over which Baker's maternal grandparents had triumphed. Baker recalled that her grandmother chose her grandfather instead of the partner the mistress had picked out. Under slavery, masters attempted to control every aspect of slaves' lives. It was not uncommon for a slave's owner to intervene in these matters, especially for a "favorite slave" and/or illegitimate offspring. Baker's grandmother's defiance created tension, both because she was the daughter of the master and because in rejecting the advice of her white owners she was banished to the fields instead of remaining a "house slave." The stories handed down strenghtened both Baker's resistance to white authority and her family ties.

Baker's family, especially her mother, played a large role in the community: "Mamma was always responding to the sick after we moved."[15] Baker's aunt was a midwife, and Baker learned about family responsibility by her example as well.

My aunt who had thirteen children of her own raised three more. She had become a midwife, and a child was born who was covered with sores. Nobody was particularly wanting the child, so she took the child and raised him. He's one of the *best* of her brood. And another mother decided she didn't want to be bothered with two children. So my aunt took one and raised him. So they were part of the family.[16]

This sense of belonging to a "wider brotherhood" than just her immediate family nurtured Baker during her youth, and she had hopes of becoming a medical missionary.

She was educated at local schools and then graduated from Shaw University in Raleigh, North Carolina, in 1927. With her college degree in hand she struck out for Harlem, in New York City, to live with a cousin, but found her education no assistance against the great wall of prejudice. Because she was African-American she was limited to jobs waiting tables or working in a factory. When the stockmarket crashed in 1929 and the depression set in, Baker watched her own dreams fade. When she moved to Harlem she had hopes of saving her money so she could pursue a higher degree in sociology at the University of Chicago, a coeducational institution with a liberal race policy. The struggles within her own community due to the depression affected Baker deeply, "The tragedy of seeing long lines of people standing waiting, actually waiting on the bread line, for coffee or handouts, this had its impact."[17] Baker began to write for the *American West Indian News*, and by 1932 had joined the *Negro National News* as office manager and editorial assistant.

Also by this time Baker was fully committed to a career in activism. In 1932 she organized the Young Negroes Cooperative League and helped coordinate activities for the Works Progress Administration (WPA) consumer education program. Baker spearheaded the effort to offer classes in settlement houses, provide lecturers to women's clubs, and help sponsor cooperatives in housing projects; Baker believed in bringing collective strategies to the people. She saw the widespread collapse of the economy as something that created an opportunity for dramatic political change. The Manhattan circles within which she traveled honed her political perspective. Baker recalled: "New York was a hotbed of—let's call it radical thinking. You had every spectrum of radical thinking on WPA. We had a lovely time! Ignorant ones, like me, we had lots of opportunity to hear and to evaluate whether or not this was the kind of thing you wanted to get into. Boy it was good, *stimulating*."[18]

By the late 1930s, Baker's activism led her into the National Association for the Advancement of Colored People (NAACP). This group, founded in 1910, was an interracial organization dedicated to improving race relations and fighting white terrorism; in particular, the NAACP sought to push an antilynching bill through Congress. This and other legislative campaigns were aimed at insuring blacks their constitutionally guaranteed rights, rights that were abridged by segregation. By the early 1940s, Baker was an assistant field secretary for the NAACP, a position that kept her on the road. Despite her peripatetic life, Baker's roots kept her anchored: "I think these are the things [community and family] that helped to strengthen my concept about the need for people to have a sense of their own value, and *their* strengths, and it became accentuated when I began to travel in the forties for the National Association for the Advancement of Colored People."[19]

Baker faced challenges within and outside the black community when organizing in the field. As an organizer she would be dispatched to specific regions; she later remembered her first contacts in Florida: "You'd call up Reverend Brother so-and-so, and ask if you could appear before the congregation at such-and-such a time. Sometimes they'd give you three minutes, because, after all, many people weren't secure enough to run the risk, as they saw it, of being targeted as ready to challenge the powers that be." She regretted that a stalwart, Harry T. Moore, a black principal, was fired for speaking out in favor of equal pay for black and white teachers. Moore later died when his house was bombed on Christmas eve—a martyr to the cause of African-American resistance. Baker remembered, "You could go into that area of Florida and you could talk about the virtue of the NAACP, because they knew Harry T. Moore. They hadn't discussed a whole lot of theory." But there was a *man* who served *their* interests and who *identified* with them."[20]

Baker attempted to build a movement among a people, like all other peoples, divided by class prejudices. She confronted well-to-do blacks who were embarrassed by being reminded of the masses of uneducated, impoverished African-Americans. Baker reasoned: "The gal who has been able to buy her minks and whose husband is a professional, they live well. You can't insult her, you never go and tell her she's a so-and-so for taking, for *not* identifying. You try to point out where her interest lies in identifying with that other one across the tracks who doesn't have minks."[21] Even more common, she encountered "the little people" who resented the paternalism of NAACP organizers. When she first came to Florida, Baker recalled, "I got a contribution for a life membership in the NAACP, which was five-hundred dollars then, was from a longshoreman's union. They remembered somebody who had been there before from the NAACP, with a mink coat. When they gave this five-hundred dollar membership, somebody mentioned it. See, they had resented the mink coat. I don't think it was the mink coat they really resented. It was the *barrier* they could sense between them and the person in the coat."[22] But wardrobe was hardly the issue; rather, Baker used these examples to illustrate the visible ways in which invisible walls would have to be broken down to bring all the people into a movement for social justice.

Baker never married; however, in 1946 she took over the rearing of her seven-year-old niece and therefore resigned from the NAACP to devote time to raising the young girl in Baker's Harlem home. Although her retirement was ostensibly for personal reasons, in her letter of resignation, Baker voiced her disillusionment with the political dissent she increasingly faced. Baker admitted she was unwilling to defer to the male ministerial leadership she encountered; many men within the organization complained of her outspoken manner and her "disrespectful style."[23] And yet she was so loved by "the people" that several urged her to voice her concerns at the annual NAACP convention. Baker refused, not out of respect for male leaders, but because she did not want *her* role or personality to become the focus of a split within the movement. Increasingly Baker's grass-roots, collectivist party politics were replaced by hierarchy within African-American leadership. Baker saw alienation between these leaders and their poor, mainly rural black constituents.

Although the NAACP continued its organizational campaigns, the major thrust of the organization was focused on legal battles. In 1954 the *Brown v. Board of Education* Supreme Court decision signaled a new era for civil rights. Although lawmakers were unsure as to what "all deliberate speed" might mean, African-Americans believed their time had come. In 1955 Rosa Parks refused to give up her seat on a Montgomery city bus to a white passenger and the subsequent boycott of the bus system in the capital of Alabama lasted for over a year. Public transportation was shut down and a new civil rights militance was born. In 1957 the SCLC developed in the wake of this resistance and King, among others, hoped to export "nonviolent direct action" throughout the South. Three years later, SNCC renewed Baker's commitment and she in turn was able to train and nurture a cadre of youthful revolutionaries.

Resigning from the SCLC to work at her unpaid position with SNCC, Baker also signed up with the YWCA in Atlanta as a consultant in human relations. Her lifelong commitment to political organization gave her little economic security, as Baker confessed in 1979, "How did I make my living? I haven't. I have eked out existence."[24] When she began working for the NAACP, her salary was $2,000 a year. During the 1950s she supported herself by working for the New York Cancer Society. She thought of her political activities as a vocation, not a means of breadwinning. Her views differed dramatically from her youthful peers in SNCC: "I think today, people's concept of political organizing is like you're really out there night and day doing it all. See, young people today have had the luxury of a period in which they could give their all to this political organizing. They didn't have to be bothered by a whole lot of other things. But most of those who are older put it in with things that they had to do."[25]

Students gave their all in 1964 in the Freedom Summer when thousands of college students moved South in an effort to register blacks to vote. Baker was invaluable during this effort. She sent SNCC member Bob Moses to Amzie Moore, her coworker from her NAACP days: "I had gone down there and stayed with them and helped with meetings, so I knew the person. I knew he knew the state, and so Bob Moses was able to have an entrée. Here was a man who had never been to Mississippi, and he had somewhere to sleep, to eat, and he had somebody who knew something that could be useful."[26] When whites resisted the registration drive and it became apparent that blacks would continue to be denied their right to vote, SNCC organized a separate political entity, the Mississippi Freedom Democratic Party (MFDP). Baker was a keynote speaker at the party convention in Jackson, Mississippi. She also moved to the MFDP office in Washington and appeared on television to support the organization. When Fannie Lou Hamer became one of the visible leaders within the newly organized party, Baker felt no spirit of rivalry;

instead she confessed to intense pride in the movement: "Great fruit came of it in terms of arousing the people and getting them involved . . . like Mrs. Hamer. There's a woman that had been a time-keeper on a plantation for sixteen or more years, and when she attempted to register to vote she lost her job, her husband lost his, and then she was badly beaten."[27]

Hamer went on to be the keynote speaker for the MFDP in Atlantic City, New Jersey, at the Democratic National Convention. When President Lyndon Johnson, in an effort to compromise, engineered a separate and partial seating of MFDP delegates on the convention floor, Hamer and her comrades refused. They wanted the all-white segregated delegation thrown out and replaced by the representative MFDP people. Johnson's hammerlock on the convention prevented the issue from getting to the floor, but Hamer and her supporters rallied outside the hall and garnered media attention. In 1967 the MFDP campaign yielded electoral victory when Robert Clark became the first African-American to serve in the Mississippi state legislature since Reconstruction.

Baker's commitment to the cause of freedom continued past the Freedom Summer, and in 1967 she joined the Southern Conference Educational Fund, a group dedicated to interracial collective action in the South. Baker continued her travels and speeches on behalf of racial justice, arguing: "I keep going because I don't see the productive value of being bitter. What else *do* you do?"[28] In 1972 she became vice chairperson of the Mass Party Organizing Committee. She also served on the board of the Puerto Rican Solidarity Committee, and by the 1980s her role as an exemplary female leader brought her national recognition.

Not only did Baker midwife the student revolutionaries of the 1960s, but she served as a force for broadening the struggle for civil rights throughout her career. Although most midwives disappear from the life of the child after its birth, Baker was a stalwart exemplary force for social struggle and justice throughout the 1960s and into the 1980s. Her nonviolent stance was one she learned from early disappointment. Late in her life, Baker recalled the first incidence of race prejudice she encountered, when a young boy called her "nigger" on the streets of Norfolk, and she struck back by slapping him across the face. As a movement elder, she counseled that striking back was not enough, that retaliatory acts were feeble. Joining a collective movement, fighting side-by-side in nonviolent protest was a more effective means of permanent revenge. Baker believed that all people everywhere would have to unite in the struggle against prejudice and injustice.[29]

Baker's global concerns, like many of the young people she inspired, led her into movements against apartheid in South Africa, for liberation in Zimbabwe, and against American imperialism in Africa generally. But her commitments remained rooted in the family and community values she inherited from her kin and her people. She explained in 1979:

> To me, I'm part of the human family. What the human family will accomplish, I can't control. But it isn't impossible that what those who came along with me went through, might stimulate others to continue to fight for a society that does not have those kinds of problems. Somewhere down the line the numbers increase, the tribe increases. So how do you keep on? I can't help it. I don't claim to have any corner on an answer, but I believe that the struggle is eternal. Somebody else carries on.[30]

Her message of collective struggle struck a chord among "the people" throughout her life, but it especially uplifted a generation in turmoil during the 1960s.

Thus Ella Baker departed from a life filled with challenge and struggle in 1986. She provided a legacy that filmmaker Joanne Grant celebrated in her 1984 documentary *Fundi*. As Vincent Harding explains in the film, *fundi* is an African term of honor and respect for a person that signifies a fountain from which knowledge and power might flow. Baker, and many older African-American women like her, nurtured the grass-roots protest movement during the struggle for civil rights. The black church may have been headed by male ministers, but it was sustained by its female membership. Records of organizations, memoirs of participants, and films and other documentation demonstrate women's widespread, steadfast, and significant participation.

The hundreds of black women who opened their homes during boycotts and protests of the early 1960s, the steady parade of domestic servants who walked to work in Montgomery for over a year to make the bus boycott effective, the hundreds of thousands of women who canvassed and counseled and made voting rights a top priority for the civil rights agenda—all these women deserve their due. The ideology, the example of empowerment, and the tactical energizing of the civil rights movement would infuse the women's liberation movement that grew from it during the 1960s and into the 1970s.

Yet much of this legacy is missing from historical reconstructions of the period. Against all odds, women seem to be simultaneously celebrated while being erased. Some commentators, sensitive to gender issues, mention appreciatively those few women leaders who emerged from the male hierarchy dominating civil rights politics, a backhanded compliment at best. Yet perhaps this historical vision is a mirror of contemporary sexual politics; one civil rights leader recalled that the video or news teams would only turn on the lights and film men giving speeches during rallies, ignoring women who might also have featured roles.[31]

The current images of "the movement" illuminate this distortion. Scholarly attention that focuses almost exclusively on men remains the standard. Even the award-winning documentary *Eyes on the Prize* (Part I, 1987, Part II, 1990) reinforces this image problem by keeping women in the background, playing up the role of male leadership (with females following), and minimizing both women's significant organizational and political contributions as well as the tensions black feminism provoked—for example, the split produced by Shirley Chisholm's presidential candidacy in 1972. It is conventional wisdom that the feminist movement of the late 1960s and 1970s stemmed from, in large part, the civil rights movement, as activist Virginia Durr explains in her autobiography.

> I believe that the struggle of the blacks against segregation led to the women's movement. The women who took part in that struggle for black emanicipation began to realize that they weren't very well emancipated either. When your husband disassociates himself from you because you have been to a prayer meeting, you're not very free to go to those meetings. . . . These sweet church women, black and white, were scared to death of their husbands. . . . If you go to any of the Southern women's movement meetings, you would be surprised at the amount of passion that comes forth. They really feel held down and they are trying to break loose.[32]

Yet the power of memory and the current renaissance of black women's literature undercuts this convenient neglect of black women's crucial part in the empowerment of blacks in the South. The lack of scholarship on these issues will soon be met by a mighty wave of work, just as the noticeable absence of African-American women's literature has been supplanted by a virtual flood of literary work.[33] Ella Baker will not be remembered merely as a "midwife," but as a full and equal parent who participated in the conception, birth, and nurturing of not one but many movements for social justice. Baker fought equally for the rights of blacks and the status of women.

When an even younger generation looks back on this dynamic era of civil rights struggle, Ella Baker will take her rightful place, at the

forefront of many movements, in the vanguard of political change—
a comrade and an inspiration.

Notes

[1]James Forman, *The Making of Black Revolutionaries: A Personal Account* (New York: Macmillan, 1972), p. 217.

[2]Clayborne Carson, *In Struggle: SNCC and the Black Awakening of the 1960s* (Cambridge, MA: Harvard University Press, 1981), p. 20.

[3]Ibid., pp. 22–23.

[4]Ibid., p. 23.

[5]Ibid., p. 20.

[6]David Garrow, *Bearing the Cross: Martin Luther King and the SCLC* (New York: William Morrow, 1986), p. 654, n. 12.

[7]Ibid., p. 141.

[8]Forman, *Black Revolutionaries*, p. 217.

[9]Ibid.

[10]Ibid.

[11]Carson, *In Struggle*, pp. 25–26.

[12]Forman, *Black Revolutionaries*, p. 24.

[13]See *Fundi*, Joanne Grant (1984).

[14]Ellen Cantarow, *Moving the Mountain: Women Working for Social Change* (New York: Feminist Press, 1980), pp. 60–61.

[15]Ibid., p. 59.

[16]Ibid., p. 59.

[17]Ibid., p. 60.

[18]Ibid., p. 61.

[19]Ibid., p. 61.

[20]Ibid., pp. 69–20.

[21]Ibid., p. 70.

[22]Ibid., pp. 71–72.

[23]*Fundi* and Cantarow, *Moving the Mountain*, p. 156, n. 3.

[24]Cantarow, *Moving the Mountain*, p. 73.

[25]Ibid., p. 74.

[26]Ibid., p. 89.

[27]Ibid., p. 90.

[28]Ibid., p. 92.

[29] See *Fundi*.

[30] Cantarow, *Moving the Mountain*, p. 93.

[31] Dudley Clendinen, ed., *The Prevailing South* (Atlanta, GA: Longstreet Press, 1988), p. 192.

[32] Hollinger Barnard, ed., *Outside the Magic Circle: The Autobiography of Virginia Foster Durr* (New York: Simon and Schuster, 1987), p. 331.

[33] Two outstanding African-American novelists, Alice Walker and Toni Morrison, have won the Pulitzer Prize in the past five years. *The Color Purple* and *Beloved* received instant acclaim and "classic" status.

Betty Friedan
(b. 1921)

Donald Meyer

Betty Friedan was born Betty Naomi Goldstein on February 4, 1921, in Peoria, Illinois. From 1938 to 1942 she attended Smith College in Northampton, Massachusetts, graduating summa cum laude *in psychology. She then went to the University of California, Berkeley, for postgraduate study but left after a year to pursue a newspaper career in New York. She married Carl Friedan soon thereafter and had three children, Emily, Daniel, and Jonathan. She continued to write, publishing articles in women's magazines. In 1963, Friedan published* The Feminine Mystique. *The book gained Friedan immediate fame, and she began to lecture widely. In 1966 she was a founding member and first president of the National Organization for Women. Friedan was instrumental in establishing one of the nation's first women's studies programs, at Cornell in 1968. She attempted to move feminism into orthodox, national politics in 1968 along with other prominent women, supporting the antiwar candidacy of Eugene McCarthy, who had been the chief sponsor of the Equal Rights Amendment in Congress. In 1971 she joined feminists Bella Abzug, Gloria Steinem, and Shirley Chisholm in establishing the National Women's Political Caucus. In the early 1970s Friedan organized the First Women's Bank and Trust Company. Friedan published* It Changed My Life *in 1976 and* The Second Stage *in 1981.*

Betty Friedan, née Goldstein, was born in Peoria, Illinois, in 1921, and grew up there, living in the same house until she went off in 1938 to Smith College.[1] As she would recall it, this girlhood was by no means unclouded. School work came easy, but she was not one of the popular girls in high school. The chief trouble appeared at home, however. Like many other midwestern small-city families, the Goldsteins weathered the Great Depression without serious blight. The tension between Betty Goldstein's parents had deeper roots than that. Before marrying, her mother had written for a local newspaper. She gave up this potential career for husband and family. Soon she had found herself restless, discontent, resentful. She had more energy, more intelligence, more ambition than would be contained in the role of housewife, even in Community Chest work and other civic activities. In effect, the first person the future feminist knew, suffering from "the problem that had no name," was her own mother: "My own feminism somehow began in my mother's discontent. . . ."[2]

Yet it was the mother who prompted the daughter not to make the same mistake. She urged her daughter to try out for the school paper, get jobs, earn money, not out of family necessity but for independence. Her mother impelled her toward Smith. In college, perhaps as though compelled to understand her own upbringing, Betty Goldstein majored in psychology. Once again the work came easy: she graduated summa cum laude in 1942. She won a grant to work with the psychologist Erik Erikson in Berkeley. After a year there she got another grant, opening a highway to a Ph.D. and a professional career in psychology. Just exactly why she chose, instead, to go to New York City and work on newspapers, Friedan never said, but presently she married Carl Friedan and soon thereafter found herself a housewife, in the suburbs of Rockland County, with three children. In an autobiographical reminiscence forty years later, Friedan noted that she had not quit her newspaper job: she had been fired, during pregnancy, with no legal recourse. But she had not, she agreed, been victimized by this lack of legal equality. Instead, she had been "relieved" to be fired. Why? "I was determined to be 'fulfilled as a woman' as my mother was not."[3] Thus, Rockland County was not to be a repetition of Peoria: unlike her mother, Betty Friedan embraced motherhood and housewifery eagerly. In short, the exemplary victim of the feminine mystique would be herself.

Some of the persuasive power of Betty Friedan's famous bestseller, *The Feminine Mystique,* published in 1963, undoubtedly inhered in the utter conviction with which she presented women's need for a complete life, a conviction drawn from personal experience. Despite her wish to live by the standards of the feminine mystique, Friedan found that she could not. She was bored. Her need for greater activity, sterner challenge, true risk-taking would not be denied. She began free-lancing articles for women's magazines. In 1957 she composed a questionnaire which she sent to the members of the Smith College class of '42, inquiring of their lives since graduation. She undertook systematic research into popular women's magazine fiction, modern psychiatry and sociology, and modern educational theories—all respecting women. Literally, she had resumed the career she had forsaken. She then brought all this individual effort to stunning fruition in her book. The book in turn launched her on a new career, that of no longer just a writer but a leader.

W. W. Norton, the publishers of *The Feminine Mystique,* had reason to hope for good sales. Exposés of tedium in the picture-window suburbs, such as A. C. Spectorsky's *The Exurbanites* (1956) and Richard and Katherine Gordon's *The Split-Level Trap* (1960) had already been modest best-sellers. As far back as 1956, in a special issue devoted to "the American Woman," *Life* magazine in its otherwise conventionally upbeat portrait included several selections indicating all was not well for this paragon. By 1962 *Esquire*'s July issue on "the American Woman" more nearly approached lamentation than celebration. The most famous career woman of the epoch, Margaret Mead, had been deploring the "return of the cave woman." Even mass-circulation women's magazines which Friedan would criticize in her book as purveyors of the mystique at its worst had begun to carry articles diagnosing malaise. But, cautiously, the publisher printed a first run of only three thousand copies. By comparison with these other discussions, Friedan's manuscript was not journalistic in style. It had very little personal, autobiographical, confessional tang. True to Friedan's own academic training, it carried a heavy freightage of scholarly quotations and references. It treated psychology and sociology on levels of high scholarly theory. Even for its intended audience, college-educated women of her own generation, it could not have been thought easy reading. Yet the book took off immediately. Norton soon printed another sixty thousand copies. In ten years, sales swelled to 3 million. Obviously, a large audience had been waiting for such a book and was receptive to Friedan's message.

Paradoxically, then, the sway of the feminine mystique had already begun to decline before Friedan's book appeared. Still, that hardly explains why Friedan's book in particular won renown. One reason was her rhetorical strategy. While the mystique Friedan attacked—of women's fulfillment through domesticity—sometimes appeared to hover everywhere in the 1950s, in every sphere of American life, Friedan did not really think women had been seduced by the fiction in women's magazines or by advertising concocted by some Madison Avenue Institute for Motivational Research. This would have been to demean women's brains, and besides, "A mystique does not compel its own acceptance."[4] While Friedan then offered several guesses why so many women had in fact apparently accepted the beliefs making up the feminine mystique, she herself shrewdly—if "unconsciously"— illuminated the most powerful one by her own procedure. While pop fiction editors and ad men were not likely to mesmerize educated women, educated women were respectful of science. The most powerful underwriters of the feminine mystique were those—both men and women—who insisted that its tenets were not a "mystique" at all but scientific, validated by "research." By far, most of Friedan's book was devoted to identifying the contribution of scientists to the mystification of women: Sigmund Freud, the psychologist; Margaret Mead, the anthropologist; Talcott Parsons, Harvard's dean of modern "functional sociology"; and so on. If the feminine mystique was purveyed by such authorities, it enjoyed prestige indeed.

The prestige of social science could not be undermined simply by citing the feelings of boredom, frustration, and despair Friedan found among her classmates and the scores of other women she had interviewed. Feelings could not stand against science. Instead, by a kind of intellectual jujitsu, Friedan turned to still more social science as counter to the social science she had identified at the heart of the feminine mystique. Freud was not the only psychologist; there were Erik Erikson, A. H. Maslow, theorists of liberation. There was not just one Margaret Mead, author of the feminine mystique's *Male and Female,* but several Margaret Meads, including the critic of the return to the cave of domesticity. Functional sociology, it appeared, was not really a science at all, but a form of circular reasoning already under fire as a "myth." Not women's complaints alone—let alone "women's intuition"—demonstrated the falsity of the feminine mystique—but rather social science's self-criticism proved her point. In chapter after chapter, the heavy majority of Friedan's references were to scholarly articles, scholarly books, academic research. She thus had it both ways, assailing the feminine mystique in its central citadel, disguised as science, while still claiming the prestige of science for herself.

Friedan improved upon this basic strength with two rhetorical contributions of her own. Obviously, the subjective feelings of the victims of the feminine mystique might have been summed up in any number of plain words. *Boredom* comes first to mind perhaps. *Frustration* and *claustrophobia* offered a quasi-clinical ring. *Alienation* resonated back through fashionable radicalism to Karl Marx himself. Friedan's "the problem that has no name" escaped the limitations of all these. It meant something far deeper than boredom, far different from some pathology open to "treatment," and it did not carry the burden of a philosophy to be learned. It encouraged each victim of the "problem" to learn more about it, not by reading about it in more articles or books but by exploring it in her own heart and soul.

The other contribution was her title itself. What Friedan was examining was in truth a mystique "of"—or "about"—femininity. Transforming the noun *femininity* into the adjective *feminine* Friedan introduced an irreducible ambiguity, but one which strongly favored her polemical intent. Clearly, a "mystique of femininity" might be held by both men and women; in Friedan's book most of its exponents were indeed men. But Friedan's whole purpose was to induce women to abandon the mystique. With her choice of "the feminine mystique," she highlighted the myth in its appeal precisely to women, and the need, therefore, of women themselves to start thinking differently about themselves. How men might be induced to start thinking differently about women, while no doubt important, was quite another matter. *The Feminine Mystique* was a call upon women.

This central purpose meshed with certain other features of the book, conspicuous only to critical reflection. The book said nothing of politics. It offered no assessments of either major party. Among politicians, only Adlai Stevenson was mentioned, but only as just another standard exponent of the mystique, not as a liberal. Nor did religion appear significantly. With only a little historical scholarship to draw on, Friedan, evidently unaware of the considerable interdependence between nineteenth-century feminists and religion, wrote as though the two had been only at odds. Secular-minded herself, she simply ignored the issue in postwar America, and thus ignored the fact that women of Jewish and Catholic origins would loom far larger in modern feminism than they had in the nineteenth century,[5] when feminism had in some ways been part of Protestant evangelicalism. Finally, Friedan wrote very little of economics. In a chapter entitled, "The Sexual Sell," she did anticipate a theme that later socialist feminists would hammer hard: "The really important role that women serve as housewives is *to buy more things for the house*." Once one realized that women are "the chief customers of American business," the feminine mystique made sense. But Friedan quickly backed away from any political implications in this. Apotheosis of the housewife-consumer had not followed from some deliberate conspiracy; "business" did not stand embattled against women's escape from the home. It was simply a "byproduct" of "our general confusion lately on ends with means; just something that happened to women. . . ."[6] In no way, then, did the feminine mystique derive from or rest on some basic structure of capitalism.

This indifference to religion, politics, and the economy both expressed and facilitated the central message of Friedan's book, the message that best explains its instant popularity: you can change yourself! In her last chapter, "A New Life Plan for Women," Friedan did not call for a new women's movement, a movement for women's liberation, a new "feminism." She did not call for a new economic system. She did not herald some new religious vision. Instead, she noted how, once a woman faced the pressure of the feminine mystique, "she begins to find her own answers."[7] True, the school system would have to purge itself of catering to the mystique of femininity. True, the collaboration of feminine mystique and the churches (and synagogues) would have to be broken. But these, as well as women's entry into politics, first at the local, then at higher levels, would follow as results even more than as causes of women's awakening. Women—a woman, any woman—need not wait for political wheels to turn, for economic revolutions, for religious transformations, before saving themselves from the deformations wrought by the mystique. The mystique was a scheme of ideas and feelings. It could be defeated by different ideas and feelings. The process of change took place in the mind and spirit. Mind and spirit were every woman's to fulfill. It was in this sense that *The Feminine Mystique* took its place among all those other perennial best-sellers in American culture, the "self-help" books according to which a *man* had only to get his mind straight and think right, think positively, in order to liberate himself from defeat. He did not need politics; he did not need—indeed, ought not want—a change in the economic rules. His religion need be simply an understanding of the powers of one's own mind. No such book had yet been written for women.

Finally, all this meshed perfectly with the historical dimension of the book. In 1963 Friedan still had only a sparse literature on which to draw for any understanding of nineteenth century feminism and of why feminism had faded away after 1920. But she did not really need it for her argument about the feminine mystique. Repeatedly, she contrasted the mystique of the fifties with previous decades when, she said, it had not flourished. Repeatedly, in her telling, the mystique was a creation of post–World War II advertisers, editors, and popular psychiatrists. (This included the somewhat paradoxical implication that Friedan herself had not grown up under its influence and indeed that her peers in the class of 1942 generally had not been its victims.[8]) In short, the feminine mystique did not have roots deep in history, deep in ancient religious myths, deep in the structures of millenial patriarchy. It followed that it would be easy to dispel. After all, why should the concoction of mere admen and popular magazine editors and pop-psychologists be hard to refute?

This foreshortening of modern women's history was a central feature of Friedan's appeal.

In 1966 Friedan helped found the National Organization for Women (NOW).[9] In 1964 congressional representative Martha Griffith (Michigan) and Senator Margaret Chase Smith (Maine) had made sure that the clause forbidding "sex discrimination"—introduced by a segregationist congressional representative in hopes of defeating the Civil Rights Act of 1964—was retained in Title VII of that act. Thousands of complaints from women were soon filed. It quickly became apparent, however, that meaningful enforcement of the act by the new Equal Economic Opportunity Commission (EEOC) depended on outside pressure. Old-line women's organizations, such as the League of Women Voters and the American Association of University women, although headquartered in Washington, did not see this as part of their purposes. The dozen or so women, several of them "closet" feminists in the federal government, who joined with Friedan to create NOW were thus primarily interested in opening to women the world of work outside the home. With Friedan as president, NOW set out to expose all forms of gender discrimination in the workplace, to insist upon a vigorous EEOC, to persuade unions and other organizations to recognize women's demands for equality, and to prompt the creation of local NOW groups for the same activities. With no money, no office, no staff, NOW in its early days relied wholly on what *The Feminine Mystique* had already revealed, a ground swell of demand among women for more opportunities. NOW's first significant success was its part in impelling President Johnson to sign an executive order forbidding sex discrimination in the federal government and by government contractors.

NOW had no particular interest in mass membership. It had no particular interest in evangelizing women themselves. Certainly it welcomed men as members; it did not proclaim "sisterhood." Friedan herself persistently linked equality for women with the equality long asserted in the Bill of Rights of the United States Constitution. Although NOW failed in seeking alliance with the black civil rights movement, its quest resembled that movement's, in striving to extend to still more persons what had remained, in effect, a right enjoyed by white men only. NOW called for no sweeping changes in political, economic, or cultural arrangements in the country. It wanted women to share equally in those arrangements. Quite consistently with this traditional liberalism, it got behind efforts to install an Equal Rights Amendment (ERA) in the Constitution. For fifty years ERA supporters had been opposed by those, including many women, who pointed out that an ERA would negate the many state laws protecting women from certain onerous conditions, laws passed often only after long struggle against crude exploitation. NOW insisted that the time had come to recognize that these protective laws had often been used to limit opportunity. Thus, the early NOW expressed women very like Friedan herself—middle class, middle aged, highly educated, ambitious, professional, white. It felt responsibility for "all" women, notably women in factories and black women, but it sought first of all the end to barriers for women most ready to seize the new opportunities awaiting.

By 1970 Friedan felt, on the one hand, that the potential for a great grass-roots women's movement had vastly increased and, on the other hand, that the women's movement was in serious danger of tearing itself to pieces. From her trips around the country, lecturing and organizing, she was convinced that eagerness for broader lives flourished among ordinary women—"Middle American" women—even more hotly than the response to her book had indicated. In addition, civil rights ferment among blacks had begun to invigorate black women ever more surely. Working-class women had begun to realize their stake in NOW's agenda. Young women on college campuses, often with links to the male-dominated Students for a Democratic Society (SDS), had begun insisting that the "New Left" purge itself of its own relegation of women to helper status. Women everywhere, it seemed, were becoming self-conscious about their marginality and determined in their readiness to do something about it.[10] But all this ferment held the potential also for division and conflict. Friedan urged young radical women to stop talking about "socialism" versus "capitalism."[11] She hoped black women would refrain from the temptations of racial confrontations. But above all, she warned against letting "sex" come to be the focus of women's liberation.

In 1970 the writer Kate Millett published *Sexual Politics*, a book instantly hailed by some women as the bible for a new feminism. In this book, relying heavily on her own reading of some American and English novelists, Millett celebrated a certain basic femininity as against various masculine propensities such as violence and power-oriented sexuality. Friedan felt sure this pointed the wrong way for women. Taking Millett to be arguing, in effect, that the explanation for women's condition consisted simply of "men," she feared that this opened the way to urging lesbianism as women's preferred escape from oppression. She was appalled when Millett allowed herself to be quoted, in a *Time* magazine cover story, as to her own personal sexual life. Any woman had a perfect right, Friedan said, to whatever sexual life suited her, but to make lesbianism into a political issue would amount to suicide for the women's movement. Middle American women were not interested in lesbian lives. Hard-pressed working women are not interested in undermining marriage and the family. Black women were not eager to attack black men. To attack men, marriage, and the family as the keys to women's oppression would lead only to defeat.

Friedan's personal history on this point was complicated. Her own marriage had long been in trouble. At the time of the publication of *The Feminine Mystique* she had been warned that a divorce would hurt her credibility. As her status in feminism grew, her status as wife suffered. She knew about the battered-wife syndrome before the feminists of the seventies made it a part of their agenda.[12] When she finally did get a divorce, in 1969, she kept it secret, flying in and out of Mexico on a single day during a lecture tour.[13] Thus Friedan had reason to sympathize with the militancy rising around her, but she never ceased deploring what she felt to be an "anti-man" feeling being vented in certain sectors of the movement.

Hoping to head off division, Friedan promoted the idea of a women's national strike for August 16, 1970, the fiftieth anniversary of the ratification of the Nineteenth Amendment to the Constitution.[14] Soon refocused as a parade in which women of every sort could share, the action would be symbolic of women's solidarity. On the appointed day, several tens of thousands of women—plus many men—marched down Fifth Avenue in New York City, in a demonstration reminiscent of the suffrage parades that had preceded the triumph of 1920. Friedan meant to follow up on this moment through an overtly political organization, the National Women's Political Caucus (NWPC), started in July 1971.[15] Any hopes she might have had for personal leadership in the NWPC were quickly dispelled. Feminist outreach to politics immediately interested women already in politics, notably a recently elected congressperson, Bella Abzug of New York. At the Democrats' National Convention in Miami in 1972, Friedan found herself effectively bypassed.

Friedan's leadership dimmed also within the increasingly heterogeneous world of feminism itself. While Millett's notoriety of 1970 soon faded, another, far more compelling figure had emerged, far more adapted than Friedan to represent feminism in the mass media. For Friedan, Gloria Steinem embodied an especially painful issue: "Gloria is assuredly blonder, younger, prettier than I am. . . ."[16] But Steinem was far more than just a pretty face. She understood the logic of modern mass media. She had a clear sense of the new constituency for feminism, women younger than those to whom Friedan had addressed her book, often better educated, not yet married, often vehement in their impatience with both the sexual as well as the economic roles still the norm for women. Steinem founded a Women's Action Alliance, obviously competitive with NOW. In June 1971 Steinem, not Friedan, was invited to address the graduating class at

Smith (Steinem's alma mater too) on feminism. The feminism she hailed resembled Friedan's hardly at all. In August 1971 Steinem made the cover of *Newsweek*: "A Liberated Woman Despite Beauty, Chic and Success." In January 1972 the first issue of *Ms.* magazine appeared, with Steinem as editor. It was an immediate hit. In the years ahead, *Ms.* proved to be feminism's one popular media success. While many radical feminists would score *Ms.* as bland, sentimental, and edited by the same yardsticks used by mass circulation organs, it gave first space to some of the best rising young feminist novelists, including Alice Walker. Friedan never appeared in *Ms.*, and was rarely mentioned. At the First National Women's Conference held in Houston in 1977, a kind of exercise to celebrate the triumphs of feminism with no fewer than three First Ladies in attendance, Betty Friedan had no official, scheduled place.

Although it had become resonably clear as early as 1969 that for feminism as a movement much was at stake in its appearance in the mass media, Friedan experienced much ambivalence about her own role. She stepped down as president of NOW in 1970, as the organization, still only three thousand members strong, in an obvious bid to widen its appeal, elected a woman of both black and Hispanic roots, Aileen Hernandez, as its new head. "I've often been asked," Friedan wrote, "if I voluntarily bowed out. . . ." Six years later she could only say: "That's a hard question to answer."[17] Retrospectively, she attributed her failures in the National Women's Political Caucus to personal deficiencies: "I was scared enough by . . . tactics used against me to stay away . . . from any confrontation whatsoever. . . . I now see that my own cowardice, my faint-heartedness, my unwillingness to compete in a really rough fight" had induced her retreat.[18] Yet there were those who had regarded Friedan as often imperious, demanding, and tactless in dealing with others.[19] On balance, Friedan did seem to have lacked those intuitions guiding an effective leader. In appearances at such high-visibility international conferences as one in Teheran in 1974, on the initiative of the sister of the Shah of Iran, and another in Mexico City in 1975, under United Nations auspices, Friedan did not seem aware, nor was she to become fully aware upon reflection, that these affairs had been completely stage-managed for ulterior purposes, her own feminist purposes not being among them.[20]

Instead, Friedan's route seemed more surely that of further thought and writing. This too did not prove easy, however. Prompted by the success of *The Feminine Mystique*, Random House had offered her a contract for a second book. Working with the title "The Unfinished Revolution," then "The New Woman," finally "Humansex," Friedan could not bring her manuscript to completion. As books that were more direct and radical about sex appeared—Millett's *Sexual Politics*, Shulamith Firestone's *The Dialectic of Sex*, Ti-Grace Atkinson's *Amazon Odyssey*, Germaine Greer's *The Female Eunuch*, among others—Friedan grew more sure of where the women's movement was going wrong than she was of some new dispensation. She was drawn to writing a column, "Betty Friedan's Notebook," for *McCall's*, a magazine she had stigmatized as one of the more blatant purveyors of the feminine mystique. Why not *Ms.*? "I always saw the women's movement as a movement of the mainstream. . . . I was interested in writing for those 8,000,000 woman's magazine readers, the suburban housewives," not for the "already convinced," "especially within the framework of a new kind of feminist conformity."[21] In 1976 Friedan cobbled together a selection from her speeches, notebooks, and other writing, together with updating comments, into a volume entitled *It Changed My Life*. Concluding that book with "An Open Letter to the Women's Movement," she noted the convulsions that had racked NOW in 1975 over a "Majority Caucus" pledged to take NOW "out of the mainstream, into the revolution." She noted the failure of state ERAs in New York and New Jersey and the stalling of the national ERA four states short of ratification. Public opinion polls still showed overwhelming endorsement, among men as well as among women, for greater opportunities for women, but this tremendous reservoir of goodwill was being wasted, she argued, by leadership preoccupied with "racism, poverty, rape and lesbian rights."[22] Antifeminist women, Friedan argued, in such groups as "Total Womanhood," "The League of Housewives," and the "Pussycat League,"—"fearful sisters," "truly vicious," filled with "icy, burning rage"[23]—were themselves symptoms rather than the cause of feminism's failure. The fears driving the antifeminist women had a taproot in reality. Almost in proportion as women were moving out into the public marketplace, women were finding themselves economically hardpressed. Indeed, what impelled far more women out of housewifery into jobs was hard necessity rather than eager ambition. Attacks upon marriage and family, upon "patriarchy," upon "compulsory heterosexuality," meant less than nothing to most women. Feminism, Friedan argued, needed a new bearing.

In 1981 Freidan published *The Second Stage*. In this book she took for granted the death of the feminine mystique. That old ideology had had but to be exposed to the light of criticism for it to shrivel away. But the collapse of the feminine mystique had not automatically been followed by equality and liberation. The ERA had been stalled. By 1981 it faced the likelihood of defeat. Millions more women were at work in the marketplace than ever before, but most of them still crowded into poorly paid "pink collar" ghettos. Millions more women with young children were at work, without help. While more kinds of careers for professional women had opened than ever before, all sorts of signs of stress and disillusion among even such privileged women had begun to appear. Supposedly egalitarian new divorce laws had backfired badly for tens of thousands of women. While the false idyll of "fifties" domesticity had long dissipated, life in 1981 fulfilled no one's fantasy.

Friedan did not doubt that forces quite independent of the women's movement had much to do with some of these problems: inflation, continuing racism, the peculiar forms of the new "post-industrial" service economy, the apparent turn to the political Right, the rise of the religious Right. But *The Second Stage* returned to what Friedan regarded as self-inflicted wounds. Citing Kate Millett, Susan Brownmiller, Mary Daly, and Shulamith Firestone among others, Friedan repeated her insistence that preoccupation with sexual issues had got feminism out of touch with the mainstream of American women who had indeed been eager to liberate themselves from the feminine mystique but had never wanted destruction of the family, repudiation of marriage, or sexual war against men. But the second-generation feminists, the daughters, as it were, younger, impatient with restraint, stimulated by media success, had generated a new mystique, a "feminist" mystique, far more dangerous to feminist success than the old, discredited feminine mystique. Still sensitive to rhetorical tactics, Friedan criticized the language both NOW and feminist radicals were using in the defense of the Supreme Court's 1973 decision, *Roe v. Wade*, invalidating states' prohibitions on abortion. Feminists had let their opponents steal the banner of "pro-life."[24] Certainly no woman should be denied an abortion, but claiming a "right" to abortion was comparable to claiming a "right" to a mastectomy or any other medical operation. Abortions ought to be defended as functions of need, failure, and despair, not of equality and sexual freedom.

Friedan was convinced that mainstream political success awaited a feminism that concentrated on family issues. Reaching out to churches, neighborhood groups, local unions, to all varieties of private associations with a stake in social health and vitality, such a feminism would far more closely approach mainstream politics than NOW, let alone the smaller feminist groups, had ever been able to do. Ultimately, the basic reason for this was that the most important collaborators with this feminism would be men. Friedan had always deplored the "anti-man" note she heard in certain radical feminists. She had felt it to be pragmatically foolish, as well as misguided sexually. Without men's goodwill, even the final collapse of the feminine mystique would not mean women's liberation. Allowed, even encouraged and urged, to move out into jobs and careers, women were already finding themselves trying to juggle two roles, two full-time responsibilities: home and work, children and office. Many women had adjusted by trying to postpone home, limit children, even abandon marriage altogether. This was the old pattern urged on college women by Bryn Mawr college's M. Carey Thomas back before World War I: do not waste your training in domesticity. Friedan felt sure the vast majority of modern American women refused to make any such choice. They would not forsake marriage, home, children. But they wanted to work, or had to work. What then was the only way to avoid exhaustion? Men had to share the homework, share "parenting," share in the private sphere.

Back in 1971, NOW itself had already set up a "Task Force on the Masculine Mystique," postulated on the idea that myths of normative "masculinity" oppressed men just as the feminine mystique had oppressed women.[25] Her own father, Friedan felt, had been such a victim. Like women, men too had only to wake up to their oppression to begin quickly to free themselves from it. The task force got nowhere. While its premise was rickety enough, its basic weakness was political. Norms of "masculinity" may or may not have weighed hurtfully on some men, but the masculine mystique had not done to men what the feminine mystique had done to women: held them out of the marketplace, inhibited them from money-making, discouraged them from competing for power. Why should men sacrifice any of these privileges? If most men had come to accept money-earning women in the marketplace, did that mean they must themselves retreat a little from the marketplace in order to spend more time at home?

In *The Second Stage* Friedan still wanted to believe that it was in men's self-interest to become a little less competitive while women became more competitive, to be a little less aggressive while women were becoming more. She did not exalt some vision of androgyny as had many feminists on the Left, but she clearly evoked a picture of the sexes sharing domesticity that, she felt, would allow women to fulfill basic needs for home and motherhood while still at work in the world. Instead of trying to construct a parallel scheme of fulfillment for men, however, she followed a quite different line, one that left her hopes—and feminism's—still adrift. The reason there was a "quiet movement" away from coercive masculinity among men was not so much that men were beginning to understand the attractions of a new sharing as that the old rewards of masculinity were being undermined. "[Many] of the old bases for men's identity have become shaky."[26] The work world was changing. Good jobs, jobs that made men "feel like men," were becoming scarce. "Only one out of every five men now says that work means more to him than lei-

sure."[27] The war in Vietnam too had undermined a certain ma-
chismo in national life. And so on. But this approach contained its
own paradoxes. If the work world was becoming less rewarding, why
should women insist upon being included in it? No doubt no more
Vietnam Wars were wanted, but women were not likely to find
reform of politics simply a matter of androgynous psychology. Still
as much a realistic observer as a hopeful reformer, Friedan could not
deny another kind of evidence also. Something like a male backlash
against the sex equalities was already in progress, as attested by the
macho heroes in the novels of John Updike, Philip Roth, Saul Bel-
low, and Thomas Pynchon; the proliferation of pornography; and a
clinically attested increase in impotence. Certainly these were as
telling as the feelings she cited among men whom she interviewed
on the waning influence of the masculine mystique. In the end,
Friedan appealed once again to the old idea that, however probable
the gender revolution might or might not be, it was not only desir-
able but necessary: the world could no longer afford leadership of the
"stereotypical male."[28]

Whether or not men were yet collaborating on the necessary "con-
vergence" of the sexes, a feminist could take hope, finally, in the fact
that the "changing sex roles of both men and women are a massive,
evolutionary development."[29] Friedan was almost surely unaware
that the same claim had been made by one of the greatest of the earlier
feminists, Charlotte Perkins Gilman, in 1898. Whatever men and
women might want, the change to sexual equality, Gilman wrote, "is
not a thing to prophesy and plead for. It is a change already instituted. . . , the same great force of social evolution which brought us
into the old relation [of inequality] is bringing us out. . . ."[30] By the
end of her life Gilman was complaining bitterly that the young
women of the 1920s had forsaken the cause. However flaming their
youth, they had wrought no "social improvement that I have heard
of."[31] Equality had not been quite so inevitable after all.

The Second Stage won no such popularity as had *The Feminine
Mystique* eighteen years before. It could not have. For the individual
woman reader, it evoked no personal awakening as had the earlier
book. For any man who might have read it, it only promoted ambivalence. The book did register the end of what might be called the
utopian phase of modern American feminism. By 1981 college
women were assuming work and careers as a matter of course, often
with little sense of the efforts that had had to be made to guarantee
them their opportunities. At the same time, a revolution had occurred in both the American marketplace and American home life:
the single wage-earner family was increasingly rare. The stresses and
pains this single fact implied for marriage, child-rearing, and home

life specifically, as well as for sexual culture at large, outran even the most radical feminist alarm. Condensed to a nub, Friedan's message constituted both a warning and a hope. If feminists followed an agenda forged only in their own fantasies of revolution, they would be reduced to the isolated sect they sometimes seemed to have become by the mid-eighties. On the other hand, so long as feminists drew their agenda from issues close to the experiences of mainstream, middle-class American women, they could not fail to prosper. If there were "massive, evolutionary" developments that would carry mainstream America on into the nineties, it seemed quite clear feminists would have plenty of problems to care about. As she herself arrived at late middle age, Friedan continued to make herself available, at conferences, workshops, conventions, encouraging activity, confident of the energies she had helped unlock.

Notes

[1]Autobiographical fragments are to be found scattered through all three of Friedan's books, but especially in *It Changed My Life* (New York, 1976). See also Paul Wilkes, "Mother Superior to Women's Lib," *New York Times Magazine*, 29 Nov., 1970.

[2]*The Second Stage* (New York, 1981), p. 93.

[3]Ibid.

[4]*The Feminine Mystique* (New York, 1963), p. 182.

[5]She did note how Catholic and Jewish women faced a "housewife image" enshrined in their churches' dogmas, ibid., p. 351.

[6]Important role, ibid., p. 206; customers, ibid., p. 207; byproduct, ibid.

[7]Ibid., p. 338.

[8]"[These Smith] graduates of 1942 were among the last American women educated before the feminine mystique," ibid., p. 360.

[9]In addition to Friedan, in *It Changed My Life*, Part 2, Jo Freeman, *The Politics of Women's Liberation* (New York, 1975), examines NOW: Rolande Ballorain, *Le nouveau feminisme americain* (Paris, 1972), is particularly interesting for its interviews with the new feminist leaders, including Friedan. Donald Meyer, *Sex and Power: The Rise of Women in America, Russia, Sweden and Italy* (Middletown, 1987), ch. 10, discusses NOW.

[10]A more or less instant history is in Judith Hole and Edith Levine, *Rebirth of Feminism* (New York, 1971); Mary Lou Thompson, ed., *Voices of the New Feminism* (Boston, 1970), offers readings including Friedan. Recent histories include Meyer, *Sex and Power*, ch. 10, and Marcia Cohen, *The Sisterhood:*

The True Story of the Women Who Changed the World (New York, 1988) is a paean in the breathless style of Tom Wolfe.

[11]Friedan, *It Changed My Life*, p. 389.

[12]Cohen, *The Sisterhood*, pp. 17–18.

[13]Friedan, *It Changed My Life*, p. 137.

[14]Ibid., pp. 137ff.

[15]Ibid., pp. 165ff.

[16]Ibid., p. 179; Cohen, *The Sisterhood*, offers many pages on Steinem.

[17]Friedan, *It Changed My Life*, p. 140.

[18]Ibid., pp. 181, 183.

[19]For example, see Germaine Greer, "Women's Glib," *Vanity Fair*, June 1988.

[20]Friedan, "Scary Doings in Mexico City," *It Changed My Life*, pp. 342ff.

[21]Ibid., p. 188.

[22]Ibid., p. 379.

[23]Ibid., p. 382.

[24]*The Second Stage*, pp. 107–108.

[25]See the discussion in Meyer, *Sex and Power*, pp. 416–420.

[26]*The Second Stage*, p. 130.

[27]Ibid., p. 134.

[28]Ibid., p. 156.

[29]Ibid., p. 142.

[30]C. P. Gilman, *Women and Economics* (New York, 1966), p. 316, quoted in Meyer, *Sex and Power*, p. 341.

[31]C. P. Gilman, *The Living of Charlotte Perkins Gilman* (New York, 1935), pp. 318–319, quoted in Meyer, *Sex and Power*, p. 347.

About the Authors

G. J. Barker-Benfield teaches history at the State University of New York, Albany. He has written *The Horrors of the Half-Known Life* (1976) and articles on medical and social history. He is completing a book on the culture of sensibility in eighteenth-century Britain.

Carol Ruth Berkin is Professor of History at Baruch College and The City University Graduate Center. She is the author of *Jonathan Sewall: Odyssey of an American Loyalist* (1977) and co-editor with Mary Beth Norton of *Women of America: A History* (1980) and with Clara Lovett of *Women, War and Revolution* (1980). She is currently working on *The American Eve: Women of Colonial America.*

William H. Chafe is the Alice Mary Baldwin Professor of American history at Duke University. His books include *The Unfinished Journey* (1986) and *Civilities and Civil Rights* (1980). He is currently completing a biography of Allard Lowenstein.

Catherine Clinton has taught at Brandeis University, Harvard University, and Union College. She is the author of *The Plantation Mistress* (1982) and *The Other Civil War* (1984). Currently she is completing a study of Fanny Kemble.

Blanche Wiesen Cook is Professor of History at John Jay College and The Graduate Center-City College. She is the author of *Crystal Eastman* (1978) and *The Declassified Eisenhower* (1981), and she is currently completing a two-volume biography of Eleanor Roosevelt.

Paula Giddings occupies the New Jersey Laurie Chair in Women's Studies at Rutgers University. She is the author of *When and Where I Enter: The Impact of Black Women on Race and Sex in America* (1984); and *In Search of Sisterhood: Delta Sigma Theta and the Challenge of the Black Sorority Movement* (1988).

Christine A. Lunardini is Adjunct Associate Professor of Social Sciences at Pace University, Manhattan. She is the author of *From Equal Suffrage to Equal Rights: Alice Paul and the National Woman's Party, 1910–1928* (1986).

618

Donald Meyer teaches history at Wesleyan University, Middletown, Connecticut. He is the author of *The Protestant Search for Political Realism, The Positive Thinkers,* and *Sex and Power: The Rise of Women in America, Russia, Sweden and Italy.* He is presently at work on a cultural history of the United States.

Annelise Orleck is Assistant Professor of History at Dartmouth College. Her dissertation, "Common Sense and a Little Fire: Working-Class Women's Organizing in the Twentieth-Century United States," is currently being reviewed for publication.

Sarah Whitaker Peters was formerly Adjunct Assistant Professor of Art History at The University of Long Island, C. W. Post campus, and a freelance critic for *Art in America.* Her book *Georgia O'Keeffe and Photography: Sources and Transformations, 1915–1930* will be published in 1991.

Rosalind Rosenberg is Associate Professor of History and Departmental Chair at Barnard College. The author of *Beyond Separate Spheres,* she is currently completing a book on American women in the twentieth century.

Ingrid Winther Scobie is a member of the history faculty at Texas Woman's University, Denton. She has written widely on twentieth-century political history and women's history. Her full-scale biography of Helen Gahagan Douglas will be published by Oxford University Press in 1991.